Luke: Interpreter of Paul, Critic of Matthew

Eric Franklin

Journal for the Study of the New Testament
Supplement Series 92

To Ed Sanders and his time in Oxford
without permission but with gratitude

Published by JSOT Press
JSOT Press is an imprint of
Sheffield Academic Press Ltd
343 Fulwood Road
Sheffield S10 3BP
England

Typeset by Sheffield Academic Press
and
Printed on acid-free paper in Great Britain
by Bookcraft
Midsomer Norton, Somerset

British Library Cataloguing in Publication Data

Franklin, Eric
Luke: Interpreter of Paul, Critic of
Matthew.—(JSNT Supplement Series, ISSN
0143-5108; No. 92)
I. Title II. Series
226.4

ISBN 1-85075-452-7

JOURNAL FOR THE STUDY OF THE NEW TESTAMENT SUPPLEMENT SERIES

92

JSOT Press
Sheffield

CONTENTS

PREFACE

Earlier forms of parts of these chapters have been presented as papers to the Oxford Society of Historical Theology and to the New Testament Seminar of the Theology Faculty. I am grateful, not only for the opportunity of testing a number of ideas, but also for many of the responses which made me go back, rethink, reshape and develop much that I offered.

John Fenton read the first section, and Bob Morgan the whole manuscript in an earlier draft. I much appreciated their comments, criticisms and encouragement. Without such, the work either would not have seen the light of day, or would have appeared with many more blemishes than it now has.

I am grateful for the toleration, interest and mild amusement with which fellow members of St Stephen's House have coped with my abiding interest in Luke–Acts and for the charity with which they have suffered no-doubt repeated expositions arising out of it. In the last resort, any contribution by me to the scholarly understanding of Luke is justified only as it helps to deepen our discipleship in the service of him who, not only for Luke, but also for us is 'Christ the Lord'.

Eric Franklin
St Stephen's House, Oxford
September, 1993

ABBREVIATIONS

AnBib	Analecta biblica
ATR	*Anglican Theological Review*
BETL	Bibliotheca ephemeridum theologicarum lovaniensium
Bib	*Biblica*
BJRL	*Bulletin of the John Rylands University Library of Manchester*
BNTC	Black's New Testament Commentaries
BZ	*Biblische Zeitschrift*
BZNW	Beihefte zur *ZNW*
CBQ	*Catholic Biblical Quarterly*
JBL	*Journal of Biblical Literature*
JSNTSup	*Journal for the Study of the New Testament*, Supplement Series
NCB	New Century Bible
NIGTC	The New International Greek Testament Commentary
NTS	*New Testament Studies*
SBLDS	SBL Dissertation Series
SBLSP	SBL Seminar Papers
SBT	Studies in Biblical Theology
SJT	*Scottish Journal of Theology*
SNTSMS	Society of New Testament Studies Monograph Series
TDNT	G. Kittel and G. Friedrich (eds.), *Theological Dictionary of the New Testament*
TynBul	*Tyndale Bulletin*
TNTC	Tyndale New Testament Commentaries
TU	Texte und Untersuchungen
WUNT	Wissenschaftliche Untersuchungen zum Neuen Testament
ZNW	*Zeitschrift für die neutestamentliche Wissenschaft*

Chapter 1

INTRODUCTION

These chapters, though I hope complete in themselves, are best approached as a development of, and in some ways as a response to, my earlier study of Luke–Acts, *Christ the Lord*, which was published in 1975.[1] That work was itself a response to the stimulation provided by Conzelmann's epoch-making approach to Luke and by Haenchen's magnificent commentary on Acts,[2] but was almost goaded into being by the overall Bultmannian evaluation of Luke's theology.[3] Luke was, after all, responsible for something like a quarter of the New Testament and it seemed to me not merely that his contribution was being denigrated by a less than fair evaluation of his meaning developed in comparison with that found in Paul, but that the witness of the New Testament itself was being impaired by what was effectively becoming an establishment of a canon within a canon. The existential approach was missing out on much of the significance of Luke's theology by forcing him into a mould which was not of his making but which was fashioned in large part by the conviction that, because he was neither a Paul or a John, his work was inevitably to be seen not merely as less insightful than theirs (a point on which not a few would agree), but that, because it was thought to add little or nothing to theirs, was to be seen inevitably as inimical to what they proclaimed. Luke, it seemed to me, was not actually in the straitjacket that such theologians, for all their magnificent insights, had made for him. He was less constrained, less clear-cut, more complex and better nuanced

1. (London: SPCK, 1975).

2. H. Conzelmann, *The Theology of St Luke* (trans. G. Buswell; London: Faber & Faber, 1960); E. Haenchen, *The Acts of the Apostles* (trans. B. Noble *et al.*; Oxford: Basil Blackwell, 1971).

3. R. Bultmann, *Theology of the New Testament*, II (trans. K. Grobel; London: SCM Press, 1955), pp. 116-18.

than they tended to allow. He had a theology which was not merely respectable but which was actually arrived at in dialogue with that outlook represented by Paul or Mark and which could in turn contribute something to our evaluation of their thought as well as that of the New Testament as a whole and which could also inform and deepen our own response to God's strange work in Christ.

In contrast to Conzelmann and to what has been characterized as the 'classical' position established by him,[1] *Christ the Lord* maintained that Luke did not reduce the importance of the parousia by removing it from its place as an imminent event to relocate it as one expected only in the distant future. He therefore did not reduce its significance for the present but, by keeping it as a happening expected in the lifetime of some at least of his contemporaries, allowed it to inform the concerns of the present as an object of hope and of expectancy. Luke therefore did not reduce eschatology by viewing it as contained only in a future event but saw both the past of Jesus and the present of his contemporaries in its light. It actually impinged upon the present and, indeed, upon the whole event of Jesus. The element of delay which is indisputably there in Luke is to be accounted for by the lengthening distance between the time of Jesus and his own. Jesus needed to be seen as allowing for a delay because that in fact had already happened. Eschatology however added its dimension to all Luke's thinking.

Though he did not reduce the eschatological dimension, Luke did, nevertheless, rework the significance of the parousia in that dimension, and he did so by moving the burden of proof, the demonstration of finality, the establishment of the kingdom and the effective Lordship of Christ which the early church had seen in the parousia, away from that to the ascension which was for Luke the determinative eschatological event. The kingdom of God was effectively established at the ascension; its sphere was a heavenly one, while the presence of the Spirit on earth proceeded from that to enable those who believed in Jesus as Lord to live out of the life of the kingdom and in response to its eschatological power. Luke's understanding of the kingdom was of a transcendent reality which empowered its adherents in this world and in this life. The parousia remained as an object of imminent hope which would make visible and complete what was already realized in the transcendent and which would, by bringing about the end of the

1. S.D. Moore, *Literary Criticism and the Gospels* (New Haven: Yale University Press, 1989), p. 57.

present age, introduce the new. It was that future which Luke put before his readers as the object of their hope and as the fulfilment of the Lord's promises.

Eschatology for Luke was not pushed to the margins of his thought and so, inevitably, *Christ the Lord* argued against Conzelmann's view of salvation history which he understood as its substitute and which divided past and ongoing time into three distinct periods. Instead, it maintained that the ascension served as the culmination of one period by which Israel's history and its climax in Jesus was caught up into a single fulfilment. The period of the church was not separate but was itself proceeding from and witnessing to what had preceded it and what continued to enable it, as the present responded to its active, living, heavenly Lord. In reality, Conzelmann's three periods coalesce into one as they see their being focused and centred upon the ascended Lord who is both the fulfilment of Israel's past and the ongoing source of the church's life.

Luke was above all a man of the Old Testament and it was his subordination to this which made him describe God's work in the way that he does. Jesus, as the fulfilment of Old Testament expectations, is controlled by its terms. He confirmed God's promises to Israel, and the width of the Gentile mission was such as to witness both to his Lordship and to the realization of God's effective covenantal concern made final in him.

Since 1975, a dialogue with Conzelmann's work has of necessity continued to dominate and inspire a large number of efforts to come to grips with the concerns of the author of Luke–Acts and most of this has, in one way or another, centred around a refining of his understanding of Luke's eschatology and of his division of Luke's salvation–historical approach into the three periods of Israel, Jesus and the church. Discussion of Luke's eschatology has been concerned with two points in particular, namely Conzelmann's assertion that Luke moved the parousia into a remote future and his belief that the kingdom of God was by him reserved for that future. Conzelmann's Luke makes the End 'endlessly remote', and the kingdom of God, 'far from being made into a historical entity, is removed into the metaphysical realm' which of course must wait for the parousia for its realization. Meanwhile, 'It is the message of the Kingdom that is present, which in Luke is distinguished from the Kingdom itself'.[1]

1. *Theology*, pp. 97, 113, 122.

C.H. Talbert, in his assessment of scholarly reaction to Conzelmann's thesis, concludes: 'General agreement is limited to this: the evangelist writes in terms of salvation history which includes within it the hope of an imminent end'.[1] Though Talbert may in fact be exaggerating the measure of the agreement about Luke's acceptance of an imminent parousia, he is no doubt correct in drawing attention to a growing recognition of this aspect of the evangelist's thought. Whether justice is actually done to the significance of this recognition, however, is another matter.

Talbert himself is able to do justice to what he believes is Luke's emphasis upon the imminence of the End because he sees it as part of the evangelist's rebuttal of those who were maintaining that the parousia had in fact already occurred. Stress upon an imminent, universal, cataclysmic event is openly contrasted with the partial, incomplete, hidden and esoteric nature of that which Luke's quasi-Gnostic opponents were advocating. Others however, who, though anxious to take account of this near-expectation in Luke, have nevertheless engaged upon a less drastic reshaping of Conzelmann, have in fact found it more difficult to do justice to that dimension within an account of what they understand to be Luke's beliefs. So Schweizer, though he maintains that references to the End in Luke 'Far more than in Mark...pervade the entire gospel', nevertheless finds the significance of this in his belief that 'exhortation has already moved its focus to responsible conduct in the interim'. So far has the balance shifted that 'in Acts 10.42 (cf. also Lk. 16.23; 23.43) it is no longer clear whether he expects resurrection and judgement only as the conclusion of each individual human life'.[2] In a similar vein, Fitzmyer, though taking account of Luke's imminent sayings, says that he has altered the End's emphasis, 'moved it off centre as it were'. Luke takes over the ambivalence inherent in the tradition but in the process, 'his sense of history blunts somewhat the imminence of the expected parousia found in the other NT writers'.[3] A further reason for

1. C.H. Talbert, 'Shifting Sands: The Recent Study of the Gospel of Luke', in J.L. Mays (ed.), *Interpreting the Gospels* (Philadelphia: Fortress Press, 1981), pp. 197-213 (204).

2. E. Schweizer, *The Good News according to Luke* (trans. D. Green; London: SPCK; Atlanta, GA: John Knox, 1984), pp. 323-34, 8.

3. J.A. Fitzmyer, *Luke the Theologian* (London: Geoffrey Chapman, 1989), pp. 129-30.

blunting its edge is his hortatory use of the Jesus sayings to make them guides for conduct to a later generation.

In actual fact, what has happened is, in a large number of responses, an implicit acceptance of Conzelmann's position that Luke has shifted the eschatological perspective of the End to allow for a continuing life of the church in the present in which discipleship and witness, as well as a call to missionary concern, have a full part. The references to the End, though taken as proclamations of an actual event, are nevertheless in reality given a symbolic referent in that their notice of imminence is translated into the need for decision, for moral urgency, for commitment. At the same time, there seems to be a strong sense that Luke has gone in for some movement in the direction of an individualization of eschatology and that the strand of thought which talks of individual judgment at death and of entry into the kingdom then is that which somehow 'deep-down' reflects the real outlook of Luke himself. Many would agree with Evans' judgment that Luke was open to a wide variety of traditions which he included but which 'cannot however be brought together to form a single coherent system of thought'.[1] It is hard to resist the conclusion that, though Conzelmann's dismissal of the imminent strand in Luke's expectation is seen to do less than justice to a number of passages, these are treated as somewhat isolated texts rather than as being accepted as part and parcel of the web of Luke's thought.

Conzelmann's evaluation of Luke's attitude to the timing of the End is much more influential than is actually admitted. Treatments which give full value to Luke's imminent expectation are in fact few even if those who actually appear to accept Conzelmann's position are not very numerous.[2] In these chapters, I take the opportunity to re-emphasize the significance for Luke of his belief in an imminent parousia and attempt to show how this continues to play a vital part in his understanding. To adapt the subtitle of Mattill's book on Lukan eschatology, it does nothing less than provide *the* 'perspective

1. C.F. Evans, *Saint Luke* (London: SCM Press; Philadelphia: Trinity Press International, 1990), p. 64.

2. See, for instance, A.J. Mattill, *Luke and the Last Things: A Perspective for the Understanding of Lukan Thought* (Dillsboro, NC: Western North Carolina Press, 1979); R.H. Hiers, 'The Problem of the Delay of the Parousia in Luke–Acts', *NTS* 20 (1973), pp. 145-55; G. Schneider, *Das Evangelium nach Lukas* (Gütersloh: Gerd Mohn 1977) tends to support Conzelmann.

for the understanding of Lukan thought'.

More consistent has been the response of a large number of scholars to Conzelmann's suggestion that Luke evacuated the present of any real eschatological involvement to remove the presence of the kingdom into the future. Attention here has been focused on those sayings of Jesus which appear to refer to the present existence of the kingdom and on the narratives of Jesus' proclamation at Nazareth and of the Pentecostal outpouring of the Spirit as themselves witnessing to the presence of the kingdom in the present age. Conzelmann's de-eschatologizing of history in Luke's plan has been widely sensed as doing less than justice to the evangelist's thought. Rather, there appears something approaching a consensus that saving history is itself caught up and embraced within an eschatological context. As Kümmel asserts, 'Redemption history is not necessarily a substitute for eschatology'.[1] Kümmel himself though is not without an element of ambiguity at this point for though Jesus is seen as the *arche* of this eschatologically significant redemptive history, Jesus' own history is not itself *the* eschatological event. Kümmel is still working within Conzelmann's pattern and is as yet unable therefore to give full acknowledgment to the eschatological significance of the whole of the Jesus event.

Others, however, have been more willing to acknowledge that Luke himself expresses an outlook which is much more in keeping with the early church's understanding of a two-stage eschatology, and to recognize his acceptance of a kingdom of God which is believed to be established, though in different ways, through both the present and the future. Helpful though this general recognition is—for it undoubtedly does more justice to Luke's thought—of itself however it actually solves little, for Schweizer is undoubtedly right when he says, 'It is less appropriate to ask whether the kingdom is present or future than *in what way is it present or future*' (my italics).[2] How does Luke think of the kingdom as being real in the present? Is it immanent in that it is actually thought to be present on earth?

Ellis, who argues strongly for a two-stage eschatology, asserts that its presence is found in Jesus and in the Spirit.[3] It is present therefore

1. W.G. Kümmel, *Introduction to the New Testament* (trans. H.C. Kee; London: SCM Press, 1975).

2. *Luke*, p. 326.

3. E.E. Ellis, *Eschatology in Luke* (Philadelphia: Fortress Press, 1972), p. 15.

in Jesus' followers who 'not only manifest the same *eschatological power of the spirit* (as did Jesus) but also have a *corporate identification* with the risen Lord'.[1] Maddox pursues the same belief in the immanence of the kingdom with such conviction as to maintain that Acts 14.22, which is usually seen as referring to some future entry into the kingdom either at the parousia or at death, actually 'suggests that the thought of "entering the kingdom of God" is still more immediate and is to be understood therefore as a present experience'. In the light of its being linked to the episode of Paul's persecution at Lystra, he interprets 14.22 to mean that 'persecution is an attendant circumstance of entering the kingdom, that is, of entering now, by faith, the kingdom which is a present reality'.[2]

However, it still remains unclear how the immanence of the kingdom is to be understood. Of just what does this present reality consist? Maddox's treatment of Pentecost suggests that it might be seen as an entry into the corporate life of the community which itself becomes the sphere of the kingdom. Elsewhere, however, he seems to individualize its presence to see it as the experience of salvation such as is attributed to Zacchaeus and to the man lame from birth (Lk. 19.9-10; Acts 3.16).[3] Schweizer, on the other hand, maintains that neither before nor after Easter is the life of the community identified with the kingdom. For him, its presence is found in a present decision to live in the expectation of the kingdom. In this way one is open to it and so receives it at least in part in the present.[4]

Luke does not envisage the life of the individual as being apart from the community. The ruler is challenged to join the disciples who follow Jesus (18.1-30) and the idealized common life of the young Jerusalem church witnesses to the corporate nature of discipleship (Acts 2.43-47). The community is the sphere of those who respond to the kingdom; that it is itself the presence of the kingdom, however, remains unlikely. At Pentecost, the 'Last days' are not identified with the 'day of the Lord' by which the kingdom is to be realized for the

1. *Eschatology*, p. 20. I argue below that Luke did not believe in the corporate Christ but that his Old Testament constraints forbade this idea. Acts 9.4 (and parallels) is an isolated reflection of Paul's thought.

2. R. Maddox, *The Purpose of Luke–Acts* (Edinburgh: T. & T. Clark, 1982), pp. 136-37.

3. *Purpose*, p. 134.

4. *Luke*, pp. 325-26.

community. Pentecost retains its future thrust. At Nazareth, Jesus' fulfilment of Scripture is seen in his proclamation of a future redemption. His presence is a guarantee of that rather than its actual inauguration on earth. His healing ministry, introduced into the passage by way of a use of Isa. 58.6, is seen as a throwing back of the power of Satan and an effective establishment of the power of God, but, within the context of the passage as a whole, it incorporates Jesus' healing ministry into that which witnesses to the significance of him as the fulfilment of the prophet's own task rather than to the immanence of the kingdom itself. In the eschatological discourse, the disciples are told to see the signs as witnessing to the nearness of the kingdom rather than to its actual presence among them (21.31). At the last supper, Jesus promises a role in the kingdom to the twelve in the same manner in which the Father had already promised the kingdom itself to him. The past promise to him is by way of his death and exaltation to be given an imminent realization: his present promise to them however is to await its resolution in the future (22.28-30). The two promises do not have a fulfilment at the same point in time. Acts 14.22 therefore points forward to that fulfilment and to the future. The kingdom is real in the present, but disciples enter into it only in the future, for it is not thought of by Luke as being immanent on earth either in the corporate life of the community or in the individual response of the disciples. In *Christ the Lord* I argued that Luke bears witness to the presence of the kingdom as that of a transcendent reality which is not actually enshrined in earthly events which rather bear witness to its nearness. I hope that these chapters will carry that argument forward and help to give further insight into Luke's message and to his method of proclaiming it.

The second main area of dialogue with Conzelmann has centred upon the categorizing of Luke as the theologian of salvation history which is unfolded in three periods, those of Israel, of Jesus and of the church. Of the importance of salvation history as an entry into Luke's understanding there can be little doubt. Of this, due acknowledgment is made by Evans when he writes, 'What is convincing is that a concept of a history of salvation which has God as its author is dominant in the construction of Luke–Acts'.[1] It makes sense of Luke's summaries of Israel's history, of his placing of Jesus in that history, and of his continuation of the story of Jesus in Acts. To quote again from

1. *Luke*, p. 53.

Talbert's assessment of the scholarly debate, 'Research since Conzelmann has generally supported his recognition of Lukan salvation history, though not his claim that it is unique to Luke–Acts'.[1] His actual dividing up of that history, however, has not gone without challenge for, on the one hand, his separation of the time of Jesus from that of Israel can be carried through consistently only by a virtual ignoring of the infancy narratives and of that element of prophecy and of fulfilment which plays such a vital role in Luke–Acts[2] and on the other, the widespread tendency of later critics to find some eschatological significance in the presence of the kingdom in the period of the church has linked that period more closely to the time of Jesus, while the more general recognition of Luke's retaining at least in part the early church's expectation of an imminent parousia has meant that the time of Jesus is not separated out to become a self-contained episode in the unfolding of God's continuing salvation through history. Again, the widespread doubting of Conzelmann's claim that Jesus' ministry was the time of the full presence of salvation when Satan was absent and so was to be contrasted with the period of the church has only increased scepticism about his categorizing of that period as the 'centre of time' and the implications he draws from it.[3]

Conzelmann's particular understanding of Luke's unfolding of the pattern of salvation history has in fact been much more severely weakened than is generally acknowledged. So for instance, Fitzmyer, though continuing in this area to give allegiance to a modified Conzelmann,[4] nevertheless has John retain a footage in both the period of Jesus and the period of Israel, Mary becomes a character within all three periods, and Jesus himself is given a part in the period of Israel as well as in his own, while his present activity makes him one with the period of the church. The period of Jesus becomes fudged at both its beginning and its end thereby breaking down any clear demarcation between the three. Indeed, the seeds of the breaking down of the three periods are contained in Conzelmann's own exposition for,

1. 'Shifting Sands', p. 203.

2. P.S. Minear's 'Luke's Use of the Birth Stories', in *Studies in Luke–Acts* (eds. L.E. Keck and J.L. Martyn; London: SPCK, 1968).

3. S. Brown, *Apostasy and Perseverance in the Theology of Luke* (AnBib, 36; Rome: Biblical Institute Press, 1969).

4. J.A. Fitzmyer, *The Gospel according to Luke* (NewYork: Doubleday, 1981, 1985), p. 185; *Theologian*, pp. 62-63.

alongside his understanding of the divisions within redemptive history, he is careful to assert its continuity. At times the passion is seemingly brought into the period of the church and so separated from the ministry which thus alone is made to constitute the period of Jesus. Jesus from the time of the ascension is in heaven and 'from this moment the church needs a substitute for his "real presence"'. Nevertheless, as Conzelmann is honest enough to point out, 'the fact that redemptive history falls into clear divisions does not mean that the community of believers has no living contact with Christ in the present'. The exalted Lord works supremely through the concept of the name. As on earth, he healed, preached and responded, so the healings and preaching are carried out in the power of his name—the power of making immediate that which is by nature transcendent—and those who call upon his name will be succoured. So, says Conzelmann, 'We can go so far as to say that to speak of the efficacy of the name is the specifically Lukan way of describing the presence of Christ'. The church therefore is not without Christ's activity, even if he is now in heaven. As Conzelmann maintains, 'His activity appears constantly. It is presupposed when the community prays to him (as it is in Acts 7.59) and above all when it acts "in the name" of Christ'.[1]

So Conzelmann himself sees much more continuity between his second and third periods than his summary statements of Luke's salvation historical understanding allow, and adjustments made to Conzelmann's divisions have had the result of further drawing the various parts together. Indeed, such are the modifications that one wonders whether the concept of the three identifiable periods can be given any continuing overarching validity. That there are three stages there is no doubt, but whether these should be seen as having the character of specific periods where one not merely follows on but actually takes over from its predecessor is much more open to question. The past is not left behind but is carried forward into the stage that succeeds it, and the character of periods two and three are only rightly understood when they are seen as embracing and bringing to some fulfilment that which has gone before. Conzelmann's own emphasis upon continuity must be accorded its full place.

This is seen most obviously in the periods of Jesus and of the church. In the first place, the two periods are not separated for the double recounting of the ascension narrative serves, not to bring the

1. *Theology*, pp. 177, 178, 177.

time of Jesus to an end and thus to inaugurate an entirely new era, but rather to link the two and to carry Jesus into the time of the church where, though he is a hidden Lord, the Spirit proceeds from him to make real the response to his exaltation which has been effected by the ascension. The story of his ascension in the Gospel, though having characteristics of a departure scene, nevertheless has the purpose, not to announce a withdrawal, but to proclaim his contemporaneity with the church. He is carried up into heaven and, as an object now of worship and thus of immediacy, is actually involved in the history of the church to which he breaks through from time to time to acknowledge its witness and to further its mission.[1] It is Luke's Old Testament christological framework rather than his understanding of salvation history which controls his unfolding of Jesus in the present and which therefore seems to give some basis for the idea of an absent Christ. But Jesus travels with his church even though it is from the vantage point of the heavenly realm. His contemporaneity is made real in the breaking of the bread (24.35), in his inspiration and acknowledgment of the witness to him (Acts 7.55), and in his directing and enabling the progress of the mission (Acts 22.18). 'Saul, Saul, why are you persecuting me?', with its implications of a corporate Christ, may well be Luke's inclusion in his story of a Pauline dimension which certainly portrays an understanding that goes further than his own, but that its basic idea of the closeness of Jesus to his community expresses what was very real to Luke is certain. For Luke, Jesus was a figure, not of the past, but of the present. He may not be in the community, but he is certainly alongside it; he may not indwell the disciple but he is certainly with him. His is not a horizontal distancing, but a vertical one.

Luke does not look back to the past as the time of salvation, for, in fact, the time of Jesus has about it a provisionality which realizes its potential only at the ascension and what proceeds from it. Until his 'exodus' he is 'constrained', hemmed in by the incompleteness, even the imperfection, which is his until he 'enters into his glory' (9.31; 12.50; 24.26). Through that, in the language of Hebrews, he is perfected. Events in the ministry from the temptation onwards point forward to the ascension as their goal; his life is a movement towards that, to the point where he is effectively 'made both Lord and Christ'

1. R.F. O'Toole, 'Activity of the Risen Jesus in Luke–Acts', *Bib* (1981), pp. 471-98; M. Turner, 'Jesus and the Spirit in Lucan Perspective', *TynBul* 32 (1981), pp. 3-42.

(Acts 2.36). From the exaltation the real work of salvation proceeds. On the journey to Jerusalem, Jesus addresses Luke's readers as the effective Lord he is to become and the Spirit is poured out as the eschatological witness to his status.

Luke's historical dimension inevitably points to differences in time and so seems to divide events and to describe the parts in terms which do less than justice to their incorporation into the whole. That is his chosen method and it is made inevitable by his decision to write Acts and so to place the duration of at least a part of early church history between the time of his readers and that of Jesus' life. But Luke does not divorce the past of his story from the present. The infancy narratives unite the two, but this unity is seen also in the Nazareth episode where the speech sums up the whole of the community's history, in the mission of the seventy, in the journey to Jerusalem which has this double aspect of past becoming and of present having become so that Jesus confronts Jerusalem not only as a past event but is seen to be addressing Israel in the present. Though the events at Jerusalem are themselves unrepeatable, they give an indelible character to the continuing life of discipleship, and the distinctive Lukan resurrection appearances become a direct address to his church as they comment upon its life of worship, belief and witness. The 'today' of the Nazareth speech is inclusive to take account, not merely of the ministry of Jesus, but also of the fulfilment of its salvation in the church.[1] Luke does not write a life of Jesus, if by that is meant an account of a past which is now ended and which affects the present only as it is recalled within the context of a movement that it has called into being. The past is not seen as a closed period but is brought into immediate relationship with the present as the living Lord continues to move his church forward into his and its future.

Talbert has pointed to Luke's concern with continuity. For him, 'the Lukan emphasis seems to be on the continuity between the various stages rather than their separateness as Conzelmann contends'. Yet he continues to talk of distinct stages within that continuity, and maintains,

> To be entirely accurate, it is necessary to recognize that Luke makes a distinction in the third stage of salvation history so that the apostolic age must be separated from the post-apostolic church. For Luke, this distinction is

1. See my discussion in *Christ the Lord*, pp. 41-47.

> so radical that it may very well be necessary to speak of a four phase salvation history.[1]

For Talbert, Luke is concerned to present the church of the problematic present with its past, to meet its need, in Drury's terms, 'for strong, historical roots'[2], to provide it with a source, to urge its members to remember their foundation in Judaism and to maintain their consciousness of continuity with the life and faith of the early church. Luke is emphasizing this oneness because he is concerned to ward off that danger arising out of an emergent Gnosticism or an incipient Marcionism which would urge it to move out into new, untried ventures and to find its hope in a present enthusiasm and freedom. Paul, of course, would have been easily claimed as a proponent of their view.

Such a reading of Luke as Talbert makes relies heavily for its outlook upon an interpretation of Paul's farewell to the Ephesian elders which sees it as a commendation of the tradition and of a handing over of that tradition's contents to the church of Luke's contemporaries (Acts 20.17-35). It is linking of Luke's church to Paul and to his teaching, to a Paul who has been legitimated by the apostles who have in turn received the tradition from Jesus himself. Luke is consciously supplying roots which will withstand the gales of enthusiasm of the moment. This says Drury is really what makes Luke somewhat bland for his is essentially a holding exercise.[3]

Such an outlook has done great service to the interpretation of Luke by drawing out that continuity which is at the heart of his thought and has made sense of his unified narrative which Conzelmann was in danger of destroying. It enables the pro-Jewish stance of Luke's work to be taken more seriously and it goes far towards giving a reason for the shape and emphases of Luke's portrait of Paul. Yet its suggestion of Luke's subordination of the present to the past seems to do less than justice to the eschatological enthusiasm of his writings and to their strong sense of forward movement in which the fulfilment of the past is to be found. Luke seems not to make the past the control of the present but rather uses it to explain the here and now. The past of course

1. C.H. Talbert, *Literary Patterns, Theological Themes and the Genre of Luke–Acts* (Missoula, MT: Scholars Press, 1947), pp. 106-107.

2. J. Drury, *Tradition and Design in Luke's Gospel* (London: Darton, Longman & Todd, 1976), p. 13.

3. *Tradition*, p. 10.

does exercise some constraint as he thinks in terms of continuity and of promise and fulfilment. But what has actually happened has issued in a newness and a moving out that has broken free from the actual limitations in which the past was enclosed. At the heart of this is the exaltation of one who came to it by way of crucifixion, and the inclusion of Gentiles into God's eschatological act without the Law. Luke's concern with continuity has to be worked at and it needs both the insights of the risen Jesus to explain the former and a scriptural interpretation of the latter to enable both Jesus' exaltation and the Spirit's Gentile outpouring to stay within its embrace. Luke knows that the real past did not itself make for a fulfilment such as actually occurred. He has to justify what he sees as the link between the two. Luke's Paul is more radical than is often allowed, and the coming in of Gentiles apart from the Law, indeed in open contradiction of it, has much bolder implications for Luke than a simple theory of continuity suggests. I argue below that his reporting of Paul's Miletus speech is a defence of Paul himself rather than of the tradition handed on by him.[1] In the last resort, Luke urges his contemporaries not to come down on the side of caution but to embrace the newness which he sees inherent in the Christian proclamation. Luke is actually a Paulinist, even if it is an interpreted Paulinism that he embraces.

Luke does not cut adrift from his roots: that is certain, but he reminds his readers of those roots, not in order to stop them from moving away from them, but because fulfilment of the past in which the past is not laid aside but caught up in and moved into the present is at the heart of his understanding of the significance of Jesus. His emphasis upon the past is not formed out of the need to defend Christianity against perversion but is of the essence of his understanding of the work of God in Christ.

For Luke does not see an easy progression from Jesus to his own time. The twelve are called upon to interpret the event of Jesus in the light of the coming of Pentecost. It takes an action of the Spirit to move the church into the Gentile mission apart from the Law. Paul's outlook (not uninterpreted) is authenticated by the apostles, but if it is James who gives it the seal of approval, it is also he who later, in the light of Paul's actual missionary stance, expresses the suspicions of others from which he himself does not entirely dissent. Luke is coming to the defence of Paul but it is a defence which, though

1. See pp. 108-20.

not necessarily made against Jewish outsiders, is nevertheless against critics who retain their links with Jewish institutions rather than against those who are severing the connection. Luke draws Paul into the concern for Judaism, not by ignoring Jewish and Jewish–Christian suspicions, but by meeting those suspicions while at the same time maintaining the validity of the stance which gave them a certain justification. Luke reinterprets Paul, not in order to save him from the clutches of enthusiastic, but unbalanced supporters, but to defend him from those who would deny his stance. He takes that stance, proclaims the truth in it, but at the same time shows that it is not inimical to the whole thrust of Jewish covenantal history as that has found its fulfilment and its rationale in the resurrection of Jesus. Luke's underlying conviction is the validity of God's covenant with Israel and of the authority of the Old Testament witness to that. He is a true exponent of its typological significance and, through his understanding of promise and fulfilment, is able to give value to its historical divisions which he never forgets. He is controlled, not by an apologetic or defensive scheme, but by a conviction. His story is itself a proclamation. The summary of that proclamation is contained in the infancy narratives and it is these which suggest that, important though the coming in of the Gentiles is to him and though this remains the ultimate source of his hope, his primary concern, indeed the primary problem and the ultimate cause of the perplexity which is found behind the writing of Luke–Acts, is with Israel and her rejection of the gospel. He writes at a time when the centre of gravity of his church has probably already moved from Israel to the Gentiles and when the church's mission to the Jews has to be pronounced a failure. Though many in Israel have come in, the vast majority have not. If the refusal on the part of many of the Gentiles is countered by the number of those who do come in to such an extent that the refusal becomes of little significance, concerning Israel, though many do come in, their inclusion is almost completely countered by the failure of the majority to respond. What of God's initial covenant? Indeed, what of *the* covenant, for Luke does not think in terms of a new covenant? Are God's promises in the end of no effect to make 'fulfilment' an empty shell? Has God in fact rejected his people?

A large number of studies, working within the framework of stages in salvation history, were able to accept just that. So Conzelmann, in his comment on the final scene with the Jews in Acts, can write,

> The scene has been constructed with the express purpose of conveying the impression that the situation with the Jews was hopeless. In contrast to Paul, Luke does not look beyond the present hardening to a future conversion of Israel. Rather, the time of the Gentile church has now broken in; the church has taken possession of the inheritance of Israel. The schema is complete'.[1]

More recently Maddox, though he does not subscribe completely to the three stages of salvation history in that he emphasizes much more clearly the theme of fulfilment in Jesus, nevertheless sees Acts as a progressive movement from Israel to the Gentile world so that at its conclusion, 'At the end of Paul's mission the opportunity offered at the beginning has been lost'. So, 'the judgment of Judaism for its rejection of the offered salvation is displayed with remarkable breadth and force'.[2] Christianity has done a takeover. *Christ the Lord* argued that this was not so, but that Luke remained, though judgmental of those who rejected the Gospel, nevertheless fundamentally convinced that God had not turned his back upon Israel but remained conscious of his covenant with her. God would in effect act to make what was begun with the proleptic restoration of Israel in those who had responded to Jesus open to Israel as a whole when the kingdom would be restored to her. Such a view was influenced by the proclamation to Israel contained in the infancy narratives which, as the prologue to the whole work, made the statement in the light of which the two volumes were to be understood.

It is significant that a number of recent treatments of Luke and the Jews which have approached the two volumes from the perspective of literary criticism have also emphasized Luke's concern with the Jewish people, a concern which many of them feel to be positive.[3] For such critics, the unity of the two volumes is such as to allow the Gospel's first two chapters to exercise an abiding influence over the whole work. For Tannehill, the story as a whole makes a tragic comment upon the hopes expressed in the infancy narratives. The

1. H. Conzelmann, *Acts of the Apostles* (trans. J. Limburg, A.T. Kraabel and D.H. Juel; Philadelphia: Fortress Press, 1987).

2. *Purpose*, pp. 44, 55.

3. L.T. Johnson, *The Literary Function of Possessions in Luke–Acts* (SBLDS, 39; Missoula, MT: Scholars Press, 1977); D.L. Tiede, *Prophecy and History in Luke–Acts* (Philadelphia: Fortress Press, 1980); R.C. Tannehill, *The Narrative Unity of Luke–Acts* (Philadelphia: Fortress Press, I 1986; II 1989); J.B. Tyson (ed.), *Luke–Acts and the Jewish People* (Minneapolis: Augsburg, 1988).

narrative therefore awaits a final resolution. Meanwhile, the church must be concerned with 'the patient and persistent preaching of the gospel in hope that the situation will change'.[1] Tiede more positively, but from the same standpoint, looks for 'the restoration, the consolation, the redemption, the repentance, the forgiveness and the reign of God which Simeon and all those other worthies in Israel expected and which has only begun to be inaugurated in the present time of Luke's story'.[2] Moessner in the same volume takes a somewhat different stance to the infancy narratives. That they speak of the fulfilment of God's promises in Israel he is quite sure, but he sees a somewhat less positive future in the light of them. Israel's expectations of God's promises are in fact reshaped by Luke for their realization is given true expression only in the expectations of Simeon. There is a tension between his hopes and those expressed by Mary and Zechariah. That is the irony of the narrative: Gabriel's promise is to be interpreted in the light of Simeon's proclamation which therefore points to the inadequacy of the other understanding. Israel's vocation is seen in terms of the Suffering Servant and of the thought of Deuteronomy as this is found in the song of Moses. The promise is thus already realized, and in it the hope of Israel is expected not at some future dramatic vindication of quasi-nationalistic hopes but in the return to the Lord. Though Moessner sees the vindication on a different level, he nevertheless sees it as hope for Israel: 'Far from sounding certain and ultimate doom for Israel as a whole, Paul in Acts 28.26-28 declares unflinchingly that the promises of God surely shall prevail'.[3]

The significance of these studies lies perhaps less in their actual conclusions (though these I would regard as providing strong support for the correctness of that view which sees a positive attitude to the Jews in Luke–Acts) than in the method of taking Luke's narrative as a whole and allowing its movement and its pointed emphases to control the significance of its individual parts. That Luke himself is aware of this dimension seems clear. It is seen for example, in his telling of the

1. 'Rejection by Jews and Turning to Gentiles: The Pattern of Paul's Mission in Acts', in *Luke–Acts and the Jewish People*, pp. 83-101 (101); cf. 'Israel in Luke–Acts: A Tragic Story', *JBL* 104 (1985), pp. 69-85.

2. '"Glory to Thy People Israel": Luke–Acts and the Jews', in *Luke–Acts and the Jewish People*, p. 3.

3. 'The Ironic Fulfilment of Israel's Glory', in *Luke–Acts and the Jewish People*, pp. 35-50 (50).

Nazareth rejection and in his story of Cornelius. In the literary approach, the story is allowed to speak for itself, especially through plot and characterization, and it is thought to do so best when it is untrammelled by externally imposed understandings of Luke's adjudged theological stresses.

When Talbert reviewed the first volume of Fitzmyer's commentary on Luke, he described it as 'in a sense marking the end of an era'.[1] That era was dominated by Conzelmann's understanding of Luke and by his search for the evangelist's theology. Now, says Talbert, there is a new approach to Luke–Acts, one which in contrast to the old, pursues a synchronic method which is concerned with the text as a whole and with the individual unit's place in it, studies the text as it is rather than in relationship to sources or parallel narratives, and dialogues with Graeco-Roman literature rather than with Conzelmann. 'The earlier method used the gospel as a window through which to see something else...the later as a mirror to reflect its own narrative world'. As has been pointed out,[2] Talbert's review is not without its polemic, but it does reflect the more recent concern to take the final form of the narrative seriously, to see it as a unified tale, and to avoid coming to it with aims and preconceptions which might distort, or at least unbalance, what the text itself has actually to tell. It attempts to sit under the text and in so doing, in Tannehill's words 'manifests a concern to understand how a text speaks not only to the mind but also to the will and the imagination'. In this way, the text is released from being a quarry for historical and theological information to become the means of the Gospel's address to the whole person—and that presumably is what Luke was trying to do!

The literary-critical approach to Luke–Acts has made an invigorating contribution towards enabling the work to speak powerfully and alluringly. It has encouraged a treatment which does justice to its religious aims and which allows it to be treated as a living voice. Somewhat less happy, however, is that outlook which contrasts the two approaches of using Luke as a window and a mirror.[3] The one

1. *CBQ* (1986), pp. 336-38.

2. Moore, *Literary Criticism*, pp. 3-4.

3. This imagery is used frequently; it is found for instance in Talbert's review of Fitzmyer referred to in n. 1. See also, R.J. Karris, 'Windows and Mirrors: Literary Criticism and Luke's Sitz im Leben', in *Society of Biblical Literature 1979 Seminar Papers* (ed. P.J. Achtemeier; Missoula, MT: Scholars Press, 1979).

may indeed be so concerned to see something beyond that which stands immediately before the viewer that it forgets the intricacies of the actual window, but the other may be so engrossed with the encounter in itself that it fails to see either the work or the addressee as related to the ongoing Christian community of which certainly the author and most probably the reader also was a part.

Discussing where literary criticism goes beyond composition criticism, which likewise seeks to look at the Gospel as a whole to do justice to the development of the narrative, Moore focuses the divergence on its rejection of concern with uncovering the author's theology as something which is propositional and which can, as it were, be extracted from the text. Literary criticism eschews this intention—at any rate it does not espouse it—as it seeks to allow the narrative to unfold from within itself.[1] It is just this declared distancing from any direct concern with the theological outlook of the author, however, which is disturbing for it suggests that such an interest is the intrusion of something which is extrinsic to the text and so does violence to it. We have seen of course that it can do just that if it fails to take account of all the text and its mixture of outlooks. It can take refuge in a belief that the author simply took over traditions that he did not incorporate into his own thinking and so ignore what is inconvenient or the possibility that the story simply proceeds through dialectic. The biblical story is not a theological textbook, a systematic theological presentation, or a contribution to a theological debate. Rather it was of the stuff of real life, of faith and doubt, of freedom and perplexity, of searching for truth and of being grasped by something greater than oneself. But theology is itself a part of this religious quest and response. Theology is quite simply the attempt to put into words the significance of the feeling that one has been grasped by God and in that constraint has actually found freedom, life, and a movement into God's future. A Gospel is the evangelist's concern to share his perception with his readers and to bring it to bear upon a situation where that perception has not yet been discovered or, more likely as in the case of Luke–Acts, where its insights have not yet been fully realized or are in danger of being lost. Luke–Acts is an attempt to share its author's understanding of the marvel of God's inclusive outreach and the equally clear but perplexing wonder at the rejection of that embrace by those who had a special place within it. All Luke's efforts

1. *Literary Criticism*, pp. 4-7.

are directed to that end, and his understanding of God, of Jesus, of the activity of the Spirit and of the make-up of the church which are worked out in the development of the story, are unfolded in the light of that wonder. Luke writes from faith to deepen faith, and his story is conceived in the light of this faith and of the situation which he deems to be in need of his message.

This, of course, is to look at the two volumes in the light of external constraints, but they are constraints imposed by the fact that the writings come out of a community of faith in general and of a specific situation in particular. Their place in the Christian community suggests that their message, to us, though inevitably transcending their original message will be impaired unless it is seen as being in some form of dialogue with that offered to the situation it originally addressed. Our response to the gospel as story still needs to be made in relation to the response it was originally hoped to arouse. As Keck maintains,[1] the absolutist claims made on behalf of historical criticism must be relativized, for it neither determines the 'real' meaning of the text nor exhausts its possibilities. But that it has some continuing contribution to make to the holistic understanding of the text is certain, for in dialogue with the literary approach there is both a challenge to, and a deepening of its own aims, and a rigorous questioning and sharpening of the newer discipline's insights. It is significant that Tannehill, in his distinguished narrative unfolding of Luke–Acts, sees his work as 'not confined to what is happening when reading for the first time with much of the text still unknown'.[2] Reflection leads to further reflection, a theology leads to narrative development which in turn leads to a deepening understanding of Luke's work which has been well categorized as 'kerygmatic story'. As Tannehill suggests, there is in Luke–Acts a narrative unity which is the outcome of a 'single author working with a persistent theological perspective'.[3] A theological perspective actually shapes the narrative and our reading of it is influenced by a prior understanding fashioned by our faith and

1. L. Keck, 'Will the Historical-Critical Method Survive?' in R.A. Spencer, *Orientation by Disorientation: Studies in Literary Criticism and Biblical Literary Criticism* (Pittsburgh: Pickwick Press, 1980), pp. 115-28.

2. *Luke*, p. 6.

3. *Luke*, p. xiii; cf. *Acts*, p. 4: 'When we study a narrative as rhetoric and discover that certain values and beliefs are consistently advocated within it theological questions cannot be ignored'.

our part in the Christian community. Neither we nor Luke's original readers came to it without presuppositions and a faith or lack of faith. We are not as ones alone going to the entirely novel.

An understanding of Luke's theology will actually help us to a balanced reading of Luke's narrative. The validity of Moessner's criticism of Tiede and Tannehill referred to above can be determined by a consideration of Luke's overall understanding of the place of Israel in God's designs. This would suggest that Tiede and Tannehill are right in their belief that the narrative awaits a formal resolution, for passages like Lk. 21.24, Acts 3.19-21 and the promise of the two young men at the ascension (Acts 1.11) suggest that Luke does indeed expect the real resurgence of Israel in terms which would fulfil the proclamation of Gabriel in the manner expected by Mary and Zechariah. The place of Mary in Luke–Acts, where she is incorporated into the believing community, makes it wholly unlikely that Luke puts her forward as an expression of wrong hopes. That would seem to go beyond irony and issue in total incomprehension.

M.C. Parsons has recently argued for a multi-dimensional approach which applies the historical–critical as well as literary methods to a biblical narrative, in this case the departure scenes in Luke–Acts.[1] He writes: 'By holding these two "radically opposed" methods of diachronic and synchronic analyses in tension, it is hoped that due consideration may be given to Luke–Acts both as first century writings and as timeless literary structures'.[2] His is a stimulating exercise, but it is doubtful whether the tension—which in the end seems to amount to virtual separation—need be as great as he allows, and it may be suggested that remembrance of Luke's theological outlook as this is unravelled in his work as a whole could have given an added depth to his literary handling of these episodes. The ending of Luke is seen as the climax of the narrative which it effectively brings to a close. It completes the journey narrative and the entry into Jerusalem and it takes the story as a whole back to its beginning. 'The temple, once the scene of heated confrontation between God's messenger, Jesus, and God's people, the Jewish leaders, has now become the site of God's new messengers, the disciples, blessing God unimpaired'. For Luke's readers, 'the image of disciples praising God, despite the

1. M.C. Parsons, *The Departure of Jesus in Luke–Acts* (JSNTSup, 21; Sheffield: JSOT Press, 1987).

2. *Departure*, p. 25.

absence of their Lord, is indelibly imprinted upon their hearts and minds. At that moment, the narrator/guide at their elbows whispers in their ears a command, "Go thou, and do likewise"'.[1]

This indeed does, as Tannehill suggests of a literary reading, appeal not only to the mind but also to the heart and emotions, and as such fulfils something of the promise of what should be expected of a Gospel. It certainly shows the strength of literary criticism and justifies its undertaking. But does it do quite enough justice to the Gospel of Luke or to the reader of it? Worship, yes; joy, certainly; an unfulfilled present which moves into the future as the narrative's ending remains incomplete. But what attitude towards those who have rejected Jesus does this return to the beginning, this conclusion of the travel narrative, of the entry story, let alone of the passion narrative expect? What is it saying about the worshipper's attitude to the opponents? Is is commending a triumphalism, a writing off of the opponents, a hostility to them? What basic understanding is to underly the mission that it is going on to narrate and to which it is calling the reader? This is important for it will determine the nature of the God seen in Jesus to whom it is that the reader is called to respond. Here again the narrative interpretation needs to be filled out with the understanding of Luke's theological concerns—how he sees the implications of God's action in Jesus. The narrative does not always in itself make this clear. It has to be read in terms of a theological stance which an earlier reading of the story has suggested.

There is a theology, a point of view, which has to be extracted from the story as a whole and it is in the light of this, which undergirds the story and actually forms the presuppositions for the way in which he tells it, that the story itself inevitably has to be read. For the story was not written in isolation from the previous beliefs of the writer and of the situation which caused him to write. These can add a depth to the understanding of the narrative and also allow the limitations of the work as a whole to be accepted and even used.

For Luke's answer and the response his Gospel calls forth will not necessarily be the one that we should be making. His response to Jesus will not necessarily be ours. Behind his writing lies a community with beliefs, expectations, hopes and perplexities which inevitably reflect the emphases and limitations put upon them by their place in time. Our use of the Gospels arises out of a dialogue with them, seen as

1. *Departure*, p. 113.

products of their age, and with our pre-understanding which is itself fashioned by beliefs and unbeliefs, insights and hindrances, our place in history and in the community of faith. They will be used in different ways and for different purposes. Our task is to plumb the depths to discover the riches which are there. Imagination is vital; the problem is however that imagination, however informed, can end up by doing a takeover. It is perhaps only that continuing critical–historical concern, which sees the Gospels within the framework of the early church and its slow response to Jesus, which can act as both a stimulus to narrative critics to go beyond its own limitations and also as a warning that the depths they fathom are neither free from hazards nor entirely uncharted.

Many insights have been gained by seeing the Lukan writings alongside the literary techniques of the ancient world as these are found in biographies, in histories and in the novel. Our understanding of the shape of his two-volume work, of his reasons for writing, of his portrayal of Jesus, and of the early church has been greatly advanced.[1] The preface to his Gospel places him among the educated men of his day and the Theophilus to whom he addresses his two volumes was also likely to have been of some social and influential standing. Luke's work certainly has contacts with literary productions of his day and their manner certainly influenced his own. A recent evaluation would be generally supported when it maintains that, 'It seems fair to conclude that the Gospel of Luke owes more to the genre of Hellenistic history writing than that of Matthew and Mark'.[2] Whether Hellenistic influences are determinative for Luke, however, remains far less certain. The actual genre of Luke–Acts is not easily determined, and Karris maintains that we must accept the limitations implied by a necessary recognition that Luke–Acts has to be viewed as a *genus mixtum*.[3] Luke himself suggests that he is at least indebted to his predecessors in the Gospel art and, though he may be critical of

1. C.H. Talbert, *Reading Luke: A Literary and Theological Commentary on the Third Gospel* (New York: Crossroad, 1984); D.E. Aune, *The New Testament in its Literary Environment* (Cambridge: James Clark, 1987); R.I. Pervo, *Profit with Delight: The Literary Genre of the Acts of the Apostles* (Philadelphia: Fortress Press, 1987); E.P. Sanders and M. Davies, *Studying the Synoptic Gospels* (London: SCM Press; Philadelphia: Trinity Press International, 1989).

2. *Studying*, p. 290.

3. 'Windows and Mirrors', p. 53.

them, he does not imply that he was leaving them behind even if he was going to adapt them and certainly extend his narrative beyond the boundaries their works marked out. Nevertheless, his *kamoi* suggests that he consciously joined their company. But Luke's decision to extend the story of Jesus into that of a part of the church meant that he gave to his work an historical dimension which inevitably entailed casting an eye back determinedly upon what had preceded it. Luke's story was rooted in history and that meant in the story of Israel as he read it. Luke was by both background and design a man of the Old Testament and it was most likely this which provided his major control. The genre of Luke–Acts it seems, once the decision to write his second volume was made, was fashioned by the Old Testament, especially its historical writings and those of the prophets, and by his predecessors as Gospel writers. Hellenistic writing techniques influenced what he wrote and it was important that his work should make contact with those who shared in the Greek and Roman cultural setting. It has long been recognised that he was at home with Roman social and political thought, and he is able to make a fair stab at entering the world of Greek philosophy. But just as his accuracy in some Roman matters was caught up in an Old Testament manner of recounting that past, and philosophy was framed in an Old Testament setting, so it seems likely that Hellenistic literary controls were caught up in his basic Old Testament pattern to be a means of communication rather than that they formed the dominant influence in his work. Luke was a man of many parts, of wide sympathies, and able to embrace many influences. Predominant among them was that provided by the Old Testament for it was this which gave him the means of expressing what was his primary conviction, that Jesus was the eschatological redeemer of Israel and, through her, of the nations.

These chapters are part of the ongoing attempt to perceive how Luke understood that primary conviction, of its implications, and how he addressed it to the church of which he was a part. Luke, it still seems, is best approached as a pastoral theologian in the sense that he is convinced of the Lordship of Jesus which he understands in a manner fashioned by his own background and by what he perceived as the salvation Jesus brought.[1] He is a man who has worked out his

1. C.K. Barrett in his earlier survey talked of Luke as a pastoral theologian, *Luke the Historian in Recent Study* (London: Epworth Press, 1961). Development of the idea is to be found in S.G. Wilson, *The Gentiles and the Gentile Mission in*

response to the work of God in Christ in a particular way in dialogue with the church of which he was a part and with those who influenced its stance. The church to which he writes is undergoing some form of a failure of nerve, brought about it would seem by the hiddenness of Jesus' Lordship—emphasized most likely by the failure of the parousia to establish that Lordship effectively—and by the rejection of the gospel on the part of the vast majority of the Jewish nation. For one such as Luke, that rejection was the more serious because it threatened the very foundation stone of his belief that Jesus was Israel's promised Lord. He therefore has to round upon the Jews who denied this, to expose their perversity, but to do so without cutting off Israel as a whole from the promises of God. Israel therefore remains central to his story. Meanwhile, his account of the inclusion of Gentiles within the people of God is seen as the fulfilment of God's convenantal promises and acts as a counterbalance to the tragedy of Israel's rejection. God's promises have been confirmed in Jesus, and Luke's story in Acts is the witness in faith to this. But the inclusion of Gentiles without the Law, though dependant upon a direct act of God through Cornelius, is not an abrogation of those promises, radical though the step is. Jewish Christians remain true to the covenant and Gentile Christians acknowledge their debt to it. So Luke can proclaim the fulfilment of God's convenantal promises and he can look with confidence to the revelation of the kingdom of God at the parousia in spite of the hostility of the Jews, the ambivalence of Rome and the actual weakness of the church.

In this story, Paul plays a large part for in some way he is Luke's hero. Luke not only uses him as the supreme witness to the power of the Spirit and so to the reality of the Lordship of Christ, but also comes to his defence against those who attacked his gospel of freedom from the Law and so accused him of despising the covenant. Luke justifies Paul's gospel by reinterpreting the significance that Paul himself gave to it.

Part One of this study is concerned with Luke and Paul for it is a balanced understanding of this relationship which will enable Luke's own beliefs to be rightly assessed. Luke is seen to be a companion of Paul for a part of his journeyings. Unlikely though it is that he came to Christianity by way of Paul, he was nevertheless deeply influenced by that apostle's thought, especially by his conviction that the coming

Luke–Acts (SNTSMS, 23; Cambridge: Cambridge University Press, 1973).

of Christ had brought to an end the situation where the Law was recognized as defining the bounds and nature of the covenantal people of God. Christ had brought this function of the Law to an end. It remained however as the identity marker of the faithful within Israel who became the basis of the community brought into being by the outpouring of the Spirit. Jewish–Christians would continue to keep the Law (though in a redefined way) and Gentile Christians would observe the apostolic decree seen, not as an imposition of a part of the Law, but as apostolic requirements witnessing to the truth of Jewish Christianity as eschatological Israel, to the nature of Gentile Christianity as having been formed upon her, and as having been enabled by God's activity within Israel. Luke, having learned and embraced Paul's fundamental conviction, nevertheless reinterpreted his outlook in terms of that continuity which Paul himself came perilously near to denying. Ongoing history, a mellowing of earlier very necessary stances, different backgrounds, and different temperaments accounted for this reinterpretation, but it was one which nevertheless remained faithful to Paul's basic convictions and which actually does more justice to the apostle's position than is often allowed.

Such an understanding of Luke and Paul allows for the distinctiveness of Luke's outlook to be more clearly seen, and this distinctiveness is given a sharper edge when his thinking is compared with that found in Mark and, more especially, in Matthew. Comparison of the different ways in which Luke and Matthew have handled a large number of parallel incidents, as well as the overall shaping of their Gospels, brings out the distinctive stances of the two writers, and more especially deepens the understanding of Luke's theology which is our basic concern. This, again emphasizes Luke's belief in an early parousia, draws out his understanding of the presence of the kingdom as transcendent rather than immanent, pinpoints his continuing concern for Israel and his positive hope for her, suggests that he does not see the Christian community as doing a takeover from her of the covenantal privileges and understands him as expressing a more relaxed attitude to the Law, brought about by something of a theological indifference to it, than that found in either Matthew or Mark. Luke appears as having a clear and consistent perspective of his own.

Part Two attempts to take no position over sources for the present state of the question does not really allow a discerning of the particular theological nuances of the individual evangelists to rest upon any one understanding of the relationships between them.[1] Nevertheless, the question of sources, though not to be used as exercising a control over the theological reading of the Gospels, must remain of serious concern not only for those who would seek to come to some position about the alleged nature and significance of a Gospel and its author's purpose, but also for those who would, albeit tentatively, try to propose some interrelationship between them and the churches of their day. As Esler has forcibly reminded us,[2] the evangelists were not armchair theologians or cushioned theorists but, as many of us would suggest, were rather pastoral theologians in the service of the churches out of which they came and to which they wrote. Therefore it is necessary to espouse some stance regarding sources and to adopt a position which makes sense of Luke's Gospel as one has come to understand it. Luke it seems to me works out a consistent, articulate and theologically sensitive understanding of the significance of God's redemption in Christ and he has come to this by way of a determined response to, and reinterpretation of, the insights of the apostle to the Gentiles. His story of Paul and his nuanced Paulinism reveals him as a freely creative interpreter of events and beliefs. He is no cypher. Since some direct relationship with Mark remains most likely, it seems that he would have handled that Gospel with the same freedom with which he handled Paul. His own creativity makes it likely that sources need not necessarily (nor indeed unnecessarily) be multiplied. Denial of all other sources seems perverse, and likely to go far beyond possibilities, but such an understanding of Luke's creativity means that they should not be multiplied unless their likelihood is virtually demanded as an explanation of particular parts of Luke's story.

Our third part therefore examines whether the Luke we have uncovered in our earlier chapters could actually have used Matthew's

1. As C.H. Talbert wrote, 'Shifting Sands: The Recent Study of the Gospel of Luke', in *Interpreting the Gospels*, pp. 197-213 (211): 'The issue before us today is, how can one study the distinctive perspective of the third evangelist without assuming any such theories'? Comparison with what is in the other Synoptic Gospels provides at least a way which allows for the sharpening of discernment of the individual writer's stance.

2. P.F. Esler, *Community and Gospel in Luke–Acts: The Social and Political Motivations of Lucan Theology* (SNTSMS; Cambridge: Cambridge University Press, 1987).

Gospel as one of his sources and whether such a use makes sense both of the use itself and of the resulting work. We believe that it does and that it in turn helps us towards a better appreciation of Luke's writings and of the actual nature of the Third Evangelist's task.

Our final chapter tries to sum up Luke's work in the light of what we have discovered about it and him. It sees him as a visionary, as one whose vision makes a continuing call to the church. It ends with a possibility, no more indeed than a probable possibility, by suggesting that Luke's work could have been a direct response to the publication of Matthew's Gospel and that it could have been written out of, or at least to, the same church from and for which Matthew wrote.

Part 1

LUKE AND PAUL

Chapter 2

THE APOSTOLIC DECREE

If Acts has left us with a problem, it is no exaggeration to say that that problem is Paul, or to be more precise, the picture of Paul that emerges from its pages. Estimates of the historical value of Acts, of the worth of its author's theological beliefs, of the use he makes of sources, and of his purpose in writing, all to a large extent revolve around his presentation of the apostle to the Gentiles.[1] Our understanding of that, of its historical and theological value, will in fact largely determine the answers we give to these and other questions surrounding Luke's story as it unfolds in his second volume. And indeed more, for its results will carry over into the way we approach his first volume, the Gospel that bears his name, and will inform the expectations and judgments we bring to bear on that also.

Well over half of Acts, and even around a third of Luke–Acts as a whole is devoted to the work of Paul so that all else falls away and he is left to fill not only the centre but virtually the whole of the stage. Luke in Acts is certainly not writing a general history of the early years of the young church. The work of the apostles as a whole is not followed up, the full story of the emerging church in Jerusalem is not revealed, and the founding and life of many prominent centres of Christianity are more or less ignored. Everything falls away so that the spotlight might fall on Paul's work, and virtually on that alone.[2]

It is just this important place Luke gives to Paul, however, which

1. See especially P. Vielhauer, 'On the Paulinism of Acts', in *Studies in Luke–Acts*, pp. 33-50; E. Haenchen, *Acts*, pp. 112-15; C.K. Barrett, 'The Acts of Paul' and 'The Acts and the Origins of Christianity' in C.K. Barrett, *New Testament Essays* (London: SPCK, 1972); U. Wilckens, 'Interpreting Luke–Acts in a Period of Existentialist Theology' in *Studies in Luke–Acts*, pp. 60-86.

2. A.J. Mattil, 'The Purpose of Acts: Schneckenburger Reconsidered', in W.W. Gasque and R.P. Martin (eds.), *Apostolic History and the Gospel* (Exeter: Paternoster Press, 1970).

compounds the problems associated with his picture of him. Paul is in some way a hero. He comes over as the ideal of Christian discipleship and of the Christian missionary. His contribution to the Church's life, strategy and theology is portrayed as being second to none. Yet that contribution is presented in terms which make it very much at odds with what can be discovered about this from Paul's letters. Compared with Paul's letters, it is often said, Luke gives us what can only be characterized as a mere domestication of both Paul's missionary stance and his theological outlook.[1]

It is in fact his presentation of Paul which leads Luke's critics to think of him ultimately as theologically shallow. Paul, the argument runs, was his hero. He wanted to present the apostle to the Gentiles to a later age, even to defend him against his critics. Yet what he arrived at was something other than the real Paul. He used a wished for Paul to serve the interests of something which was very different from Pauline theology. If the very fact of Acts is enough to bring down upon his head the wrath of his existentialist interpreters, his picture of Paul is such as to question the innate ability of the theologian of redemptive history.[2] The attack on him at this level ranges much more widely and with far more devastating consequences. Luke becomes not merely a rogue elephant, but a rogue elephant impelled by naivity. So Haenchen in his great commentary on Acts, can write, 'Luke is no systematic theologian. He does not seek to develop any unified doctrine, the product of thorough reflection!'.[3]

Haenchen's words find a remarkable echo—though perhaps 'echo' is the wrong word, for it represents a magisterial judgment on its own right—in the approach of Professor Barrett. In a paper which confessedly moves forward from some earlier reactions to Luke, Barrett nevertheless still writes, 'It would perhaps be wrong to describe Luke as either a *theologus gloriae* or a *theologus crucis*. He is not sufficiently interested in theology (beyond basic Christian convictions)

1. See the overall stances in the various works cited in n. 1 p. 40. Wilckens' defence of Luke represents what is very much a minority position and it is doubtful if he does justice to the very real differences between Acts and the Pauline letters.

2. My old tutor, Geoffrey Lampe, was wont to point out that NT interpreters did scant justice to Luke. He pointed to their own lack of understanding of the Third Evangelist by suggesting that they tended to see him as little more than 'a dim-wit'. His own writings on Luke show the inadequacy of the more usual response to him.

3. Haenchen, *Acts*, p. 91.

to be called a *theologus* of any colour'.[1]

What ultimately is at stake is Luke's theological understanding of Paul. Did Luke admire Paul, as it were, at a distance, but did what he admire amount to something other than the real beliefs of Paul and issue in a picture of the apostle which is other than that of the real Paul? In a spirited defence of Luke's picture of Paul, F.F. Bruce can answer the question 'Is the Paul of Acts the real Paul?' by saying, 'Yes, he is the real Paul, seen in retrospect through the eyes of a friend and admirer whose own religious experience was different from Paul's and who wrote for another public and purpose than Paul had in view when writing his letters'.[2]

Yet it is hard here to share Bruce's confidence. Did Paul not only have a mission to Jews as well as Gentiles, but did he seem almost always to go to them first with a priority which expressed not merely their priority in the eternal plans of God, but also in the actual missionary strategy and missionary concerns of the apostle?[3] Was he as subservient to Jerusalem as Luke suggests? Did his undoubted concern to be linked in some way to Jerusalem and to the wider church actually allow him to submit to the apostolic decrees and commend them to his churches? Was his theology so at one with the rest of the church that he could preach in the manner of Peter[4] and show by a simple act

1. C.K. Barrett, 'Theologia Crucis—in Acts?' in C. Andresen and G. Klein (eds.), *Theologia Crucis—Signum Crucis* (Festschrift E. Dinkler; Tübingen; Mohr [Paul Siebeck], 1979). Barrett rightly categorizes Luke as a pastoral theologian but says, 'There is no doubt that Luke was more interested in the ways people lived than in formal theology'. But was not Paul himself interested in 'formal theology' and was not his theology essentially a pastoral theology? Earlier, in 'Paul's Speech on the Areopagus' in M.K. Glasswell and E.W. Fasholé-Luke (eds.), *New Testament Christianity for Africa and the World* (London: SPCK, 1974), p. 70, Barrett had written, 'This may lack the profundity of Pauline theology, but it is hardly a betrayal of it'. Certainly Barrett's appreciation of Luke would contrast with Koester's suggestion, 'GNOMAIDIAPHOROI' in H. Koester and J.M. Robinson (eds.), *Trajectories through Early Christianity* (Philadelphia: Fortress Press, 1971), p. 153, that 'Without doubt, Luke in all his admiration of the great apostle of the Gentiles, was a student of Paul's opponents rather than of Paul himself'.

2. F.F. Bruce, 'Is the Paul of Acts the Real Paul?', *BJRL* 58 (1975–76), pp. 282-305 (305).

3. On J.T. Sanders' questioning of this, the usual reading of Acts, see below, pp. 146-47.

4. E. Schweizer, 'Concerning the Speeches in Acts', in *Studies in Luke–Acts*, pp. 208-16.

of Jewish piety that rumours that he was teaching his fellow countrymen to forsake Moses were obviously untrue? Did he have such a positive view of mankind's religiosity that he could see movement from that into Christianity as a natural progression whereby the one is caught up into the other?

Questions such as these make it hard to share Bruce's confidence that Acts presents us with the real Paul, if by that is meant Paul as he actually was and as he would actually have appeared to his contemporaries. At point after point there appears a tension, if not a conflict with the picture gleaned from Paul's letters. This tension is such that it cannot adequately be accounted for by suggesting that it is merely seeing Paul through other eyes, out of a different experience, for different purposes, and at other times. The differences are more fundamental than such an explanation allows.

Above all, Bruce's confidence cannot do justice to the very real problem of the Lukan account of the Jerusalem Conference in Acts 15. Here, Luke's picture of Paul really is at stake.[1] Bruce himself acknowledges the gravity of the problem, although it seems without giving full weight to the significance of his own suggested solution, when he writes,

> But if in fact Paul was unhappy about the invocation of the Decree in his own Mission field, we may suspect that his own close association with the Decree in the narrative of Acts could be due to the amalgamation of a Jerusalem meeting at which he was not present with one at which he was present.[2]

Acts 15 is in every sense pivotal for Luke's picture of Paul in Acts. If he has got Paul to a meeting at which he was not present and doing something which he is wholly unlikely to have done—let alone then going around and imposing that something on others—there seems little room left for defending the historicity of Luke's picture of Paul.

1. Maddox, *The Purpose of Luke–Acts*, pp. 36-39.

2. 'Is the Paul of Acts the Real Paul?', p. 291; cf. M. Hengel, *Acts and the History of Earliest Christianity* (trans. J. Bowden, London: SCM Press, 1979), pp. 111-26. Hengel recognizes the bias present in Paul's account in Gal. 2.1-10 but nevertheless, albeit reluctantly, has to acknowledge that 'Luke's narrative, with its tendencies towards harmonization, is even more questionable'. We would maintain that Luke's narrative is both freer than Hengel allows and that its freedom is caused by something much more radical and more pervasive than the cause of 'harmonization'.

In some way, the Paul of Acts is not the real Paul.

Nevertheless, allowing this and accepting it, we still need to go on to ask about the legitimacy of the picture that emerges from Luke's hands. Paul did not really do some of the things in the way Luke says that he did. He did not necessarily think or act in the way Luke presents him as doing. Yet Luke believed that he could have done, indeed that he would have done and that in fact he should have done them. As far as Luke is concerned, Paul 'must' have acted in this way.[1]

Is the basis for these beliefs of Luke one that shows an understanding of the real Paul, a knowledge of what the apostle to the Gentiles really was about, and is it made in dialogue with the real Paul? Is Luke's a considered re-interpretation based on a theological position which understands Paul's own (at least insofar as anyone was actually able to make his own Paul's particular insights and understanding)[2] or is it a trivialization in which the theology of the apostle is debased in the service of some idealized conception of Christian theology and history? Is Paul domesticated and trivialized, or is he perhaps revealed to another time and saved for another public? Did Luke understand Paul and is what he wrote about him a determined re-evaluation of the apostle's thought or is his picture of the apostle based on a misunderstanding of his subject?

The heart of the problem is Acts 15, for here seems to be the place where Luke appears unashamedly to have either misunderstood or deliberately domesticated Paul to such an extent that he appears actually to have lost sight of him. How could Luke have thought of Paul's not only accepting the imposition of the decree, but of then going on to argue that it should be adhered to by his converts?[3]

1. I owe this description of the evangelist's thinking to the insights of C.K. Barrett and his expression of them in his NT seminars at Durham.

2. J. Fitzmyer, *Luke*, pp. 47-51; J. Nolland, *Luke 1–9.2* (WBC, 35A; Dallas, TX: Word Books, 1989), p. xxxvi.

3. Though see the argument of J.C. Hurd, *The Origin of 1 Corinthians* (London: SPCK, 1965) and I.H. Marshall's defence of Luke's accuracy in *Acts: An Introduction and Commentary* (TNTC; Leicester: Inter-Varsity Press, 1980), pp. 260-61. G. Lüdemann (*Early Christianity according to the Traditions in Acts* [trans. J. Bowden; London: SCM Press, 1989], p. 175) notes that 'Luke does not report later that the communities founded after the conference received the apostolic decree' and thereby suggests that he might have seen it as having far less continuing significance than is usually suggested.

The attitude demanded by the apostolic decree is quite other than that

The usual account of Luke's understanding of the decree is that it amounts to an imposition of some part of the Mosaic legislation upon the Gentiles. Moses is seen as having some continuing and universal

expressed by Paul in 1 Cor. 8 and 10 and Rom. 14 and 15 where he makes no reference to such regulations in spite of their immediate relevance to the situation he was addressing. It is hard to come to any conclusion other than that arrived at by C.K. Barrett when he says of Paul, 'At no point in 1 Cor. 8; 9; 10 does he admit the view that a Christian must never eat meat that has not been slaughtered in conformity with the Jewish regulations. On the contrary, he specifically states that sacrificial food may be eaten.' *Essays on Paul* (London: SPCK, 1982), p. 46. Cf. E.P. Sanders, *Paul, the Law, and the Jewish People* (London: SCM Press, 1983), p. 101, '1 Cor. 8 and 10, especially 10.27, show that Paul expected Christians to eat Gentile food, and in Rom. 14.1-4 Paul indicates that what food is eaten is basically a matter of indifference'. The more cautious approach of N.T. Wright (*The Climax of the Covenant* [Edinburgh: T. & T. Clark, 1991], p. 135) still maintains that Paul 'is asserting the independence and full validity of his own apostleship over against any suggestion that his pagan converts should be bound by the so-called Apostolic Decree'. Attempts have been made to link him more closely to the decree. Marshall (*Acts*, pp. 244-47) says, 'Once the basic issue had been settled, namely that Gentile converts were not required to be circumcised and hence to keep the whole law as a means of salvation (Gal. 5.3), it seems wholly likely that Paul could assent to some measures for the sake of peace with Jewish Christians which involved no real sacrifice of principle'. C.J. Hemer (*The Book of Acts in the Setting of Hellenistic History* [WUNT, 49; Tübingen; Mohr (Paul Siebeck), 1989], p. 269) deals with these passages by suggesting that the decree was not applied by Paul outside a limited geographical area. These attempts to defend Luke's historical accuracy however ignore the fact that the Antioch incident suggests that the food regulations were for Paul a matter of principle for they represented some form of continuing authority for the Jewish purity laws as bounding the people of God. He could not have limited their significance in the way that Marshall and Hemer suggest. This general consideration together with the thought of 1 Cor. 8 and 10 suggests that Paul could not have advocated the decree at Corinth (*contra* J.C. Hurd, *The Origin of 1 Corinthians* [London: SPCK, 1965]).

A novel treatment which allows Paul to accept the terms expressed in the decree as an ethical concern is put forward by P. Borgen, 'Catalogues of Vices, the Apostolic Decree, and the Jerusalem Meeting', in J. Neusner *et al.* (eds.), *The Social World of Formative Christianity and Judaism* (Philadelphia: Fortress Press, 1988), pp. 126-41. Paul continued to proclaim the ethical dimension of what had been associated for Gentiles with the physical act of circumcision and the keeping of the Law. Abstention from pagan vices was implied in the relaxation of the physical demands. The decision of the council was that Jewish proselyte traditions should be taught without the necessity of physical circumcision. Acts 15 makes this explicit. It does not involve a contradiction and Paul could actually have proclaimed these ethical

significance which is acknowledged in the Jewish–Christian community's observance of the Law and in the requirement, which though it might be seen as amounting to a concession, nevertheless demands that Gentile Christians should keep a minimum rule. These rules are then understood as having a cultic significance. As Haenchen puts it: 'These legal obligations do not concern morality, but are requirements from what we would nowadays call the "ritual sphere"'.[1] It is usual to see their origin as in some way determined by Leviticus 17–18 which contain rules for the 'stranger in the land' for those who are associates with Israel.[2] They therefore are seen as having a typological significance which Luke would have understood, accepted, and intended to convey to his readers. He would have understood them as necessary for the Gentiles in order to maintain the purity of the community so that relationships with the Jews and the Jewish mission could be continued, and in order to assert that the community, though not wholly controlled by it, was in fact related to the Law which had a continuing part in its definition. Though the Jewish mission was no longer in practice a really viable option by the time Luke wrote, he was anxious to maintain the church's links with its beginnings in Judaism and to keep its concern with the Jewish people open. All this, it is maintained, is contrary to the thought of the real Paul who would totally have repudiated the idea that the Law had a part in defining the people of God. For him, the Law was at an end and was in no way acceptable for maintaining the holiness of the people. Though the Law had some continuing validity on the moral side, Paul did not appeal to

requirements. However, Galatians and 1 Corinthians make this suggestion unlikely. Circumcision in Galatians is a cultic entry into the people of God, and the whole tenor of Paul's report makes it almost certain that the Antioch food requirements centered around and were later interpreted in a cultic context; they were about those which witnessed to and enabled entry into and continuation within the people of God. That the apostolic decree witnessed to this dimension seems clear from Paul's stance in 1 Corinthians. 6.9-11 does indeed talk in ethical terms and 10.19-22 suggests ethical consequences. On the other hand, the argument of chs. 8–10 as a whole clearly has cultic implications and these for Paul are primary. Any limitations on cultic freedom were resisted by him, and his dealings with constraints parallel to those envisaged in the terms of the decree show that he could not have emptied it of this dimension and that he would therefore have refused its imperatives.

1. Haenchen, *Acts*, p. 469.
2. *Acts*, pp. 469-70.

it even on ethical questions[1] and it was completely void as far as the question of idol meat was concerned.[2] Luke therefore stands far apart from Paul here and virtually in opposition to him. He has not really entered into an understanding of the principles by which the apostle was motivated.

A recent questioning of this interpretation of the Lukan understanding of the cultic intentions of the decree has been made by Stephen Wilson.[3] He questions whether the cultic background is primary for Luke on the grounds that, seen in this way, it conflicts with the Cornelius episode of chs. 10 and 11, that had Luke viewed it in terms of Leviticus 17–18 he would undoubtedly have spelled this out in accordance with what Wilson sees as his usual practice, and that, as far as Luke was concerned, the ordinance is apostolic rather than Mosaic in both intention and authority. By the time of Luke, Mosaic commands are viewed in a basically ethical light. Wilson therefore writes: 'It is improbable that Luke and his readers would have understood the decree exclusively as a set of Levitical or cultic regulations'.[4] By Luke's time they would have been given either a significance in respect of pagan cults or, and Wilson thinks this more likely, an ethical interpretation.[5]

Wilson's treatment contains a number of valuable insights and should certainly give pause to too easy an assumption that either Luke or the original framers of the decree had Leviticus 17–18 uppermost in mind. Nevertheless, his treatment fails as a whole to carry conviction. There is in fact little ethical concern in Acts as a whole.[6] Peter

1. See E.P. Sanders' discussion in *Paul, the Law, and the Jewish People* (Philadelphia: Fortress Press, 1983), pp. 93-105; H. Räisänen, 'His ethics converged with that of the Law even though Rom. 12.1-2 shows that when Paul gives an independent account of the basis of Christian ethics, he does it without any reference to the Law—the Decalogue included', *Paul and the Law* (WUNT, 29; Tübingen: Mohr [Paul Siebeck], 1983), p. 77.

2. Räisänan, *Law*, p. 236.

3. S.G. Wilson, *Luke and the Law* (SNTSMS, 50; Cambridge: Cambridge University Press, 1983).

4. *Law*, p. 94.

5. *Law*, p. 101.

6. C.F. Evans (*Saint Luke*, pp. 93-94) notes that though there is a great deal of ethical instruction in the Third Gospel, in Acts 'although Christianity is here called "the Way" and apostles are said to teach in the name of Jesus and about the kingdom of God, there is scarcely any ethics at all'. This may bring into question Barrett's

acknowledges such an approach in his encounter with Cornelius (10.35) and it is found in Paul's discussion with Felix (24.25). But at Lystra and Athens it does not appear, and idolatry is not said to lead to immorality. Acts appeals to the Gentiles in order to link them to the God of the Jews who is now declared in Jesus. There is no talk of repentance from the immorality of the past. The appeal is based upon an acknowledgment of the true God in place of what is represented as idols.

Luke sets the terms of the decree in a speech of James, and it is this which puts forward his own justification for it and also his understanding of it (15.13-21). God has brought the Gentiles into association with renewed Israel. Conversion of the Gentiles follows from, and is in effect a part of, the restoration of the tabernacle of David.[1] It is not a new event, but was inherent in the old covenant to the fulfilment of which it witnesses. The new community is based upon a remaking of the old and is therefore continuous with the old to such an extent that Luke himself would not actually have thought in terms of 'old' and 'new'. Wilson separates the decree from the context in which Luke sets it and so divorces it from Luke's understanding of the nature of the people of God. He writes, 'Luke's view of the Law and his view of the Church and Israel are developed in different ways and for different reasons and, as far as I can see, the one has nothing to do with the other'.[2] James' speech in Acts 15, however, shows the inadequacy of this view. The setting of the decree in the context of James' speech means that Luke understands it, not as ethical rules, but as an acknowledgment of the nature of the community and its relation to God's former activity in Israel.

Whatever the original concerns of the decree, Luke sees them as cultic in that they have a part in defining the boundaries and nature of the people of God brought into being by the coming of Christ. He probably understood them as related in some way to the outlook of Leviticus 17–18.

How though did Luke actually understand their significance? For

suggestion that Luke was interested in how people lived rather than in theology as such. See also below, pp. 119-21.

1. J. Jervell, 'The Divided People of God' in *Luke and the People of God* (Minneapolis: Augsburg, 1972), pp. 41-74; N. Dahl, 'A People for His Name', *NTS* 4 (1957–58), pp. 319-27; Franklin, *Christ the Lord*, pp. 95-99.

2. *Law*, pp. 104-105.

Haenchen, that significance is theological. It is found in the belief that the Gentile mission should be conducted without the full constraints of Law.[1] Yet, he maintains, that did not involve for Luke an actual break with the Law.[2] These are Mosaic rules for Gentiles based on Leviticus 17–18 and so the Law has continuing validity. Moses remains an authority and the Law still in some way defines the people of God.[3]

How then can Haenchen square this with his belief that Luke viewed the Gentile mission as being now without the Law, as it must be since Gentiles became part of that people of God which is no longer determined by circumcision? Haenchen must maintain that Luke did not understand the real significance given to the Law by the Jewish people. He saw circumcision and its accompaniments, not in the Old Testament sense as determining the people of God, but as a particular custom of the Jews which could be laid aside without actually denying the Law.[4]

If this really is what Luke meant, Luke is seen as being guilty on two counts. His particular theological understanding of the Law is said

1. Haenchen, *Acts*, pp. 440ff. He titles his discussion of the Council in ch. 15 'Gentile freedom from the Law admitted in Jerusalem'.

2. *Acts*, p. 471 where the decree is described as being 'the four commandments which Moses himself gave to the Gentiles'.

3. *Acts*, p. 470. The mission to the Gentiles is in full accord with Moses himself, 'who demanded just those abstinences of the Gentiles'.

4. Haenchen's denial to Luke of any real understanding of the theological significance of the Law as that was asserted by Paul is perhaps most clearly seen when he writes: 'We only understand the coherence of the narrative if we grasp the fact that the burdensome nature of the law lay in circumcision and beyond that only in the sheer multiplicity of the legal prescriptions. From Luke's point of view these four requirements were thus not a burden: the Apostolic Council's edict is rather the final recognition of the mission free from the law, hence of Gentile Christianity free from the law' (p. 459). Yet, in the light of his understanding of the significance of the decree as Mosaic regulations for Gentiles, it seems that Haenchen's assertion that it represents freedom from the law is an overstatement. It would rather have to be seen as freedom from almost the whole of the law, but not completely so. Haenchen says ('The Book of Acts as Source Material for the History of Early Christianity', in L.E. Keck and L.J. Martyn [eds.], *Studies in Luke–Acts* [London: SPCK, 1966], pp. 258-76) 'If one is to understand correctly Luke's attitude at this point (the Cornelius–Council complex), one must consider the fact that Luke was no longer able to grasp theologically, as Paul had, the legitimacy of the mission to the Gentiles free of the Torah'. This, however, represents precisely that understanding of Luke that we are arguing against.

to negate totally Paul's insistence that Christ and Christ alone bounds the people of God, while his lack of real theological depth is said to stop him from appreciating the Pauline evaluation of the positive claims of the Law.

J.T. Sanders' recent discussion of Acts 15 seems to be aware of the problems raised by Haenchen's evaluation of the decree without however managing to resolve them.[1] He recognises that the break is much greater than Haenchen allows. Gentiles do not have to be converted to Judaism, that is, to an observance of circumcision and the Law. They do, however, have an obligation to obey the requirements that God has given for Gentiles. Are not these, though, the requirements demanded by the Law? Sanders struggles at this point. In his main discussion, he acknowledges that the regulations of the apostolic decree are Mosaic. So, he says: 'Thus Luke, by the use of this list, is able to demonstrate the proper fidelity of *Gentile* Christianity to the Law of Moses while at the same time freeing Gentile Christians from any need to be converted to Judaism, especially from any need to be circumcised'.[2] Later, however, the fact that, biblically understood, they are Mosaic laws is quietly dropped. 'Inasmuch as God had prophesied the existence of the church as a *Gentile* religion he also saw fit to include a few laws for that Gentile church'.[3] Later in the book, these laws are separated from Moses altogether and are related rather to the later Jewish discussion of Noachic laws.[4]

Sanders has the same problem as Haenchen. He wants to see the decree as marking the end of the Law for Gentile Christians, yet has to acknowledge that it seems to be based on the Law itself. In the end, he has to try to resolve the issue by making it a question, not of tension within the biblical revelation, but of conflicting interpretations of that revelation, on the one hand by Luke's Christians, and on the other by Jewish contemporaries.[5] Does Luke see the decree as binding Gentile Christians in some way to the Law or not? If the half-way

1. J.T. Sanders, *The Jews in Luke–Acts* (London: SCM Press, 1987).

2. *Jews*, p. 116.

3. *Jews*, p. 118. Sanders goes on to say, 'By keeping those laws the Gentile church demonstrates its continuity with and fidelity to the Bible. Circumcision is a Jewish affair.'

4. *Jews*, p. 267. They are not then seen as part of what he describes as 'Mosaic customs'.

5. *Jews*, p. 268.

house offered by Haenchen and Sanders issues in ambiguities of interpretation, can these be removed by suggesting that Luke is more radical in his interpretation than that allows?

Some attempt to defend Luke's theological consistency is made by Jervell[1] who sees Luke as working with the concept of a people and an associate people, both controlled by the demands of the Law. He writes: 'The apostolic decree is nothing but Mosaic Law which is applied to Gentiles living together with Israel'.[2] Luke sees this as the fulfilment of Old Testament expectations which control his understanding of the renewed convenantal people. Jervell's is certainly a consistent theological interpretation and as such gives more value to Luke's theological ability, but it does so at a great price. What emerges is simply not indebted in any way to Paul.

Jervell's picture of the situation, however, again does less than justice to Luke. Above all, it fails to take into account the fact that Luke's understanding of what occurred at the apostolic council is controlled by the significance he gives to the Cornelius episode—and the significance of that for him is very great indeed. Jervell actually undervalues the radical stance adopted by Luke in his description and defence of Peter's dealings with Cornelius. He writes: 'Luke labours to prove that the salvation of Gentiles occurs in complete accordance with the law: no transgression has taken place: the law is not invalidated, abridged, or outmoded'.[3] For him Cornelius 'keeps the law'; Cornelius's 'Jewishness' is demonstrated; God has cleansed him and his company. They have become, for Jervell, honorary Jews. Yet this cannot be the significance that Luke is placing here. It is true that he has no clear definition of 'God-fearers'.[4] In Acts 13 they are brought closely into relation with Jews by v. 26. But this is not so in the Cornelius episode. There they are Gentiles and remain so. The meats Peter is called upon to eat remain in Jewish eyes 'common'; the Gentiles with whom Peter eats remain, quite rightly in Jewish terms, unclean. The Spirit comes in place of incorporation into Jewish propriety, and it is this which causes astonishment.[5]

1. 'The Law in Luke–Acts', *People*, pp. 133-52.
2. *People*, p. 144.
3. *People*, p. 143.
4. A.T. Kraabel, 'The Disappearance of the "God-fearers"', *Numen* 28 (1981), pp. 113-26.
5. *Christ the Lord*, pp. 124-34.

Jervell has defended Luke's clarity at the expense of his real theology. Luke's consistency cannot be defended by making him into the most conservative of the New Testament writers in his attitude to the Law. His consistency can be established only by acknowledging that at the basis of it is his recognition of the radical significance of the revolutionary act of admitting Gentiles into the people of God without circumcision. Commentators rightly see that Luke realizes that to be a radical act.[1] He defends it, but he does so, not by underplaying its radicality, but by acknowledging and explaining this.

For Luke, the Cornelius episode is fundamental for settling two different yet totally related questions, that of the place of circumcision for Gentiles and that of table fellowship rules. The complaint of Peter's critics, 'Why did you go in to uncircumcised men and eat with them?' (11.3) is neither a misunderstanding nor a trivialization of Peter's action.[2] Luke's omission of the Antioch incident from his narrative, though no doubt convenient for his picture of early church harmony, is quite deliberate, for he could not have envisaged separate, independent missions which did not express a total unity of understanding and acceptance. Table fellowship was the mark of the unity of the one eschatological people of God, and the divine will on this is made perfectly clear in the Cornelius episode as well as the complete irrelevance of circumcision for Gentiles. The two questions are solved as far as Luke is concerned in one single indisputable act.

And this act is seen to be an irrefutable demonstration of the divine will. 'Then to the Gentiles also God has granted repentance unto life' (11.18). Why, in the face of such a demonstration and of such a conclusion, should later groups reopen the issue? Partly, no doubt, because Luke knows that the issue was not easily settled, and partly for the sake of his readers to enable the whole established work of Paul and Barnabas to be included in the conclusions. However, these later events, including the promulgation of the apostolic decree, are brought under the umbrella of the Cornelius

1. This is the whole basis of Conzelmann's and Haenchen's arguments as opposed to those of Jervell. What is at issue though is whether they have actually done justice to Luke's understanding of the radicality of the act.

2. Wilson, *Law*, p. 72: 'While for Luke Cornelius' conversion is in some senses exceptional, much more important is its paradigmatic significance. What applies to Cornelius applies to all Gentiles and decisions made in his regard establish principles appropriate to them all.'

incident and are interpreted wholly in terms of that.

The nature of that event for Luke is clear. Repeated accounts of visions, of angelic visitations, and of apostolic insights are but the accompaniments, the necessary preludes to and preparations for the decisive intervention of God in the bestowal of the Holy Spirit upon uncircumcised Gentiles.[1] It is in this where the overriding, compelling nature of the incident is to be found. Three times Peter points to its significance. To his companions he asks, 'Can anyone forbid baptism to those people who have received the Holy Spirit just as we have?' (10.47). Of his critics he demands, 'If God gave the same gift to them as he gave to us when we believed...who was I that I could withstand God?' (11.17). At the Council he proclaims, 'God who knows the heart bare witness to them, giving the Holy Spirit just as he did to us' (15.8). It is this thrice-repeated καθὼς καὶ ἡμῖν which is vital for Luke. The Cornelius episode becomes another Pentecost. Then, as the Joel quotation makes clear, the bestowal of the Spirit enabled the eschatological renewal of Israel (2.17-21). The one covenant was completed and caught up in this fulfilment. All present then were Jews (2.5). It was the reassembling of Israel for which the prophets hoped.[2] Henceforth, Israel was to be a divided people, summoned to become what she was meant to be and to enter into her heritage promised to her through Abraham. So the appeal of Peter's speech reached out from 'Men of Judaea and all who dwell in Jerusalem' by way of 'Men of Israel', to 'all the house of Israel' (2.36). It was a closed event which did not hint at a Gentile outreach. Before anything else Israel

1. Luke sees the presence of the Spirit as an irrefutable guarantee of incorporation into the eschatological people of God. This is his understanding of the Pentecostal outpouring. See, *Christ the Lord*, pp. 97-99.

2. Acts 2.5, 11. Sanders is surely right to acknowledge this and to reject the efforts of the authors of *The Beginnings of Christianity* to make it a predominantly, if not exclusively, Gentile audience. There is little reason for his further comment, however, that Luke included Jews in order 'to attest to the universal Jewish guilt in the death of Jesus'. Verse 23 implicates them in the actual crucifixion of Jesus, but some three thousand of them do repent and so, by receiving the gift of the Spirit, enter into eschatological Israel. Lampe suggests that the scene probably symbolises the future world-wide church, and this may be true. But it is limited to world-wide Jewry as the fulfilment of scriptural expectations of the renewal and ingathering of Israel rather than to a foretaste of the Gentile mission. G.W.H. Lampe, 'Acts' in M. Black and H.H. Rowley (eds.), *Peake's Commentary on the Bible* (London: Nelson, 1962).

had to be remade. The universal outreach, the breaking of the barrier, was to occur later, at Caesarea. Only then were Gentiles to have a part in the eschatological people of God.

If what has happened to Cornelius is perfectly clear, its complete significance however is less so. How is the Cornelius event related to the Jerusalem outpouring of the Spirit? Is it an extension of that event or a repetition of it? If Pentecost is the renewal of Israel, is Caesarea an incorporation of Gentiles into that renewal? Peter's defence to his original critics does not actually settle the matter. Certainly the Law no longer bounds the people of God: the gift of the Spirit has broken through such a presupposition in a divine action which has made the Law redundant for Gentiles. It is in fact no longer necessary either for inclusion within the eschatological people of God or for sharing in that unity which is expressed in its fellowship meals. It has been bypassed. Nevertheless, what is not essential, may not thereby be necessarily obsolete. Law may not be necessary to enter the people of God but it may still be desirable in order to witness to the origins of that people in Israel and to the nature of the community as eschatological, extended Israel.

That is obviously the position of those who at the Council are described as belonging to the party of the Pharisees. 'It is necessary to circumcise them and to charge them to keep the Law of Moses.' Luke, by and large, is favourably disposed to the religious position of the Pharisees even if he gives full prominence to their weak points, and the understanding of the Christian Pharisees, is not necessarily meant to represent a perverse interpretation of the Cornelius event.[1] The Law is not required to bound the people of God but it is required to witness to the nature of that community called into being by Pentecost and Caesarea.

Such an understanding of the Cornelius event is, however, totally ruled out by Peter in a speech which advances considerably upon his previous insight (15.7-11). At Caesarea, God showed that he made no distinction between Jews and Gentiles. Both groups entered the eschatological people of God by an act of grace. Both had been prepared; the Jews by the observance of the Law, the Gentiles by their piety. But neither Jewish Law nor Gentile piety had actually enabled them to be included. In the infancy narratives, Luke's pious Jews all need an

1. The gift of the Spirit did not necessarily exclude circumcision. For Luke, however, it is a perversion of the truth to argue thus.

action of the Spirit to enable them to acknowledge Jesus. The only exception is Anna and she comes in as it were at the side of Simeon. Zechariah without the Spirit, though engaged in the work of the Law, does not respond. He needs a further lesson. Luke's Pharisees need more than the Law to bring them to Jesus. So Peter points to the inadequacy of the Law. No doubt Luke's words are those of a Gentile looking in to the operation of the Law from without,[1] but Peter is made to express very Pauline sentiments. The Law is contrasted with grace and with faith. It is oppressive compared with the new freedom of universality in Christ. In going in to Cornelius and eating with him, Peter has acted not unlike Paul's Peter who 'lived like a Gentile' (Gal. 2.14). Any imposition of Law upon Gentiles is seen as 'making trial of God'.[2] The same language is used of Sapphira when, by her deceit of the eschatological community, she 'tempted the Spirit of the Lord' (5.9) and so was cut off from that Spirit-filled community. In the same way, imposition of the Law would destroy the whole basis and nature of that community. You cannot really have Law and Spirit—at least in so far as Gentiles are concerned. Luke, unlike Paul, has no wish to take such a thought to its logical conclusion to include the abolition of Law for the Jewish people.[3] The Law still has a positive role for them.

And so the way is prepared for the definitive interpretation of the Cornelius episode to be made by James (15.13-21). He accepts the

1. Haenchen, *Acts*, p. 458.

2. J. Nolland ('A Fresh Look at Acts 15.10', *NTS* 27 [1980], pp. 105-15) denies that Luke's use of 'yoke' here has a negative connotation and suggests that this verse does not express an 'outsider's' view of the Law. Rather, he maintains, the verse represents the usual outlook of Acts on the Law, namely, that it is irrelevant as salvation but remains a continuing mark of the Jewish people. The situation in Luke's time is continuous with that seen in Jewish history as a whole. However, 'yoke' as used here is more likely to be pejorative and its use would in fact seem to represent the outlook of an outsider on a particular issue of the Law—namely, the question of the nature of circumcision and the food laws. It refers to the Law's bounding of the people of God and to the separation from outsiders. Paul in Gal. 2.14 had already expressed himself in this way on this particular issue for Peter was already 'Living like a Gentile'. Now Luke takes up this same point. Some Gentile Christians did find it a burden at this particular point and on this particular issue. It separated them off in a way that they found ultimately unacceptable; Peter has in Acts acted in a Pauline manner.

3. It is unlikely however that Paul actually took the argument he uses to its logical conclusion, 1 Cor. 8.20-21, 7.18, Gal. 6.15.

validity of Peter's verdict and actually goes further than the apostle. For James, the significance of the Cornelius episode is that 'God has visited the Gentiles to take out of them a people for his name'. This sees the Cornelius event as witnessing, not to an extension of Israel, but to a Gentile people established with her, coming into being because of her, owing its origin to her, and formed in relation to her as it responds to her traditions and draws from her life. But this people exists alongside eschatological Israel, she is one part of the total people of God brought into being by the outpouring of the Spirit. She is not a separate people, she could not exist on her own, but she does have an existence and a life in her own right. Eschatological Israel needs her just as much as she needs eschatological Israel. The community of the Spirit is one in two interlocking parts. This is more than Jervell's people and an associate people. It is one people in two interrelated, interdependent parts.[1]

This is seen as the fulfilment of Scripture. The quotation from Amos is significant in that it goes further than most of the Old Testament expectations of the eschatological pilgrimage of the nations

1. Jervell, *People*, p. 147. This position represents a slight, but nevertheless significant movement on from that which I took in *Christ the Lord*. There, pp. 124-26, I saw the apostolic decree as both concession and obligation. Gentiles enter into 'Israel renewed and restored'. She 'gives identity to the new people of God as they enter into her covenantal life'. Though I still see the Gentiles as entering into the sphere of eschatological Israel which alone enables their salvation and their incorporation into the covenantal people of God, the full significance of Luke's account of the Cornelius episode seems now to demand more emphasis upon the Gentiles in their own right and as their own people. They come in alongside Israel but not merely as associates with her for they are now seen to have a more determined part of their own. Eschatological Israel, really to be shaped to that happening, needs them as much as they need her. She remains their source and she alone gives them identity, yet they are more than associates of her for they have a significance of their own. They are therefore seen to accept the requirements of the decree as a concession on their part which enables them to make a theological statement about the source and nature of the eschatological community but which at the same time, by recording it as an apostolic rather than as a Mosaic requirement, frees it from any hint of suggestion that Mosaic requirements in any way have a part in defining the people of God. By them, they give witness to their theological beliefs while themselves being aware that they come in as Gentiles who are themselves not under the Law but under the Spirit. Such an understanding Luke seems to have learned from Paul and it is this learning from the apostle to the Gentiles that I failed to acknowledge adequately in my earlier work.

to see the rebuilding of the house of David as a preliminary to the Gentile response which becomes the climax and even the reason for the final act of God (15.16-18; cf. Amos 9.11-12).[1] In this, Luke comes close to Paul's use of Scripture in Rom. 15.9-12. He too could have said that Christ became a 'Servant to the circumcised to show God's faithfulness, in order to confirm the promises given to the patriarchs and in order that the Gentiles might glorify God for his mercy'.[2]

So the Gentiles exist apart from the Law. James' judgment is a refutation of the Pharisees and of their understanding of the place of the Law in the new community. James' speech takes up Peter's stance. As Haenchen expresses it, 'James is now speaking as forcefully about

1. Luke's quotation from Amos 9.11-12, LXX, has a different balance from that found in the majority of OT expectations of the future where the centrepiece is in the restoration of Israel into which some Gentiles are incorporated (Isa. 2.3; 19.23; Zech. 8.21; Isa. 60.11). These take much more the form suggested by Jervell's 'people and an associate people'. In Amos, however, the conversion of the Gentiles becomes virtually the climax and reason for the restoration of Israel. Luke is sometimes understood as using Amos 9.11-12 to refer, not to the remaking of Israel, so much as to the resurrection of Jesus who in himself and in the people established upon him takes the place of historical Israel as the object of God's convenantal activity. Haenchen, *Acts*, p. 448 writes, 'He does not see this as the restoration of the Davidic kingdom, nor does he even see it in the image of the true Israel. He conceives it as adumbrating the story of Jesus, culminating in the Resurrection, in which the promise made to David has been fulfilled'. Cf. G. Schneider, *Die Apostelgeschichte* (2 vols.; Feiburg: Henden, 1980), II, pp. 182-83. But, as Tannehill (*Acts*, p. 188) points out, the absence of ἀναστήσω in Luke's form of the quotation weakens the link with Jesus' career. Luke rather sees it as pointing to a remaking of Israel which climaxes in the incorporation of Gentiles. The 'hut of David' becomes Israel as she is founded on Jesus and remade, at least in her nucleus, at Pentecost. Though the verse does not talk primarily at this point about the remaking of Israel, it does include that event as it becomes an inevitable part of the outcome of the exaltation of Jesus, and as the Ascension in Acts finds its rationale in the Pentecostal remaking of that people. The Amos quotation holds together a remaking of Israel and an ingathering of Gentiles, and bases both on Jesus' exaltation.

2. J.D.G. Dunn, *Romans 1–8, 9–16* (WBC, 38A, B, Dallas, TX: Word Books, 1988), pp. 847-48, 853, emphasizes that Paul is here envisaging the grand sweep of God's saving action. His discussion of Wilckens' suggestion that v. 9 contains Paul's own critical twist to a Jewish–Christian tradition found in v. 8 shows how the emphasis rests upon the Gentiles.

freedom from the Law as Peter'.[1] Gentiles are not to be troubled, and God is not to be tested. The decree therefore is not to be seen as an imposition of a part of the Law but is rather a substitute for the Pharisaic demand. It moves within the qualitative interpretation of the Law rather than being a return to quantative considerations. It is not a compromise with the Pharisees but a rejection of their position. Verse 21 sees it, not as a Mosaic imposition, but as a substitute for Moses.[2] In rejecting a Mosaic imposition, however, upon the Gentiles, it is not to be seen as a threat to Moses. Many still respond to him and Jewish Christians will continue to keep his customs. Verse 21 justifies the terms of the decree to Jewish Christians and defends it against them, against those indeed who would later see it as an imposition of Law upon Gentiles. When the decree is actually sent to the Gentiles no mention is made of Moses. Its cultic rules are apostolic, not Mosaic.[3]

So, how does Luke understand them? His clearest expression of this is found in Acts 21. Paul's ministry has been seen as a threat to the Jewish Christian understanding of the continuity of the people of God which his preaching is thought to undermine. His action in the temple is to show them that this is not so. It is a concession on the part of

1. *Acts*, p. 449.

2. See Wilson's discussion of this in *Law*, pp. 83-84. He connects it with the preceding verse so that the requirement is made because of Mosaic preaching in the synagogue. It becomes a mark of respect to that. This however fits ill with his insistence that the decree is apostolic rather than Mosaic and with his true recognition that the terms are ultimately controlled by Luke's understanding of the significance of the Cornelius episode. Sanders (p. 123) keeps the idea of obligation but has to assert that the decree is merely maintaining those obligations which were already laid upon Gentiles in their pre-Christian state. But presumably Gentiles did not then acknowledge them, so it amounts to a new imposition of an unrecognized Mosaic law upon Christians. It is more likely that v. 21 points to no Mosaic obligation. Verses 14 and 17 assert that, because of their reception of the Spirit, Gentiles are now called into the sphere of God's people without any obligation to the Law and it is this assertion which becomes the climax of James' speech. The 'therefore' of v. 19 responds to this assertion and draws from it the truth that 'we should not trouble those from the Gentiles who turn to God'. The 'for' of v. 21 picks up this 'therefore' which is itself quite deliberately climactic. Moses is not taken on board, but neither is he despised. He is acknowledged both by continuing Jews and by Jewish Christians and the decree becomes a mark of respect both to them and to that from which the church has sprung. The decree is seen by Luke as a concession on the part of Gentile Christians to these beliefs.

3. See once again the comments of Wilson, *Law*, pp. 77-78.

Paul, going further than he would normally go, to show that he himself retains his respect for the Law seen as the bounds, not of the eschatological people of God, but of Israel.[1] It is a concession made in the interests of continuity, of historical Israel, and is the recognition that her history has made possible the fulfilling act of God. Israel as Israel still has a place in the people of God which is derived from her. Moses is not forsaken. But Paul is a Jew. Gentiles do not keep the Law.[2] Nevertheless, they do recognize Israel's priority, her concept of purity, and that her history and calling give shape, definition and meaning to what has come into being by way of it. So the apostolic decree consists of rules whereby Gentiles can acknowledge that, and Jewish Christians can show their loyalty to their part in what they believe the new community to be. The terms of the decree witness, not to Mosaic requirements for the Gentiles but to continuing respect for the Mosaic faith on the part of the whole community. They are undertaken by Gentiles so that Jewish–Christian beliefs can be acknowledged and the nature of God's new people can be proclaimed. For Luke (and of course we are not concerned with their original intention) they are not a compromise regarding the keeping of the Law, for they witness to its end for Gentiles rather than to partial acceptance by them. He does indeed see them as a concession which has real theological significance—but it is a concession made by Gentiles for the sake of the unity of the church and as a witness to that by which

1. Neither here nor in 1 Cor. 9.19-23 is it suggested that Paul habitually kept the Law. The position taken here has much in common with that advanced by M.A. Seifrid, 'Jesus and the Law in Acts', *JSNT* 30 (1987), pp. 39-57. He sees the decree as concession to Jewish sensibilities and writes, 'The prohibitions of the decree are directed toward protecting Jewish concerns about defilement by Gentiles'. Seifrid relates Luke's attitude to the Law to the question of ethics to a greater degree than I would allow. For Luke, the question of the Law is rather concerned with the nature of the new community and its relation to the covenant established in Israel. Jewish concerns are acknowledged as matters of legitimate interest for them, and Gentiles accept the provision of the decree as recognizing their point of view without having in any way to take that outlook upon themselves. They have no ethical significance other than as an expression of Gentile respect for their Jewish–Christian brethren. See also the discussion in Tannehill, *Acts*, pp. 190-93 where he writes, 'James is proposing that Gentiles be asked to abstain from certain things especially offensive to a Jewish sense of cultic purity so that Jewish Christians may remain in the fellowship of the church without being forced to give up their way of life'.

2. 21.25 suggests a contrast with the previous verse.

she was enabled and from which she was hewn. When they received the decree the church at Antioch rejoiced (15.31) for it was seen as being derived from the Spirit's eschatological action and as witnessing to that.

Chapter 3

CONTINUITY AND DISCONTINUITY

Our reading of the significance Luke gives to the apostolic decree suggests that he has a clearer appreciation of Paul's position on the Law than is often attributed to him. Above all, he has learned from Paul that the Law no longer had a part in defining the boundaries of the people of God for he views the decree, not as rules linking Gentiles to the Law, but as concessions which are made by Gentile Christians in order to enable Jewish Christians to be true to their inheritance. In so doing, Gentile Christians also bear witness to the nature of the community which has come into being by virtue of the universal outpouring of the Spirit: it is a community enabled by God's action in the Jewish people and by his eschatological activity in Israel. Based upon Israel, it is nevertheless wider than Israel. The outpouring of the Spirit upon Cornelius, though enabled by eschatological Israel in the person of Peter, represents not an extension of Israel but a decisively new act of God. Cornelius and his fellow Gentiles do not enter the community by way of Israel, however eschatologically and differently conceived, but by virtue of a new outpouring of the Spirit. Circumcision is thereby made redundant to such an extent that its imposition would be an act of apostasy on the part of both the imposers and the imposed, and any table fellowship regulations regarded as requirements demanded by Jewish reading of the Law would have come under the same condemnation, for they too would have spurned the significance of the Spirit's gift as Peter by his action in eating with Gentiles rightly discerned it. As a mark of the people of God the Law is redundant for it has been wholly superseded in this new action.

In this, Luke has learned from Paul and, even if he has had Paul accept and proclaim the apostolic decree in a way that Paul himself did not do and indeed would not have done, he has so redefined the significance of that decree as to evacuate it of any idea of containing Mosaic rules for the Gentiles which seemed to be the essence of its initial propagation. Luke's Paul accepts the decree as a concession made by Gentile Christians for the sake of the unity of the people of God, for the sake of acknowledging the legitimacy of the Jewish-Christian understanding of the nature of their place in the new community as that of eschatological Israel, and to encourage Gentile Christians to recognize the significance of the community as being both centred upon Israel and enabled by historical Israel.

The historical Paul did not accept the apostolic decree. Whether he would have denied its implications as redefined by Luke, however, is far less certain. It is by no means obvious that the Paul of 1 Cor. 9.19-23; 8.7-13; 10.23-33 and of Rom. 14.1-23 would necessarily have disassociated himself from Luke's outlook even if it did not in reality form a part of his historical situation and thinking. Luke was altering the Paul of history but, on this point, he certainly was not obviously denying him.

But would Paul have been such a good continuing Jew as Luke makes him out to be? Again, of course, we could appeal to 1 Cor. 9.19-23, to the alleged misunderstanding of the Galatians (5.11), and to his submission to the 'forty stripes save one' (2 Cor. 11.24). Further, recourse could be made to the alleged development in Paul's understanding which suggests that he moved away only gradually from his basis in Judaism.[1] However, even when due allowance is made for all these features, it remains unlikely that the Paul of history envisaged such a slight change in his ancestral faith at the point at which he embraced Christianity. Paul's apologies before the Council (Acts 23.6), Felix (24.14-15), and Agrippa (26.22-23) have little in common with his own accounts of the significance of the change (Gal. 2.19; Phil. 3.7-8). Luke's understanding of the Law as finding its logical fulfilment in the acceptance of Christ in an inevitable and obvious continuation seems alien to Paul's thought, and his presentation of Paul's new life style as an extension of that which had been his as a Jew is a clear simplification of the action of Paul himself. That the Paul of history ceased to practise the Law, at least when he was with Jews, is not obvious, but that he continued its practice as a virtual

1. F. Watson, *Paul, Judaism and the Gentiles* (SNTSMS, 56; Cambridge: Cambridge University Press, 1986); J.D.G. Dunn, 'The Incident at Antioch', *JSNT* 18 (1983), pp. 3-57.

requirement of his new-found faith is very unlikely.[1]

Nevertheless, even here, Luke is well aware of the ambiguity in Paul's position as he presents it. James asserts that the apostle's outlook can be construed as 'teaching all the Jews who are among the Gentiles to forsake Moses, telling them not to circumcise their children or observe the customs' (21.21). Luke knows that Paul was executed by the Romans on a charge which had its basis in that sort of accusation,[2] and he is equally aware that Jewish Christians did little to save him from Jewish antipathy. Moreover, he knows that Paul's loyalty to the Law did not so obviously lead him to Christ for he three times describes Paul's 'conversion' which was needed to break the strangle hold of the Law which had made him persecute Christians as a pious activity (22.3-5).[3] It might, in Luke's considered theology, have been continuing Jewish perversity which made them disobedient to that Law throughout their history and which reached a culmination in the rejection of Jesus by 'lawless men' (2.23), and it was certainly in his scheme, as evinced in the infancy narratives, that those who recognized Jesus were led to do so by reason of their Law-centred piety. So, Zechariah and Elizabeth, Simeon and Anna were models of such piety, but nevertheless Zechariah had to have an angelic input, Elizabeth to have Mary's greeting, and Simeon an action of the Holy Spirit. Mary herself is not said to be an example of Law-piety and she too needs an angelic visitation to move her into the eschatological sphere. John the Baptist's Law-piety has actually to be challenged by the ministry of Jesus to give him a new perspective (Lk. 7.23).

Luke was not unaware of ambiguity in relation to the Law. However it is understood, the apostolic decree is not seen by him to meet the desires of the Pharisees to continue in obedience to the Law. Peter recognizes the newness of his position which is accepted by James, and Paul's meals do not seem wholly determined by the decree's requirements. Luke struggles to resolve the ambiguity but he cannot hide it with complete success, and it is indeed made inevitable by his desire both to recognize the end of it as authoritative for the

1. Sanders, *Law*, pp. 171-210.

2. See below, pp. 125-30.

3. Luke describes the Damascus Road event in terms which do justice to the break in Paul's relations with Judaism. He does not underplay the drastic nature of the event and its results even though he has Paul himself in his speeches appear to do so.

Christian dispensation and also to see Christianity as the fulfilment of Judaism by being one with it and carrying over its gifts into the present. He recognized the part of Law in enabling the Jewish faith but he was conscious that its strength was also its weakness insofar as that which prepared the way for Christ had also excluded others from the sphere of God's people. So the gift of inclusiveness which for Luke was at the heart of Christianity inevitably passed a judgment upon what before had excluded so many from the covenantal community.

Nevertheless, in spite of the ambiguity of which he was aware, Luke placed all his emphasis upon presenting the Law as the definer of Israel and so as the enabler of Christ's coming and the prelude of the redemption effected by him. Jesus came out of the Law, it produced him, and, even if now it had no saving significance, it was not discarded as being of no further use. Jesus did not deny the past of Israel of which it was a part. Jewish Christians therefore did not opt out of its sphere even though inevitably their keeping of it had to be redefined in the light of Christ, and Gentiles respected the Jewish-Christian obligations to it even as they acknowledged what it had achieved. Yet they themselves were wholly free from it for, while honouring it, they could not but be aware that it had excluded them so that any embracing of it would be nothing other than a yoke (15.10). In this, Luke's Peter was very close to the Paul of Galatians. Indeed, in one respect Luke seems inclined to go even further than Paul. Though Jewish-Christians still keep the Law and see it as that which enables the love of God and man (Lk. 10.27), as a moral code it is not regarded as either distinctive or determinative but rather as an expression of that universal morality by which 'in every nation anyone who fears him and does what is right is acceptable to him' (10.35). In this in fact he seems to be less certain than Paul that the Law was in some way a universal moral indicator.[1] It reflects universal right morality rather than indicating what that morality should be. Luke does not see Gentiles as entering into some new ethical understanding through their embrace of Christianity. Apart from Christ, they are not wholly without some response to God (Acts 17.16-34). What is new in Christianity is not any ethical standard but a revelation of the true God.

Luke sees the Law as reduced in significance now that Christ has come. It does not define the people of God and it is now no longer of

1. Sanders, *Law*, pp. 93-122.

saving value for either Jewish or Gentile Christians for it has been caught up in the work of Christ to which it can add nothing. Jewish Christians will continue to keep it but only as a sign of their Jewishness and all that that entails in the light of Christ. Gentile Christians must not be brought within its embrace and to do so would be tantamount to apostasy for it would deny the significance of the Spirit. On this, Luke was no less certain than Paul. For the apostle, it was Christ or Law; for Luke, it was the Spirit or Law. Neither Paul nor the evangelist was prepared to compromise.[1]

It is in the light of this that Luke's account of Paul's circumcising of Timothy must be seen (16.1-5). Luke does not understand Timothy's circumcision as having been made necessary by virtue of the fact that he was a Jew: the Jewishness of his Christianity did not demand it. Rather, it was undertaken as a concession to Jewish susceptibilities, not as a mark of cynical expediency in the service of some missionary concern, but because the Jews 'all knew that his father was a Greek'. Timothy's non-circumcision was an offence to the Jews for it represented an open denial of his Jewishness, a refusal to incorporate him into the historical people of God. It seems likely that Luke regarded it as a deliberate scorning of Judaism on the part of mother or father or, indeed, of both.

Luke therefore regards the circumcision as the removal of an offence, as the recognition of the historical place of Judaism in God's plans and as a sign that Jewish embrace of Christianity entails, not an abrogation of the Jewish historical covenant, a by-passing of its gifts and traditions, but a completion of its promises and a fulfilment of its blessings. But, he is clear that he does not regard it as a necessity laid upon Timothy by his Christian discipleship. It is a concession rather than an obligation and one which by reason of its nature as expressing sensitivity to Jewish religious scruples, in so being, actually reduces the significance of the act and treats the sign itself with a certain indifference. Luke again certainly does not see the Law as having any continuing necessary part in defining the requirements of the people of God. It is given an historical significance as that which has enabled the present to be and as showing the nature of that which now is.

Nevertheless, it remains unlikely (though one must emphasize it is not necessarily certain) that the historical Paul would have engaged in such an act. Though he can say, 'neither circumcision counts for

1. Sanders, *Law*, pp. 149-59.

anything, nor uncircumcision' (Gal. 6.15), this is to talk of pre-Christian religious marks whose value is at an end. In the light of the new, the old is superseded so that it ceases to have any continuing significance. Indifference only serves to emphasize the negative value of everything other than Christ. Circumcision after the acceptance of Christ, however, is quite another matter and amounts to entering the sphere of slavery (Gal. 5.1). In this sense, Paul could not have treated circumcision with that theological near-indifference with which Luke treats it. As Haenchen asserts, 'Paul could not disregard the religious significance of circumcision'. Circumcision evacuated of its full theological content 'would have been for him a lie and at the same time a blasphemy against God'.[1]

Luke however divests the act of circumcision of its Pauline significance. He has learned from Paul that it does not in any way contribute to inclusion within the people of God. On that point at any rate there is no argument. But whereas Paul could not see it as being used without that significance—he could not demystify it for it had that implication deeply embedded in both Jewish understanding and his own consciousness—Luke was able to do so and to treat it as having a different value and a different import. For him, it was a matter of Jewishness which was not negated by Christ. Unlike Paul, he could subordinate it to Christ as a continuing mark of the Jewish people and of their part in God's one saving act which culminated in Jesus. This was not Paulinism, but it was a conscious and understanding reinterpretation of Paulinism to give value to what was prior to the whole event of Jesus without in any way devaluing the fulfilment.

Luke understands Paul and the significance he gave to the Law. Nevertheless, he entered upon a conscious reinterpretation of that position to give to it, not a saving value, not continuing validity in the Christian dispensation, but to endow it, first, with a continuing historical significance as the mark of God's covenant with Israel and, secondly, to make it witness to the nature of the community brought into being by Christ. Gentiles entered into that community in their own right and by virtue of the universal outpouring of the Spirit, but they came in nevertheless on the backs of Israel[2] and shared in the wide

1. *Acts*, p. 481.

2. J.L. Houlden uses this idea in 'The Purpose of Acts', *JSNT* 21 (1984), pp. 53-65.

expanse of God's eschatological promises to her. Historical Israel had enabled the church to be, and eschatological Israel witnessed to what it was. To this end Luke reshapes both Paul's thinking and his actions. What emerges is not the real Paul, but neither is it an illegitimate interpretation. It is rather one made in the light of Paul's basic conviction about the Law—that it no longer had a part in defining the boundaries of the people of God—but which nevertheless reinterprets Paul's understanding of the relation of what has come into being with what went before. Where Luke and Paul differ is over the question of the parts played by continuity and discontinuity in God's act of salvation.[1] What Luke does is to shift Paul's emphasis upon the newness of Christ's saving event to see it rather in terms of promise and fulfilment, to see the work of Christ as the climax of what has earlier been begun in God's saving work in Israel.

It is generally accepted that Luke works within the scheme of promise and fulfilment and therefore emphasizes the unity of God's saving action begun in the appearance of Abraham and completed by the coming of Christ. The Law is brought into his scheme—'everything written about me in the law of Moses and the prophets and the psalms must be fulfilled'—and the fulfilment is widened out to include, not merely the event of Christ, but the preaching to all nations (Lk. 24.44). More however than mere promise and fulfilment, Luke sees the essential wholeness of God's saving action as meaning that the promise actually controls and determines the way in which the fulfilment is understood. Jesus is one with Jewish history, the supreme prophetic figure, characterized as actually conceived by the Spirit's

1. It is true that not all Pauline scholars stress Paul's emphasis upon discontinuity. For E.P. Sanders this is primary while the other leading English-speaking interpreter of Paul, W.D. Davies, puts more stress upon continuity; *Paul and Rabbinic Judaism* [London: SPCK, 1965]). C. Rowland (*Christian Origins* [London: SPCK, 1985]), stresses the continuity when he writes, 'We cannot suppose any more that Paul's conversion involved him in the transference from one religion to another... It was a change *within* Judaism, parallel to the change which might take place when an adherent of an Essene group became a Pharisee (pp. 194-95). Yet Rowland has Paul advance beyond such a limited move when he says, 'It is difficult to resist the conclusion that Paul *has* in fact helped to give birth to a very different religion, with different concepts and concerns from those of most Jews' (p. 196). Here he seems to part company with Davies' stress to come much closer to Sanders. Though Sanders may at times state this in an extreme way, it does seem that it is his emphasis which does most justice to Paul's thought.

action, but nevertheless of the same kind as Moses, Elijah, John the Baptist and the general prophetic tradition. One with them, he is their fulfilment and becomes other than them only at the point where the resurrection enables his exaltation to the right hand of God. But David prophesied even that for it is controlled by Ps. 110.1, and the Son of David takes up Israelite convenantal history into his exaltation. The cross is merged by Luke into Jesus' whole career of suffering of which it is the focus and climax, but it is not isolated and so treated as something distinct from the overall Old Testament tradition. Though Luke places more emphasis upon Jesus as suffering servant than do the other evangelists,[1] he does not take over the picture of that figure's vicarious death, for to do so would be again to distinguish Jesus from the prophetic line as a whole and to give the death a value which he refuses to assign to it. The resurrection and ascension are of course seen as fulfilling scriptural expectations and Pentecost is understood as that which the prophet foresaw (2.16-21). Joel's prophecy actually controls Luke's account of Pentecost. Its eschatological perspective is emphasized, those present are Jews for the Jewish covenant is realizing its potential, and the Spirit is thought of in impersonal terms. Glossolalia is associated with prophecy and the various languages give expression to the worldwide Jewish ingathering.[2]

Prophetic expectations are being fulfilled, and so far Luke has had no difficulty in showing how the events of Jesus can be accommodated to, and actually controlled by, the Old Testament and its hopes. In the process he has had to cut some corners so that the cross is undoubtedly underplayed, there is little room to do justice to the Christian experience of the corporate Christ, and the Spirit is constrained by being understood in essentially impersonal terms.[3] Nevertheless, it is a considerable achievement and gives significant expression to Luke's belief in the unity of God's single developing saving action.

Difficulties arise, however, when he seeks to bring the universal mission within this scheme and to see its shape as witnessing to the fulfilment of scriptural expectations. The Old Testament thought primarily in terms of the eschatological pilgrimage of the nations to Jerusalem. Luke could actually have conformed to this scheme had he thought of the Pentecostal outpouring of the Spirit as being extended

1. *Christ the Lord*, pp. 61-64.
2. *Christ the Lord*, pp. 95-99.
3. *Christ the Lord*, pp. 132-34.

to Gentiles in Jerusalem as well as to Jews. The Cornelius episode could then have been seen as an extension of Pentecost and the apostolic decree as unifying Gentile Christians with Jerusalem and its renewal by means of a partial imposition of the Law. All could then have been proclaimed as the fulfilment of Isa. 2.2-4. In this he would have been adumbrating what Jervell suggests is his outlook when he characterizes it as a belief in a people and an associate people. It would have made a clear and consistent picture.

It is just this, however, that Luke refuses to do. Pentecost is not for him an inclusion of Gentiles within Israel, Cornelius does not represent simply an extension of Jewish covenantal renewal, and the apostolic decree does not relate Gentiles to the Law. Paul is not an advocate of Gentile law-keeping, his mission threatens the Jewish law, and his Christianity causes him to make a radical reversal of what before his conversion was seen as the direct result of his keeping of it (26.5, 14, 19).

Luke does not allow the Law to have any part in defining the boundaries of the people of God. It does seem to have some actual say in influencing the lives of that people for Jewish Christians still keep it, even if only after a fashion and certainly only in the manner of those who have seen its significance in a new light. Gentile Christians are made to be aware of it in some way by the apostolic decree. Nevertheless, Gentile acknowledgment is a voluntary concession on their part. Even then, however, it is acknowledged as apostolic constraints rather than as those actually suggested by Moses. The Law, qua Law, is no longer accepted as having a part in determining the actual holiness of the Christian community.

Such an outlook is not uninfluenced by Paul's distinct contribution to early Christian thought. More than that though, it seems likely that it is Pauline influence which has actually determined it. Without such a constraint, Luke's overall theological position would have allowed the Law more say in controlling the boundaries and nature of the eschatological community. His downgrading of it at these points suggests in fact that he has learned from Paul.

Nevertheless, he has reinterpreted Paul in the interests of his belief that the Christian dispensation rose out of, and was continuous with, that earlier action of God to which the Old Testament witnessed. How great a reinterpretation this entailed is shown when what is characteristic of Luke's thought is compared with the related outlook of Paul.

Paul so stresses the originality of the work of Christ and so emphasizes the greatness of the work of God through him, that everything else is seen as contrasted with it, even alien to it. It has been usual in much recent thought to locate the main impact of Paul's experience on the road to Damascus in his compulsion to preach Christ to the Gentiles and to characterize it as a call rather than a conversion.[1] An erstwhile tormented soul did not suddenly find peace and security, nor did he change from one religion to another. Whilst this is undoubtedly true, the radical change which the event initiated should not be underplayed, for it involved both a reversal of his previous manner of life and a drastic re-appraisal of his earlier convictions. Whether the appearance of Jesus to Paul is understood as revealing the Lord's messiahship, his saving significance or his universality,[2] it demanded a total upending of Paul's attitude to the Law for it proved it wrong in its judgment of Jesus, denied its saving value, and annulled its status as the definer of the area of God's covenantal activity. Paul's earlier zeal for the Law was seen to be both misguided and misplaced. Membership of God's covenantal people was not coterminous with membership of the Jewish nation; Paul's experience on the Damascus road caused him to see that in fact it never had been (Gal. 3.19-20). If his attack on 'works of the law' was directed against the view that the covenantal community was to be identified with the boundaries of Israel, its implications mean that Israel as a whole had radically to rethink that national pride and exclusiveness which such an identification made virtually inevitable.[3] Paul may not have accused the law of encouraging legalism on the part of its practitioners, but his complaint centring on national exclusiveness meant an inevitable

1. K. Stendahl, 'Conversion or Call?' in *Paul among Jews and Gentiles* (Philadelphia: Fortress Press, 1976).

2. J.D.G. Dunn, 'A Light to the Gentiles: The Significance of the Damascus Road Christophany for Paul', in L.D. Hurst and N.T. Wright (eds.), *The Glory of Christ in the New Testament: Studies in Christology in Memory of George Bradford Caird* (Oxford: Clarendon Press, 1987).

3. J.D.G. Dunn, in 'The New Perspective on Paul', *BJRL* 65 (1983), pp. 96-122, and in other essays collected in *Jesus, Paul and the Law* (London: SPCK, 1990), sees Paul's attack on Judaism centred upon its social exclusiveness. While this does seem to be true, such a religious exclusiveness was almost bound to lead to some national pride which would not indeed pass by at least some individuals within the nation and which would not make some residual charge of legalism entirely inappropriate.

denigration of Israel's covenantal self-consciousness (Rom. 4.2-5; 10.1-4). Religious particularism had to be broken down, though perhaps it is more correct to say that Paul replaced one religious particularism, that of unity under the law, with another, that of unity in Christ (Phil. 2.8-9).[1]

Paul therefore contrasts the fading splendour of the 'dispensation of death' and 'of condemnation' with the unfading glory of the 'dispensation of righteousness'. So great indeed is the contrast that the former dispensation is now seen in fact to be devoid of splendour. When the veil that was over both the face of Moses and the minds of Israel is removed, it enables the glory of the Lord to be seen only as it discloses the lack of glory in Moses (2 Cor. 3.11-18). Paul is called to be a minister of a new covenant for 'if anyone is in Christ, he is a new creation; the old has passed away, behold, the new has come' (2 Cor. 3.6; 5.17).[2]

This represents a great contrast to Luke's understanding where the infancy narratives, seen as the prologue of his two volumes, proclaim the unity of God's one work of salvation. Both John and Jesus do their work 'in the spirit and power of Elijah' (Lk. 1.17; 4.25-26) and those who acknowledge Jesus are the true in Israel (Lk. 1.30, 54; 2.25, 36). Even the shepherds, though religious outcasts, are following in the steps of David, and Jesus himself finds his natural place in the temple which receives and acknowledges him (Lk. 2.22, 49). He is one with Jewish history and the Jewish religious institutions which find their positive fulfilment in him. After his ascension, his followers find their natural home in the temple (Acts 2.46; 3.1; 5.12). The Hellenists are brought within this understanding, for those who accuse Stephen of speaking against the Law and the temple are described as false witnesses (6.11-14) and his speech is understood by Luke, not as an attack upon the temple as such, but as a denial of its finality.[3] Law and temple point forward to Jesus by whom they are affirmed and in whom they find their positive fulfilment.

So for Luke it is axiomatic that Jesus is the Christ of Israel and

1. E.P. Sanders, *Paul and Palestinian Judaism: A Comparison of Patterns of Religion* (Philadelphia: Fortress Press; London: SCM Press, 1977).

2. Sanders, *The Law*, pp. 176-88, 'We must recognise the extent to which the church constituted, in Paul's view, a third entity, which stood over against both the obdurate part of Israel and unconverted Gentiles'.

3. *Christ the Lord*, pp. 99-108.

that his sufferings were in accordance with scriptural expectations (Lk. 24.26, 46). He is therefore one with Israel and the fulfilment of that to which her faith and history pointed (Acts 2.29-36). His coming affirms her history, her beliefs, and those who fashioned her religious insights. Paul, however, does not see Jesus as following the path of scriptural expectations. Scripture foresees the gospel of justification by faith (Rom. 1.2; Gal. 3.8) but it does not foretell the career of Jesus for his death means not the fulfilment of the Law's expectations, but the reversal (Gal. 3.10). Only at 1 Cor. 15.3-4 does Paul give scriptural justification for the death and resurrection of Jesus, and it seems most likely that at this point he is using an earlier credal statement.[1] But Paul does not express the heart of his belief in this way for 'he saw more clearly than any other early Christian the destructive consequences of a crucified Messiah for the fabric of Judaism'.[2] By his characteristic use of 'Christ' as a proper name, Paul gives to Jesus the significance of the eschatological redeemer of Old Testament hopes, but by his avoidance of the term as a predicate, he fails to proclaim it as a title of Jesus and so points to the fact that he does not actually fulfil those hopes in the way that the Old Testament expected. He preaches rather 'Christ crucified, a stumbling-block to the Jews and folly to the Gentiles' (1 Cor. 1.23). The difference between the expectations and the reality is such as to call the expectations wholly into question and to put a large question mark over the symbols of the covenant which fostered them.

Because of their contrasting emphases upon continuity and discontinuity, Luke and Paul make very different uses of the Abraham tradition.[3] Both see him as a sign and guarantee of God's promises to Israel (Rom. 9.7; 11.1; Lk. 1.55, 75), but whereas Paul sets these within the context of the promises' universality (Rom. 4.1-25), Luke rarely draws out this aspect of the Abraham tradition. At Acts 3.25, Abraham's significance is found first and foremost in the covenantal promise to Israel, and universal implications are a clear second to that. Israel, indeed, must not presume upon the promises, for God is

1. J. Héring, *I Corinthians* (trans. A.W. Heathcote and P.J. Allcock; London: Epworth Press, 1962), p. 158.

2. J.J.C. Beker, *Paul the Apostle: The Triumph of God in Life and Thought* (Edinburgh: T. & T. Clark, 1980), p. 184.

3. N.A. Dahl, 'The Story of Abraham in Luke–Acts', *Studies in Luke–Acts*, pp. 139-58.

able to raise up other children to Abraham (Lk. 3.8) and the evangelist traces the ancestry of Jesus back through Abraham to Adam (Lk. 4.34, 38). Gentiles however do not for Luke become sons of Abraham whereas, of course, in Paul they do. Jews alone for Luke are Abraham's sons and their sonship is not actually dependent upon their faith in Jesus but rather upon their natural Jewishness. The crippled woman is already a daughter of Abraham, Dives in torment can still call Abraham 'father', and Zacchaeus's sonship in Abraham is based, not upon his response to Jesus, but on his participation in Israel which encourages his response (Lk. 13.16; 16.30; 19.9).[1] Luke's Jews have a built-in advantage as sons of Abraham which is denied them by Paul. Though Paul does not explicitly deny sonship of Abraham to non-believing Jews, his stress on faith as the indispensible requirement for that sonship means that he comes close to doing so, and he certainly does not see the Jews' sonship as privileged by reason of their possession of the Law. They are placed virtually on the same footing as Gentiles.[2]

Luke on the other hand interprets Abraham as a sign of God's continuing concern for the Jews and of the continuity of his action in Israel leading up to the coming of Christ. Abraham is given the covenant of circumcision (7.8) which embodies the effectiveness of God's promises in his descendants who will actually worship God 'in this place', namely in the Holy Land (7.7).[3] So the rites of Israel's covenant affirm and guarantee her continuing within the promises made to Abraham. They become ineffective only when their fulfilment in Jesus is denied, for it means then that they cease to be filled with that movement towards the future which God's initial activity and Abraham's response revealed as an essential part of the covenant. Luke's understanding of the Law and of the temple is that both carried forward God's promise to Abraham to find its fulfilment in Christ. They embodied that promise insofar as they were seen to contain within themselves that movement forward characteristic of Abraham and his looking ahead to the future which was actually realized in Jesus.

In this he differs substantially from Paul who sees God's covenantal

1. I.H. Marshall, *The Gospel of Luke* (NIGTC; Exeter: The Paternoster Press, 1978), p. 698.

2. Sanders, *The Law*, p. 176.

3. Dahl, 'Abraham', pp. 143-45.

activity as moving forward, not in some single developing sweep, but in a series of disjunctures. For Paul, God gives circumcision to Abraham as a seal, not of the promise but of the faith which was necessary for inclusion within the promise (Rom. 5.9-12). Circumcision and the Law express no benefits in themselves for they do not contain within themselves the ability to move the recipients forward to Christ who alone stands as the inheritor of God's promise to Abraham in contrast to the peoples embodied by the Law (Gal. 3.25-28). Indeed the works of the Law seem to be a disadvantage for they move the recipients into the sphere of slavery (Gal. 4.21-31) so that the outlook which was characteristic of them has actually to be thrown off in order that the sonship of Christ might be put on.

Luke and Paul then represent two very different positions on the relation of God's work in Christ to that of his action in the Jewish people. Luke thinks in terms of continuity and fulfilment; Paul in terms of discontinuity and newness. As far as Paul is concerned, historical Israel has real advantages since God's promise to Abraham cannot be rendered ineffective, and she has been the means of enabling Christ to be freed for the world (Rom. 9.4). However he does not see Jesus as the Christ of their expectations and the one for whom they had prepared. The coming of Jesus has actually brought a break in their religious pilgrimage for he must occasion a reversal of the attitudes engendered by a large part of their history. To receive Christ, they have to leave behind a large part of their particular identity and of their covenantal hopes; they have in fact to lay aside the basic outlook of their covenantal understanding and return to seek again the true significance of God's promise to Abraham. They have to learn Paul's own evaluation made in the light of the cross of Christ: 'I through the law died to law, that I might live to God' (Gal. 2.19). Luke on the other hand, sees the Law, rightly understood, as leading to Christ. Those who rejected Jesus were lawless men (2.23). Jews, linked to that rejection, must repent (3.19) to see the true significance of the Law and how it should be leading them to the one who is the Christ (3.22). God's is one continuing action and the Christ completes and affirms what has been begun in Jewish history and its covenantal pledges.

Luke sets out his understanding of Christianity as the fulfilment of Israel's religious pilgrimage in the speech which he puts into Paul's mouth at Antioch of Pisidia (13.16-41). A number of things make it clear that it is Lukan thought which fashions the speech as a whole. It reproduces the shape of the programmatic speech of Jesus at Nazareth to present him as one with Jewish history, to explain Jewish rejection of him as following in the pattern of that history as it is found in the Old Testament, to make the rejection appear inevitable if not actually willed by the divine plan, and to present Jewish perversity as the means by which God's universal outreach is furthered.

If the hand of Luke is revealed in the shape of the speech, the unity of ideas between this speech and the other kerygmatic speeches of Acts suggests that it is Luke's voice which expresses the theology of its various parts.[1] Israel has the primary place in God's plans (13.26; cf. 2.39; 3.25-26; 10.36). Her history has led to Jesus (13.34; cf. 2.29-31) and he is linked to her through the ministry of John the Baptist (13.24-25; cf. 10.37). The Jewish condemnation of Jesus—though not to death for the actual death sentence is the responsibility of Pilate (13.27-28; cf. 3.13)—is compounded by making the Jews the real agents of his crucifixion (13.29; cf. 2.23, 3.15; 4.10; 10.39). All however is seen as the fulfilment of scriptural expectations (13.29; cf. 2.23; 3.18). The resurrection is the reversal of men's judgment and its actuality is guaranteed by Jesus' appearances to witnesses who saw and recognized him (13.30-31; cf. 2.32; 3.15; 4.10; 10.40-41). It established him as God's eschatological agent (13.33; cf. 3.15-16, 22; 4.10, 10.40-43). Since the incorruption, promised but denied to David, was actually realized in him, he is revealed as the embodiment of God's covenant with David (13.34-36; cf. 2.25-31). From the time of the vindication of Jesus, the proclamation of the forgiveness of sins can be made (13.38; cf. 2.38; 3.26; 4.12; 10.42-43).

Jewish history and faith are taken up into Jesus. The speech gives a resumé of that history which, like that expressed in Stephen's speech, is designed to show the working out of God's purposes through what appears to be its 'riddle' (Ps. 78.2) and to point to Jesus as its climax. God's faithfulness is able to use the nation's perversity to move Israel forward into the realization of his promises to her. Earlier history found its climax in David whose hope was realized, not in himself, but in Jesus: 'Of this man's progeny God has brought to Israel a saviour, Jesus, as he promised' (13.23).

That the speech expresses Luke's understanding of the apostle's

1. E. Schweizer, 'Concerning the Speeches in Acts', *Studies in Luke–Acts*, pp. 208-216.

theology rather than Paul's own is seen clearly in its version of Paul's proclamation of the resurrection, belief in which is grounded, not in any experiential compulsion and affirmation, but in the witnesses in Jerusalem. Paul, of course, is quite able to refer to other appearances when he wants to stress the unity of his proclamation with that of his predecessors in the faith (1 Cor. 15.8), but he then unites his experience to theirs in a way which affirms and validates theirs and also serves to determine his understanding of the continuing action of the risen Christ. Jesus' appearance to him is presented by the apostle as an encounter which is expressed in a continuing initiative and which determined the nature of his own enduring response. Paul had been grasped by Christ and it is inconceivable that he could have left out this dimension from any proclamation to his fellow Jews.

Jesus here, however, is proclaimed rather than directly encountered. Paul at Antioch asserts 'that through this man forgiveness of sins is proclaimed to you' (13.38). This does not mean, however, that Jesus as Luke here envisages him is not active or that, in Conzelmann's words, 'the community of believers has no living contact with Christ in the present'.[1] Jesus has enabled and empowered the proclamation, and its working out remains under his control. His direct, personal activity is seen supremely at the time of the conversion of Paul and of the reaching out of Peter to Cornelius (9.5, 10-17; 10.14), but he is also immediately active in visions, dreams and through angels at other times (12.11; 13.11; 18.9; 23.11). He pours out the Spirit (2.33) and, since the Spirit is sometimes referred to as 'his Spirit' (1.2; 16.7), it is likely that Luke means him to be associated with the Spirit's general work, particularly when a personal activity is implied (8.29; 10.19; 11.12; 10.18). To persecute Christians is to persecute him (9.4) and he is in some way acknowledged as present when the community is engaged in the breaking of bread (Lk. 24.35; Acts 2.46). Above all, Luke expresses the sense of Jesus' present activity through the use of the Old Testament concept of 'the name'. Here, the Lord's powerful intervention and actual activity among men is directly affirmed. Disciples call upon his name and thereby receive his direct help and grace (2.21; 4.7; 16.18). Baptism is in his name (2.38; 8.16), and it is likely that the complications of 3.16 are to be accounted for by Luke's attempting to use name imagery to make possible some present activity of the ascended Lord.

1. Conzelmann, *Theology*, p. 177.

Luke does not have the depth of Paul's understanding of the present indwelling Christ, and this is undoubtedly the point at which he does least justice to the apostle's thought. No doubt he is constrained by his own experience which is likely to have been very different from Paul's own but, in the end, the basic reason for his reshaping Pauline thought at this point remains the constraints imposed upon him by his portraying Jesus in Old Testament terms. Luke's greatest strength becomes at this point the occasion of his primary weakness.

As elsewhere, Luke does not focus redemption in the cross.[1] He is

1. So Conzelmann, *Theology*, p. 201, 'There is no trace of any Passion Mysticism, nor is any direct soteriological significance drawn from Jesus' suffering or death. There is no suggestion of a connection with the forgiveness of sins'. This is not to say that Luke has no soteriology but to deny that for him that soteriology includes belief in the vicarious and redemptive nature of the Cross. Such an estimate has, however, recently come in for some criticism. So, Fitzmyer, *Luke*, pp. 219-27; *Aspects*, pp. 203-33; R. Karris, *Luke: Artist and Theologian: Luke's Passion Account as Literature* (New York: Paulist Press, 1985); J. Neyrey, *The Passion According to Luke: A Redaction Study of Luke's Soteriology* (New York: Paulist Press, 1985); D. Senior, *The Passion of Jesus in Luke* (Wilmington, DE: Michael Glazier, 1988); D. Moessner, *Lord of the Banquet: The Literary and Theological Significance of the Lukan Travel Narrative* (Minneapolis: Fortress Press, 1989), pp. 322-24. Yet it seems that Conzelmann's estimate stands:

a. Acts 20.28 is part of a speech which is a conscious and sustained attempt on the part of Luke to give a convincing defence of Paul against those who, from a Jewish–Christian angle, are attacking both him and his message. Luke here is determinedly reproducing the authentic Paul.

b. Though the evidence of the longer text of Luke's institution narrative is overwhelming, it seems likely that Luke himself wrote the shorter text for it is hard, otherwise, to explain its coming into being. Jeremias's view that it was in the interests of secrecy has little to commend it. The shorter text reflects Luke's view of both the Last Supper and the church's meal as eschatological anticipations of the heavenly banquet and a bonding of a link with Jesus. It has been lengthened by the community to make it conform to the eucharist of the Pauline church. The first cup was not excised because it supported the eschatological orientation which formed a part of the Pauline church's understanding.

c. Luke has nothing to equal Mk 10.45 and its Matthaean parallel. It is unlikely that the whole episode was avoided in the interests of cushioning the disciples for his near-equivalent at the Last Supper is no less critical of them, 22.24. Its positioning makes it refer to the attitude found in the post-Pentecostal community and so allows it to be addressed directly to

of course, aware of Paul's emphasis (20.28), but he does not choose to make it his own, largely one suspects because he thought in terms of continuity and knew that it was Paul's understanding of the significance of the cross which threatened that aspect of Jesus' relation to Jewish piety. Paul had made the cross the point of discontinuity and Luke is therefore unlikely to have embraced his understanding of it.

What Luke makes Paul proclaim is 'the forgiveness of sins', a concept which does not appear in the undisputed Paulines. At Col. 1.13-14 and Eph. 1.7 it is found in contexts which suggest its use as a transfer term expressing movement into the sphere of the people of God. This same aspect is uppermost in Luke's understanding. In the Gospel, its corporate dimension is present in the song of Zechariah where the salvation of God's people is found in the forgiveness of

them. It contrasts with the outlook prevalent at Pharisaic anticipations of the eschatological banquet. Luke has Jesus point to his own way of service. The cross is not seen as the actual point of service even though it no doubt focuses that which is characteristic of him.

d. Jesus is indeed pictured by Luke as Second Adam, however distinctive is his understanding of this from that elaborated by Paul. The story of the penitent thief is one with other stories of Jesus' attraction and reception of the outsider to issue in a redemption. Luke's crucifixion scene was almost bound to include some kind of episode like this but it has no status other than that accorded to earlier scenes of acceptance and forgiveness. 'Today you will be with me in paradise' parallels earlier sayings, 'Your faith has saved you'. There are no soteriological differences, or indeed any different result. Both bestow forgiveness, acceptance and a relationship with Jesus.

e. Moessner has seen some saving significance ascribed by Luke to the death of Jesus in the evangelist's portrayal of him as the antitype of Moses. The necessity of the sufferings includes Deuteronomy's evaluation of the death of Moses which is understood as 'enabling the people to cross over to their promised inheritance'. Yet such an interpretation goes beyond the meaning of Deut. 1.9; 3.23-29; 4.21-22. These verses talk of the necessity for Moses' death but they do not see it as itself redemptive. Moses enabled the people to enter the promised land but the death itself does not achieve that. Indeed, the death itself is rather the result of Moses' own weakness. Moses was not actually punished for the people's sins rather than his own. His death was the result of sin, but it is not actually said that it was redemptive. Had Luke seen Moses' death as redemptive, it is unlikely that he would have avoided references to the redemptive value of the death of the Suffering Servant.

their sins (1.77), in the proclamation of John the Baptist where the baptism of Jesus associates him with a people (3.7, 21), and in the risen Lord's command where the proclamation of forgiveness of sins is linked to the promise of the Pentecostal gift of the Spirit (Lk. 24.47). The same idea of inclusion within the people of God is expressed at Acts 2.38, 5.31 and 10.43, while at 26.18 the thought of transfer from the power of Satan to the sphere of God's reign is made explicit. Forgiveness of sins has for Luke a primary sense of inclusion within the active sphere of God's rule which for the Jews had been marred by the nation's wilfulness and which was in danger of being lost by reason of their rejection of Jesus (3.23-26). For Gentiles, the universal outpouring of the Spirit had universalized the covenantal community.

The final promise of the speech makes use of Pauline language: 'and by him everyone that believes is freed from everything from which you could not be freed by the law of Moses' (13.39). This may be Pauline terminology, but how far does it express Pauline thought? Certainly, it expresses the universality of the work of Jesus and grounds that hope in faith. On the other hand, 'the righteousness of faith is not clearly formulated in antithesis to righteousness by works'.[1] However, is this last judgment itself based on a misunderstanding of Paul? Was Luke necessarily wrong in having Paul, when making a first approach to Jews, omit such a contrast?

Much recent writing on Paul would seem to suggest that he was not and that to see such a contrast as a *sine qua non* for a right appreciation of Paul's outlook is in fact over-emphasizing one aspect of the apostle's thought to the exclusion of its primary intention.[2] Nevertheless, given that, is Luke here giving to the Law a more positive value than Paul himself would have allowed? Vielhauer argues that the verse expresses belief in 'only a partial justification: one which is not by faith alone, but *also* by faith',[3] for it is at least possible that it allows some saving significance to the Law and that it therefore runs contrary to Paul's thinking when he is contrasting the two religious systems. It is true that Vielhauer's understanding has not met with universal approbation. Conzelmann maintains that it is 'not

1. Lüdemann, *Early Christianity*, p. 154.

2. Sanders, *Paul*; F. Watson, *Paul, Judaism and the Gentiles*; J.D.G. Dunn, *Jesus, Paul and the Law* (London: SPCK, 1990).

3. P. Vielhauer, 'On the "Paulinism" of Acts', *Studies in Luke–Acts*, p. 42.

legitimate to suggest that this verse allows partial justification through the law; it expresses not a considerably different theology from Paul, but a clumsy attempt to express Paul's own'.[1] This is Haenchen's opinion for he writes that speculation on Luke's meaning 'imputes a venture into problems which were foreign to him'.[2] Luke, the subject of such judgments, remains the superficial exponent of Christianity.

There remains, however, the possibility that Luke was aware of what he was doing which was to present his own version of Paul's thought which, though undoubtedly lacking the creative depth of the apostle's teaching about justification, nevertheless did justice to Luke's own understanding of the continuity which he believed lay at the heart of God's one ongoing, saving action. In his infancy narratives, Luke speaks of Zechariah and Elizabeth as 'both righteous before God, walking in all the commandments and ordinances of the Lord blameless', and of Simeon as 'righteous and devout, looking for the consolation of Israel' (Lk. 1.6; 2.35). Such examples of Jewish piety were already within the sphere of the people of God and, by their response to God's action in Jesus, showed that they were looking for the eschatological fulfilment which he brought (Lk. 1.32-33). Within the people of God, they nevertheless were conscious that its reality was not yet fully realized.

Jesus was one with Israel's history so that his work completed what was there begun. The lawyer is told that he would find life in his keeping of the Law (Lk. 10.28), though, by his attempt to justify himself, he puts bounds around its demands which stop him from fulfilling it. The ruler who observes the commandments needs to find their fulfilment in Jesus to whom they should have been leading him (Lk. 10.22). The parable of the Pharisee and the tax collector makes much the same point (Lk. 18.10-14). The Pharisee's prayer must have been thought of as genuine for, if it was not, the parable's conclusion would come as no surprise, and this therefore suggests that the comparison is not between justification and non-justification, but rather between complete and partial justification, or perhaps between various grades of partial justification.[3] Since, presumably, full justification is only through Jesus, the latter would seem more appropriate though the parable in Luke is no doubt to be read in the light of the whole

1. *Acts*, p. 106.
2. *Acts*, p. 412.
3. Evans, *Luke*, pp. 644-45.

work of Christ. The complaint against the Pharisee is that, having virtually asserted that he had already 'arrived', he was not open to receive God's eschatological action in Jesus.

It therefore seems that Acts 13.39 is not an inadvertent misunderstanding of the Pauline teaching about justification but is rather a re-application of that teaching made in the light of Luke's interpretation of God's work in Jesus as bringing to fulfilment that which he had begun in the Jewish people. Jesus complements that earlier work, and the righteousness conveyed through that becomes unrighteousness only at the point where its fulfilment is denied and when Jesus is rejected in favour of a remaining within the sphere of that which, rightly understood, pointed forward to him. This is not Pauline thought and it lacks that distinctiveness and intensity which arises out of the contrast between the old and the new, but it is not necessarily to be seen as a trivialization for it actually does justice to God's work outside of Jesus and to mankind's religious quest which the Pauline thought does not.

The ideas developed in Paul's speech at the Areopagus (17.16-34) have surprisingly close parallels to those of the Antioch speech. On the whole, its fundamentally Hebraic outlook and the use of philosophy as an ally has tended to be seen as supporting those who would argue that the speech could represent, if not what Paul actually said at Athens, then at least how he approached Gentile audiences and the stance he took with them.[1] We do not elsewhere have any account of his actual missionary preaching to Gentiles and, as Bruce points out, there would inevitably be a different balance in that from what is found in his letters to established converts where he is dealing with tensions that have emerged in the young communities. And so Bruce maintains that the author of Romans 1–3 could quite probably have presented his initial preaching in the way suggested by Acts 17.[2] It

1. Marshall, *Acts*, pp. 282-83.

2. 'Is the Paul of Acts the Real Paul?', pp. 301-303. D. Wenham ('The Paulinism of Acts Again', *Themelios* 13 [1988], pp. 53-55) thinks that Acts 17 legitimately reflects Paul's actual evangelistic preaching as that is suggested by 1 Thess. 1.9-10. This certainly suggests that the absence of any mention of the cross need not imply Lukan rather than Pauline thought. Luke's overall understanding of idol worship need not necessarily be different from what Paul suggests in his epistles and Paul may not always have been as negative in his estimate of the past as Romans might suggest. Luke may be reflecting Paul's initial preaching though he does so in his own way and in a manner which moves in a rather different direction from the

would, of course, be a mistake not to see Romans conditioned by its particular purpose and by the results of Paul's own missionary endeavours. In Romans his sense of the overwhelming need of all for Christ is recounted both in the light of Jewish rejection of his message and of his own success with the Gentiles. The gratitude of the response as well as the perversity of rejection would make him speak in the way that he does. In any case, Romans 1–3 does include ch. 2 which talks of Gentiles fulfilling the law by nature and therefore of being in some way acceptable (Rom. 2.14-15).[1]

If it is true therefore that there is in Romans 1–3 a less wholly negative judgment on earlier beliefs than first appears to be the case, it is equally true that Acts 17 is by no means wholly uncritical. In view of v. 16, Paul's assertion in v. 22 that Athenians are 'very religious' is not without ambiguity. Idolatry misses the mark and must be given up when the light of Christ reveals its misunderstandings. Light brings judgment as well as knowledge. God has overlooked the ignorance of the past, but he does so no longer, for the arrival of Christ demands repentance before a coming judgment.

Nevertheless, however much of the gulf between Romans 1–3 and Acts 17 can be narrowed, even those who discern the thoughts of Paul in the Areopagus speech have to allow for a different emphasis which can only be explained by the conclusion that here we have these thoughts brought to expression through the voice of Luke.[2]

As Wilson points out, the tone of the two emphases is completely different. He summarizes: 'For Luke, the Gentiles' religiosity is the first stage on their way to salvation: for Paul, it is the basis of their condemnation by God'.[3] If we could alter Wilson's first 'is' into 'can

overall approach of Paul. However, 1 Thessalonians is not a summary of Paul's initial preaching but rather a statement of his converts' movement from one sphere of authority to another: it summarizes his converts' stance rather than the initial preaching which occasioned that stance. The basis of that initial preaching must, of course, have been the resurrection for that alone could validate any claim to authenticity that the preaching might have. Yet that the initial preaching of Paul could mention the resurrection without the cross and its significance is scarcely conceivable, for it would have said nothing about the change of stance which for Paul determined and demonstrated the reality of the change of spheres.

1. See the problems this presents for Sanders, *Paul, the Law and the Jewish People*, pp. 125-29.

2. Bruce, 'Real Paul?', pp. 302-302, 305.

3. Wilson, *The Gentiles and the Gentile Mission in Luke–Acts* (SNTSMS, 57;

be', then his reading of the differences is correct.[1] As far as Paul himself is concerned, God has given the idolaters up in a positive act of rejection which, even if it is to move them to something better, nevertheless can be brought to an end only by a complete denial of the past. For him, the Gentiles knew God but perversely refused to honour him (Rom. 1.21). They are therefore guilty.[2] Luke's Paul, however, ascribes ignorance to them, and this, though misguided, is not in itself culpable since their worship is rightly intentioned and presumably therefore at least partly effective.[3] 'What therefore you worship as unknown, this I preach unto you'. They did not really know God, but they were nevertheless offering him worship. He is near them and in them and, fundamentally, they are one with him. Paul in Romans can talk of God's hiddenness and forbearance, but it nevertheless means that the past is fundamentally guilty, that God and man are apart from each other. There is a gulf between the two. This seems to be fundamental to Paul's outlook. For him there has to be a radical break with the past.

Acts 17 calls for repentance, but it bases its call upon a different understanding of the human predicament. In men there is a basic response which is God-given and derived from the close link between God and men. Man has not lost his way but has taken a wrong turning which his true nature and right instincts should show as wrong. There is need of repentance because he has not followed his instincts correctly. But what can be accepted as ignorance apart from Christ now becomes blameworthy in the light of him. There is therefore a mixture of blame and excuse, just as there is in the speeches directed to Jews. The Christian proclamation reveals the truth about man himself and his own situation. Response to it will amount to a fulfilment of himself and his natural aspirations while rejection of the message will take him away from his beginnings and reveal the real culpability of idolatry.

There is no mention of the cross, for its radical rejection of the past

Cambridge: Cambridge University Press, 1973), p. 218.

1. Luke is in fact more critical of Gentile religiosity than Wilson allows.

2. Rom. 3.23.

3. Their previous view of God and their worship of him has been inadequate, born out of ignorance. It only becomes blameworthy and so to be repented of in the light of Christ. In this they parallel the history of the Jews.

and its denial of continuity is out of place.[1] Instead, there is the proclamation of the resurrection which is presented as a moving forward from the past which however takes up the past into its sphere. The enormity of this claim, however, should not be underplayed or the full significance of its challenge denied. As Haenchen reminds us, 'Even in the Areopagus speech Luke has let the doctrine of the risen-one stand as the stumbling block'.[2] It represents a new age, not indeed one which cancels out the positive side of the old, but one which nevertheless proclaims a leap forward in God's revelation of himself and which demands an equally great advance on the part of those who accept. Paul's listeners ought to move forward. Their own understanding, their own background, their own teachings, even their own inclinations and natural goodness derived from their closeness to the God who indwells them ought to lead them on. But, just as their built-in tendency led men as a whole to misrepresent the necessary stance so that they were diverted from the right way, so now there is an equally strong built-in resistance to respond. Response demands faith, it demands believing in the witness of others, it demands an abandonment of self-sufficiency, it makes a great challenge to those whose religiosity finds an outlet in either philosophy or idolatry. It demands assent to the resurrection of one unknown and not totally able to be comprehended. Just as the speeches to the Jews suggest that the resurrection of Jesus illuminates the Old Testament so that it can then be seen as pointing to him,[3] so Greek philosophy needs the resurrection to make its good assertions into saving knowledge. Without that, the speech suggests that philosophy itself leads to idolatry. Though philosophy contains a built-in safeguard against the belittling of God, it nevertheless leads to that from which it ought to be protecting its adherents. The speech does not suggest a separation of philosophy from idolatry. Both ultimately are actually one.

The speech therefore is not really as easy-going in its account of the Gentiles' past as Vielhauer, for instance, accepts when he says, 'The repentance which is called for consists entirely in the self-conscious-

1. For Luke, the cross has significance as a historical problem rather than as a theological event.

2. *Acts*, p. 530.

3. One of the purposes for Luke of the great forty days is to enable the risen Lord to unpack the Scriptures so that they can be seen in a new light, Lk. 24.24-32; Acts 1.3.

ness of one's natural kinship to God'.[1] To say that is really to fail to give due notice to the significance Luke sees in the proclamation of the resurrection of Jesus. It is the resurrection which proclaims the inadequacy of religiosity and philosophy. Jews refuse the resurrection (2.22; 3.13; 13.30). The Pharisees who seem to side with Paul when he proclaims the resurrection, though closer than the Sadducees, nevertheless wholly misunderstand the significance of the declaration (23.9), and, earlier, when at Ephesus the town clerk denied that Paul's message really threatened Ephesian religiosity (19.37), he was plainly further from the truth than was Demetrius's own assessment of the situation, 'that gods made with hands are no gods' (19.26). There is, indeed, a tension and the resurrection demands a leap forward. Nevertheless, it is not one which is of quite the same order as that demanded by Paul's proclamation of the cross. It is not a reversal, but a moving forward—a leap forward—in the light of a real understanding, which though there in origin from the beginning, had been clouded and even lost. The cross cancels out the past: the resurrection is not simply the past's confirmation since it transforms what it confirms and judges what should not have been accepted. It demands a radical moving forward, though not a reversal. That Paul would have preached a resurrection without a cross is indeed very unlikely. Here, we have Luke's understanding and Luke's message.

Haenchen has suggested that the Aeropagus speech put forward a kind of programme for the missionaries at the time of Luke's writing. *Heilsgeschichte* has been left behind in a turning away from the Jews. The gospel is now free to go to the Gentiles.[2] Wilson has accepted this to see the speech as 'influenced by the ideas and missionary attitudes of Hellenistic Judaism and the post-apostolic Church'.[3] Yet this seeing of the speech as a programme of what to preach in the service of the edification of Luke's church is surely negated by the fact that Luke does not present Paul's visit to Athens as a success. True, he wins some followers, but Luke is careful to point this out even at those places where Paul appears to turn aside from the Jews (e.g. 18.8). Verse 33—'So Paul went out from among them'—reads like a statement witnessing to lack of success, and a mention of a few names of converts suggests the refusal of the many. Paul leaves Athens for

1. *Studies in Luke–Acts*, p. 36.
2. *Acts*, pp. 529-30.
3. *Gentiles*, p. 215.

Corinth where he himself calls the church there 'the first-fruits of Achaia' (1 Cor. 16.15). It is therefore unlikely that Luke meant this to be a pattern of how his contemporaries were to preach. It is rather his statement of how Paul himself preached. The stumbling block of the resurrection should not be forgotten in the search for substantiation of Luke's supposed *theologia gloriae*, nor should the relative failure of the visit be overlooked in the service of alleged Lukan triumphalism. In correction of such stances, Conzelmann writes:

> On the contrary, Luke intends to show how this unique Paul at that time dealt with the philosophers in Athens in a unique discussion. If the philosophers were not even converted by a sermon of Paul, they will certainly not be converted today... the truth of the faith is established in spite of its being rejected by the wise.[1]

1. 'The Address of Paul on the Areopagus', *Studies in Luke–Acts*, pp. 217-30. The quotation is on p. 227.

Chapter 4

PAUL AS PREACHER TO ISRAEL

In the speeches at Pisidian Antioch and Athens, we have Luke's version of what he believed Paul would have preached to Jewish and Gentile audiences. Both manifest the Lukan stance in that they both work from the perspective of continuity which is so different from what seems to have been the outlook of the historical Paul. Again, both base the Christian hope on the resurrection of Jesus which is in fact understood as the confirmation of God's eschatological promises to Israel. Gentiles join in through acceptance of the resurrection of Jesus. Repentance is an acknowledgment of and a response to the one true God, and this enables incorporation into the people of God brought under his sway by his work through Jesus.

Luke, because of that theological perspective, will go on presenting Paul as a preacher to Jews as well as to Gentiles. The priority of the Jews in the purposes of God means preaching to them first, and only then to the Gentiles. He is aware of Paul's increasing break with the Jews but he presents this, not as the fault of the apostle or of the radicality of his message, but as the result of Jewish perversity. Given his stance on the relation of the new to the old (and even the use of 'new' and 'old' would really be alien to him), that is the only way left to him of accounting for the break. Refusal to put the blame on the Jews or to draw out the depth of their perversity would leave him only with the alternative of saying that God himself brought about the break, and that, because of his overall perspective, Luke cannot do. The more the continuity of the Jesus event with the earlier work of God in Israel is emphasized, the more Jewish perversity has to be pointed to as the explanation of their refusal of the Christian proclamation. It is this which accounts for the presence in Luke–Acts in general and in the career of Paul in particular of both a strong pro-Jewish bias and an equally strong anti-Jewish bias. The presence of both has to be explained, and this can in fact be done from the perspective of Luke's idea of continuity.

Since Paul is the subject of a large part of Acts (and the reason for that must be discussed later),[1] these things have to be put forward constantly about him. Paul's continuing concern with the Jews is for Luke a theological necessity. It is in Luke's picture, not just to bring Paul into conformity with the outlook of an idealized early church, nor even as a preliminary to his preaching to the Gentiles.[2] It arises rather out of two things; first, Luke's overall theological perspective and, secondly, out of the fact that by Luke's time the Jewish nation as a whole had rejected the Christian proclamation. It comes out of both Luke's abiding concern with the Jewish people and the need to explain to Christians the highly problematical rejection of their faith by the vast majority of the nation.[3]

This overall view of Paul's ministry is worked out by Luke in his accounts of the apostle's conversion. This is recounted three times (Acts 9.1-19; 22.1-21; 26.2-23), the two accounts set in the context of Paul's captivity speeches being supplemented by further speeches in chs. 23 and 24. There are of course differences in the three accounts centering on the appearance of Jesus, the nature of the commission, and the part of Ananias. These should not however be accounted for by crediting Luke with slavishly including and following different sources. While sources may be found in Acts, Luke was certainly no slave to them. His use of Mark shows precisely the opposite; he revised and omitted from his sources.[4] What is there is presented in the way it is, and placed in the context it is, to further Luke's narrative purpose. The differences in the three accounts arise from the way Luke uses them to contribute to the developing stages of his story.

This is especially true of the differences between the account given in ch. 9 and those contained in chs. 22 and 26. A single developing theological stance is to be found in all three accounts. In ch. 9, there is an appearance to Paul but no direct commissioning of him. Indeed, the significance of the appearance itself is given only by way of Ananias—'He is a chosen instrument of mine to carry my name before the Gentiles, and kings, and the sons of Israel' (9.15)—and it is through

1. See below, pp. 136-38.
2. Jervell, 'Paul the Teacher of Israel', in *People of God*, pp. 153-84.
3. See the discussion in Section 2, pp. 210-22.
4. See below, pp. 290-27.

him that Paul is enabled to receive the Holy Spirit (9.17). Paul will learn of his task, not from a direct revelation, but by way of the church's ministry into which he is incorporated. For Luke, Paul is neither an individualist nor an initiator. He is one with the church and his commission comes, not in a moment of revelation, but through the church. It will come by way of Barnabas and in response to the Antiochene church after Luke has recounted the story of Peter and Cornelius (11.25). The manner of Paul's Gentile mission is not the work of an individual. It is foreseen from the beginning by God and accepted by the church through the conversion of Cornelius. Paul after his conversion must, as it were, wait in the wings as far as his part in the Gentile mission is concerned. Meanwhile, as he waits, he takes part in the early mission of the church to Jews, first in Damascus, and then inevitably in Jerusalem itself. Here is Luke's schematized narrative, but it is one worked out for no trivial purpose but from a consistent theological outlook.

The other two accounts of Paul's conversion are told within the context of his apologetic speeches and have to be interpreted accordingly. That in the temple (22.1-21) is a defence against Jews from Asia who allege that Paul's missionary work results in his 'teaching men everywhere against the people, and the law, and this place'. What actually though occasions their complaint? What actions on the part of Paul have caused them to make it? Haenchen believes that the cause of the accusation is the Gentile mission. What the speech contains is therefore a justification of that mission.[1] Jervell objects to this because in Acts it is Peter not Paul who is the instigator of the Gentile mission. For Jervell, the issue is actually the justification of the church's existence. 'Luke wants to show that the twelve and Paul represent Israel, while the unrepentant Jews no longer have a claim to be designated "Israel"'.[2] It is true that Haenchen does not really give enough weight to the Cornelius episode, but he is surely right that acceptance of Gentiles without circumcision, fellowship with them, and inclusion of them within the eschatological people of God in their own right is fiercely threatening to Israel. It is Paul's part in the Gentile mission which is at stake and under attack here. It is concentration on them which threatens 'the people, the law, and this place' (21.27). The Gentile mission of Paul is the problem here for Luke. Luke knows

1. *Acts*, p. 630.
2. *People of God*, p. 174.

that it was actually more climactic and more law-free than his unfolding of the story allows. What he therefore has to show at this point is that the mission to the Gentiles was divinely commissioned and that Paul could do nothing else.

The speech in ch. 22 does not underplay the radicality of Paul's action. It is however demanded by two things, his commission to preach Jesus, and the Jewish refusal of his message. Verse 18 speaks of the refusal, though it must be noted that as yet it does not seem that the Jews have actually been approached. The speech rather builds on the earlier conversion account and above all on the pattern of Paul's activity that Luke has constantly displayed. It really points forward to the events contemporary with the speech. Paul protests that the Jews must respect his past life and acknowledge the compulsion of his witness to Jesus (vv. 19-20). His turning from persecutor to proclaimer must by seen by them for what it is, and it can be accounted for only by a direct intervention on the part of God himself. The Jews however, will not acknowledge this. Jewish perversity will stop them from accepting the authenticity of his call.

And so while he is actually in the temple he receives a further direct commission: 'Depart, for I will send you away to the Gentiles'. In this way, the movement away from Jerusalem and the movement to the Gentiles are seen as the inescapable response to the direct intervention of God. Luke does not underplay the radicality of Paul's action. What he does do, however, is to justify the shape of his ministry and its climactic concern with Gentiles by the refusal of the Jews to listen. Paul's ministry, described in accordance with the shape demanded by Luke's theology, should have been to both Jews and Gentiles, but Luke knows that in actual fact it was not. It therefore did seem to threaten the Jewish covenant. Nevertheless, this was not actually inherent in it. It was Jewish perversity which caused it to have the shape that it actually acquired.[1]

Paul had to move out. The Gentile mission was demanded by God and its actual shape called into being by God in the light of the foreseen Jewish lack of response. Paul's career followed an inescapable must. The apostle could do no other than obey. But its implications are great. The speech gets a fierce reception for it has done nothing to turn aside the Jews' initial charge made in 21.28. All Paul can offer in

1. This explains the pro-Jewish stance and the anti-Jewish stance in Luke's description of Paul.

defence is the divine compulsion. It is out of his hands. His is an inevitable response under God to the sociological situation.[1]

The final stage in Luke's understanding and defence is unfolded in the three further speeches Paul makes in captivity (23.6; 24.10-21; 26.4-23). The first two speeches deal with Paul's conversion to Jesus. His embracing Christianity is justified as in his earlier speeches by the resurrection of Jesus, here given an existential immediacy in the appearance to him. Jesus' resurrection marks the fulfilment of Israel's hope and the establishment of the people of God. He serves Jesus therefore as a good Jew. Justification of the Gentile mission as part of that service is given in the defence before Agrippa and Festus. Paul here is positive about the Gentile mission which he explains as part of the eschatological hope of Israel. Jesus' resurrection makes him the one in whom the Old Testament promises are fulfilled. Again, Paul's basis for this belief is his own encounter with the risen one. That encounter contained a commission to go to Jews and to Gentiles who become his primary concern and who make the main response. They are now joined to the people of God as they receive 'forgiveness of sins and a place among those who are sanctified by faith in me' (26.18). Again, Paul could do nothing but obey.

But now the speech makes the final climactic justification of Paul's career. He has proclaimed effectively 'both to small and great'. The success of the mission shows its basis in God. And what he has preached is 'nothing but what the prophets and Moses said would come to pass; that the Christ must suffer and that, by being the first to rise from the dead, he would proclaim light both to the people and to the Gentiles' (vv. 22-23). The universal mission is given scriptural justification. Because Jesus is the fulfilment of God's eschatological promises to Israel, a universal response must follow. Equally, because of the universal response, the proof of that messiahship is given.

The risen Jesus had in Luke 24.47 pointed to the mission 'to all nations' as being grounded in Scripture. This for Luke is an important function. He is, of course, the pre-eminent New Testament witness to the worldwide mission, yet he handles it in a way more subtle than

1. F. Watson, *Paul, Judaism and the Gentiles* emphasizes the sociological constraints which determined both Paul's practice and his theology. Luke's theology itself is determined in part at any rate by the actual situation of the predominant Jewish rejection of Paul.

that used by Matthew. Matthew grounds the mission in the words of the glorified Christ (Mt. 28.18-20). It is an eschatological commission.[1] Luke however grounds it, not primarily in the commands of Christ, but further back in the promises of Scripture so that it becomes an inevitable part and proof of the eschatological remaking of Israel. The Gentile mission is not the climax but the authoritative witness that the last days have begun. It is recounted for a purpose which is not wholly contained in itself, for it rebounds to Israel's glory and witnesses to what is happening. So here, in Paul's most detailed justification of his mission, what he has done is said to be nothing other than what has fulfilled Old Testament expectations. The Gentile mission is justified by the messiahship of Jesus, by the establishment of the eschatological people of God, by the direct command of the risen one, and by the authority of Moses and the prophets. The Gentile does not understand the significance of these things. The Jewish ruler recognizes their validity even if he rejects their implications (26.24, 28, 32).

So Luke gives these three accounts of Paul's conversion and uses them as three steps in his developing defence of Paul. In ch. 9, Paul's mission is presented as no individualistic whim but is rather put forward as communicated to him by way of the church and as learned from his predecessors in the faith. In ch. 22, his concern with the Gentiles is explained. The shape his mission has taken is justified to validate its paramount attention to the Gentiles and its seeming lack of concern with the Jews. It comes about as a response to a divine commission and to the failure of the Jews to accept his witness. What else could Paul do? And then finally in ch. 26 the mission itself is presented as part of the eschatological hope of Israel. Paul can engage upon the Gentile mission as a good Jew. He himself remains a Jew, and what he is doing is to rebound to the Jewish covenantal promises for it is in fact to be seen as an ongoing part of the fulfilment of that covenantal position which has been affirmed and realized in the resurrection of Jesus.

For Luke the Gentile mission is grounded ultimately in the Scriptures, and its success rebounds to Israel's glory and to the truth that Jesus is Israel's lord. The period of the church recorded in Acts demonstrates the validity of the Christian proclamation. The Gentile

1. J.P. Meier, *The Vision of Matthew: Christ, Church and Morality in the First Gospel* (New York: Paulist Press, 1979).

mission arises inevitably out of God's promises to Israel from the beginnings of his dealings with her. Yet Luke knows that the mission in general and Paul's part in it in particular have not completely fulfilled Old Testament expectations for these would have envisaged the coming in of Israel as a whole as well as the Gentile incorporation into her. So he labours to show that the eschatological event really has been manifested in Israel but that Jewish perversity has stopped a large part of Israel from acknowledging it. This remains his primary problem and is largely responsible for what is often described as his anti-Jewish stance.[1] If Paul's ministry focused and intensified the problem, he has to show that it was not Paul's fault. He underplays the radicality of the apostle's message while acknowledging the radicality of his actual career. He can do so, again, only in one way, and that is by emphasizing Jewish perversity. Paul is thus brought into Luke's theological scheme. The positive value of that scheme is that it does credit to the religious history of Israel: its price is that, by underplaying the newness of the Christ event as that is focused in the cross, it has to seize upon and expose, even to exaggerate, Jewish perversity. Only so can Luke bring together his theology and his situation.[2]

Luke therefore has yet one more speech of Paul, and that is his final witness to the Jews at Rome. What for Luke is the significance of that episode? How does he resolve this tension in his presentation of Paul's overall ministry?

The climax of Luke's account of Paul is the apostle's preaching in Rome, though from a prison, about 'the kingdom of God' and his 'teaching about the Lord Jesus Christ quite openly and unhindered' (28.31). Luke here is careful to point to two factors. First, Paul's

1. Maddox, *Purpose*, 1982, pp. 42-46.

2. The Jewish rejection of both the messiah and the kerygma about him is perhaps the primary problem for Luke and his theological scheme. C.A. Evans, 'Is Luke's View of the Jewish Rejection of Jesus Anti-Semitic?', in D.N. Sylva (ed.), *Reimaging the Death of that Lucan Jesus* (Frankfürt am Main, 1990), pp. 29-56, notes that compared with contemporary internal Jewish inter-party disputes, Luke's writing falls far short of the polemic issuing in hatred that is there often expressed and is 'much more akin to the polemic of Paul'. 'Luke emphasizes Jewish responsibility for Jesus' death, not because of anti-Semitic hatred, but because of his desire to place the Messiah's death firmly within the framework of biblical history... the struggling emergence of the Christian faith is ultimately a Jewish affair. And it is on a Jewish note that the book of Acts closes as the Lucan Paul continues to preach the "kingdom of God"' (p. 55).

actually being in Rome witnesses to the power of God in his ministry and so through that to the Christian witness of which it is a part. In spite of the hostility of the Jews and the ineptitude of Roman justice, in spite even of the hostility of nature itself, Paul arrives at Rome. The fact of his arrival at Rome, as at Jerusalem before, is highly significant. Here, as there (21.15, 17), Luke includes what is sometimes seen as a confusing double notice of his arrival (28.12, 16).[1] The first notice is given as a pointer to the fulfilment of an earlier hope of Paul and of a promise of God to him. In 19.21 Paul had 'resolved in the Spirit' what he must do and which would climax in his arrival at Rome. In 23.11 'the Lord stood by him'. In vocabulary used only here and by Paul when he arrived at Rome in 28.12, he proclaims 'Take courage, for as you have testified about me at Jerusalem, so you must bear witness also at Rome'. Paul, by his presence at Rome, shows the power of the Spirit. His being there is the direct result of the appearances of the Lord to him at his conversion, at the temple commission, and at the time of the promise made to him at the beginning of his captivity.

But, in the second place, Paul's presence in Rome is the climax of his preaching. He does not bring Christianity to Rome since it is already established there.[2] His preaching in Rome is rather the climax of Paul's own ministry and of his part in the universal witness. Rome, however, is the capital of the empire, and so his preaching there and his making of converts in that city is seen as the fulfilment of Paul's part within the working out of the eschatological expectations. What is to happen afterwards is no part of Luke's story. The proclamation in Rome is the climax; anything else could only be anti-climax. There he preaches the kingdom of God (28.23, 31). His preaching thus points back to the question of the apostles at the ascension, 'Lord, will you at this time restore the kingdom to Israel?' (1.6). The mission has taken place. Is it the kingdom? Is it a substitute for it? Or is it a guarantee of it? In the light of Luke's eschatological expectations as a whole, it is to be seen as a witness of its reality and a guarantee of its coming. The church is now waiting for it. But what of Israel?

1. Haenchen, *Acts*, p. 718; Conzelmann, *Acts*, p. 224.

2. Maddox, p. 77 struggles at this point. He recognizes that Luke does not suggest that Paul brought Christianity to Rome, but he wants to maintain that Paul nevertheless is the significant figure in the Roman fulfilment of the Lord's missionary charge.

The main content—though it is not the climax—of Luke's account of Paul's time in Rome is given in the apostle's dealings with the Jews. To them he testifies 'to the kingdom of God' and 'tries to convince them about Jesus both from the law of Moses and from the prophets' (28.23). Paul pleads earnestly with the Jews. They disagree amongst themselves. Because they are at variance, Paul uses against them the prophecy of Isa. 6.9-10. Jewish perversity has led to an emphasis upon the Gentile mission. This will be successful (28.28).

What exactly though for Luke is the significance of this episode? Determining it depends upon our evaluation of the Isaiah quotation, the statement of a successful response among the Gentiles, the meaning of the disagreement among the Jews, and whether the episode is deemed to be climactic or illustrative of Paul's dealings with the Jews as these are recorded in Acts.

Haenchen's view of the significance of the episode for Luke has been highly influential. For him, it marks the final rejection of Israel and her replacement by Gentiles.[1] His understanding is summed up by his assertion that at Rome 'Luke has written the Jews off'.[2] Most recently, J.T. Sanders has developed and even sharpened this understanding. For him, there are no real conversions of Jews at Rome. The episode rather exhibits a 'monolithic anti-Judaism which questions whether Luke considers it possible for any Jew to be converted after the end of Acts'.[3]

1. 'Judentum and Christentum in der Apostelgeschichte', *ZNW* 44 (1963), pp. 155-87.

2. 'The Book of Acts as Source Material for the History of Early Christianity' in *Studies in Luke–Acts*, pp. 258-78. Haenchen's outlook runs counter to our understanding of Lukan theology to enable him to write, 'Luke has no inkling of the extent to which he thereby (10.35) eliminates the continuity of the story of salvation between Jews and Gentiles. It certainly is not Pauline theology that appears here... It is rather the theology of Gentile Christianity toward the end of the first century in which Luke lived not only outwardly but theologically'. The ending of Acts however does not express such an outlook nor does 10.35 which is seen rather as a response to the Cornelius episode in the light of all that has been asserted about the restoration of Israel's nucleus and the means of that as the extension of God's activity among the Gentiles. Luke thereby does not forget the priority of the Jews and the continuity of God's saving work. It is the wonder of Gentile inclusion, the widening of God's work to include them alongside Israel which is paramount for Luke.

3. *The Jews in Luke–Acts*, p. 299. Sanders criticizes me (p. 82) for a failure to accept his negative view of Luke's attitude to the Jews and in particular for my assertion (*Christ the Lord*, p. 79) that Luke's Old Testament outlook meant that he could

This last understanding however is extremely doubtful. Verse 24 maintains that 'some were convinced'. This must mean converted for it fulfils Paul's expressed aim as this is stated in the previous verse where it is said that he was 'trying to convince them about Jesus from the law of Moses and the prophets'. Of Paul's ministry at Corinth Luke has written that 'he argues in the synagogue every sabbath and persuaded (convinced) Jews and Gentiles' (18.14). At Thessalonica 'some were persuaded' and one part of the group is said to be made up of 'brethren (17.4, 10). At 28.25 ἀσύμφωνοι δε ὄντες is given emphasis as the first phrase of the sentence and, by its tense, suggests that it is not merely causal, so explaining why Paul turned upon them,

never 'have turned his back upon the nation whose hopes it recorded'. My alleged 'serious flaw in method' is a failure to ask *how* he used Jewish Scripture. Sanders' estimate is that he used it against the Jews: 'The Jewish Scripture is quoted in Luke–Acts against the Jews'. This, however, is less than half-correct. Isaiah 61 is used by Luke at the Nazareth episode as an inclusive statement of God's concern. It can be seen as being in itself against the Jews only by having it in the control of the Elijah, Elisha references. But in fact it is to control them rather than the other way round. At Pentecost, Luke uses Joel 2.28-32 to express the eschatological hope of Israel. It has a wider reference, but its significance is seen in the first place as referring to Israel and to her remaking. The promise has to be grasped, it is true, but it remains directed in the first place to Israel (Acts 2.36, 39). At the Apostolic Council, James uses Amos 9.11-12 as, though expressing a wider hope, a statement of Israel's remaking. It may confound the Pharisaic demands of some, but it is in no way against the Jews as such. It sees the inclusion of the Gentiles without the Law as a result of Israel's confidence in her place in God's saving concern. Luke's scriptural quotations are often used in the service of pointing to Israel's perversity and are as such critical of her. But they explain her present rejection of the proclamation and are not propounding a consequent rejection of her by God. Indeed they do the reverse for they point rather to God's use of the perversity and to his continuing concern for her. The quotation at Rome does not suggest a change. Sanders' attempt to separate out the speeches from their context and to take the two independently makes for a clarity of result which goes much further than Luke himself allows. Conzelmann has pointed to the need to interpret the speeches in their contexts and to see a development and inter-relatedness between them ('Luke's place in the development of Early Christianity', *Studies in Luke–Acts*, p. 309). Recent literary interpretations of Luke have emphasized such concern. Luke's is a theology of movement and this entails the unity between speeches and the incidents in which they are set. Failure to treat Luke's work as a whole will result in a clarity of outlook which is achieved only by a partial exposition. Sanders' assertion that there is a consistent attitude in the speeches of Jesus, Peter, Stephen and Paul which is one in its hostility to the Jews is achieved only by a method of 'divide and conquer'.

but has a continuing temporal sense. Their being at variance continued after Paul's dismissal of them. Some of them could well have been among the 'all' who came to him (28.30).

So at the end of Acts not all the Jews refuse the proclamation. Conversion of individual Jews cannot be ruled out, and Luke's church is likely to have contained Jewish as well as Gentile Christians. Nevertheless, the end of Acts undoubtedly witnesses to the end of an organized ongoing mission to the Jews in Luke's time. The last scene in Acts is to explain why this is so. Our question though must be, does that explanation go beyond an emphasizing of a factual situation which can be explained by Jewish perversity, to embrace a theological explanation which expresses God's rejection of the Jews? Does Luke ground the lack of a mission to the Jews in a theological scheme proceeding from, and witnessing to, the will of God?

It is widely accepted that he appears to be doing just that. So Conzelmann sees Rome as witnessing to a change of epochs. 'We can see quite clearly how that Luke thinks of the Christians, according to plan, taking over the privileges of the Jews as one epoch is succeeded by the next'.[1] Christian lack of movement towards the Jews reflects the Christian lack of concern with them which, in turn, arises out of God's rejection of them. Whether God has actually brought about that rejection of the message in a hardening of Jewish hearts or whether he has rather responded to Jewish perversity is regarded ultimately as beside the point. What is important is that he has rejected. The historical position is seen to be grounded in a theological scheme which is arrived at as a result of Luke's understanding of salvation history.

More surprising is Jervell's estimate of the significance of this final scene. He, of course, sees the Gentile inclusion within the sphere of the people of God as coming about as a result of a Jewish acceptance of the gospel. The Gentile mission comes, not out of Jewish rejection, but out of Jewish inclusion. It is the fulfilment of Old Testament promises and of Israel's eschatological expectations. Nevertheless, for him Rome still marks a decisive change as it becomes the point where the mission to the Jews is brought to an end. Israel has now actually been remade. 'As much of Israel as is able has now come in'.[2] Henceforth, 'there can be no talk about a renewed mission to Jews

1. *Theology*, p. 163.
2. *People of God*, p. 64.

without misunderstanding the right to Gentiles of the promises' (64, 69).[1]

So, for Jervell the age of Israel and the concern with Israel is now over; it is now the turn of the Gentiles. This schematization however seems to come out of an over-wooden approach to Luke's understanding of the fulfilment of the Old Testament promises. For Luke, it is not simply a question of Jews first and Gentiles only afterwards. It had to begin in that way, it is true, but from the time of Cornelius there has been a continuing mission to both. Paul's Jews still come in even after he has declared an end of the mission to the people as a whole (18.7-8). Luke's theology makes it quite unnecessary for him to have suggested that the Jewish mission was closed before that to the Gentiles could really take off.

The reception of the preaching by the Jews in Rome is a mixed one. The Jews are divided and that division continues even after Paul's response so that it is apparent even in their leaving him. The door to all the Jews is not actually closed. Nevertheless, for Luke the main problem is the rejection by the majority, and it is to this that Paul's Isaiah quotation is directed (28.26-28). Of some importance is the fact that the prophecy is not said to find fulfilment in the Rome event.[2] Indeed, the quotation is explicitly taken out of the scheme of prophecy and fulfilment to be instead a witness to the past as well as to the present. The Holy Spirit spoke to the fathers. For Luke, the Spirit was not simply the Spirit which enabled prophecy but was one also to empower the witness to Jesus and to God's action in him (Lk. 24.48-49). It is this latter function which is primary here. The Spirit witnessed that the people of Israel were hard and rebellious towards God. His is a continuing witness to a continuing state. As were the fathers, so are they. The point here is precisely that made earlier by Stephen: 'You stiff-necked people, uncircumcised in heart and ears, you always resist the Holy Spirit. As your fathers did, so do you' (7.51). The quotation becomes a comment on the situation at Rome, and therefore on the situation of Luke's own day. By the time he writes, the mission

1. *People of God*, p. 69.

2. Luke makes it quite clear when he is using his prophecy-fulfilment scheme. See for instance Lk. 4.18-21; Acts 2.16-21, 25-28; 8.32-35; 13.33-35, 15.14-18. There is nothing like this here. Indeed there is a clear contrast for here, as at 13.40-46, past and present are rather used as illustrative of each other. They are parallel rather than climactic.

to the Jews has come to an end; Jewish rejection of the gospel by the nation as a whole has been cemented. The Isaiah quotation becomes a comment on that situation which it justifies by seeing the present Jewish perversity as one with their previous perversity and as arising out of it. It becomes climactic only in that it is a culmination of a longstanding situation, that it is now expressed against the eschatological happenings, and that it has resulted by Luke's time in unprecedented sufferings for the Jewish nation. But it is of one piece with Israel's history and it does not necessarily mean that God has now rejected her or brought his concern with her to an end.

The form of the quotation follows the Septuagint which had already made the imperatives of the Hebrew into indicatives. While this may, as Haenchen suggests, emphasize the obduracy of the Jewish people and increase the guilt of those who reject the divine message,[1] it nevertheless releases God from the responsibility of determining that hardness. It is not represented as God's will and is therefore not seen as part of God's design in bringing about the rejection of Israel. Israel rather than God rejects and determines a turning away from salvation. As such therefore, Luke understands these words as a comment upon Jewish perversity rather than as a proclamation of God's rejection of her. The episode records a fact rather than an intention: it is a statement explaining a situation rather than a proclamation of a determination to bring that situation about.

In this Luke agrees with that use of the quotation made by Matthew where, in 13.14-15, it differs from its use in Mk 4.12. Matthew alters the Markan emphasis upon the use of parables as a means of causing hardness to make it into a comment upon the results of such hardness, to become even an attempt to deal with it. Matthew and Acts represent a different handling of the Isaiah pericope from that found in Mark and John and this suggests that Haenchen's assertion that this Old Testament passage was understood in the Hellenistic community 'purely as God's judgment of rejection' is in fact an oversimplication.[2]

Paul's speech ends with the assertion that 'this salvation of God has been sent to the Gentiles: they will listen' (28.28). The climax of the speech, and what takes the place of Jewish response, is the Gentile acceptance of the gospel. Their response is contrasted with the Jewish lack of response. The climax is the response of the Gentiles to a

1. *Acts*, p. 724.
2. *Acts*, p. 724 n. 1.

mission that will go to them. It is the response rather than the mission which is primary in the thinking of Luke at this point.[1] It does not necessarily mean that a Gentile mission has taken over from a Jewish one. The thought is with the contrasting responses of Jews and Gentiles rather than with necessarily successive areas of missionary concern.

Nevertheless, does Luke understand the Gentile mission and its response as 'taking the place' of a Jewish concern, or does he see it rather as 'making up for' the lack of success with the Jews? If it is the former, then it entails a rejection of the Jews; if on the other hand it is the latter, it means that the Gentile mission and its success are seen as consolations for the failure with the Jews, and a justification of the truth of the proclamation which the Jewish rejection might seem to deny. Its reference to a successful Gentile mission is not in itself a declaration of a new departure, of a new stage in the witness, for the Gentile mission has long since begun; its pattern has been consistent from the time of Paul's preaching and indeed before then;[2] it has not so far entailed a refusal to deal with Jews. Verse 28 is therefore not necessarily a witness to a new departure. The pattern that has been followed so far and into which it fits, the fact that some Jews have responded even in Rome, and the already established successful mission to Gentiles suggest that this is a continuation of Paul's missionary stance rather than a new development in it and the church's proclamation. The mission to the Gentiles, therefore, is not a substitute for, but a counterbalance to the failure of the Jews to respond. The successful mission to the Gentiles is pointed to, not merely as a fact of history, but as a sign of the truth of the proclamation and as the fulfilment of scriptural expectations. It buttresses the failure of nerve brought about by the Jewish refusal of the gospel. Rome represents and confirms the cycle and the message of Luke's account of Paul's dealings with Jews and Gentiles.

1. Cf. R.L. Brawley, *Luke–Acts and the Jews: Conflict, Apology and Conciliation* (SBLMS, 33; Atlanta: Scholars Press, 1987), p. 75, 'In Acts 28.28 Gentiles hold no exclusive proprietorship over the gospel'. G. Schneider, *Die Apostelgeschichte* (2 vols.; Herders theologischer Kommentar zum Neuen Testament; Freiburg; Herder, 1980, 1982) II, p. 414, notes that Paul appears to have had dealings only with the leaders of the Jews. The 'all' of v. 30 does not then exclude all Jews from dealings with Paul.

2. Stephen's rejection does not mean the end of Jewish conversions in Jerusalem. At Corinth, Crispus the ruler of the synagogue believes even though Paul has already declared his intention of going to the Gentiles.

Nevertheless, is Paul's dealings with the Jews at Rome more than a repetition, even if in a climactic way, of a cycle? Is it in fact a climax which goes beyond earlier rejections at Antioch and Corinth to announce, even to bring about, a final break with the Jewish people? Does Luke say at this point that God has finally turned against the Jews in a way that he has not done before? Maddox has argued that he does. He writes, 'We must note that the three passages about Paul's "turning to the Gentiles" are not merely parallel; there is a progressive intensification of the theme'. He speaks of Paul's reluctance to turn aside from Jews in Antioch of Pisidia, of frustration and impatience with the Jews at Corinth, and of a solemn air of finality at Rome. So 'at the end of Paul's mission, the opportunity offered at its beginning has been lost'.[1]

This however is to fit these episodes into an alleged progressive intensification which is in fact not there. It is true that only at Rome does Paul use a long Old Testament quotation to account for the lack of response,[2] though he has already in his initial appeal to Jews at Antioch and before their refusal used an Old Testament quotation to point to the seriousness of the appeal (13.41).[3] The Isaiah quotation at Rome explains the fall into what the quotation at Antioch warned about. Its use at Rome marks the importance of the scene, but that importance lies in its being used as a summary of the whole Acts situation rather than in its marking of a new stage in the drama. At Antioch, the quotation from Habakkuk is also used to point, not to a time of fulfilment, but to a characteristic Jewish perversity. That is shown at 13.45. The Jews reject and Paul goes to the Gentiles, not merely because of that rejection, but also to be acting in accordance with Old Testament expectation (13.47). In v. 48 their acceptance of the gospel is recorded.

There is no more reluctance on Paul's part at Antioch than there is at Rome. Indeed, there he is nearer to the pattern of Jesus' Nazareth sermon where the attitude of the speaker comes close to actually causing the rejection by the listeners.[4] At Rome, however, the initiative is not Paul's. The Isaiah quotation comments upon rather than causes

1. Maddox, *Purpose*, p. 44.
2. Sanders as in n. 3 p. 95 above.
3. Maddox, *Purpose*, p. 44.
4. Jesus acts to bring out and to explain their outlook but in doing so he is actually seen to be causing it.

the Jewish response. What gives the episode at Rome its air of finality is simply its place as the last episode in the book. Had Acts ended at 13.49, the Antioch episode would have seemed no different.

If the rejection at Antioch is parallel with that at Rome, that at Corinth (18.5-7) is actually stronger than the Roman one. The Jews oppose and revile Paul and the apostle rejects them personally: 'Your blood be on your own hands! I am innocent. From now on I will go to the Gentiles'.[1] Here is Paul washing his hands of his Jewish opponents in a violent confrontation. Yet many of the Corinthian Jews do believe and the harshness is directed only to those who deliberately revile the apostle and his message. Here is Paul shaking the dust from off his feet (Lk. 10.10-11).

There is not a progressive intensification of hostility towards the Jews in Acts. The final rejection of Paul in Jerusalem continues their history of disobedience yet it is no greater than that entered into at the time of Stephen (6.8–8.3). That event itself takes up themes that are present in the city's rejection of Jesus. Jesus' plea for forgiveness 'for they know not what they do' (Lk. 23.34)[2] is paralleled by one of 'Lord, do not hold this sin against them' (7.59). The martyr's plea following upon that of the Lord himself means that Luke must have

1. This is sometimes compared with the response in Matthew of the crowds to Pilate's willingness to release Jesus, Mt. 27.25. Luke however does not say that the Jews are cursed for the blood of Jesus but that the exclusion from the people of God which will be theirs because of their rejection of the kerygma is their fault not Paul's or, indeed, God's. The responsibility lies with them and with no one else. They are not bringing Paul's curse upon them but a necessary rejection (awful and bloody though that may be). Luke of course does accept dire consequences for those who refuse the proclamation. This however is merely a continuation of the prophetic outlook and of the prophets' message to Israel of old. It is not however a rejection of Israel as such for the mission to her continues both in Corinth and wherever else Paul goes. His mission produces divisions within Israel rather than an exclusion of her and witnesses to her actual response rather than to God's rejection of her.

2. Sanders (*Jews*, p. 63) argues that this verse extends only to allow for the mission in the early part of Acts and that Jewish action thereafter is regarded as blameworthy. Yet he himself sees this verse as linked to the plea of Stephen. The Jewish action is now sinful for they no longer, because of the gift of the Spirit, have the excuse of ignorance. Nevertheless, Luke sees their sin as being open to God's forgiveness. The great rejection by Jerusalem at that time does not bring concern for the city to an end. Her rejection of Paul cannot be more blameworthy than her rejection of Stephen and it is unlikely therefore to be met with any harder response. Stephen sees the Jewish lack of response as blameworthy but not unforgivable.

acknowledged God's mercy even here. There is nothing to suggest that Rome marks the end, either of God's concern, or of his mercy towards the Jews.

Luke then has a continuing concern with the Jewish people so that this final episode in Rome is not an indication that he has written them off. It does indeed acknowledge the facts of life as Luke's own period experiences them. Israel as a whole has rejected the mission; she has in fact turned her back on her Lord. As such, she continues and brings to a head that perversity which has marked the whole of her history. Her actions in the present are one with her stance throughout her history and Luke's attitude stands firmly alongside the stance taken, say, by the Deuteronomistic historians.[1] Yet God has actually used that perversity in the past to move forward his plans to enable the Christ to be realized (7.51-53; 13.47), and in the present to bring about a thrust out into the Gentile world. The Gentile response makes up for the lack of it on the part of the Jews and actually has a positive role in being dangled before the Jewish people as a challenge, almost as a provocation.[2]

How does all this compare with Paul's own concern as he reflects in Romans 9–11 upon the situation of his day?[3] It is in fact remarkably parallel. Luke, of course, does not express that anguish which introduces and motivates Paul's thinking on the matter. This is primarily because of their different ethnic backgrounds. Recent suggestions that Luke might have been a Jew are not compelling.[4] He was certainly a

1. It is by no means certain that Deuteronomy for all its condemnation of Israel's recurring attitude of apostasy, ends with final rejection of her. The Deuteronomic cycle, the continuing guidance of God, and the ending of the overall narrative would suggest to Luke rather a hope of continuing care and of the permanence of the covenantal relationship.

2. Cf. Rom. 11.13-14.

3. U. Wilckens, 'Interpreting Luke–Acts in a Period of Existentialist Theology', *Studies in Luke–Acts*, p. 76; 'The question asked by Ernst Fuchs, 'But does salvation have a history?' must be answered in the affirmative both for Paul and Luke, however different the details may be. For the thinking of both rests upon Old Testament belief and Jewish belief according to which God realises his salvation in historical events'. See J. Jervell, *The Unknown Paul: Essays on Luke–Acts and Early Christian History* (Minneapolis: Augsburg, 1984), p. 65.

4. E.E. Ellis, *The Gospel of Luke* (NCB; London: Nelson, 1966), pp. 52-53; B. Reicke, *The Gospel of Luke* (trans. R. Mackenzie; London: SPCK, 1965), pp. 21-24.

man of the Old Testament, and his intellectual—we might even dare say spiritual—sympathies lay with the Jews. He had learned from them. But his emotional ties are rather with the Gentiles.[1] If he looks at the Jews wonderingly from without, it is with the Gentiles, and more especially with those who had formed a link with the Jews, where his real empathy lay. Luke's concern with the Jews is more detached. He can wonder at them and be infuriated by them, but he cannot become emotionally entangled with them. He is just too easily aroused to wonder and to incredulity by their turning away from their heritage, which he at least appreciates, for his considerations to lead to any kind of emotional turmoil or involvement in them.[2] Yet it must not be forgotten that, if he alone among the evangelists has Jesus pray for their forgiveness (Lk. 23.34), he, also alone, has Jesus weep over Jerusalem (Lk. 19.41-44). He would expect Jesus as a Jew to do just that. He though, as a Gentile, would not be expected to share the same sentiments.

Paul's is also a cerebral concern. This is centred upon his desire to vindicate God's power, righteousness and constancy (Rom. 9.6). He embarks upon a theodicy.[3] Luke's intellectual problem however is of a different kind. His emphasis upon continuity and upon the fulfilment of God's covenantal purposes in Jesus means that the problem of God's power and consistency does not arise since he knows that his purposes are being fulfilled. His intellectual problem rests upon the fact that the Jewish people as a whole have not acknowledged this. Their disavowal of Jesus as Lord presents a real problem to Christian belief for it by itself calls into question the correctness of the Christian assertion. Luke therefore is virtually forced by his own presuppositions to answer the problem, sharpened by those very presuppositions, by a constant assertion and intensification of the nature of the Jewish perversity. Their rejection of Christ becomes wholly blameworthy; it seals what has to be seen as their continuing rejection

1. *Contra* P.E. Esler, *Community and Gospel in Luke–Acts: The Social and Political Motivations of Lucan Theology* (SNTSMS, 57; Cambridge: Cambridge University Press, 1987), pp. 30-45 who sees Luke's community as composed primarily around former adherents of the synagogue.

2. There is an emotional detachment in the way he describes Paul's denunciations of the Jews.

3. J.C. Beker, *Paul the Apostle: The Triumph of God in Life and Thought* (Edinburgh: T. & T. Clark, 1980), pp. 351-67. Cf. P. Richardson, *Israel in the Apostolic Church* (SNTSMS, 10; Cambridge: Cambridge University Press, 1969).

of God's approaches to them. A harsh judgment on their rejection is demanded by Luke's basic approach to the nature of the God-event in Jesus.

On the other hand, Paul's emphasis upon discontinuity leads him in a very different direction. He pursues the idea of a remnant.[1] 'For not all who are descended from Israel belong to Israel'. The remnant depends 'not upon man's will or action but upon God's mercy' (Rom. 9.6, 16). In the first place, it is a negative idea—'Though the number of the sons of Israel be as the sand of the sea, only a remnant of them will be saved' (Rom. 9.2). Scripture is fulfilled and God's honour is vindicated, but in the end Paul is unwilling to pay the price, which is the virtual ending of the covenant with Israel as a people and an arbitrariness on the part of God which calls into question the real nature of his covenantal initiative. So Israel must be at least in part responsible for their stumbling and falling over Jesus. They did not pursue God's righteousness 'through faith, but as if it were based on works' (Rom. 9.32). Their admitted zeal for God took a wrong turning. They were 'ignorant of the righteousness that comes from God' (Rom. 10.3). That was a culpable ignorance, for Paul uses the same term for those Gentiles who would not see the real significance of the Jewish–Gentile situation of his day (Rom. 11.25), of those who did not perceive the nature of baptism (Rom. 6.3) and of those who failed to perceive the true meaning of the Law (Rom. 7.1). The Jews should have known and entered into the righteousness that comes from God. They should have responded to Christ but, though this offence is primarily a christological one, a criticism of their attitude to the Law is included.[2] Christ not only universalizes salvation, he also reveals the incorrectness of the Jewish understanding and pursuit of law. They 'did not submit to God's righteousness' when it met them in Christ because their response to the Law had led them into a wrong understanding of its purpose. Her present disobedience is not unprepared for by her earlier history (Rom. 10.21 quoting from Isa. 65.2).

But God has not rejected Israel (Rom. 11.1). Chapter 11 is wholly positive to Israel. The remnant is no longer a cutting down to the exclusion of the rest, but a guarantee of God's continuing concern for the whole, since it now has something of the nature of the first-fruits

1. This of itself can be very negative about Israel as his use of the quotation from Isa. 10.22 shows.

2. Rom. 4.1-8; 10.1-4.

which thereby becomes the pledge of the redemption of the whole (Rom. 11.13, 15-16, 23-24). There will be an eschatological action which will not only make Israel jealous but which will actually point to the restoration of Israel as a whole. Israel will be seen to be both prior and pre-eminent in God's plan of salvation (Rom. 11.25-26).[1]

Is Luke as positive as this? Certainly Israel is blamed for disobedience (Acts 13.27). Yet she is still God's people throughout Acts; she is in her faithful ones the nucleus of the eschatological people of God. Those who refuse Jesus are in danger of being 'cut off from the people' (3.23). Before Agrippa, Paul declares God's promise to deliver him 'from the people and from the Gentiles (26.17). He stands for the hope and belief that God 'would proclaim light both to the people and to the Gentiles' (26.23). At Rome, and before Jews, Paul defends his conduct towards 'the people' and quotes Isaiah's description of 'this people' (28.17, 26, 27). Unbelieving Israel is not outside the sphere of God or excluded from his covenantal concern. Repentance of at least some of the Jews means an eschatological refreshment and will enable the sending of the Christ and a complete eschatological renewal. Then will be the time 'for establishing all that God spoke by the mouth of his holy prophets from of old' (3.21). This must mean the restoration of Israel and the inclusion of the Gentiles. It is the fulfilment of God's promise to Abraham, 'And in your posterity shall all the families of the earth be blessed' (3.25 quoting from Gen. 22.18).

Though Luke's hopes for the redemption of Israel are expressed mainly in his Gospel and will therefore be discussed in our chapter dealing with his relationship to Matthew's thought,[2] there is enough in Acts to make it certain, not merely that he had not shut the door upon 'the people' but that he expected that people's inclusion at the parousia. At the ascension, the disciples' question, 'Lord, will you at this time restore the kingdom to Israel?' (1.6) is not declared illegitimate in its hope. Rather, it is the timing which is re-expressed. The Spirit, so far from being a substitute for, is rather a guarantee of the restoration, and the universal mission under the Spirit's power is a necessary prelude to it.[3] The twelve have to be made up by the

1. Beker, *Paul*, pp. 334-35.
2. See below, Chapter 10.
3. *Christ the Lord*, pp. 95-99.

inclusion of Matthias before the Pentecostal gift.[1] They are a symbol of the potential wholeness of Israel and represent, not a nucleus of a new Israel,[2] but the first-fruits of eschatological Israel which witnesses by its number to the nature of the Spirit-filled community, which challenges its members to remember both its source and its character, and confronts Israel as a whole with its fulfilment in it. Acts as a whole does nothing to deny the proclamation made in the climactic episode of the infancy narratives which, as we have seen, as the prologue to Luke's whole narrative, asserts that Jesus is not only the 'light for the revelation of the Gentiles' but is also 'for glory to thy people Israel' (Lk. 2.32).[3] As in Romans 9–11, the inclusion of the Gentiles rebounds in the end to the unity of Israel in God.

1. *Christ the Lord*, pp. 96-97.
2. Beker (*Paul*, p. 330) maintains that Luke sees the church as the new Israel.
3. Sanders (*Jews*, p. 48) dissociates use of 'people' for Israel from Luke's use of 'people of God' or just 'people'. While they are to be distinguished in that they are not identical, they are nevertheless not separated. Gentiles are now also 'a people for his name' but they do not take the place of Israel who remains potentially part of the people as she enters into her heritage. Israel has to realize her true nature.

Chapter 5

THEOLOGIA CRUCIS

We have argued that Luke's picture of Paul, though it does not give us the real Paul, is not one that is based upon a lack of understanding of the real Paul so as to point to incompetence on the part of its originator, be that judged either understandable or blameworthy, but that it is a determined and consistent re-interpretation of the apostle's outlook, based upon a knowledge of it, but reshaping it for a later time and bringing it into line with Luke's own theological message to that later period. It arises, not out of ineptitude, but out of a learning from and a moving on from the master. It is an interpretation which demands respect in its own right and of which our own appreciation of Paul and response to him needs to take account.

The point at which Luke seems to show his greatest understanding of Paul's own theological position is often seen to be his reporting of Paul's farewell speech to the Ephesian elders (20.17-38).[1] This speech is distinctive in that it is the one post-Pentecostal sermon in Acts which is addressed directly to members of the church rather than to outsiders. It carries the situation it is addressing directly beyond its own time into the period after Paul and therefore enables the possibility of immediate confrontation with the situation for which and out of which Luke himself is writing. Verses 28 and 29 bring the speech firmly into the orbit of Luke's contemporaries. So C.K. Barrett sees the significance of the speech as a whole as putting forward Paul as the 'chief and exemplary evangelist and pastor who by word and example instructs the new generation in their duties'.[2] It is often viewed as expressing Luke's salvation-historical perspective by means of which

1. Marshall, *Acts*, pp. 329-30.

2. C.K. Barrett, 'Paul's Address to the Ephesian Elders', in J. Jervell and W. Meeks (eds.), *God's Christ and His People: Studies in Honour of Nils Alstrup Dahl* (Oslo: Universitetsforlaget, 1977).

Paul's own ministry is incorporated into that of the apostolic age which is then distanced from Luke's own time when the shift of periods has taken place. The early untroubled church life is contrasted with the perplexities of the present, and the doctrinal irregularities of some of Luke's contemporaries are said to be countered by the church's *depositum fidei* which has been entrusted to it by the first generation of Christians.

A strong exposition of this kind of approach has recently been given by Lambrecht[1] who bases it upon a determined attempt to uncover the structure of the speech. It is seen to fall into two major parts, the break occurring at v. 28 which then points forward to the future and is completed with the commendation of v. 32. This verse in fact forms the climax of the speech as a whole so that the two elements, that of Paul's self-defence with its announcement of his impending suffering on the one hand, and that of exhortation and farewell to his disciples on the other, come together with the former being subordinated to the latter: 'The whole first part has a subsidiary function with respect to the second; both Paul's self-defence and his references to the future have to be seen in the light of the paraenesis of the second part'.[2] As a result of this structural explanation, Lambrecht can assert that the 'image of Paul which emerges from the apologetical passages is meant by Luke more as an example for others than as a personal apology'.[3] Exhortation of Luke's contemporaries is primary.

Such an approach, of course, takes full account of the centrality of the warnings to later generations in vv. 28 and 29 and of the Pauline commendation of v. 32. However, it must be asked whether it does real justice to Paul's apology for his past and to the announcement of his forthcoming sufferings in the first part of the speech, and whether it does not leave his references to the service of others in the second part as little more than bathos.[4] It is just possible that the biographical details of the first part of the speech serve to rescue Paul from the

1. J. Lambrecht ('Paul's Farewell Address at Miletus [Acts 20.17-38]', in J. Kremer [ed.], *Les Actes des Apôtres: Traditions, redaction, théologie* [BETL, 48; Gembloux: Duculot; Leuven: Leuven University Press, 1979], p. 314) can say that recent authors agree that the 'discourse is of importance as a witness to the way in which Luke endeavours to represent his own time as in continuity with that of Paul'.

2. 'Farewell', p. 318.

3. 'Farewell', p. 318.

4. Conzelmann, *Acts*, p. 176.

clutches of those who, in the service of their own teachings of a Gnostic outlook were making him into some form of a *theios aner* and who were claiming him as their authority. They could then serve as a legitimation by Luke of the kind of preaching that Paul had delivered and of the tradition he had handed down to the evangelist's church (vv. 20, 27).[1] Nevertheless, it has to be said that if this were Luke's aim, he makes his point only very indirectly. The speech appears, at least on the surface, to represent a defence of Paul rather than a rescue of him. Paul stands out as being under attack by opponents rather than as misused by supporters. If Luke's aim had been to defend Paul from proto-Gnostic enthusiasts he would have written his whole account of the apostle much more carefully to guard against a *theologia gloriae* which his contemporaries are alleged to be ascribing to Paul and which so many interpreters have seen in his own work. Professor Barrett has recently pointed out that there is much more of a *theologia crucis* in Acts than is often allowed to Luke.[2] Nevertheless, the way he works it out does not suggest that combating a false teaching with its emphasis upon a *theologia gloriae* was the primary aim of his telling the story of Paul.

It is even harder to see how the final verses of the speech serve the cause of exhortation. It is possible of course that Luke's opponents were actually using their position to lord it over their contemporaries, that they were so misusing their authority that the divine gifts they claimed were being manipulated to promote their own welfare at the expense of their fellow Christians and to the neglect of any real pastoral concern. This could account for the Lukan emphasis upon the weakness, surrender and service of Jesus (Lk. 22.27) and for his attacks upon Pharisaic ease. It could also have shaped his picture of the early church's care of the poor and needy (Acts 4.32-37).[3] Nevertheless, again such a concern does not appear to have determined his telling of the stories of Peter and Paul as a whole. They are not overall pictured as concerned pastors of the church and they do not make extended provision for its life. Apart from here, only 14.21-26 suggests such an interest, for the way of life attributed to the church in Jerusalem is not said to have been repeated elsewhere and is

1. This is how these verses are usually taken.
2. See n.1 p. 212.
3. For this, see L.T. Johnson, *The Literary Function of Possessions in Luke–Acts* (SBLDS, 39; Missoula, MT: Scholars Press, 1977).

not so set out as to provide an example for others to follow. Why Luke should have conceived of Paul's ending his farewell address in this way if exhortation were his main aim is not easy to perceive. As exhortation, the speech is, as Barrett notes, both 'formless and repetitious'.[1]

Two other more general considerations would also make us wary of the view that the speech was designed primarily as direct exhortation to Luke's readers in the service of a true teaching derived from Paul and put forward specifically in contrast to that of a false 'Gnostic' type of belief. Such an approach would, in the first place, seem to mark off this address from the speeches in Acts as a whole. As far as one can judge, these are all related to their context in Luke's historical narrative, and their message for Luke's contemporaries can be discovered, not by a direct response to them as isolated pericopae loosed from their links in the narrative as a whole, but more indirectly as they are seen as related to, shaped by, and in part even controlled by the context in which they are set.[2] So the early speeches are more varied in the parts of the proclamation they contain than the kerygma approach of C.H. Dodd, for instance, would allow,[3] and their different emphases are shaped in response to their historical context on which they form a commentary. Stephen's speech finds its attitude to the temple controlled by the fact that it represents the final, and known to be unsuccessful, challenge to Jerusalem as a whole to acknowledge the significance of its own history while Paul's various accounts of his initial encounter with Jesus are (as we have seen) shaped to conform to their function and place in Luke's narrative. Paul's farewell speech to the Ephesian elders is, it is true and as we have seen, distinctive insofar as it does consciously relate past and present, yet to make it primarily concerned with direct unmediated exhortation to Luke's contemporaries is to separate it out from Luke's overall strategy and to loose it from its place in Luke's work. It is in fact to isolate it and give it a universality which it would seem in its setting it was not meant to have.

Luke sees Paul's work at Ephesus as the heart of his third missionary journey. His address to the Ephesian elders, however, takes place

1. 'Address', p. 110.

2. See above, p. 95 n.3 and *Christ the Lord*, p. 206.

3. C.H. Dodd, *The Apostolic Preaching and its Development* (London: Hodder & Stoughton, 1936).

at Miletus. Luke's explanation that it was in order to save time appears a little thin, and there is much to be said for the view that Paul himself was under threat if he actually returned to Ephesus.[1] Luke at any rate determines to emphasize a farewell to the Ephesian elders. It is true that it refers back more widely than to the Ephesian ministry alone and therefore seems to bring the whole of Paul's missionary enterprise in view. As Luke's story stands, the Jews of Ephesus are not particularly hostile—they are in part more positive than in most other places Paul visited—and nothing is said about Paul's working in Ephesus to maintain himself or of his actual pastoral concern. But the reference in the speech to the hostility of the Jews brings the Ephesian episode in line with Luke's overall pattern, and the failure to describe any of Paul's pastoral concerns is also characteristic of Luke's work as a whole.

Yet Luke does spend more time on Ephesus than on any other of Paul's churches. It is the only place where events of two visits are recorded, where a number of unrelated episodes are described, where one incident—that of Apollos and Priscilla and Aquila (18.24-28)—unrelated immediately to Paul is included, and it is the place where Paul announces well in advance his intention of going to Jerusalem and Rome (19.21). In addition, it becomes the occasion for two of Luke's overwhelmingly triumphalist assertions: 'All the residents of Asia heard the word of the Lord, both Jews and Greeks' and 'So the word of the Lord grew and prevailed mightily' (19.10, 20).

Nevertheless, Paul had to leave Ephesus in a hurry (20.1). At this point his exhortation to the disciples is not recorded. Later, on his way to Rome, he decides to sail past Ephesus (20.16). The Ephesian church has to be content with a second-hand token of concern delivered to it by way of the church leaders. Is it any wonder therefore that Paul has to concentrate to justify his past ministry and his singleness of purpose, and to express his concern vicariously by way of the elders whom he commissions virtually on his behalf? His commendation of them seems to be given urgency in that the end of the address suggests that they will have to come in some way to Paul's defence. 'I coveted no one's silver or gold or apparel' (v. 33). Paul gave an example of toil and of service in the help of 'the weak' and so led them in the acknowledgment of the Lord's words 'It is more blessed to give than to receive'. Paul himself in his own letters suggests that

1. Marshall, *Acts*, p. 328.

he had a trying time in Ephesus. The 'beasts' with which he fought seem to have been opponents of his preaching. If that verse in its context (1 Cor. 15.29–34) suggests Christian opponents of a Gnostic stamp,[1] 1 Cor. 16.9 talks of many adversaries and these would most likely have included opposition from both Jewish and Gentile quarters. In Rom. 16.4 Prisca and Aquila are said to have risked their lives for Paul and this could well refer to incidents at Ephesus where Paul himself declared that he was delivered from 'so deadly a peril' (2 Cor. 8.10). Though this might have been a near-fatal illness, it is equally likely a danger brought about by human hostility.[2]

Luke's account of Paul at Ephesus does not present a picture of unity. For all his well-known harmonizing tendencies, the rough waves of turmoil are allowed to break through so that the time of Paul there is not presented as one in total contrast to the hostilities of later years. Luke's report of Paul's first visit to Ephesus is odd (18.19-21). He argues with the Jews but they do not openly oppose him. On the contrary, they ask him to stay, a request which he refuses and for which no reason is given. There may well be substance in Haenchen's suggestion that there was already a Christian presence in Ephesus and one with which Paul was not altogether happy.[3] This suggestion gains some support from the fact that on his return visit he enters the synagogue and 'pleads' about the kingdom of God. His opponents are not actually said to have been Jews. They could well have been from some form of Jewish Christianity which was hostile to Paul. Further support for this is given in the preceding episode where Paul encounters the twelve disciples who had 'never even heard that there was a Holy Spirit' (19.1-7). If these disciples, for Luke at least, represent a non-Pauline form of Christianity, Apollos would seem to stand for a form of Christianity which as Luke saw it did not know the full meaning of the Pentecostal era of the Spirit (18.24-28). He could not deny him the possession of the Spirit but he maintains that he did not understand the significance of the gift, that it brought about the eschatological renewal of Israel and united the Gentile community to her. It is significant that after Priscilla and Aquila had 'expounded the way of

1. C.K. Barrett, *I Corinthians* (BNTC; London: Adam & Charles Black, 1968), pp. 362-64.

2. C.K. Barrett, *II Corinthians* (BNTC; London: Adam & Charles Black, 1973), pp. 61-66.

3. *Acts*, p. 547.

God more accurately', he then went on to proclaim Jesus as the Christ of Jewish and Old Testament fulfilment.[1]

Apart from internal dangers, there were the external ones. Jewish exorcists are routed (19.11-20) but the Jewish danger remains and when the Gentiles rise against 'the Way' (19.23-41) there is a perplexing Jewish involvement (19.33-34) which can be taken as a Jewish attempt to dissociate themselves from, and perhaps disown, the Pauline mission.[2] That Paul's encounter with the civil powers was not so easily resolved as Acts suggests has well been argued by Bruce.[3] At any rate, Paul deems it wise to leave hurriedly and can only make his apologies to Ephesus at a later time and from a distance.

In its context the speech at Miletus represents a defence of Paul and an apologia for his Ephesian ministry which Luke has to strive hard to present as legitimate. Paul found opposition and difficulties both from without and within. His version of the gospel was not accepted without opposition. His ministry there saw the beginnings of what was to deepen after his death. Verse 29 of the speech does not contrast Paul's time with what is to happen afterwards, for the beginnings—more in fact than the seeds—of the opposition were encountered by him, and

1. While it is relatively easy to understand the situation of the 'twelve disciples', discovering the significance of Luke's account of Apollos is more difficult. Luke is favourably disposed to him, though the episode is not without some apologetic significance on behalf of Paul and may reflect some knowledge of the Corinthian situation: E. Käsemann, *Essays on NT Themes* (trans. W.J. Montague; London: SCM Press, 1964), pp. 136-48; M. Wölter, 'Apollos und die ephesinischen Johannesjünger' *ZNTW* (1987) pp. 49-73. Luke however is not critical of Apollos (Tannehill, *Acts*, p. 232), at least in his later preaching after instruction by Priscilla and Aquila. However he is brought into the Lukan/Pauline understanding as the contrast between ἀκριβως and ἀκριβέστερον in 18.26 shows. But in what was he deficient? G. Krodel (*Acts* [Proclamation Commentaries; Philadelphia: Fortress Press, 1981], p. 63) makes him virtually of the same kind as the 'twelve disciples' and believes that he lacked the Spirit. However, the description of his being 'fervent in spirit' and the lack of any reference to an added gift of the Spirit suggests that he must be distinguished from them. What he was deficient in seems to have been an understanding of the significance of the gift of the Spirit as Luke unfolds that through his Pentecost and Cornelius incidents. Apollos's charismatic life had lacked an understanding of the historical implications of the Spirit's presence. He now preaches in the way of Luke's Paul.

2. Schneider, *Apostelgeschichte*, II, p. 277.

3. F.F. Bruce, *Paul, Apostle of the Free Spirit* (Exeter: Paternoster Press, 1977), pp. 294-99.

his ministry had not quelled the growing discontent. Paul had spoken the truth; the ensuing troubles cannot really be blamed upon him. God really had worked through him and what could be interpreted as failure or indifference was really not so. Again, it was the Spirit who determined Paul's journey to Jerusalem (19.21). Paul's failure to return was not a sign of pastoral insensitivity or neglect on his part. He had not cut and run, even though his enemies could so interpret his actions. Paul's speech therefore defends his ministry at Ephesus and is part of Luke's overall defence of Paul and his justification of his career as the outcome of the action of the Spirit.

A second point which tells against interpreting the speech as direct exhortation to Luke's readers is a questioning of the assumption that he uses it in the service of an alleged anti-Gnostic stand which is to be found in the work as a whole and which determines his presentation of Jesus. Talbert[1] has advocated this over the years in a number of publications and has seen this as controlling the pattern of Luke's Christology which he finds centred in his account of the baptism and ascension which are designed to counter any docetic or dualistic presentation of Jesus. But these two events as Luke describes them cannot bear this weight. His realism in the story of the ascension is in fact balanced by his presentation of the crucifixion which reduces the realism of the cross and moves the Markan narrative in a Johannine direction, while his account of Jesus' baptismal anointing of the Spirit 'in bodily form' (Lk. 3.22) is balanced by his story of the virginal conception of Jesus which could be taken as pointing away from his real humanity. Even the grossly materialistic account of Jesus' resurrection appearance before the disciples (24.36-43) is set in tension with the mysterious presence found on the way to Emmaus with his apprehension 'in the breaking of the bread' (24.35). Luke does see the ascension as the mark of continuity between the earthly Jesus and the heavenly, especially as it is recounted at the conclusion of the Gospel (24.50-53), but even this has to be set against his view that Jesus was actually advanced by that event to become, not other, but certainly more than he was before. He now 'enters into his glory' (24.26) and

1. C.H. Talbert, *Luke and the Gnostics: An Examination of the Lucan Purpose* (Nashville: Abingdon Press, 1966); *Literary Patterns, Theological Themes and the Genre of Luke–Acts* (SBLMS, 20; Missoula, MT: Scholars Press, 1974); *What is a Gospel*? (Philadelphia: Fortress Press, 1977); *Reading Luke: A Literary and Theological Commentary on the Third Gospel* (New York: Crossroad, 1982).

he is now 'made both Lord and Christ' (Acts 2.36). In some way he has become what he was not before as he achieves his 'being received up' (Lk. 9.51). In Luke the transfiguration prefigures the ascension.[1] Its language of 'alteration of countenance', of appearances 'in glory' and of 'accomplishment' of his 'exodos' (Lk. 9.29-32) would merit charges of carelessness if an anti-Gnostic outlook were Luke's concern. The resurrection is important for Luke. Jesus has to 'present himself alive after his passion by many proofs over a period of forty days' (Acts 1.3). The resurrection is the lynchpin of Luke's whole apologia for Jesus; without it the exaltation would have been impossible, and its reality is entrusted to witnesses who saw (2.32; 3.15; 10.41). Luke lives as a second generation Christian and he is incorporated into the people of God through the witness of others. The church is for him the people of God, but both his Christianity and the sense of the people of God arise out of his Old Testament understanding of what has happened in Christ rather than out of an opposing of false tradition. He does link the apostles to Jesus, Paul to the apostles, and the elders to Paul, but he makes no real provision for a continuing ministry, a continuing sacramental action, a single self-contained statement of faith, or a clearly defined universal church. Paul is not actually legitimated by the apostles in any irrefutable manner and he is not said to mark a change of aeons in the ongoing life of the church. Luke just does not point out the principle of succession in such a clearly defined manner as the concept of legitimation demands. Paul's speech at Athens does not represent a pattern for the proclamation to the Gentiles, while that at Antioch shows too much the marks of its special place in the growing mission for it to be put forward as a model to future generations.

It is by no means certain therefore that Paul's Miletus speech is primarily concerned with safeguarding and guaranteeing the correct handing down of a settled tradition from Paul to his successors. Paul in fact has not been credited with the appointment of the elders, he makes no provision for continuing the line which is not said to depend upon him, he does not give them a full explanation of their duties—there is for instance no command to engage upon a continuing mission or even on a continuing proclamation—and his charge to the elders in v. 28, though it may be closer to Pauline language than are the other

1. J.G. Davies, 'The Prefigurement of the Ascension in the Third Gospel', *JTS* NS 3 (1955), pp. 229-33.

speeches in Acts, is, by virtue of that difference, removed from what he is said to have proclaimed in the book as a whole. Luke does not seem to have been concerned to set out a continuity of proclamation. Verses 20 and 27 refer to Paul's initial responsibility in proclamation rather than to the actual contents of what he proclaimed. It is the fact of a proclamatory coming among them which is the subject of Luke's defence of Paul rather than the shape and contents of that preaching. We may well question therefore Haenchen's confident assertion that the opponents of Luke's presentation here were clearly Gnostic,[1] or Lambrecht's belief that 'Luke wants to underline Paul's ecclesial orthodoxy',[2] and may equally hesitate to accept Talbert's view that Luke wanted to say that 'the true tradition in his time was located in certain successors of Paul'.[3] Neither the speech nor Acts as a whole gives such clear guidelines as to the nature either of the beliefs or of the way of life of Paul and his successors.

The view that the speech is addressed to the defence of Paul and that it speaks only indirectly and in its context to Luke's readers is given credence by the fact that it makes sense of the last verses of the speech which otherwise appear only as an anticlimax. There is much to be said for Nickle's suggestion[4] that 20.33-35 contain paraphrased echoes of Paul's collection project. He had carried through that enterprise in spite of the reluctance of some and the opposition of others, and Rom. 15.31 makes it clear that both Jews and Jewish Christians could view it with suspicion. There is little doubt that Paul himself saw it as more than a charitable exercise, that he viewed it as a sign of the unity of the church, and of the Gentile response to what they owed to the Jewish people and its history. But it is possible that it was not entirely without some character of a demonstration and that at any rate it could be viewed thus by both Jews and Gentiles. Paul's Corinthian correspondence shows that some at least of his opponents were using it as an excuse for attacking him and his alleged money consciousness (2 Cor. 8.20; 12.14-18). Resentment at the collection was transferred to a certain antagonism towards the apostle. The silence of Acts (other than 24.17) suggests that it may not have been accepted and the obscurity of that verse may hint that the collection itself somehow

1. *Acts*, p. 596.
2. 'Address', p. 323.
3. *Literary Patterns*, p. 135.
4. K.F. Nickle, *The Collection* (London: SCM Press, 1966).

proved the point of opposition to Paul in Jerusalem.[1] Intended or not, it may have been a point of provocation of Israel (and of Jewish Christians) to that jealousy of which Paul speaks in Romans 11.13-14. Altogether then, the collection proved productive of complaints about Paul, and the most likely explanation of Acts 20.33-35 is that it is a defence of Paul in the light of accusations which his obsessive preoccupation with the collection may have caused to be levelled against him. Luke was aware of the outcome in Jerusalem and of the complaints that had been made against him and, in this way, comes to his defence.[2]

Luke then is concerned to give the speech an historical setting and, in so doing, he does not set out to make it that direct legitimation of the present that is often found in it. It becomes rather a defence of Paul himself and of what Luke wants to contribute by way of his picture of him to the message of Acts as a whole. Who though were the opponents? Against whom is Paul being defended? Lampe talks of an anti-Pauline mission in which Paul was regarded as the arch propagandist of the church and as the ultimate threat to Judaism as his teaching was seen as designed so determinedly to break down the old boundaries of the people of God.[3] The 'grievous wolves' were probably outsiders of a Jewish persuasion even if their beliefs may have been expressed in something of a Gnostic outlook. Equally though, the Pauline influence was under attack from within the church for, whenever the church felt still related to its Jewish antecedents, his teaching was bound to be regarded as threatening to these.[4] Moreover we know from such evidence as that provided by the Galatian and Corinthian letters that Paul's proclamation left ethical and practical problems which often cried out for resolution but which his missionary zeal did not always allow to be resolved.[5] Paul may not have been a complete

1. Rom. 15.31.

2. 2 Corinthians 9 suggests that the Corinthians did not take kindly to the collection and it may well be their attitude to this which focussed their opposition to Paul and left them open to the beguilements of his opponents.

3. G.W.H. Lampe, 'Grievous Wolves', in B. Lindars and S.S. Smalley (eds.), *Christ and Spirit in the New Testament: Studies in Honour of C.F.D. Moule* (Cambridge: Cambridge University Press, 1973), pp. 253-68.

4. One of Paul's aims in Romans was no doubt to justify his position in the light of the problems it raised for those of a different outlook in respect both to their own attitude to the Law and to the hostility he aroused in the Jewish people.

5. See for instance the discussion of this issue, at least in so far as it is reflected

opportunist, but his theological position did not always result in carefully and consistently worked out practical applications.[1] Opponents, particularly those of a more cautious and conservative stamp, would have had plenty about which to complain and would not have found it hard to draw up support for an attack upon an alleged lack of pastoral concern, sensitivity or constancy. It was against such attacks that the Miletus speech seems to have been designed by Luke.

In a positive and persuasive study of the speech, Professor Barrett says, 'The content of the preaching is given in terms that are curiously both Pauline and un-Pauline'. It is, he says, 'a fair summary not quite Paul's'.[2] In the same vein, Lambrecht can say, 'Luke wants to imitate Paul here, and to a certain extent he does succeed in doing so'.[3] Luke at this point goes to the heart of Paul's career and presents him clearly as 'accomplishing a course' which is successful in its working out of the obligations that God has placed upon him but of which the very success is measured finally in terms of ultimate surrender and suffering. Here he comes very close to Paul's own estimate of his vocation and its working out and in this he is not far from Paul's own understanding of the marks of true apostleship (2 Cor. 3.1–6.13). He uses the language of Paul—faith, grace, gospel, church—in a slightly unPauline way. As Barrett sees it, his use lacks 'the creative, disputatious, theological energy of the epistles...and it is no substitute for this that the Pauline inheritance is cast in unexceptional phrases'.[4] This is undoubtedly true, but whether theological application can survive fully only in situations of conflict, and whether it does not have to be engaged in continuing life is open to discussion.[5] Excitement and opposition cannot always be the hallmarks of relating the gospel to daily living which accepts reality because it has to live with ambivalence in both the church and the world. Apocalyptic confrontation has sometimes to be mellowed by continuity both of the world and with it.

in Galatians, in J. Barclay, *Obeying the Truth* (Edinburgh: T. & T. Clark, 1988). Though for a more positive assessment, see Tannehill, *Acts*, pp. 180-81.

1. H. Chadwick, 'All Things to All Men', *NTS* 1 (1954–55), pp. 261-75.
2. 'Address', p. 112.
3. 'Farewell', p. 320.
4. 'Address', p. 119.
5. Paul's other interpreters, as these are seen in Ephesians and the pastorals, had to make their own interpretation of his teaching in order to allow it to be relevant to their times. In this, Luke would appear to be closer to Ephesians than to the pastorals.

Nevertheless, the question really is whether Luke's undoubted stabilizing of the Pauline language has led in fact to fossilization. Barrett admits that v. 28 does indeed ground exhortation in theology[1] and, if we are right in our interpretation of the speech's final words, then his accusation of a division of ethics and theology is at least partly met for, if it refers to Paul himself rather than to those who are to follow after him, its basis is the theological assessment which undergirds the speech as a whole. Again whether fossilization is to be seen really depends upon the idea of a *depositum fidei* which provides security and salvation and which is often found in vv. 20 and 27. We have argued however that these refer to Paul's own pastoral ministry rather than to an ongoing belief guaranteed and retained in succeeding generations and so shaped as to include the true and exclude the false. The speech is then seen to be a much more limited, but nevertheless a much more radical and understanding defence of Paul designed, not as a guarantee of his faith, but as an interpretation of Paul's stance against those from within and without who were making quite specific charges against him. If they were right, Luke would have been hard pressed to put forward Paul's career as exhibiting the marks of the Spirit which he so clearly claims for. Luke understands Paul, even if he has not entered into the resultant depths of his theological genius to reproduce it in himself and for his own times. He has nevertheless learned from him so that he is able to defend him with much sympathy and no little insight.

Paul's speech to the Ephesian elders contains Luke's one reference to the saving value of the cross of Christ and it is no doubt placed here to show his knowledge of the Pauline understanding of the cross even though he does not make it is as his own.[2] Indeed Luke's failure to speak of the atoning value of the cross of Christ has been put forward as one of the strongest reasons for believing that he failed to understand Paul's theology.[3]

As part of God's plans, the cross was essential for Jesus (Lk. 24.26). Nevertheless, Luke refuses to isolate it from the whole suffering and servant life of Jesus or from that to which it leads. It is not the focusing event but is rather one vitally important stage in that

1. 'Address', p. 119.

2. See p. 77 n.1.

3. Vielhauer, 'Paulinism', pp. 44-45. C.K. Barrett has taken a more positive view in 'Theologia Crucis—in Acts?'.

series of events—each in its own way essential—beginning with the baptism which leads up to and culminates in the ascension of Jesus. If Luke had had to pinpoint one event that could be called the saving act, he would undoubtedly have pointed not to the cross, but to the ascension, for it is that which for him becomes the means of the remaking of the people of God within which salvation is effected and guaranteed. For Luke, salvation is understood essentially in corporate terms.[1]

Why otherwise Luke avoids giving atoning value to the cross, we can only guess. Perhaps any tradition which seeks to set the whole life of Jesus within the saving purposes of God inevitably places less emphasis upon the cross as the actual point of redemption. The Markan tradition does not say a lot about the actual atoning value of the cross, and if Luke refuses to isolate the cross, he would seem to be sharing in an outlook which is at least in part represented by the Fourth Gospel. For Luke no less than the Fourth Evangelist, however, the cross was determinative of the whole life and manner of Jesus. It determined his way and revealed his glory.

But primarily it would seem to be Luke's emphasis upon continuity which caused him to refuse either to isolate the cross or to pinpoint it as of saving significance. Jesus is one both with the earlier servants of God and with those of the renewed people. He fulfils the pattern laid down by the lives of the Old Testament servants, and determines the way to be followed by those who are to take up their cross daily and follow him (Lk. 9.23). He is both climax and source. His life in a real sense completes the work of the leaders of the old covenant and is itself furthered by the witness of the leaders of his church. And it is the whole work of God which enables the redemption of his people. In this, Jesus is the focus and the means of its complete realization, but he is not isolated and separated out from the whole. Stephen's witness is his preaching rather than his martyrdom (7.54-56), for it is the proclamation which causes the heavens to be opened and the Son of Man to be seen. Paul's witness might lead to his death—and Luke makes it pretty obvious that it does (20.38)—but that in itself is neither here nor there; it is the decision to follow through and to

1. See below, Chapter 12.

embrace the sufferings which is important and which enables him to witness at Rome.

But this does not mean that Luke has reworked Paul's theology of the cross in the service of one of glory.[1] The cross casts its shadow over Luke's Gospel no less fully than it does over Mark's. True, Luke's passion narrative does not have the utter desolation of the Markan and the glory is never far away, but the suffering of the present is fully embraced and the longer text of the agony in the garden reflects Luke's concern with its reality.[2] Again, the Acts of the apostles should not be read as an unambiguous success story in order to make it conform to some expectations which view it as a first chapter in ongoing church history, a prototype of Victorian missionary concerns, or a pattern for the somewhat dubious programmes of church growth. In fact, it gives a rationale for none of these. It opens with an ascension story which proclaims an exaltation but one which is, nevertheless, hidden, so that the disciples are left with no little perplexity,[3] and it closes with Paul preaching in Rome, but nevertheless as a prisoner and meeting disbelief and rejection on the part of the Jewish leaders while facing death at the Gentile hands.

In between, Jerusalem as a whole has rejected the proclamation for, in spite of James' assertion to Paul of the numbers of those who have turned to Jesus, the rejection of Stephen's witness by the establishment seals its own fate and guarantees that disaster which Jesus according to

1. E. Käsemann, 'Ministry and Community in the New Testament', in *Essays on NT Themes*, p. 92.

2. 'The textual evidence for omission is strong... omission in so many different branches of the tradition is hardly due to accident', Marshall, *Luke*, p. 831. Nevertheless, he adds, 'On the whole, the internal evidence inclines us to accept the verses as original'. On the other hand, Evans (*Luke*, p. 813) says, 'On balance the verses should probably be deleted'. J. Neyrey, *The Passion according to Luke*, accepts them as part of Luke's own text, being an expression of Luke's soteriology where Jesus as Second Adam undergoes the return attack of Satan for which his peculiar ending of the temptation narrative has prepared the reader. We shall see below, pp. 214-15, that Luke does indeed see Jesus as Second Adam and that he revises some of his early narratives in the light of this. Now at the eschatological climax, the battle is truly engaged; Jesus himself enters into the sphere of *peirasmos* which he will successfully withstand. This scene has been prepared for by 9.51, 12.49-50, 13.31-33. 22.53 sets the scenes against the transcendental battle and Psalm 110.1 sees them in this light.

3. See *Christ the Lord*, pp. 29-41.

Luke saw so clearly and could do nothing to avert.[1] Continuing Jewish rejection wherever Paul goes remains a constant source of perplexity. And Paul's mission among the Gentiles is by no means presented as one of unambiguous success and acceptance. Only in its beginnings on Cyprus (13.4-12), at Troas (16.8-10) where the 'we' passages begin, and at Corinth (18.17-18) where a vision points to the distinctiveness of the pattern there—'I am with you and no one shall attack you to harm you'—does Luke proclaim unhindered success. Elsewhere churches are established in the context of and in spite of misunderstanding, hostility and constant attacks. The authorities are uncomprehending and almost universally unhelpful and Paul is having to be constantly on the move with his work in the individual churches incomplete. Even in Philippi where he is rescued in a dramatic way and where the authorities are routed, he is nevertheless asked by them to move on (16.39). One near-disaster follows another at Antioch, Iconium, Lystra, Thessalonica and Beroea. In all these places it is a case of Christianity being established in the midst of hostility. What he leaves behind must, it seems, be a very tender shoot. Athens hardly represents a success story and, even at Ephesus, after the Demetrius episode, Paul deems it wise to pack his bags and move. His farewell speech to the Ephesian elders talks of hiddenness, sacrifice and suffering (20.17-38).

What contributes to the appearance of a success story is primarily the Lukan summaries and his stories of miraculous interventions and rescues. This latter element should not be overplayed however. Paul's escape from death at Lystra should not be turned into some Lukan urge for one more resurrection story. It is one rather of real suffering, and as a result, Paul has yet again to move on (14.19-20). In its light Luke can, a few verses later, summarize Paul's exhortations to his newly-founded churches in a reminder that 'through many tribulations we must enter the kingdom of God' (14.22). If this is one of the few references in Acts to the kingdom of God, it is a pointer to both the futurity and the other worldliness of the kingdom. The present is a time of trial. Peter and Paul it is true both have their miraculous escapes, but these are only in order that their work may be completed—their suffering is real and will come to its climax in good time. Until then, however, their rescues are only partial. Peter has to leave Jerusalem at this point, Paul to move on from Philippi, and the

1. See below, pp. 236-40.

rescues on the way to Rome still lead to his ultimate suffering there.

What ultimately gives Acts the appearance of one great success story and the expression of a theology of glory is the Lukan summaries. They do tend to act as a framework and to express something like a recurring theme. They should, however, be taken in their context for they are never far from descriptions of failures and disasters. That of 6.7—'And the word of God increased and the number of the disciples multiplied greatly in Jerusalem and a great number of the priests were obedient to the faith'—leads directly into the Stephen episode with its break, its persecution, and its rejection. In 12.24—'But the word of God grew and multiplied'—is a confident reflection on the outmanoeuvering of Herod and his subsequent drastic downfall. But James is dead and Peter has to flee. In 19.10 'all the residents of Asia hear the word of God' which 'grew and prevailed mightily', but this leads into Paul's rejection by the vast majority at Ephesus (20.1-7). James tells of the myriads in Jerusalem who believe, but they are nevertheless unable or unwilling to rescue Paul from his attackers. Paul preaches in Rome 'quite openly and unhindered', but he is in prison, Jews have rejected him, Christians do not know much about him, and what lies ahead does not seem mentionable.

Luke's vision is one of success in spite of seeming disaster. It is a vision in faith that the story he tells can in fact be seen as what he believes it to be, a sign that God's promises are being fulfilled in the work of Jesus and that the events after the resurrection can be seen as witnessing to the reasonableness of that which faith affirms. If he is seen to be banging the drum, it is because the drum needs to be banged if its message is to carry conviction and if that which it proclaims is to be heard above the rest of the noises which might in fact be felt to be proclaiming a contrary message. Luke shouts loud because he has to. He strives to show that what he proclaims can in reality witness to the faith in which he proclaims it, but he is aware only too well that the story he tells could be seen in a very different light. The life of the early church has its own cross, its own hiddenness just as did the life of Jesus, and both have to be seen through the eyes of faith if God's promises can be accepted as fulfilled. Lk. 24.47 brings the universal witness of the community as well as the life of Jesus into the sphere of the fulfilment of Old Testament promises. Neither the one nor the other makes its fulfilment obvious. For both it has to be spelled out as faith can see through the external to the underlying pattern and truth.

This indeed, is not very different from what Paul himself does in Romans 15 where he comes closest to that overall vision which Luke expresses. There he writes:

> In Christ Jesus then I have reason to be proud of my work for God. For I will not venture to speak of anything except what Christ has wrought through me to win obedience from the Gentiles, by word and deed, by the power of signs and wonders, by the power of the Holy Spirit, so that from Jerusalem and afar round as Illyricum I have fully preached the gospel of Christ, thus making it my ambition to preach the gospel of Christ, not where Christ has already been named lest I build on another man's foundations.

It seems that the strivings of some of Paul's friends on behalf of his modesty can easily be overdone!

It must not be forgotten however that Paul comes to Rome as a prisoner, that the climactic statement about his preaching is made when he is in a prisoner's lodging (28.30-31), and that Luke says nothing about his release. Suggestions that Luke pictures Paul's shipwreck and subsequent arrival at Rome in terms of symbolic death and resurrection give to Luke's ending a triumphalist outlook which is just not there.[1] Victory indeed is present, for Rome has been reached in spite of the machinations of the Jews, the ambivalence of many of his fellow Christians, the incomprehension of the Roman authorities, and the evil of the elements. God's purposes have been, not thwarted, but carried forward, but the terms in which Luke presents Paul's arrival at the city—'On seeing (the brethren) Paul thanked God and took courage' (28.15)—suggest relief and trust and a willingness to face the dangers that lie ahead, rather than a triumph arising out of the past and unrestrained confidence in the future. And that death awaits him there Luke has made very obvious (20.22-24, 37; 23.11).[2] Over six chapters of Acts tell the story of Paul as a prisoner in the hands of Rome and, apart from in Rome itself, during all that time, no one is converted to Christianity. The speeches are apologetic rather than proclamatory; they may show the lack of blame on the part of the apostle and may suggest that Rome recognizes his innocence, but he

1. M.D. Goulder, *Type and History in Acts* (London: SPCK, 1964).

2. The whole tendentiousness of Acts makes it sit too loosely to the historical realities for it to have been a work near contemporary with the events it describes.

nevertheless remains a prisoner. It is however that very imprisonment which enables his appearance at Rome so that what to the eyes of the non-Christians and of the Christian doubters seems disaster, is in fact a victory, for it enables the Lord's promise to be fulfilled and shows the power of the one who makes it (23.11). Nevertheless, it is a power revealed in weakness; and it is a victory which has to transform seeming defeat. For it is the eye of faith alone which can see Paul's witness under constraint as enshrining a legitimate proclamation of the lordship of Jesus. The constrained manner of the preaching befits a kingdom which in the present is that of a very hidden Lord. The way of the cross is the way of victory for both Lord and disciple, so that Paul's witness is of one piece with the work of the Lord to whom he witnesses. Jesus himself characterized his way as that of a 'baptism to be baptised with' and spoke of 'constraint' until its accomplishment (Lk. 12.50). When his choice of Paul is first announced to Ananias, the terms of the commission are clear and of the same order: 'He is a chosen instrument of mine to carry my name before the Gentiles and kings and the sons of Israel: for I will show him how much he must suffer for the sake of my name' (9.15-16). The witness can be made only by way of the suffering which becomes an integral part of it. Lord and disciple follow the same way and the way itself is the means of the glory which will follow. Of Paul, as well as of his converts, it is true that 'through many tribulations we must enter the kingdom of God' (14.22).

The way Luke tells his story raises a question mark against the widely accepted view that Acts expresses some political concern on the part of its author,[1] that he writes his account in the service of an apology directed either to some Roman citizens outside the Christian community in order to make them more favourably disposed to the Christian message, or to those already Christian to given them a message of comfort about the attitudes and activities of the Roman state as it might be expected to affect them.[2] Luke is then thought of as being

1. C.K. Barrett, *Luke the Historian in Recent Study* (London: Epworth Press, 1961).

2. Acts may well be a defence of Paul against those critics who attacked him for driving a wedge between Christianity and Judaism. Luke maintains that his renunciation of the Jews is forced upon him by his opponents: he could do nothing else but concentrate upon the Gentiles. Sociological circumstances rather than purely theological ones accounted for the actual balance in his work. A defence of Paul in his life-

concerned to help the church live effectively and with confidence by enabling it to come to terms with the state's real intentions and its basic legitimacy.[1]

Any sort of political apology seems, however and in the end, to be ruled out by the fact that Luke's overall picture is not one which is such as to inspire real confidence in Roman authority. It is true that no Roman official actually condemns Paul. At Corinth, Gallio recognizes that it is matters of Jewish law only which are stake, and refuses to accede therefore to Jewish demands that he sides against Paul (18.16-17). At Ephesus the Christian proclamation is judged not to be sacrilegious and so is said to pose no threat to the Roman state (19.41). Nevertheless Paul deems it wise to move on. Christians are in a perilous position. At Philippi 'customs which are not lawful' are deemed sufficient cause for Roman intervention. Roman citizenship comes to Paul's aid but he is, nonetheless, asked to leave (16.39). His teaching does pose a problem, if not a threat, and is unwelcome to Roman authority which, when confronted with it is always likely, when it is deemed expedient, to act in a constraining capacity for the sake of law and order. When the good order of the state is threatened it will bow before hostile accusations even if they are not always verifiable. At Thessalonica (17.8-10), where the apostles are accused of 'acting against the decrees of Caesar', the authorities are disturbed and although they do not act against them then, they take security which is thought to be so at risk that the brethren deem it sensible to send them away secretly and by night.

The Christian proclamation meets hatred, opposition and incomprehension from all sides. It represents at least a threat to the Pax Romana and it seems that Rome does not entirely understand the nature of the threat. She acknowledges that it is not a movement in direct opposition to herself. She can recognize Jewish misrepresentaion and perversity when she wants to. Nevertheless, she does act against Christianity when she is faced with a confrontation which she cannot avoid. Only at Corinth is there clear and objective discrimination which declares

time or very soon afterwards would have had to play down his actual rejections and would no doubt have pictured them in a gentler hue.

1. B. Easton, *Early Christianity: The Purpose of Acts and Other Papers* (London: SPCK 1954); P.W. Walasky, *'And So we Came to Rome': The Political Perspective of St Luke* (London: SPCK; SNTSMS, 49; Cambridge: Cambridge University Press, 1983).

for the rights of Paul and his companions. But Corinth is distinctive. Gallio is being used by God and his objectivity is so unusual that it is seen to be the direct and total response to that divine initiative declared beforehand to Paul, 'Do not be afraid, but speak and do not be silent, for I am with you, and no man shall attack you to harm you; for I have many people in this city' (18.10).

Luke's Rome is certainly not evil. She is an instrument in God's hands. But she is uncomprehending rather than cooperative; she is perplexed rather than clear-sighted. It does not seem that Luke's portrait is such as to deserve Walasky's vote of confidence in Rome when he says: 'Rome is not only just and powerful: Rome can abide the Christian message'. It is into the hands of this power that Paul is committed to enable his appearance at Rome. As Walasky maintains: 'The Christian community, especially the community of Rome, may rejoice that God has worked out his purpose and extended the Gospel to them by means of the imperial order'.[1] This is no doubt true, but of itself it begs the question of the nature of the imperial instrumentality. God is able to use the Roman power to achieve his purposes, but this does not mean that her part is either willingly positive or laudatory.

The same ambivalence on the part of Roman authority that was evident in its earlier dealings with the apostle is seen in Paul's journey to Rome. The tribune, Claudius Lysias, acts completely correctly and he is always seen in a wholly favourable light. He twice rescues Paul from Jewish enemies, is open to reason, fair in his judgments and, as far as we can judge, determined to be impartial. His verdict on Paul to the governor deserves to be accepted—Paul could be charged with nothing deserving death or imprisonment (23.29). His superiors, however, do not measure up to the same standards. Felix, though not directly declaring Paul to be innocent, is however persuaded by him of the correctness of his message (25.25-26). Nevertheless he is himself open to corruption and for a space of two years keeps Paul a prisoner, not merely to satisfy his own philosophical interests, but in the hope of material gain in the form of a bribe. When he is to be replaced, he leaves Paul in prison, not out of conviction, but in order that he might build up some goodwill with the Jews. Festus comes over little better. He starts off admirably with a court at Caesarea. Jews appear with charges which Luke declares to be unproven and unprovable. Yet Festus now determines on a trial at Jerusalem. Such

1. 'Rome', p. 62.

an option is refused by Paul, presumably on the grounds that the imperial power will ensure neither safe conduct for the prisoner nor a fair trial when he gets there. He sees Festus's offer as a sop to the Jews and can have little confidence in its outcome. He is therefore forced to appeal to Rome, and Festus's defence of his own actions before Agrippa and his declaration of Paul's innocence (his withdrawal in fact from responsibility for Paul's continuing captivity) do nothing to further the correctness of his earlier actions. Paul's appeal to Caesar can be seen only as the act of one who mistrusts the local rulers, has little more reason to trust the final outcome, but who can use the state in spite of itself to further his own journeyings and to bring them to that conclusion which the ascended Lord has promised to him (23.11). In view of the notices of Paul's impending death (20.25, 36-38; 21.4-6, 7-11, 14), there can be little doubt as to how Luke expects his readers to interpret the narrative he puts before them. God works mightily through the state even though he works apart from its intentions and often in spite of its nature. Walasky suggests that Luke has suppressed the (if true) death of Paul at the hand of Nero because he 'wanted to maintain his positive perspective on the imperial government'.[1] It would seem rather that Luke all the way through Paul's dealings with the state presents what is at best ambivalent and at worst fickle. Confidence in Roman power would not seem to express one of the reasons for his writing as he does.

It seems likely that Luke knew, and that he knew his readers knew, that Paul had not been released but that his imprisonment had ended with his judicial execution at the hands of Rome. Had it been otherwise, he could hardly have failed to recount a release for, had it been either an acquittal with the routing of the Jewish complaints or even a dismissal because the Jews had failed to appear to substantiate their charges, it would have witnessed to the power of God at work in Paul and so have contributed mightily to Luke's thesis. Any further missionary activity say in the west or even as a recapitulation in the east, would certainly have been an anti-climax, but preaching in Rome in freedom would not. Luke stops where he does because Paul's preaching as a prisoner in Rome witnesses to the truth he is proclaiming in his two volumes. The external facts, seen in the cold light of day, may not be enough to guarantee the Lordship of Christ, but seen through the eyes of faith, they can witness to just that and to its

1. 'Rome', p. 63.

fulfilment in its own way of the Old Testament promises. At the heart of that fulfilment is a pattern controlled by a cross, and Paul faithfully follows in the way of his Lord.

But why does not Luke then point to Paul's death? Does he in the last resort forsake the *theologia crucis* for one of glory? In the light of his whole account of Paul's career, it can be asserted confidently that he does not. Luke isolates and pinpoints neither the death of the Lord nor those of his followers. The death of Jesus is significant, not in itself, but for the sufferings and way of life of which it is the climax and for the exaltation to which it leads. It is the witness rather than the death of Stephen which enables his vision of the exalted Lord, merits his approval, and makes for the furtherance of the mission (7.54-60). It is Paul's witness in Rome to the Lordship of Jesus which marks the climax of his work. But Jesus' exaltation is achieved only by way of his death which enables the resurrection. Stephen's witness issues in his death which becomes the inevitable price of it. Paul's witness in Rome is made possible only by way of suffering which culminates in his death. But the deaths are never isolated, separated out, as the inescapable and vicariously effective means of the extension of salvation. They witness to a way followed by the Lord and by every disciple, to a way of constraint, of suffering, of a daily taking up of the cross and of following in the way of him who came into our midst as 'one who served' (Lk. 22.27).

Chapter 6

WHY THIS PAUL?

Acts ends with Paul triumphant in Rome though within the shadow of execution. God's promises to him have been fulfilled; his witness in the capital points to the Spirit's power. However, this very emphasis upon Paul forces us to ask the question: why does Paul have such an important part in Acts? Why is the spotlight on him and, in the end, virtually on him alone. Though there have always been advocates of this position, it remains wholly unlikely that Paul was actually the purpose of Acts.[1] The ultimate reason against this is the fact that Acts itself does not stand alone but as a part of Luke's two-volume work. Luke's literary preface, as well as the way that stories such as the martyrdom of Stephen complement and complete stories in the Gospel, in this case the crucifixion of Jesus, suggest that Luke had Acts in mind from the beginning even if Luke's Gospel was first published on its own.[2] The fact that Acts represents a new departure does not mean necessarily that Luke did not include it in his scheme to add to the number of 'narratives' that had been written about 'the things which have been accomplished among us' (Lk. 1.1). He extends his narrative of Jesus to include the universal proclamation among Jews and Gentiles, and it is just this universal proclamation which is incorporated among those things which have taken place as the fulfilment of scriptural expectations and so which thereby witness to the messiahship and Lordship of Jesus (Lk. 24.46-47; Acts 1.8). Acts becomes in

1. A.W. Gasque, *A History of the Criticism of the Acts of the Apostles* (Grand Rapids: Eerdmans, 1975), pp. 268-76.

2. Evans, *Luke*, p. 4, 'Luke's [Gospel] appears to have been the first half of what the author had conceived from the first as a two-volume work'. See, however, Nolland, *Luke 1–9.20*, pp. 33-34. He resists the idea that 'we have part one and part two of a single work' and accepts that 'the Gospel was issued first and was freestanding'. He nevertheless says that 'Luke did not write [the Gospel] without having Acts already in mind'.

this way the confirmation of the proclamation which the Gospel expresses and which is summed up in the angelic announcement to the shepherds, 'For to you is born this day in the city of David a Saviour who is Christ the Lord' (Lk. 2.11).

Paul therefore is not the purpose of Acts, let alone that of Luke–Acts, but is used in the service of Luke's purpose in writing Luke–Acts. While this has been widely recognized, it has also been maintained, not merely that he is illustrative of Luke's purpose, but that he is in fact climactic of it. For Haenchen, Luke's aim was to show the spread of the gospel from Jerusalem to Rome. This explains his concentration on Paul, the emphasis upon his final journey, and the ending of Acts in Paul's unhindered preaching in Rome. 'The path of the gospel from Jerusalem to Rome formed a complete story, a rounded whole in itself. It brought comfort and reassurance to the faithful, for it showed them how God's ways continued even after the departure of Jesus'.[1]

Yet the spread of the gospel from Jerusalem to Rome cannot be either the determining factor in Luke's story or the reason for his concentration on Paul. Haenchen can make his claim only by going on to assert that Luke downplays, to such an extent as virtually to ignore, the existence of an already believing group of disciples in Rome.

> That he practically eliminates the Roman community by his silence has another and deeper reason: he wants Paul to proclaim in Rome the Gospel up to that point unknown... Although Paul comes as a prisoner to Rome, he there marks a beginning with the last proclamation and so in the world's capital city crowns his work as the great missionary of Christianity.[2]

This, however, is plainly a misunderstanding of Luke's purpose. Luke, and certainly Haenchen's Luke, was no slave to his sources and, had he wished to present Paul as the missionary to Rome, the establisher of Christianity in that city, he could quite easily and clearly have omitted all references to the disciples who already existed there. But this he does not do. More than that though, he presents Paul's meeting with the Christians at Rome as the actual climax of his journey, the fulfilment of what had been promised. 'On seeing them, Paul

1. *Acts*, p. 98; cf. H.C. Kee, *Good News to the Ends of the Earth; The Theology of Acts* (London: SCM Press; Philadelphia: Trinity Press International, 1990).

2. *Acts*, p. 720.

thanked God and took courage' (28.15). Arrival at Rome is not the climax of the church's preaching but of Paul's own last journey. Paul's arrival at Rome is of concern, not primarily for the universal witness to the gospel, but for Paul's own particular career under the guidance and direction of the risen Lord through the Spirit. Paul's preaching at Rome climaxes, not with the spread of the gospel from Jerusalem throughout the world, but Paul's own witness as the instrument of the exalted Lord.

Conzelmann sees a more limited purpose in Luke's climactic use of Paul. For him, the emphasis is upon Paul's break with the Jews and on the church's movement out into the Gentile world. 'We can see quite clearly how Luke thinks of the Church, according to plan, taking over the privileges of the Jews as one epoch is succeeded by the next'.[1] I have, however, already argued against that view which sees Rome as the climactic point of the break between Jews and Christians. Rome does not represent a new stage in what Luke sees as God's developing plan, but is rather a continuation of the pattern that is to be found in Paul's activity in Acts as a whole. But is that pattern itself in the service of a demonstration that Christianity must move out from its Jewish matrix? O'Neill has argued forcibly that this is so. He writes, 'The Gospel was breaking out from its entanglement with organized Judaism, and breaking free to be the universal religion. Jerusalem is left behind and Rome is entered'.[2] But Luke's Paul does not break free from his Jewish background. As Luke makes him preach, he proclaims an essentially Jewish message which is shaped by his belief that the resurrection shows that Jesus is the messiah and which is at odds with Jewish history only in his acceptance that circumcision no longer defines the people of God. That is defined by the Spirit which is, however, the eschatological realization of Jewish hopes and is therefore brought within their terms. Paul himself is a good Jew. He stands on trial 'for hope in the promises made by God to our fathers, to which our twelve tribes hope to attain, as they earnestly worship night and day. And for this hope I am accused by Jews O king! Why is it thought incredible by any of you that God raises the dead?' (26.6-8). Paul nowhere departs from this position. Jewish hostility does not

1. *Theology*, p. 163.

2. J.C. O'Neill, *The Theology of Acts in its Historical Setting* (London: SPCK, 1961).

make him change his message or alter its emphasis. He remains tied to his Jewish background:

> But this I admit to you, that according to the Way, which they call a sect, I worship the God of our fathers, believing everything laid down by the law or written in the prophets, having a hope in God which these themselves accept, that there will be a resurrection of both the just and the unjust (24.14-15).

There is nothing in either Paul's actions or his words, to suggest that he would in any way dissent from the correctness of the stance described by James of those Jews who are zealous for the Law for themselves. Failure to demand circumcision of the Gentiles is the result, under God, not of Paul but of the insights of Peter and James. Paul is wholly at one with them for at no point does he go off on a line of his own or express a view which could not be served by any of Luke's Christian leaders.

Luke then clasps Paul to the wider Christian community and to the ancestral Jewish faith which has produced both it and them. But is he by this consciously defending Paul? There can be no doubt that Paul is at least the subject of a sub-plot in Luke–Acts and that, whatever Luke's overall purpose in using a narrative of him, that story is so shaped as to come in some way to the support of Paul. But is that support the determining stance of his picture of the apostle?

This in the end is unlikely. Luke's emphasis upon continuity into which he draws his picture of Paul is determined, not by any immediate, practical considerations occasioned by some purpose of defending his hero, but by his overall theological understanding of Jesus as Israel's messiah and of the Christian dispensation as the eschatological fulfilment of Israel's hopes. Paul is presented as a good Jew who believes in the resurrection of Jesus because that according to Luke is precisely what he is, since it is belief in the resurrection of Jesus which for Luke affirms a man's place in the Israelite people and marks him out as a good upholder of that for which the Law stands. Here is no artificially contrived scheme serving the defence of Paul, but a picture determined by theological conviction. So, Paul's links with Jerusalem, and through them with the Jesus of history (Acts 13.30-32), are determined by Luke's own theological understanding rather than by any external demands placed upon him by a need to refute false teaching or to counteract pre-Marcion Marcionites who would drive a wedge between past and present.[1] It is true that by Luke's time some such groups may have appealed to Paul for support. But Luke is not setting out to legitimate Paul or the tradition of his church against them. Had he intended to do so, not only would he have been more careful in his portrayal of Jesus so as to avoid scenes which could have been read in Gnostic terms, but he would undoubtedly have modified the way in which he speaks of Paul's moving out from the Jews. These movements away from the Jews are determined however by the need to explain the Jewish problem of Luke's own day, and his portrayal of the human Jesus is determined by his presentation of him in terms dictated by Old Testament categories and expectations.

Paul, then, is not climactic for Acts, let alone for Luke–Acts as a whole. He is rather supremely illustrative of the purpose of Luke–Acts. He is drawn into Luke's overall purpose which is to express his understanding of the significance of Jesus and of the events which have come about as a result of him. Luke's aim is to encourage Theophilus in holding on to the 'truth' of those things 'which have been accomplished among us' in the face of disappointments, tensions and doubts caused by the passing of time and by the failure of the Jews to respond. There may have been more immediate reasons which determined the actual point at which Luke took up his pen and set about writing his 'narrative'. These may have shaped the actual form which at least some of his account took. But such causes—and criticisms of Paul may have been one of them—were incorporated into the development of his overall theme rather than being the reason for that theme. Luke's primary purpose was nothing less than a presentation of the truths of the gospel as he understood it.[2]

1. J.L. Houlden, 'The Purpose of Luke', *JSNT* 21 (1984), pp. 53-65.

2. P.F. Esler, *Community and Gospel*, p. 1 protests against the idea of Luke as a speculative theologian and its assumption of him as 'a glorified armchair theorist, who ponders over purely religious questions before issuing forth from his scriptorium to enlighten his fellow-Christians as to the correct attitude which they and their community should adopt to their social and political environment'. Esler is of course quite right to insist that Luke was no disinterested theorist but that his theology was shaped by his own situation and that of those around him. His was certainly not a predominantly cerebral concern. But Luke stood in a tradition, a faith, and his work was not merely shaped by the response which the situation called forth. He came to the situation with beliefs, a faith and experience, and with a conviction that he had been grasped by God through Jesus. Past experiences contributed to his

Why then is there so much about Paul? For some reason Paul is Luke's hero. He knew about Paul, admired him, and was enthused by his work. He felt himself to be a follower of Paul and a legitimate exponent of his beliefs and practices. Our understanding of Luke's exposition of Paul's beliefs would not lead us to deny the legitimacy of his presentation.

Could Luke then have been a companion of Paul? Are the 'we passages' meant as claims by Luke to have been the companion of Paul for at least a period, or are they to be taken, as in the sea-voyage genre of ancient literature, as claims rather to vicarious participation in the events the narrative as a whole describes?[1] The most natural explanation of these passages is undoubtedly the former of these possibilities. As Hengel expresses it, 'From the beginning, this is the only way in which readers—and first of all Theophilus, to whom the two-volume work was dedicated and who must have known the author personally—could have understood the "we" passages.'[2] Though this is in fact vastly overconfident, there does not in itself seem to be reason to dissent from his further assertion that '"We" therefore appears in travel accounts because Luke simply wanted to indicate that he was there'.[3] Reasons for questioning this, the most obvious understanding of the 'we', are really twofold, namely the presentation of Paul's theological stance in Acts, and the more historically dubious statements in it about him. If our understanding of Luke's presuppositions in his theological presentation of Paul are correct, then there is nothing in them to suggest that he could not have been the apostle's companion. What though of his presentation of Paul's history?[4]

Again, the really difficult episode is Luke's assertion that Paul was

understanding of God's action in Jesus to give him a belief which had to be applied to his situation which no doubt gave emphasis and nuance to that belief. Esler is right to protest against the divorce of theology from its context but that context is formed from the totality of experience that he brings to bear upon his situation. Luke approached the community and the task of writing his two volumes with a theology that was formed by his own understanding. He was in fact a pastoral theologian, one whose beliefs were directed upon a situation rather than actually controlled by it. In the last resort we must say that Esler's picture of Conzelmann's Luke is in fact a caricature.

1. Aune, *Literary Environment*, pp. 122-24.
2. Hengel, *Acts and the History of Earliest Christianity*, p. 66.
3. Hengel, *Acts*, p. 66.
4. Hemer, *The Book of Acts*; Lüdemann, *Early Christianity*.

present when the Jerusalem church drafted the decree, that he accepted its demands, and that he advocated loyalty to them from at least some of his churches. We have seen why Luke could have believed that Paul 'must' have done these things without his doing an injustice to the apostle's basic insights. But if he was writing as one who was not far removed from the time of Paul, how could he have asserted these things as facts without fear of open contradiction of such a kind as to invalidate his whole case?

If in fact Luke were writing at a time when an open attack was being made upon Paul, if he were writing in the context of concerted and determined controversy, then it seems that he must have been writing at a temporal or geographical distance from the events he was describing. Only so could he have avoided direct refutation. On the other hand, if he were writing within the context, not of confrontation but of differing evaluations of the past, if Paul was being criticized rather than actually rejected, then Luke's account of Paul's presence at the time when the decree was being promulgated, is more easily understood. This is in fact made easier if the apostolic decree was seen as a compromise healing the dispute centred upon the incident at Antioch rather than being itself the cause of the dispute.[1]

Luke himself does not include the Antioch incident. Indeed his narrative leaves no room for it. This, however, does not mean that he was ignorant of it. It seems rather to have been the presupposition behind the whole of his account focusing upon the conversion of Cornelius and the promulgation of the decree. Luke's readers would have been aware of the incident but it was the background to, rather than the definer of, the differences they themselves were facing. Time had moved on. As C.K. Barrett has reminded us,[2] the deaths of the old protagonists, the fall of Jerusalem, the appearance of new problems as well as the coming to terms with them or at least with ways of living with them, caused the old problems to be seen in a new

1. Hengel, *Acts*, p. 117; J.D.G. Dunn, 'The Incident at Antioch'; *JSNT* 18 1983), pp. 3-57; L. Goppelt, *Apostolic and Post-Apostolic Times* (trans. R.A. Guelich; London: A. & C. Black, 1970). Others see the decree as being the cause of the Antioch incident: D.R. Catchpole, 'Paul, James and the Apostolic Decree', *NTS* 23 (1976), pp. 428-44; Krodel, *Acts*, pp. 95-97: A. Weiser, 'Das Apostelkonzel', *BZ* 28 (1981), pp. 145-47.

2. C.K. Barrett, 'Pauline Controversies in the Post-Pauline Period', *NTS* 20 (1974), pp. 229-45.

light. Luke writes out of a situation which is not controlled by a continuation of the old attitudes aroused at the time of the Antioch incident, but from one where reconciling developments have taken place which nevertheless allowed for differing outlooks and approaches. It is not any more a question of opposing stands and contrary approaches but of varied attitudes and different emphases. Tensions remain, but it is a question of different nuances rather than of outright contradictions, of the weighing and balancing of probabilities rather than of mutually exclusive certainties.

In these circumstances, Luke is able to assert that Paul supported the decree as it was now being interpreted by Luke and those in the church who agreed with him. That Paul was being presented as an advocate of the decree's terms would in fact present little difficulty. In 1 Corinthians, Paul does not mention the decree and he does in fact in pure theory take a line which is opposed to its requirements (1 Cor. 8.8; 10.25).[1] Yet in practice that freedom is not pursued; it is constrained both by the need to remember and acknowledge the scruples and the beliefs of other Christian brethren and also by the necessity of stopping freedom from turning into unrestrained and presumptuous licence. Paul does not follow out the logic of his own theological presuppositions nor, though accepting the actual basis from which his questioners (or even opponents) build up their arguments does he follow through their reasoning to support their conclusions. Paul in fact argues for constraints upon freedom and for a recognition of the validity of the traditions by which some members of the community have come to their Christian faith.[2] In this sense Paul could be presented as accepting the position advocated by the apostolic decree which itself could be seen as acknowledging a legitimate desire for the continuing purity of those who saw themselves still as linked to Israel after the flesh. Paul could be accepted as being not far removed from the outlook of Luke's contemporaries who interpreted the decree as a concession in this manner.

So Luke is actually able to picture Paul as being present at the time of the original promulgation of the decree. Paul himself is not described as having a part to play in the actual drawing up of the

1. C.K. Barrett, 'Things Sacrificed to Idols', in *Essays on Paul* (London: SPCK, 1982), pp. 40-59.

2. One need not accept J.C. Hurd's particular thesis (*The Origin of I Corinthians*) in order to appreciate the strong advocacy of this outlook in Paul.

decree, though it is promulgated as an acknowledgment of the validity of the Pauline mission which is seen as wholly Spirit inspired (15.12). The decree is a response to this, yet its outlook is determined solely by the divine initiative enabled by the actions of Peter in accepting Cornelius and his household. The Jerusalem church can do nothing other than acknowledge the hand of God so that the terms of the decree are seen as bringing once and for all a freedom from accepting the Law as in any way bounding the people of God. It is a total victory for what was in fact the Pauline position. Yet that freedom was itself to be constrained. For the sake of the Jewish matrix, for the sake of those who valued their links with the historic people of God, for the sake of those who were Jews, and for the sake of those whose Gentile background left them still open to temptation, the freedom was to be controlled. Freedom was not to become licence; liberty was not to turn into uncontrolled presumption.

Luke then looks back thirty years to see those earlier events in the light of the interpretation of a later time. Old controversies have mellowed. In a sense, the Antioch incident is the presupposition of his narrative, but it is the Antioch incident as it bears upon the thinking of his contemporaries. Table fellowship in itself is no longer an issue.[1] That is now accepted. Equally, all now accept that the Law does not in itself any more define the people of God. But there is still a place for the Law within the Christian community, and it is the nature of that place which remains a matter, not necessarily for total dispute, but certainly for differences of opinion. And how that place is defined will to a large extent determine the community's attitude to continuing Jewry. It will in fact determine whether the community is now prepared to see itself as a *tertium genus*, set alongside and apart from Jews and Gentiles. Luke for his part is quite certain that it should not.

Luke's story of this early period of the young church's life, though itself a theological construction, can nevertheless be seen as a comment upon the events in so far as they can be recovered from Paul's letter to the Galatians.[2] Dibelius argued for historical bases for Luke's stories of Peter and Cornelius, believing that older narratives with some factual content lay behind both Peter's visions and the Cornelius

1. *Contra* Esler, *Community*.

2. This is even more true when it is recognized that Paul's historical account in Galatians is itself tendentious. Hengel, *Acts*, pp. 115-16.

conversion.[1] Though a factual basis for both has been denied,[2] this seems an unnecessarily negative response. The vision is a private affair and it does fit in with Luke's overall understanding. His version of the Cornelius incident has been written up in the light of his belief that it unquestionably settles both matters. That does not mean however that the Cornelius incident itself has no basis in either church tradition or history. It cannot be accounted for solely by Luke's overriding Gentile concern or his interest in Roman officers. His Gospel account of the healing of the centurion's servant contains a description of the centurion which is likely to have been influenced by the Cornelius episode rather than the other way round (Lk. 7.2-5).[3]

We therefore see a basis in history for Luke's assertion that Peter had some sort of Gentile outreach. This however seems to go beyond Paul's description of the conclusions reached at the apostolic council (Gal. 2.7). It seems that something happened to encourage Peter to move on from its compromise. Peter, probably as a result of some involvement with Cornelius, had dealings with Gentiles and ate with them. For this, both Paul and Luke say that he was criticized (Gal. 2.12; Acts 11.3). In Galatians he draws back; in Acts he does not. We have already seen why Luke could have omitted the Antioch incident. Its story of open, unresolved hostility would not have been acceptable to his vision. It is unlikely however that Peter would have been unaffected by the quarrel or that he would have turned his back entirely upon his relations with Gentiles.[4] He has been criticized

1. M. Dibelius, *Studies in the Acts of the Apostles* (ed. H. Greeven, trans. M. Ling; London: SCM Press, 1956). Cf. Lüdemann, *Acts*, pp. 131-32, 'The historical nucleus of the Cornelius tradition which is markedly legendary, is that Peter had been involved in the conversion of a Gentile called Cornelius in Caesarea'.

2. Haenchen is critical of Dibelius's suggestion of traditions, *Acts*, pp. 360-62. In 'The Book of Acts as Source Material for the History of Early Christianity', *Studies in Luke–Acts*, pp. 258-78 (265-67), he appears to suggest that Luke built up his narrative on a tradition of a baptism of Gentiles by Peter.

3. Though see, Lüdemann, *Acts*, pp. 125-26.

4. It would seem likely that some contact with Cornelius happened before the incident at Antioch. We have suggested, however, that the decree was promulgated after that. If Acts 11.27-30 is the Council, then Luke's story of Peter's departure from Jerusalem, 12.17, could refer to Peter's move to Antioch and form the setting for the incident, though it would seem that the first journey of Paul and Barnabas occurred before that event, Lüdemann, *Acts*, p. 138. Catchpole ('Decree', p. 438) suggests that the journey could as easily have followed the conference as precede it.

severely by C.K. Barrett who suggests that the Antioch incident reveals his 'lack of theology'.[1] This seems unduly harsh. He lacked Paul's particular understanding of the newness of the Christian dispensation. But this, in itself, is only one interpretation of the significance of Jesus.[2] In practice, Paul himself was prepared to limit the outward marks of this newness, and it seems likely that Peter's position was based on an understanding of Jesus as continuous with the old dispensation and on his appreciation of the need for maintaining the unity of the eschatological people of God. If the first principle caused his withdrawal when messengers arrived from James, the second principle would mean that he could not acquiesce in that position. It seems likely that he returned to Jerusalem to argue his case. Acts 15 could well be Luke's theological reconstruction of that situation. It resulted in the decree which was a compromise.[3] Luke interprets it in terms which are not unPauline. Just how Peter himself interpreted it we do not know, or whether his interpretation differed from that of James. His possible presence in Corinth suggests that Jewish–Gentile unity continued to be his concern.[4] Luke's interpretative history of those times is not so far divorced from the likelihood that it left itself open to easy refutation by those who saw the past through different eyes.

If this assessment of Luke's account in Acts is at all correct, it suggests that though his story can be accepted only as interpreted history, it has nevertheless a closer relation to the facts which gave rise to it than is sometimes suggested. It is a response to the facts as these were 'remembered, told, and interpreted' by a later generation. Paul's letter

It is hardly possible to decide once the decree is separated from the conference.

1. C.K. Barrett, *Freedom and Obligation: A Study of the Epistle to the Galatians* (London: SPCK, 1985), p. 13. On the other hand, see J.D.G. Dunn, *The Parting of the Ways* (London: SCM Press; Philadelphia: Trinity Press International, 1991), pp. 132-33.

2. R.E. Brown and J.P. Meier, *Antioch and Rome: New Testament Cradles of Catholic Christianity* (London: Chapman, 1983).

3. Haenchen, *Acts*, p. 449. J.T. Sanders (*Jews*, pp. 117-19) on the other hand, says, 'The Apostolic Council, as it is presented in Acts, throws out the position of the Christian Pharisees'. Jervell (pp. 23, 32) sees the decree as part of a gradual hardening of the demands on the Gentiles by the Jerusalem church. It 'imposes demands on the Gentile Christians, demands that were not there from the beginning'. Cf. Krodel, *Acts*, p. 98.

4. C.K. Barrett, 'Cephas and Corinth', in *Essays on Paul*, pp. 28-39.

to the Galatians suggests how these were handed down, recounted, slanted and argued about within a very few years. When Luke wrote, time might have mellowed the arguments, but it would also have dimmed the actual recollection. Nevertheless, it remains unlikely, however creative Luke was, that he was simply free to ignore the events or the interpretations that others were putting upon them. He had to relate to these, even though, as in his Gospel, he set out to see through them to the pattern as he saw it behind them and as he viewed them, and so created around them his own particular narrative in the light of his vision of how it must have been. Nevertheless, his could not be just a free construction; there had to remain a dialogue with what had been. The interpretative nature of Luke's work must not be underestimated. However, if his stress on Paul is best accounted for by seeing him as a close admirer of the apostle, if the 'we passages' can be accepted as suggesting that he was an actual companion of him, if his interpretation of Paul can be acknowledged as springing from a legitimate stance and if his account of the apostolic council can be seen, not as correct factual history, but as a reconstruction by which a number of historical events have become the basis for a careful interpretation which writes up their significance in historical form, then it seems that Luke's narrative cannot be simply addressed as pure fiction in the service of the edification of later generations. The use of Acts as a source in the reconstruction of events of this period cannot simply be declared illegitimate on the supposition that because some narrative is the result of Luke's theological creativity, everything could have been and therefore is to be spurned as a source for what might have been. If we are right, Luke, though highly creative, did not lack all form of external control over his narrative.

Yet, the difficulties in the use of it are real and his creativity is of such a kind as to call in question the confidence with which Hengel, for instance, approaches Luke's work in Acts. He writes:

> The radical redaction-critical approach so popular today, which sees Luke above all as a freely inventive theologian, mistakes his real purpose, namely, that as a Christian 'historian' he sets out to report the events of the past that provided the foundation for the faith and its extension. He does not set out primarily to present his own 'theology'.[1]

1. *Acts*, pp. 67-68. See also Hemer, *The Book of Acts*.

Yet the way Luke presents his account of the events surrounding the apostolic council shows beyond doubt that Hengel's categorization of his aim as that of being 'to report the events' is an oversimplification. These events are told in the light of his theology which enables him to see a pattern in them, to see through them to a significance behind them, and then to recount the whole in the light of that significance. Hengel himself believes that the decree was promulgated without Paul and that he himself 'never acknowledged it or practised it'.[1] His own use of Acts has to rely heavily on possibilities, probabilities and assumptions, and these go far in negating the declared confidence with which he sets out upon his task of reconstruction.

Does this mean, then, that in the end Luke's account of Paul's activity is of such a kind that it cannot be used to throw light on the questions of the apostle's relations with Jerusalem and those who were Christians before him, and of his possible ministry to Jews? Confident answers to these questions would contribute substantially to our understanding of the apostle.

Francis Watson, appreciating the difficulties in using the Acts account, has asserted roundly, 'Acts therefore gives us virtually no reliable information about the origins of the mission to the Gentiles'.[2] Luke's account is seen to be the result of his view that everything was centred in Jerusalem and moved out from there; he brings Paul within this understanding. That Luke's concern is to centralize everything in Jerusalem and to have the mission going out tidily from there is undeniable. The manner in which he deals with the resurrection narratives and the way he has the mission to the Gentiles go out from Antioch, dependent upon Jerusalem, and brings Paul on the Gentile scene only after the Cornelius episode, points to his freedom with the facts and to his subordination of these to his vision of what in fact has been. Resurrection appearances were certainly in places other than Jerusalem, the Gentile mission may have begun independently, and Paul may have been concerned with Gentiles at a date earlier than Luke suggests. Here there is no certainty; only a Lukan scheme. That Antioch was actually the initiator of the Gentile mission remains hidden by that Lukan scheme.

Yet just how far does the Lukan schematization go? To see it carried further as Watson does to account for Luke's assertion that

1. *Acts*, p. 117.
2. Watson, *Paul*, p. 28.

there were Hellenists in Jerusalem is to go beyond reasonable interpretation of the narrative.[1] The presence of Hellenists in Jerusalem remains something of an embarrassment for Luke. He would like to see them purely as Jews from the dispersion who were wholly at one with the Hebrew Christians. But, in actual fact, he is unable to hide tensions between the two groups. The appointment of the seven in order to serve at tables is plainly a cover-up made in the light of Luke's idealization of the eschatological unity of the young community. His description of the witnesses against Stephen as 'false' (and his omission of such a presence at the trial of Jesus) is Luke's own assessment of the worth of their evidence. Their charge against Stephen of proclaiming a future attack by Jesus on law and temple is witness to the Hellenists' denial of the permanence of these institutions and as such is an attack upon the nature of both. Luke works hard on Stephen's speech to play down its criticism of the temple and of its failure to surrender to him who is the true fulfilment of Davidic covenant. But it seems to have some traditions behind it, and these were certainly not less critical than the final shape of the speech makes them. Finally, Luke does all that he can, though without real success, to hide the fact that the persecution was directed at Hellenists rather than against the whole Jerusalem church.

It seems then that there were in fact Christian Hellenists in Jerusalem at this time and that even if Räisänen is right and that they were not actually hostile to the Law, they were nevertheless in his words 'radical enough within the spectrum of Judaism to arouse the anger of Paul, and not of him alone'.[2] Luke's account of Stephen's speech suggests that they were pointing to the temporary nature, the ultimate lack of finality, of both law and temple. It is true that the speech itself, while containing an underlying criticism of the temple, has no such critical attitude to the Law. It presents Christians as being more positive in that respect than the Jews themselves. Christians are the true defenders of the Law (7.53). This may of course, be a concealed counter-attack which actually witnesses to some substance in the charge. In any case, it represents Luke's own point of view that Christians were upholders of the intention of the Law and that Jewish Christians remained loyal to it by reason of their incorporation into God's covenantal history. At his conversion, Paul learned from the

1. *Paul*, pp. 26-28.

2. Räisänen, *Paul and the Law*, pp. 251-56.

Hellenists' stance which he took over and which he developed by way of controversy to establish his own peculiar root and branch radicalism.[1] 1 Thess. 2.15 suggests that he associated himself with them in at least some stage of his career.[2]

Paul's efforts in Galatians are directed at asserting his own independence of the Jerusalem apostles who are being enrolled against him rather than at affirming his complete independence of others. Luke, of course, has him go up to Jerusalem immediately and works hard to make him one with the whole Jerusalem church. This is plainly an interpretation in the interests of his own theology, both of his concern for the unity of the Jerusalem church and for Paul's unity with her. Paul's was obviously a less public ministry than Luke allows. Yet the fearfulness of the Jerusalem church over Paul (9.26) may have been caused, not by his pre-conversion stance and worries over the genuineness of his new way of life, but by his adoption of that attitude to Law and temple which had been advocated by the Hellenists. Luke here is idealizing in the service of his own ideas.

Paul goes up again to Jerusalem after 14 years. Why had such a long period elapsed, and why was the journey undertaken then? As C.K. Barrett says, it cannot have been a question of his getting cold feet.[3] The length of time that had passed is probably Watson's strongest point in favour of his assertion that Paul's Gentile ministry took off only after his failure with the Jews. But neither Luke nor Paul himself suggests this as a possibility, and Luke's presentation of Paul's earlier dealings with the Hellenists tells against it. Gal. 2.2 suggests that Paul, as a delegate of the Antiochene church was actually wanting validation in the light of what was most likely a developing concern with the Gentiles and with a new stage therefore in the make-up of the church at Antioch. On the other hand, both Gal. 2.4 and Acts 15.1, 5 may suggest the emergence of an ultra-conservative element in Jerusalem as being the immediate cause of the conference.[4] As the later concern with the collection suggests, identification with the Jerusalem church was necessary if the acknowledgment of the source of the new act of God was not to be disallowed completely and

1. M. Hengel, *Between Jesus and Paul* (trans. J. Bowden; London: SCM Press, 1983).

2. Räisänen, *Paul and the Law*, pp. 251-56.

3. Barrett, *Freedom and Obligation*, pp. 10-11.

4. See above, p. 141 n. 3.

if the unified nature of God's eschatological act was not to be denied. Both sides, at least in the mainstream, recognized the presence of the eschatological in the other and declared the legitimacy of each other's approach. But it was only a first step in reconciliation and its superficiality left too many loose edges. At any rate, neither Paul nor Peter could be content with its half-way house. Neither could acquiesce in the existence of two independent missions which remained unrelated and ununified with merely a nod from a distance towards the principle of unity. Luke has treated the council in two parts. In ch. 11 he has recounted the visit and Antioch's concern. The concern is repeated in ch. 15 but now the outcome of the council is carried forward to include the results of the Antioch incident without which the work of the council, at any rate as far as Luke is concerned, was incomplete. Paul is represented as both accepting and commending the decree. Such a presentation is obviously wrong historically and bears all the marks of Luke's attempt to draw Paul into the consensus of the early church's outlook as that was viewed by Luke himself.

The tentativeness of such a reconstruction, the possibility that events may have been very different, and the way in which all suggestions have to diverge from Luke's actual presentation in Acts witnesses to the thoroughness of his theological presentation and to the freedom, though not unrestrained licence, with which he dealt with the hard facts at his disposal. This recognition makes an equally tentative approach necessary in considering his presentation of Paul's missionary stance. This is put forward as expressing an overriding concern on the part of the apostle with a mission to the Jews, a limited though definite response by Jews and related Gentiles, the hostility of the vast majority of the Jewish people, the consequent determined turning to the Gentiles, and the acceptance of the proclamation by large numbers of them. J.T. Sanders has recently pointed to the over-stylization of such an evaluation of Luke's overall stance and has advocated rather a lack of uniformity in the accounts of Paul's attempts to evangelize.[1] It is true that such a pattern does not appear at every point on Paul's missionary tours. There are occasions where Paul does not make contact with Jewish audiences (13.6; 14.6-8; 14.20-21). He is not always opposed by the Jews (13.4-5, 6-12; 14.20-21; 16.11-40; 17.16-34), his success with diaspora Jews is varied, and he is not always met with large-scale Gentile conversions (16.35-50; 17.33-34). While this is

1. *Jews*, pp. 75-78.

true, these incidents are all set within the overall development of the pattern as it is outlined above. The three rejections of the Jews (13.46; 18.6; 28.28) set out its rationale, the visit to the synagogue at Thessalonica is explicitly stated as being in accordance with Paul's customary practice (17.1-2), and this is pinpointed by the non sequitur that at Athens when Paul beheld the city full of idols he countered this, not merely by speaking in the market place, but also and in the first instance in the synagogue with the Jews (17.16-17). Before Agrippa he declares his ministry as being 'to those at Damascus, then at Jerusalem and throughout all the country of Judaea, and also to the Gentiles, that they should repent and turn to God and perform deeds worthy of their repentance' (26.20). His active concern with the Jews is, as far as Luke is concerned, unambiguously clear.

But equally clear is the climaxing of his missionary activity upon the Gentiles. This has in fact been questioned recently by Philip Esler who believes that Luke pictures as recipients of Paul's concern, not Gentiles as such, but Jews and associates of them. Only at Philippi, Lystra, Athens and Ephesus does he describe Paul's dealings with people without Jewish connections. Only at Ephesus is the 'one favourable report in Acts of missionary preaching to an audience which may have included pagan idolaters'.[1]

However, Luke's story as a whole does not support this understanding of Paul's missionary stance in Acts. It is true of course that Cornelius is closely associated with the Jewish people (10.2). He is in fact a God-fearer and it is in the light of this that the responses to his conversion have to be understood. 'Then to the Gentiles also God has granted repentance unto life' (11.18). Yet the three accounts of Paul's turning to the Gentiles make it clear that it does not mean a concern limited to Gentiles who had previously had some attachment to the Jewish faith. At Antioch, Paul in the synagogue addresses 'Men of Israel and you who fear God' (13.16). Here the God-fearers are firmly included among those who should be responsive to the Christian proclamation. The barrier of circumcision has been broken down so there is nothing to distinguish them from the Jews. They are the first recipients of and responders to the fulfilment of the Old Testament promises. Many of them in fact do respond (13.43) and enter into their inheritance for which their links with the Jewish people have prepared them. But 'the Jews', those who will not believe,

1. *Community*, p. 41.

turn against the apostles. Paul and Barnabas break with them and move away from the synagogue and out into the Gentile world as the Old Testament predicted. Verses 48-49 record a moving out into the Gentile world, to those who had no connection with Judaism. In contrast, 'the Jews', 'devout women of honourable estate', and civic authorities turn against them. Here we have a whole series of groupings; believing Jews and God-fearers, believing Gentiles, unbelieving Jews and God-fearers, and unbelieving authorities. It is clear that the Gentiles are much wider than those who had previous links with Judaism. As at Ephesus, it includes Jews and Greeks, among whom were many who were themselves unattached to the Jewish faith (19.18-20).

At Corinth, after Jews and Greeks have been persuaded in the synagogue, Jewish hostility causes Paul to move away. He goes in to the house of a worshipper of God whose 'house was next door to the synagogue'. A ruler of the synagogue makes the same break, 'and many of the Corinthians hearing Paul were baptized'. The God-fearer's house, though a link with the synagogue, witnesses to a break with it and becomes a stepping stone for a ministry which reaches out into the Gentile city and in contrast to the Greeks in the synagogue who had believed (18.4-11). Jewish rejection means a turning of attention away from the Jews and a movement out into the Gentile world (28.28). The ministry to the God-fearers is always linked to the ministry to the Jews. Some Jews and God-fearers in the synagogues believe, yet not all God-fearers respond, and the vast majority of the Jews do not. Overall, the God-fearers receive a good press. They are the means of the movement out into the Gentile world and are emphasized as being ethnically one with it. They are not, however, the climax of the mission which is always characterized as being more extensive and to the Gentile world as a whole.

Esler's conclusions therefore cannot be accepted. Nevertheless, he has brought to the fore an important, and not often noticed, point about Luke's narrative. Paul's ministry to the Gentiles is not actually described in detail, and it is not successful at all points. Luke in fact does not often tell of it for its own sake and, when he does, he does not usually describe its actual successes. At Athens, he meets with rejection, at Lystra with misunderstanding, at Ephesus with hostility and divisions within the church. The ministry to the Gentiles is always present, it is the backcloth against which the narrative is worked out, but its fact is assumed, accepted, generalized rather than described for its actual circumstances. There is a wonder that the Gentiles have been included but its actuality, how it happened, is simply accepted rather than finely pinpointed and detailed. The main concern is actually upon the failure with the Jews and how, in spite of all efforts to bring them in, they effectively cut themselves off from the people of God as it was being reconstituted and so refused their birthright.

Luke knows that Paul went primarily to the Gentiles and that he had virtually no response from the Jews. His accounts of Paul's defence of his missionary stance make that clear. In the temple, when he is under attack, he has the apostle justify his overriding Gentile concern by a direct command from God made inevitable by Jewish refusal of his witness (22.17-21). Before Agrippa, though a ministry to the Jews is declared, the climax is found in a mission to the Gentiles (26.18-19). Luke labours to give Paul a ministry to the Jews and tries to give him some success. But in actual fact he knows that he is swimming against the tide of historical reality. Luke's is a theological pattern arising out of his own perception. He knows the overwhelming Gentile concern of Paul and he labours, not to underplay it, but to deny any idea that it was an exclusive concern and that it came out of a denial of the place of the Jews in God's plans. Paul's lack of results with the Jews arose out of no theological intention on his part but out of necessity. It was determined, not by belief, but by pragmatism. In actual fact, says Luke, Paul's beliefs meant an overriding concern with the Jews. That he did not have an abiding actual concern with them came about solely because he was prevented from doing so by their perversity.[1]

Here there is a clear-cut reinterpretation of Paul's outlook in the cause of Luke's understanding of the continuity of God's saving act. That he has rewritten the programme of Paul's missionary strategy is clear. Certainly there was no determined and continuing ministry on the part of Paul to the Jews. The Lukan pattern is obviously imposed. But did Paul have some contact, some mission to Jews, at some stage at least in his career? Can we use Luke's picture to influence our evaluation of Paul's stance? Can it be used to illuminate,

1. In part, Luke would understand Watson's sociological approach because he sees Paul's concentration upon the Gentiles as brought about by sociological considerations. It is this which makes him hard upon the Jews for it is the only way that he can make the actual situation square with his theological beliefs.

to give perspective to, even to correct what can be learned from the evidence of Paul's letters?

E.P. Sanders has presented a powerful case for seeing Paul's mission as exclusively a Gentile one and for taking seriously Knox's belief that Paul must be interpreted on his own terms and from his own writings.[1] It is undoubtedly true that the absolute priority of Paul's own writings must be acknowledged and, if Acts appears to clash with what they explicitly say, that it must then be laid aside as a historical source. On that there can be no doubt, for we have seen the abundance of the evidence for acknowledging the all-pervasive character of Luke's interpretative concern. Yet, Paul's own evidence does not seem to be quite as unambiguous as Sanders suggests. Certainly, 1 Cor. 9.9 must not be used as an all-embracing means of making room for Acts. Sanders rightly gives it an oratorical evaluation which he finds expressed in hyperbole. It certainly talks neither of an actual mission to the Jews nor of a continuing determined attitude on the part of Paul. It points rather to exceptional actions and suggests uncharacteristic occasional events when Paul had to bow to necessity. It represents something of an apology for his actions rather than a statement of conviction. But he did not cut himself off entirely from the Jewish people. His collection does not suggest isolation, his action at Antioch does not mean that he was indifferent to other Christian groupings, and that this outlook was not brought to an end by his development in the light of that incident is made likely by his references to the weak and strong not only in 1 Corinthians but also in Romans where his Gentiles are to 'receive the weak' (Rom. 14.1).[2] His account of the purpose of his call as being 'that I might preach him among the Gentiles' (Gal. 1.16) is made in the context of a controversial justification of his later stance and does not thereby necessitate a belief that Paul from the beginning saw his mission as an exclusive one to the Gentiles alone. Pragmatic considerations and theological convictions are here interwoven. So, even if Acts has shifted the focus of Paul's missionary endeavours, it

1. J. Knox, *Chapters in a Life of Paul* (London: A. & C. Black, 1954).

2. The 'weak' and the 'strong' may refer as much to groupings of Gentile Christians as to Jewish–Gentile Christian attitudes, Kümmel, *Introduction to the New Testament*, pp. 310-11; R.J. Karris, 'The Occasion of Romans' in P. Donfried (ed.), *The Romans Debate* (rev. edn; Peabody, MA: Hendrikson, 1991), pp. 65-84.

does not necessarily mean that it is wrong to suggest that he had some missionary concern for the Jews. For all its interpretative stance, if the modern interpreter thinks that Paul's own witness allows that possibility, Acts may be used as witness to Paul's missionary interest in the Jews, at least when opportunity presented itself. It may in fact just shift the interpretation of Paul in that direction if on other accounts his own witness seems to be indecisive. But, in the last resort, it can do no more than point to occasional sorties in that direction, and it certainly does not allow for any strong Jewish–Christian presence in Pauline churches. The proclamation of movement out to the Gentiles may mean that Paul actually in the end parted company with many Jewish and God-fearer Christians who had originally joined with him.[1]

On the other hand, Luke's account in Acts does suggest that Paul's mission was directed to the Gentiles from the beginning.[2] The Hellenists whom he was persecuting had probably moved in that direction as a result of their initial stance in Jerusalem. Luke's inclusion of Ananias's vision in his initial account of Paul's conversion may, as we have seen, have been determined by his concern to see Paul at one with the early church, but it may well be that Paul actually did receive the commission to the Gentile mission by way of a part of the church. Galatians would not necessarily deny this. However, on this again we must be guided by our response to Paul's own account. Acts can contribute little to our understanding of how Paul came to his belief. All it can do is to support the view that that belief was there from the beginning. Luke's account does not support the view that there was a time when Paul did not preach to the Gentiles. Paul's account of his conversion as he tells it in the temple does not suggest that he preached to the Gentiles only because of the failure of a mission to the Jews. It is the completion of the commission given in the first place by Ananias. Reference to its occurring in the temple is dictated by its place in Luke's story, Paul's own defence in the temple, rather than by any determined witness as to the nature of Paul's career. It does not suggest that Paul had not already preached to Gentiles; it witnesses rather to his lack of success with the Jews.

1. This would make for a very different situation from that described by Esler. See above, pp. 147-49.

2. For this see K. Stendahl, *Paul among Jews and Gentiles* (Philadelphia: Fortress Press, 1976); Sanders, *Paul and the Law and the Jewish People*.

Ananias had already declared Paul's task to be 'a witness for him to all men of what you have seen and heard' (22.15). It points, not to an extension of the sphere of the missionary concern, but to its limitation which arises however, not out of theological determination, but from practical constraints.

Yet even Luke's pointing to Paul's Gentile concerns from the beginning may arise out of his own response to Paul's understanding rather than to his concern for the facts. In the end, in practice he makes Paul's Gentile work arise out of the work of the church in Antioch, a movement among Gentiles which takes place only after the Cornelius episode (11.20, 25). Here again, Paul is brought into Luke's scheme. He is commissioned through the church (9.17), preaches as the church preaches to Jews (albeit of the dispersion) in Jerusalem (9.29), joins the church at Antioch and from there extends his preaching to the Gentiles. Yet, as we have seen, in Paul's witness to himself, Luke presents the apostle as engaged upon Gentile missionary work from the beginning (22.15; 26.17). This discrepancy can be accounted for in one of two ways. Either Luke knew that Paul was not engaged in Gentile work from the beginning but, in the light of his knowledge of Paul's own assessment, represented him in the apostle's own terms, or he knew that Paul was at work among the Gentiles from the beginning but chose to work out its implications in the light of his own pattern brought about by his understanding of the nature of the Christian proclamation and of the oneness of Paul with the whole church. The second of these possibilities seems to fit more satisfactorily into the way Luke has worked in Acts as a whole.

Acts then contains a consistent but determined re-interpretation of both the outlook of Paul and also of the actual pattern of the apostle's career. It results in a presentation which is very different from that of the real Paul. His theological stance is refashioned and this has resulted in a reshaping of his actions. The principle behind both the refashioning and the reshaping is, we have suggested, a re-evaluation of the discontinuity, of the newness, which Paul saw in God's action in Christ in the direction of continuity with, and as the fulfilment of his earlier acts in the Jewish people above all, but also in the Gentile world.

Why should Luke have engaged in such a determined and drastic reshaping of Paul's outlook? Why should he differ so strongly from his mentor and hero? Fitzmyer, in his monumental commentary on

Luke, seeks to account for such a difference by pointing to the relatively short acquaintance of Luke with Paul. If the 'we' narratives are to be taken seriously at their face value then Irenaeus's characterization of Luke as Paul's 'inseparable' companion has to be drastically revised. Luke then 'was not with Paul during the major part of his missionary activity or during the period when Paul's most important letters were being written'. Luke was not with Paul during the major crises in his evangelization of the eastern Mediterranean world. So, 'Luke would not have been with Paul when he was formulating the essence of his theology or wrestling with the meaning of the Gospel'.[1]

This understanding, however, accepts the evaluation of Luke's interpretation of Paul as superficial, and this is one which we have denied. Luke's picture of Paul is much deeper and more coherent, and shows a greater understanding of its subject than such an evaluation allows. His is not the real Paul, but his picture builds upon the real Paul, having learned from the real Paul, to present an interpretation of him which makes him relevant to later circumstances without trivializing his message. That message, it is true, is different, but it is one which comes out of a real understanding of the apostle and his thinking to reshape it to become a vehicle of Luke's own theological concern. He does for Paul what he does for Mark, that is, engage in a drastic reshaping of the material and a re-presentation of the message. What emerges is different, yet its differences come out of a determined design. What though accounts for this act of reinterpretation? Explanation has to centre around the different circumstances of both Luke himself and his community from those of the apostle and his churches. In part the differences are accounted for by the obvious comment that time had moved on. Pauline controversies had either been settled or the manner in which they presented themselves had been altered. As far as we can tell from Luke's two volumes, he was writing no longer for times of fierce conflicts. Some form of early Gnostic outlook, what Houlden calls 'pre-Marcion Marcionism',[2] may have been gaining ground and there may have been some over-zealous apocalyptic enthusiasts on the horizon. But the general tone of Luke's writing seems to suggest that he was encountering, not an abundance of enthusiasm, but a lack of it, not a surfeit of confidence but its

1. Fitzmyer, *Luke*, pp. 47-51.
2. Houlden, 'The Purpose of Luke', p. 62.

diminution.[1] The community he faced was encountering something of a failure of nerve brought about by the non-appearance of the parousia and the non-acceptance by the Jews of the Christian claims on behalf of Jesus. Pauline controversies had taken on gentler contours. Old battles no longer needed to be fought. These new problems may not be characterized as requiring 'shadow-boxing'[2] but they did not demand, or even suggest as an appropriate response, the confrontational attitude seen in, and so necessary to, the ministry of Paul. Circumcision of Gentiles was no longer an issue, for the Law was no longer actively advocated as necessary for defining the people of God. There were still of course varying attitudes to the place of the Law within the new community. The apostolic decree was no doubt seen by some as advocating loyalty to the Law however redefined that Law was seen to be.[3] Again, there were varying attitudes to the Jews and to the question of the relation of the new community, not only to the past of Israel, but to Israel after the flesh in the present. The community to which Luke responds was a mixed community and this no doubt allowed for varieties of responses on all these issues. Gentile Christians and Jewish Christians, and within them groups of varying persuasions, had still to learn to live together in real accord. How the community was to regard the differing pasts of its various groups of members was still open to different interpretations.

Philip Esler has recently attempted to determine the make-up of Luke's community in a more comprehensive manner than this somewhat general survey allows.[4] Reacting against that dominant approach to Lukan studies which means that they have been conducted in dialogue with the writings of Hans Conzelmann, he characterizes these as being in danger of approaching Luke as a 'glorified armchair theorist who picks over purely religious questions'. He is, of course, right to remind us that social and political needs played a vital role in the making of Luke's theology and to emphasize that he was shaping his

1. The apocalyptic discourse of Luke 21 and the account of the Ascension in Acts suggest this clearly.

2. Barrett talks in these terms when he discusses Luke's reporting of Paul's farewell address to the Ephesian elders. See above, pp. 119-20.

3. I argue below that Matthew took it in this sense, pp. 385-86.

4. Esler, *Community*. This is not to deny the very real insights that Esler has revealed but to suggest that there are not the grounds for making that direct link that he suggests.

traditions in response to the overall pressures experienced by his community. Luke certainly did not write either in a vacuum or merely as an act of self-expression. He, like all the evangelists, was a pastoral theologian and his own particular theological emphases were undoubtedly arrived at in response to a varied number of pressures upon the community or communities with which he was in relationship.

Nevertheless, at least two factors make it likely that Luke's story and the community with which he was concerned cannot be easily correlated in such a way to allow the nature of the community to be read off directly from Luke's writings. These two factors do actually mark Luke off from the other evangelists and mean that he has to be treated as somewhat of an individualist among them.

The preface of Luke's Gospel suggests that his is not only a self-conscious writing of a particular individual, but that he himself is consciously aware that his approach is worked out in deliberate reaction to others.[1] He is in some way at variance with his predecessors in the field and his claim to accurate research in order to give an authoritative presentation of the true significance of the teaching which Theophilus has received suggests that he himself is not entirely at one with that teaching. Luke is making claims to an authoritative position. The 'we' passages in Acts are included to back up the legitimacy of those claims.

The preface suggests that Luke wrote as an individual and that he was not a cypher of either the life or the beliefs of a community.[2] His was a self-conscious piece of writing in which the beliefs and personality of the individual writer determinedly shaped whatever traditions he was handling to mould them into a carefully nurtured work. The literary preface introduces a literary production which, as has been frequently pointed out, comes closer to the literary forms of its day and contains more artistic and literary devices than the other Synoptic Gospels.[3] Luke's are the hands of an artist. But his work is also consciously the work of a theologian. His drastic reshaping of Mark suggests that his was a deliberate theological work. The distinctiveness of his presentation of the career of Jesus, the conscious shaping of the story of that part of the life of the church which he

1. See below, pp. 170-73.

2. Aune, *Literary Environment*, pp. 120-21.

3. H.C. Kee, *Christian Origins in Sociological Perspective* (London: SCM Press, 1980).

includes in Acts, his reshaping of Paul's position to make him one with the overall approach of the author of the two volumes, the re-casting of the whole to express it as the fulfilment of Old Testament promises, and the use of the first two chapters of the Gospel to serve as a comprehensive prologue to the two volumes, suggest that Luke was himself a theologian of no little significance and result in a work which bears the hall mark of an individual rather than of a community.[1] It was no doubt not unaffected by the political and sociological pressures upon the community with which it was connected. But these were not its primary controlling factor which is to be found rather in the theological stance of its author whose presence is allowed to come across so obviously in the preface with which he introduces his work. His is less a direct response to social and political factors of a particular community and less a direct legitimation of its practices against pressures from without and within than Esler allows.

A second point against a too easy correlation between Luke–Acts and the community with which it is connected is provided by the fact that Luke is consciously putting his story of Jesus and of the particular part of the early church that he includes in the form of history which records development and progression and which distinguishes not only between past and present but also between various periods in the past. He writes of the past not merely, and certainly not only, to explain how the church has come to be that which now it is, but to justify a faith in Jesus as the church's Lord. History is used in the service of theology. The Old Testament, the career of Jesus, the life of the early church and the story of Paul are all used in the service of a faith that at the ascension Jesus was installed at the right hand of God. If Luke's preface gives us his justification for writing, the last chapter of his Gospel tells us of his overall purpose. That purpose is christological. Again, this means that the present of Luke's church cannot be read off directly from the past as Luke unfolds it.

This of course is not to deny that past and present are related, or to suggest that the story of the past is not to illuminate the present of Luke's church. Past and present must meet if there is to be any significance in the story of the past. But past and present are not the same; the situation of the present cannot be reconstructed directly from Luke's picture of the past. Luke does indeed, as Esler maintains,

1. K. Stendhal, *The School of Saint Matthew and its Use of the Old Testament* (Philadelphia: Fortress Press, 1954), p. 32.

'shape the history of first-generation Christianity to speak to the concerns of his own contemporaries',[1] but the actual shape of those concerns is seen through the eyes of Luke the individual rather than through the eyes of the community itself, and they have to be read out of, rather than read off from, a work which differentiates quite clearly between past and present and sees both through concerns which are primarily theological and less immediately political and sociological.[2]

If this conclusion makes it difficult to be as certain about the ethnic make-up and political stance of Luke's community as Esler suggests, it means that his assessment of the internal interests of that community is also less obvious than he allows. He writes:

> One issue in Luke–Acts towers above all others as significant for the emergence and subsequent sectarian identity of the type of community for whom Luke wrote: namely, table fellowship between Jews and Gentiles. An almost universal failure to appreciate the centrality of this phenomenon, both to Luke's history of Christian beginnings and to the life of his own community, is one of the most outstanding deficiencies in Lukan scholarship.[3]

Yet there is little in Luke–Acts to suggest that table fellowship was one of Luke's major concerns. His accounts of Paul's eating with non-Jews (16.15, 34; 18.7) are given no special emphasis, and the possible eucharistic action of Paul on board ship (27.35-38) bears little relation to Jewish–Gentile controversies. But, above all, Luke does not point to table fellowship as an issue independent of that of circumcision and having to be resolved separately. Peter's visions at the time of the Cornelius episode may have had significance for the question of Jewish–Gentile common meals, but Luke incorporates such a concern into the whole business of God's acceptance of people of all races. Though he is aware of the complaints against Peter's eating with uncircumcised men (11.3), the issue is not separated out from the wider one and, at the council, any alleged irregularities over table fellowship are contained within the issue of circumcision and not identified apart from that (15.1, 5). The two together are decided once and for all by a council in the light of the Cornelius incident and,

1. *Community*, p. 2.

2. Conzelmann writes (*Theology*, p. 1650) 'Thus Luke is the first writer who deliberately describes the past of the community as "the past"'.

3. *Community*, p. 71.

when the decree is sent out, it is seen, not as relating specifically to the question of table fellowship, but to the wider question, of which table fellowship is a part, namely, that of the obligations of Gentiles to the Law of Moses. Table fellowship is not separated out as a specific issue in Luke's story. He himself could not have envisaged an eschatological community which did not eat together (2.46). As an issue it is not isolated but is included within, even to the extent of being submerged by, the wider concern of the boundaries of the people of God.

Table fellowship is not put under the spotlight in Acts. It does not appear to have been a live issue to Luke and it seems therefore wholly unlikely that it was a major interest to Luke's contemporaries. Luke's writings do not suggest that it 'had been a matter of intense controversy in the early church'. It had of course been just that, but Luke gives no indication that this was so, for as an issue he maintains that it was easily settled. It is therefore wholly unlikely that it 'was still of concern for Luke's contemporaries' or that its legitimation 'forms a vital arch in the symbolic universe which Luke creates for his community'.[1] Past controversies had rather been mellowed and allowed to take on more gentle contours as these were made to reflect a situation where they were no longer lively issues. They had been solved by an undeniable direct act of God which had been accepted by the united response of the early church.

So the different situation of Luke and his contemporaries from that of Paul and his churches enabled him to emphasize the continuity between the old and the new in a way that was certainly not open to Paul as he engaged in what were then life and death struggles for the truth of Christianity. Luke no longer had to fight over old issues; he could afford to bathe them in a gentler light.

But the differences between Paul and Luke rise not only out of the different situations of the churches with which they were connected but also out of the differing backgrounds and temperaments of the two men. Paul, on his own estimate, was a Hebrew of Hebrews, one whose glory and boast was in the inner circle of the Mosaic covenant (Phil. 3.4-6). All its blessings and privileges were open to him and he was conscious of their appropriation. His coming to Christianity was seen as a reversal of his past; it resulted in an upending of his previous attitudes, in a total reassessment of what before had been his pride and privilege. Luke's background was entirely different. Recent attempts

1. *Community*, p. 109.

to picture him as a Jew have not been successful. His Old Testament concerns are those of someone who has entered into its thought-world rather than of one born into its community. His concern with the Jewish people is cerebral rather than emotional; his own sympathies are rather with the Gentiles and it is with them where his strongest ties are to be found. His wonder is that Gentiles have been brought in to have a share in their own right in that which previously had been exclusively the prerogative of the people of Israel. Hence his concern in his whole work with the outcast and with those on the fringe of the covenantal community. His joy is that of an outsider who has been brought in. It arises out of the wonder of fulfilment, out of the freedom that unhoped for blessings have made available.

Given both Luke's sense of inclusion and his appreciation of Old Testament concerns, his earlier life is best characterized as that of a God-fearer,[1] who stood near the fringe of the Jewish people yet who consciously was not one of them. Circumcision remained the bar to full inclusion; the Law was that which bounded the covenantal community and he, as a continuing Gentile, was ultimately excluded by it from a real place in the people. The coming of Christ had changed

1. I believe that the outlook of Luke–Acts is best accounted for by seeing Luke himself as a God-fearer rather than, as Esler suggests, that his community was one with a large number of God-fearers. Luke's Gospel is influenced by a community composed largely of Gentiles rather than of God-fearers. By the time Luke wrote, the distinctiveness of God-fearers as a group had largely broken down and Luke himself already witnesses to the beginnings of this development. I have assumed the more usual view here to allow that Luke is referring to a distinctive group of 'God-fearers'. M. Wilcox ('The "God-fearers" in Acts—a Reconsideration', *JSNT* 13 (1981), pp. 102-22, has challenged this approach to suggest that since Luke uses the term of Jews (Lk. 1.50), of proselytes (Acts 13.43), and of a less defined group (Acts 10.2; 13.16), its meaning is more fluid and less circumscribed. However, it seems that Luke's use of it of Cornelius does imply a technical term, at least for Luke himself. Cornelius is distinguished both from Jews and proselytes. The whole narrative depends upon his being neither of these. In 13.16, 26 it is likely that people like Cornelius are being addressed alongside Israelites. In 13.45 Luke talks of 'devout proselytes'. Since the Cornelius episode has made circumcision redundant, the distinction between God-fearers and proselytes has been abolished. Luke can now speak of two groups rather than of three; proselytes can now be included among the God-fearers and God-fearers among the proselytes. It was probably for this reason that Luke moved on from φοβούμενοι to use σεβομένοι. It is more inclusive, less technical, and enables the characteristics of φοβούμενοι to be applied to the whole group.

everything. He was now able to enter into the sphere of that which before he had admired, whose beliefs he had upheld, and in whose story he had delighted. All that was best in Gentile religiosity could be envisaged as finding its fulfilment in Israel's God (14.15-17; 17.23). In Christ therefore he found the fulfilment of both his natural past and his adopted religion. His inclusion did not demand a letting go or a turning aside from his earlier hopes, beliefs or partial acceptance. These were now caught up in Christ, to find fulness and realization, in the extended, unbounded, covenantal people of God.

The influence of their different backgrounds is increased by the different temperaments and religious experiences of the two men. Recent Pauline scholarship has reacted against those earlier interpretations of the apostle's religious career which it saw, in Stendahl's terms, as over-influenced by the 'introspective conscience of the West' to be over-categorized in Reformation-style terms.[1] Nevertheless, such a right reaction is, if it is carried too far, in danger of interpreting Paul almost exclusively in cerebral terms which forget that Paul's letters are religious, practical, pastoral documents, and that he himself approaches his beliefs in the light of one who has become a new man in Christ. Whatever its exact nature, Paul underwent a deeply-felt experience which, not only committed him to a universal mission but also recreated him to give him a freedom and a re-birth which before had not been his (Gal. 2.15; Phil. 3.7; 1 Cor. 15.10). In Christ, he found a new life, 'knowing this that our old man was crucified with him, that the body of sin might be destroyed, so that we should no longer be in bondage to sin' (Rom. 6.5-6). The experience can be divorced from the temperament only by making it either wholly cerebral or by seeing it as a completely external event. Neither would be consistent with Paul's own assessment of the relationship as one which can be expressed only as 'I...yet not I but the grace of God which was with me' (1 Cor. 15.10). Theissen, whose sociological studies have done so much to illuminate Paul's thought, has more recently pursued a psychological approach which itself becomes a part of the wider sociological concerns and which adds to an appreciation of that symbolic universe which both expresses and forms Paul's thought.[2] Paul himself is included within the experiences of universal man as these

1. *Jews and Gentiles*, pp. 78-96.

2. G. Theissen, *Psychological Aspects of Pauline Theology* (trans. J.P. Galvin; London: SCM Press, 1987).

are described in Romans 7. It is significant that Luke emphasizes no corporate Christ, no recreative incorporation into him, and no atoning cross. The risen Christ incorporates the individual into the community which is, however, defined by possession of the Spirit rather than by a relationship with him.

Luke found not recreation but fulfilment in Christ. This met his deepest need, and it was this, alongside the quieter situation of his community, which enabled him to engage in a full-scale reinterpretation of the apostle's thought which allowed Paul to speak to a new generation with insight and effectiveness. This was not the real Paul. It was a message which was at least open to superficiality in a way that the real Paul's was not nor never could be. Yet, at the same time, it presented Paul to a later age when it was just that reinterpreted Paul who alone could be relevant. The problems of those days could not be addressed by the unadulterated voice of the earlier confrontations and, by presenting Paul to a later age, Luke showed how Paul could still address those who were more open to the various ways and diverse manners in which God has spoken outside of his address through Christ. Luke helped to make possible a dialogue with Paul and to show how his message could be seen as a part of that response to Christ which itself has to test the spirits and to allow the ascended Lord to address ever-new situations and men and women of differing styles, temperaments, experiences and hopes.

Part II

LUKE AND MATTHEW

Chapter 7

COMPARING LUKE AND MATTHEW

My first section was a reconsideration of Luke's picture of Paul in an attempt to see what he was actually saying about his hero and to consider how that related to the 'real' Paul insofar as he can be discovered from his letters. By trying to understand how that particular portrait was arrived at, I hoped to determine what it suggested about Luke's interpretation of the Christian gospel and how that related to Paul's own. We concluded that Luke's distinctive picture emerged because it was controlled by particular presuppositions. These owed much to Paul, understood him (insofar as it was possible for anyone really to understand his genius), but reinterpreted Paul's theological position in the light of Luke's own perception of Christianity as the fulfilment and logical outcome of Judaism which he regarded as the presupposition for it and the expectations of which he believed controlled the way in which God had acted in Jesus. Such an understanding helps us to take more seriously Luke's picture of the apostle to the Gentiles and thereby to give greater value to his witness to Jesus and to his story of the early church. His becomes a considered response to God's work in Jesus and one which demands to be accepted as a valuable contribution to the New Testament understanding of this.

My aim in this section is to use some areas of comparison between Luke and Matthew in an attempt to come to a fuller understanding of Luke's particular point of view. That they have so much in common suggests the special value of such an exercise. There is of course most obviously the large range of material that is common to both. The fact that source criticism can still suggest that both were independently using Mark and Q as the basis for their works shows just how important that common material is.[1] Even if their use of Mark and Q be

1. R.H. Stein, *The Synoptic Problem: An Introduction* (Leicester: Inter-Varsity Press, 1987).

denied, they still share in a common tradition which is expressed in a large amount of close verbal agreements and common order. Yet the fact that there are large differences within these common presentations suggests just how much adaptation there is, most likely in both works.[1]

In the second place, Luke and Matthew share a common perspective. Their stories of Jesus' ministry follow a common outline. Each has not only a 'Markan framework', however much again this is reshaped by them, but also includes infancy narratives which criss-cross at significant points only to go on their individual ways at others. While it is important at this stage to look at them free from commitment to any particular version of the 'solution' of the Synoptic problem, the fact that both have been seen as independent revisions of Mark, so that their works can be accepted as genuine second editions of his, suggests again that they share something of a common stance.

All this suggests that they each share something of a common setting in the life of the early church, or rather, and to put it more accurately, that their Gospels reflect something like similar stages in the development of the lives and outlooks of the congregations for which they wrote. Both Gospels are written for mixed communities where what was a strong Jewish outlook is moving out into a situation where the church is becoming predominantly Gentile in its concerns. For both, the future is with the Gentile world.[2] At the same time, the failure of the Jewish mission impinges hard upon the thinking of each writer. The Jews by and large have rejected the message about Jesus, and the proclaimers of that message have met with opposition, abuse and sometimes death. Jerusalem has fallen and its fall has resulted in a growing hostility on the part of continuing Jews to the young Christian community and in the placing of heightening barriers around legitimate Jewry.[3] Both works are written from the point of view of those who are conscious of the break with Judaism, of an exclusion from it, and meet its adherents from a position of outsiders in receipt of antagonism. Both Gospels are attempts at self-definition

1. E.P. Sanders and M. Davies, *Studying the Synoptic Gospels* (London: SCM Press; Philadelphia: Trinity Press International, 1989).

2. For a survey see W.D. Davies and D.C. Allison, *A Critical and Exegetical Commentary on the Gospel according to Saint Matthew*. I. *Commentary on Matthew* (7 vols. Edinburgh: T. & T. Clark, 1988).

3. Mt. 10.16-18; 22.7; Lk. 21.12, 20-24.

of the young community in the light of this hostility.

Both Gospels therefore are grappling with the same problems brought about by this situation. How do they respond? How does the response of one compare with and illuminate the response of the other? How do they see the old in relation to the new? How much of the old is carried over into the new? What is the attitude of each to the Old Testament in general and to the Law in particular? How do they react to the Jewish failure to believe? Are the Jews now to be excluded from the people of God or is there still a hope that they will come in? Both Gospels provide ample evidence that Munck's oft-quoted dictum that Israel's lack of response was 'the greatest problem faced by primitive Christianity' was at least no exaggeration as far as the communities reached by the works of Matthew and Luke are concerned.[1] Their thought is never far from it.

But if each is concerned with this, it is also true that both Matthew and Luke are caught up in the problem of relating eschatology and history. Though Conzelmann's assertion that the failure of the parousia to happen caused something of a crisis for the early church has not been without its critics,[2] there is little doubt that both Matthew and Luke have to come to terms with the fact that history has gone on, that earlier hopes were not realised in the way they had expected, and that what moved in the direction of a failure of nerve was evident in some quarters, while in others there was what could only be described as over-confident reaction amounting almost to unreality. Both Matthew and Luke therefore have to respond to the situation brought about by the passing of time and by the continuing hiddenness of the reign of God. They have to justify the time that was past in such a way as to embrace the time that is left and to relate both to a continuing hope of the parousia. The church that had now come into being had to be related to the parousia, and both had to be brought into the activity of the establishment of the kingdom of God. Eschatology and the kingdom of God had to be explained and retained in the light of the passing of time, and the ways Matthew and Luke do this are illuminated as the approach of the one is brought into relation with the approach of the other.

1. M. Hooker, 'In His Own Image?' in M. Hooker (ed.), *What about the New Testament? Essays in Honour of Christopher Evans* (London: SCM Press, 1975), pp. 28-44 (40-41).

2. Ellis, *Eschatology*, pp. 17ff.

Our concern here is primarily with Luke, and Matthew and his answers to all these questions are considered only from the standpoint of the light they throw on our attempts to understand the third Evangelist. If these three main reasons suggest the value of the exercise, there would seem also to be two additional bonus points to be derived from it. The first is mentioned at this stage with some hesitation lest it should be deemed to threaten such objectivity that can be mustered by one whose declared aim is to encourage an enhanced appreciation of the Lukan writings! I shall be approaching Luke by way of comparing him with Matthew (and to a lesser extent with Mark) without making any direct use of any one particular source-critical theory. That approach to redaction criticism which sometimes goes by the name of composition criticism and passes gently into literary criticism will be my overall aim[1] and I shall not base my understanding of Luke upon any particular source-critical point of view. Yet no approach can be presuppositionless. My view of Luke—in the light of his handling of Paul in Acts—is that he is a free handler of materials that come his way and that he is often a creator of incidents and expresses his understanding of their significance in the light of what 'must' have been. He is not a slave to his sources and his narrative is used in the service of his theology which provides the ultimate control of the way he writes. Following on from this, our comparison of Luke and Matthew will, it is hoped, throw light on what Luke's attitude to Matthew would have been had he known it and so will be of use to our third section when we shall consider this possibility.

Looking at how Luke is related to Matthew in his ideas may give us a second (though even more tentative) bonus point in the shape of some further illumination of the possible setting of each Gospel in the life of the early church. Relation of ideas may lead to relatedness in actuality and may suggest some possibilities of a further understanding of the life of at least one of the early church communities. In the conclusion to their studies of how the histories of the churches at Rome

1. C.C. Black, *The Disciples according to Mark* (JSNTSup, 27; Sheffield: JSOT Press, 1989), p. 243, 'The approach I envisage depends little, if at all, on the actual discrimination and analysis of a Gospel's tradition and redaction... Though I shudder at its syntactic clumsiness, this interpretative approach might be referred to as a *schriftstellerische Tendenzkritik*, an authorial-theological criticism of the Gospels (or other biblical literature)'. Cf. J. Barton, *Reading the Old Testament: Method in Biblical Study* (London: Darton, Longman & Todd, 1984), pp. 57-58.

and Antioch might well be illuminated by the New Testament writings which could be linked to those churches, Brown and Meier write that 'the Christianity of the works we have discussed was interrelated, and an adequate interpretation of these works requires an effort to discover the interrelationship'.[1] While they stress that such links are bound to be hypothetical, they nevertheless lay down a strong challenge to others to build in dialogue with their work. It is possible that a discussion of the relationship between Luke and Matthew may help to do this.

Nevertheless, there are certain problems to be taken into account in any comparison of the thought of Matthew and Luke. Though they have so much in common, it would be unwise to assume that they are necessarily of the same kind, seeking to do the same things and to accomplish them in the same way. At this point in time there was no such thing as a single, recognized Gospel genre, nor are they necessarily related in the same way to the churches with which they are linked. They do not necessarily have the same functions to fulfill.

Matthew's is undoubtedly a church book; there is much to be said for the suggestion that not only was it addressed to a church but that it actually arose out of a church situation so as to reflect and even encapsulate that situation. The situation of its contemporary local church can be read off from it. Its tensions in the areas of attitudes to Jews and Gentiles, to the Pharisees, to the Law, and to Israel are often pointed to as evidence for the beliefs of various groupings within the church,[2] not only as they are, but as they came into being. Though these tensions may be exaggerated and though it is right to seek for some consistency in the Gospel as a whole[3]—a consistency which is capable of taking up and embracing these differences to allow for a unified outlook in the work as it stands—they nevertheless do mean that, because of them, due value has to be given to the point made for instance by Stanton when he says that 'we may simply have to accept that the evangelist was less creative as a theologian and less consistent than some of his modern students have supposed'.[4]

1. Brown and Meier, *Antioch and Rome*, pp. 213-14.

2. S.H. Brooks, *Matthew's Community: The Evidence of his Special Sayings Material* (JSNTSup, 16; Sheffield: JSOT Press, 1987).

3. J.P. Meier, *The Vision of Matthew: Christ, Church and Morality in the First Gospel* (New York: Paulist Press, 1979).

4. G.N. Stanton (ed.), *The Interpretation of Matthew* (London: SPCK;

Luke on the other hand by his preface reveals the presence of an author who is working out a consistent point of view.[1] It is that of an individual and is arrived at consciously in response to the point of view of others. He is not a cypher for a church's beliefs but shows himself to be both an author in his own right and distinctive in his individual outlook. It is true that such a consistency is often denied him when it is suggested for instance that he included different and ultimately contradictory Christologies or that he had no overriding view in his attitude to the Law, or yet again that his ideas on eschatology developed between the writing of his Gospel and Acts.[2] Luke's picture of Paul in Acts, however, argues against both his slavishness to sources and his ineptitude. Luke developed a consistent point of view and expressed this in a work which showed literary and theological skills. On the theological side, his picture of Paul reveals this clearly, while as far as his literary ability is concerned, it is significant that Talbert's attempts to claim the Gospels as Hellenistic literary biographies have worked most successfully in the case of Luke. As H.C. Kee expresses it, 'Although Talbert wants to claim all the Gospels for this genre, his evidence and his remarks in passing point to Luke–Acts as the New Testament writing most closely akin to the model'.[3]

Luke lays out his literary and theological concerns as well as his attitude to the writing of history in his preface (1.1-4). It is a literary piece, distinctive and cultivated.[4] If it is more than a following of a literary convention for convention's sake—and Luke's work would suggest that it is—then Luke is making considerable claims both for himself and his writing. His use of κάμοι brings himself in relation to his predecessors in the field and, at the least, claims his work as worthy to be set beside theirs. His is at least to supplement their

Philadelphia: Fortress Press, 1983), p. 16.

1. G. Schneider, 'Zur Bedeutung von καθεζῆς im lukanischen Doppelwerk', *ZNW* 68 (1977), pp. 128-31; G. Klein, 'Lukas 1–4 als theologisches Programm', in E. Dinkler (ed.), *Zeit und Geschichte: für R. Bultmann* (Tübingen: Mohr [Paul Siebeck], 1964); R.J. Dillon, 'Previewing Luke's Project from his Prologue', *CBQ* 43 (1981), pp. 205-227. T. Callan, 'The Preface of Luke–Acts and Historiography', *NTS*, pp. 576-81.

2. Fitzmyer, *Luke*, p. 200; Wilson, *Gentiles*, ch. 3; *Law*, pp. 43-51.

3. H.C. Kee, *Christian Origins in a Sociological Perspective* (London: SCM Press, 1980), p. 146.

4. Aune, *Literary Environment*, p. 121, 'Historical prefaces allowed an author to display his rhetorical skill, and this carefully drafted sentence does that for Luke'.

works. He is neither an 'eyewitness' nor one of the original 'ministers of the word' but he bases his claim for writing an authoritative account and one to be reckoned with on the completeness, accuracy and thoroughness of his research. Such strengths enable him to produce an account which is καθεζῆς. Since again his handling of Paul shows that the order that is stressed is not likely to be an historical one, Luke is rather claiming authority for his presentation of Jesus and his understanding of what has come about through him. His picture in both the Gospel and Acts is a step by step unfolding of a thesis; it is an orderly development of his message, a careful presentation and justification of his witness. And the witness itself is no casual presentation. It is rather a statement of what has been 'accomplished among us'. These events are presented as the acts of God himself which conform to his earlier actions and fulfil what earlier he had promised.They are unfolded as God's plan and as such are determined by his promises. It is small wonder that immediately after the preface Luke launches into what is best understood as his prologue[1] in episodes which are described in Old Testament terms as the outcome of Israel's history and the fulfilment of her expectations. So Luke points forward to what is to follow as being in the nature of theological reflection.[2] He thereby expresses confidence in the rightness of his presentation. As Fitzmyer expresses it, 'He clearly sets out his own proper contribution. He has done his "homework" in investigating the story of Jesus and its sequel with a claim that rivals the boast of any historian.'[3]

But is Luke doing more than this? He is associating himself with his predecessors and claiming that his work is worthy to be set alongside theirs. But is he associating himself with them only to distance his work from theirs by asserting its completeness and superiority over theirs? It cannot be ruled out that this claim to accuracy implies that it conflicts at some points with what Theophilus had previously heard. Those interpreters who have seen Theophilus as some Roman official or the like and who have seen Luke as making some apologetic attempt in the Gospel and Acts to sooth, educate or persuade him would inevitably have read the preface in this way.[4] But if an audience

1. *Christ the Lord*, pp. 80-87.
2. Klein, 'Lukas 1–4', p. 193.
3. Fitzmyer, *Luke*, p. 289.
4. Evans, *Luke*, p. 136.

of non-Christians or fringe-Christians is ruled out by the presentation of the Gospel as whole,[1] there is still the possibility that Luke is writing to counteract or exclude certain outlooks within the Christian community. While docetically minded Christians or 'pre-Marcion Marcionites' are unlikely to be the object of Luke's attentions in Luke–Acts, some form of defence of certain ideas cannot be ruled out for the work as a whole. We have already seen this as in some way contributing to Luke's picture of Paul.

Yet it is unlikely that Luke was writing to ward off a sustained attack upon what he understood as the true presentation of Jesus and his work. The vocabulary of the preface is too ambivalent for that and there is little evidence of this in the work as a whole. All the words that Luke uses in the preface can be given a neutral meaning, yet, when this is done, there remains the feeling that the preface as a whole is less neutral than its neutered parts.[2] It mounts to a climax in τὴν ἀσφάλειαν, and it seems to do so as more than a literary device. Theophilus may be wavering in his faith, he may be open to Jewish persuasion or to doubts brought about by misplaced hopes, he may be sharing in Christianity's failure of nerve at this point in time. Nevertheless, Luke–Acts does not suggest that warding off attacks either from those who would deny Christianity or from those who would totally pervert it was anything like its main aim. Direct, overriding apologetic is not suggested by the preface as its main concern.

Yet this does not rule out differences of emphasis, differences within the Christian response which make for tensions, for different ways of relating Christianity to the past and for different outlooks in the common search for self-definition. Luke was not hostile to his

1. Luke's overriding consideration seems to be a theological one, such as to make his a primarily pastoral concern.

2. J. Nolland (*Luke 1–9.20*, p. 6) maintains that the suggestion that Luke was in some way countering the positions of those who had earlier written Gospels must be excluded because of his use of ἐπειδήπερ and the fact that 'even a notion here of "attempts to be improved upon" would require an "although"'. If Luke thought that he was unable to improve upon earlier attempts, one wonders why he was concerned to write, and certainly why he thought it worthwhile to write, what must at least have been taken as a second edition of Mark. The ἐπειδήπερ simply acknowledges his being of the same genre as his predecessors: it does not mean that he felt at one with them, their stances and their teaching. ἐπειδήπερ is less consciously critical than καίερ would have been. He nevertheless makes their works the reason for his writing and, by his alterations to them, suggests that his is actually a more authentic work.

predecessors. He lines up with them. Yet, in doing so, he nevertheless appears to be critical of them and to mark out his contribution from theirs. In some way he appears to stand over and against them while standing alongside and with them.

The very strength of his claims for the basis of his narrative suggests that it is written, not only in relation with those of others but also in tension with theirs. The forcefulness of his assertions suggests that these are likely to meet denial or at least stern scrutiny, for it seems that his account is to differ from those of others in certain important respects. His claim that his work is καθεξῆς means that it will have to justify itself since it will differ at important points from those other accounts to which Theophilus is accustomed. Luke knows that his διηγήσις is the presentation of a case and that that case will not go unchallenged within the Christian community. It will have to commend itself by its authenticity.

Luke characterizes the work of his predecessors in the field by the use of the verb ἐπιχειρέω. From the time of Origen, this has often been seen as having some pejorative significance. Though Moulton and Milligan emphasize that any idea of failure expressed by means of it is to be found in the context rather than in the word itself,[1] it is used so frequently in contexts where failure is implied that it is seen at least to have a bias in that direction. Luke himself uses it twice in Acts. At Acts 9.29 the Hellenists ἐπεχείροῦν to kill Paul but are thwarted when Christians remove him out of their clutches. At Acts 19.13 some itinerant Jewish exorcists ἐπεχείρησαν to have control over evil spirits by the use of the name of Jesus. They meet with significant lack of success. Both these instances point to unfulfilled expectations and it would seem that Luke is likely to be using the verb in his preface in a formal, emphatic way to make something of the same point. There is something incomplete or inadequate about his predecessors' accounts which he now sets out either to complete or to correct. κἀμοὶ becomes more than just an identifying of himself with them; it expresses a certain claim over and against them.

But it is in the last verse of the preface where it can most firmly be suggested that Luke is setting out to modify, if not correct, that which has been communicated to Theophilus.[2] While ἀσφάλεια is not used

1. J.H. Moulton and C. Milligan, *The Vocabulary of the Greek New Testament* (London: Hodder & Stoughton, 1930).

2. *The Beginnings of Christianity*, II, pp. 489-510.

elsewhere in Luke–Acts to convey the idea of truth or certainty, Luke does use the related ἀσφαλής. When Paul is arrested in the temple, the various contradictory reports of his accusers stopped the truth from being ascertained. Their statements are not satisfactory, either because they are incomplete or because they are misinformed or misinforming (Acts 21.34). At Acts 22.30 the tribune takes steps to find out the real reason behind the accusations, and this again suggests a certain distrust of what he has already heard. Later, Agrippa is asked to hear Paul because Festus has no reliable case to put before the emperor. What he has been given already is either inadequate or biased (Acts 25.26).

If therefore Luke's use of ἀσφάλεια in the preface would seem to convey some pointer to the partial nature of the previous information given to Theophilus, this aspect is further strengthened by his use of κατηχέω to describe that information. He uses it three times in Acts, once to talk of Apollos's knowledge of Christianity which, on any understanding of the verse as a whole, he plainly deems to be deficient since Priscilla and Aquila have to 'expound to him the way of God more accurately' (Acts 18.25, 26), and twice to describe the incorrect nature of the reports that have been brought to Jerusalem about Paul (Acts 21.21, 24).

All this suggests, therefore, that Luke is doing more in his preface than simply lining up with his predecessors. He does indeed associate himself with them and his is not a totally other presentation. It is, however, a distinctive one which is calculated to move beyond theirs either by way of supplementary explanation, which is nevertheless bound to call in question the completeness and satisfactoriness of the earlier offerings in Luke's situation, or by way of a distinctive outlook which in some important areas at least offers something of another, opposite point of view. In making the claims he does, Luke sets out to capture the centre of the stage and puts forward his own work as the standard by which all others must be judged.

Chapter 8

THE PHARISEES

I come first to consider Luke's attitude to the Jewish people and to determine how it is nuanced and how far its distinctiveness is clarified when it is set alongside similar presentations in Matthew and, more sparingly, in Mark. I begin by considering his picture of Jesus and the Pharisees.

Luke's outlook here is not easy to unravel. Wilson sees a difference in attitudes between one that is friendly in Acts and one that is ambivalent in the Gospel.[1] Such an estimate however arises out of an oversimplification of the Acts portrayal. It is true that there Paul is said to have been a Pharisee and to have regarded Christianity as the logical outcome of such a position. The Pharisees restrain attacks upon Christianity and they themselves make a more favourable evaluation of the Christian proclamation (Acts 23.9-10). Christians and Pharisees have a common basis. Nevertheless, the Pharisees' interpretation of Paul's explanation of the significance of the resurrection of Jesus is plainly perverse through its inadequacy. They need to make a definite move forward if they are to grasp the real meaning of Jesus and so to respond to him. The difficulty they have in making that response is seen in Acts 15 where Christian Pharisees are unable to grasp the significance of the outpouring of the Spirit upon the Gentiles (Acts 15.5). Their outlook would have destroyed the whole basis of the Christian proclamation.

So Luke sees the need for them to take a radical leap forward. They can, and in fact do, remain 'zealous for the law', and that is a perfectly legitimate response for they themselves to make provided that they see that it no longer defines the people of God and therefore cannot in any of its parts be imposed upon others and that they realize and respond to the newness and the radicality of the demand that Jesus places upon them. This in fact inevitably leads to a tension. So,

1. Wilson, *Law*, pp. 111-12.

throughout, Luke has what can rightly be termed an ambivalent attitude to them. Yet in this he is much less negative to them than is Matthew or, indeed, than is Mark.[1]

1. D.A. Neale, *None but the Sinners: Religious Categories in the Gospel of Luke* (JSNTSup, 58; Sheffield: JSOT Press, 1991), has taken a contrary position on Luke's portrait of the Pharisees. Earlier J.A. Ziesler had written ('Luke and the Pharisees', *NTS* 25, p. 153) 'Without doubt, Matthew is more anti-Pharisaic than Luke' and my conclusions would be in accord with his. Neale however maintains, 'It is not the case that Luke is less harsh than Matthew in his portrait of the Pharisees' (p. 105) and suggests 'Far from being soft on the Pharisees, Luke's treatment is more organized and negative than any of the other Synoptic evangelists' (p. 106). He believes that Luke caricatures to give them a literary role which pits them over and against 'the sinners'. Both groups are given a sociological and theological part in Luke's story. Yet is Neale really doing justice to Luke? He notes that he omits Mt. 23.2-3, yet this surely is not because of hostility but because he does not share Matthew's continuing concern with the Law and the tradition. Though Luke does not have the Pharisees come to John's baptism and Jesus holds this against them, their failure is one of eschatological discernment rather than ethical concern. To speak of them as 'the enemies of God's purpose' (106) is to mistake Luke's point. Simon is not 'the prototypical blind religionist' (147) and the parable Jesus used to illustrate his attitude is not condemnatory of him. Neale does not seem to do justice to his own understanding of the significance of Luke 15 of which he says, 'In fact, for the purposes of the parables, the Pharisees are the righteous. One would not guess on the basis of these parables that the Pharisees are represented elsewhere in the gospel of Luke as the enemies of God' (p. 163). He would have done well to have given more heed to his own comment, 'It shows us that the categories we have observed cannot be pressed in all cases' (p. 164). He oversimplifies Luke's attitude as this is to be discerned in the parable of the Pharisee and the tax collector. Comparing this with 5.30 and 7.29 he says, 'These other Pharisees opposed Jesus in a dark and malevolent way. Here, the Pharisee is still a negative figure, but in a more boorish, almost buffoonish sort of way' (168). Such a view leaves no room for any message to come via the parable but would make its conclusion obvious, even trivial, if not otiose. It leaves a picture of a Pharisee which is at variance with earlier portraits. B.E. Beck (*Christian Character in the Gospel of Luke* [London: Epworth Press, 1989], pp. 127-44) also believes that Luke presents the Pharisees in a far from sympathetic light. He writes, 'We therefore have to conclude that the Pharisees are not presented favourably in any passage in Luke–Acts'. 'Favourably' is of course an ambiguous term. If it means that as they stand they are acceptable and to be approved of, then Beck is right, but if it means that Luke does not regard them as potentially open to Christianity, Beck is wrong. Luke's Pharisees do not follow Jesus. As a group they have inherent weaknesses which work against any response. Jesus' meals are dismissed by Beck as being merely a part of Jesus' wide outreach. But for Luke the meals mean more than this for they are part of the anticipation of the eschatological

This can be seen in the Lukan version of the series of conflict stories which is to be found in Mk 2.1–3.6. In Mark there is considerable hostility expressed between Jesus and the scribes and Pharisees. While Matthew's version is such as to deepen that to make it more explicit, Luke consistently tones it down in such a way as to enable some dialogue between them.

The section begins with the story of the healing of the paralysed man (Mk 2.1-12; Mt. 9.1-8; Lk. 5.17-26). Matthew, like Mark introduces the scribes only at this point of conflict; they do not appear in the narrative until then; their presence centres wholly upon their complaint. Whereas in Mark the form of their complaint can be seen as making a reasoned if misguided value judgment, Matthew sharply and without explanation makes them condemn Jesus completely, 'This man blasphemes' (Mt. 9.3). Jesus' judgment of their reply is equally stark, 'Why do you think evil in your hearts?' He has no qualms about a total condemnation of their outlook. As far as Matthew's version is concerned, their hostility is wholly to be explained by their perversity. And so, at the conclusion of the episode, whereas Mark allows for the scribes to be included within what can only be seen as some form of positive response to the event (Mk 2.11), Matthew, by restricting any positive response to 'the crowds' (Mt. 9.7), excludes them from any hope.

Luke, on the other hand, has a picture which has moved in the opposite direction from that taken by Matthew.[1] Pharisees and teachers of the law are introduced at the beginning of the episode so that their presence is not noticed purely to pinpoint their hostility. The episode is in fact of the nature of a revelation, for Luke notes that the 'power of the Lord was with him to heal' (5.17).[2] Their reaction is a

banquet. Jesus' reaction is one of disappointed expectations. He exposes their weaknesses ruthlessly, but he does so, not to write them off, but to explain what stops them from responding.

1. This again runs counter to some assessments. L. Gaston ('Anti-Judaism and the Passion Narrative in Luke–Acts' in P. Richardson with D. Grauskov [eds.], *Anti-Judaism in Early Christianity*. I. *Paul and the Gospels* [Waterloo, OT: Wilfrid Laurier University Press, 1986]), says of the Lukan redaction of Mk 2.1–3.6 that it shows an increased tendency to portray the Pharisees as the enemies of Jesus', p. 141. Cf. E. Schweizer (*Good News according to Luke*), says of Lk. 5.27-32, 'Here, too, Luke intensifies the conflict'.

2. That Luke introduces a deliberate gathering of Pharisees and scribes from all parts at the beginning of the episode is sometimes seen as a heightening of the

more open one for it expresses less a reaction of closed minds than a genuine perplexity: 'Who is this that speaks blasphemies? Who can forgive sins but God only?' On the face of it, Jesus is blaspheming, yet if he is a prophetic figure, then he is speaking in the name of God. They therefore in Luke refrain from actually affirming (as is the case in Matthew and Mark) that Jesus is blaspheming. They are less closed and less hostile. The conclusion includes them: 'Amazement seized them all, and they glorified God and were filled with awe, saying, 'We have seen strange things today' (5.26). They recognise the magnitude of the event and they glorify God because of it.They should therefore be led to acknowledge the person of Jesus through whom God's power has been bestowed. The question, of course, is, will they?

Something of the same pattern occurs in the rest of the series of narratives. At the dispute with Pharisees when Levi is called (Mk 2.13-17; Mt. 9.9-13; Lk. 5.27-32), Matthew attacks them directly by telling them to come to terms with the meaning of Hos. 6.6. Luke, on the other hand, brings their attitude into a closer relationship with that of Jesus. The scribes and Pharisees object not merely to Jesus' but also to the disciples' eating and drinking (the last a Lukan addition). It is a continuing attitude which is the subject of dispute. Luke adds, 'they murmured'. Elsewhere in Luke, this represents less the determined hostility of a closed mind than a genuine complaint of one who is in fact capable of being met by argument and so is not entirely beyond persuasion. At 15.2 their murmuring is met by parables; Zacchaeus defends himself against the crowd's murmurings (19.7), and those of the Hellenists are recognised as legitimate (Acts 6.1). Murmurings are not entirely unjustified or unanswered. So here in Luke Jesus actually defends himself in a manner which by the addition of the words 'to repentance', narrows the gap in outlook between the Pharisees and himself. Their outlook is not entirely ignored, nor is it declared completely invalid.

Nevertheless, Luke does not underplay the radicality of Jesus nor the leap forward that the Pharisees are to make if they are to become

confrontation. On the contrary, in the light of the conclusion of the narrative, it is to be seen rather as a revelation to them in which they acknowledge God's action, appreciate that it has implications, and remain open to its significance. The next two incidents show the tension inherent in the situation and the Lukan version of the parable of the patch points to the leap forward that the coming of Jesus demanded and the natural religious resistance to this.

one with him. In the discussion over fasting, his version of the new patch on the old garment, by its emphasis upon the harm done to both new and old in any attempt to join the two, accentuates the points of the Markan and Matthaean versions (Mk 2.18-22; Mt. 9.14-17; Lk. 5.33-39). Matthew at the end talks about preserving both the old and the new. Luke here is significantly different. He rather emphasizes the need to leave the old, if not behind, at least as no longer the main object of concern. The new is there to be accepted but the failure of the Pharisees to do so, though greatly to be deplored, is at least understandable: 'No one after drinking old wine desires new; for he says, "The old is good"'. They are held back by their concern with the old from embracing the new age. What ought to have been their inheritance is denied them by reason of their satisfaction with the old and their failure to let it lead them forward as it should.

Luke like Mark follows these incidents with two sabbath day conflict narratives, those of plucking corn and of the healing of the man with the withered hand (Lk. 6.1-11; Mk 2.23–3.6). In Matthew these incidents come later (Mt. 12.1-14). In Matthew the pettiness of the Pharisees, their total perversity, is seen to be accentuated. The sabbath is retained, but Jesus is Lord of the sabbath who acts about it, not indiscriminately, but in a manner in conformity with that of both David and the priests. The Pharisees accept neither him nor the significance of the actions of those who were the upholders of their own covenantal position. They need to learn from their own prophets for, if they had, they 'would not have condemned the guiltless'. They had not begun to learn that the Law had its rationale in mercy; their attitude therefore was bound to lead to a wrong application of its commands.

In Luke, the situation is different. The episode is determined wholly from a christological perspective for, by not containing Mark's 'the sabbath was made for man, not man for the sabbath' and Matthew's references to Old Testament attitudes to the sabbath, he simply bypasses it as being caught up in the new era which is determined by Christ alone. Jesus has a freedom towards the sabbath which comes out of his place as messiah of Israel. He neither points out the sabbath limitations as does Mark nor does he justify Jesus' attitude as does Matthew. The attitude of his opponents is not condemned; they are rather presented with a new fulfilment in Jesus with which they must come to terms.

In Mark, the story of the man with the withered hand which follows has Jesus 'look around at them with anger, grieved at their hardness of heart' (Mk 3.5). At the end, Pharisees go with the Herodians to determine how to destroy him. Matthew accentuates this (Mt. 12.9-14). There is an open conflict with them. They ask questions of him only to accuse him and he confutes them with a Pharisaic-type argument, 'So it is lawful to heal on the sabbath day'. Their opposition rests, not on the Law, but on perversity. Jesus has proved them wrong on their own terms. In Luke, however, the dialogue is different from that found in Matthew. Jesus refutes them, not so much by a form of scribal argument, as with a direct question which not only goes to the heart of the interpretation of the sabbath law—'I ask you, is it lawful on the sabbath to do good or to do harm, to save life or to destroy it?'—but which, because he does not have Mark's reference to Jesus' anger, also assumes that they are capable of seeing the point. Jesus appeals to the light which is in them. They are angry because Jesus' action, as they see it, does not actually conform to a real saving of life. He is in fact going further than he can openly justify, but, in doing so, he is bringing his action into a christological perspective which claims to be the eschatological fulfilment of the Law. Again, Christology rather than the Law is the defining standard. In Luke, as opposed to Mark and Matthew, they do not set out to destroy him. Rather, it is a question of 'what they might do to Jesus'. There is not a total rejection. That may come but it will be perversity in the end rather than a rejection of his way because it is one of abiding conflict with their own. So in Luke perversity stops them from acknowledging what really they should acknowledge, for their tradition should have prepared them for it.[1]

Luke then has mellowed the depth of the antagonism between Jesus and the scribes and Pharisees which is so apparent in this section of Mark and even more so in Matthew. It is in keeping with this outlook that he leaves them out from his Passion narrative. Mk 12.13 has no

1. 'Luke completely reformulates here. He brings to the fore the degree to which the Pharisees and scribes were upset by Jesus' action, but tones down any suggestion that fixed plans for Jesus' destruction are now already set in place' (Nolland, *Luke*, p. 262). This is not just because Luke wants to make a climactic confrontation later (Beck, p. 128). It is rather that he wants to keep relationships open. It is in the end a question of whether they will be able to acknowledge the eschatological significance of Jesus.

place in his Gospel. Matthew on the other hand introduces more references to them at this point. The parable of the wicked tenants is against the Pharisees as well as the chief priests (Mt. 21.45). Pharisees send their disciples to attack him (Mt. 22.15), and it is they who are challenged by Jesus to come to some true christological understanding (Mt. 22.45). In both Mark and Matthew, but not in Luke, the scribes mock Jesus on the cross (Mk 15.31; Mt. 27.41).

Yet Luke does have some very strong anti-Pharisaic material. The hard core of it is found in 11.37–12.12, much of which is parallel to some of the invective of Matthew 23, though it is nevertheless significantly different. He does not express the positive evaluation of the Pharisaic approach to tradition that is found in Mt. 23.1-3, so that his respect for a traditional interpretation of the Law is seen to be far less high than is Matthew's, and no abiding necessary place for that tradition is allowed in defining the ways of the Christian community.[1]

On the other hand he can still see the tradition as having value for those who have practised it. He affirms it for them as offering a valid relationship with God provided that it leads to a deeper awareness of God and a concerned outlook to men (11.42). He does not actually demand an abandoning of their outlook on tradition nor does he attack that tradition as inculcating an attitude which is contrary to God's revealed will in the way that Mt. 15.1-20 and 23.16-22 do.[2]

Nevertheless he does not see the tradition as necessarily having a continuing validity. His discussion of the cleansing of cups (11.39-41) is more radical than its counterpart in Mt. 23.25-26. Matthew declares the uselessness of cleansing the outside without doing the same for the inside, but the cleansing of the outside is not thereby declared superfluous. In Luke however, it is. The cleansing of the inside makes everything clean so that the requirement of the tradition is made redundant at this point; not necessarily wrong, but unnecessary.

For Luke then the tradition is both less affirmed and less attacked than it is in Matthew. If it is seen as less of a threat to the Christian stance, it is because it is downgraded in importance. It does not have any continuing validity for Christians and so it does not become an actual battleground between Christians and Jews in which the Christian interpretation of a tradition is affirmed at the expense of

1. See above, n. 1 p. 175.

2. Lk. 15.31 represents the underlying stance towards the Pharisees. Luke's theme is one of disappointed hopes.

a denial of the interpretation of that of their opponents. Jewish interpretation is inadequate but, if its defects are met, it can presumably continue to be observed by Christian Pharisees. This however becomes now of little importance, for the coming of Jesus has made it superfluous. There is, in fact, a certain indifference in Luke to its continuing practice.[1]

But, if Luke is somewhat indecisive about the tradition, he is nevertheless hard in this chapter upon its non-Christian practitioners. He takes over the Matthaean woes, though, by dividing them three and three between Pharisees and lawyers, he avoids the finality of the build-up that the Matthaean version suggests and, in this way, softens the Matthaean attack upon the Pharisees as such. He avoids the Matthaean repeated designation of them as hypocrites and, by not having some of the starker of the Matthaean denunciatory sayings (Mt. 23.15, 16-22, 24), makes his passage less of a sweeping, overriding denunciation of them. Luke's discourse does not have the climactic positioning that ch. 23 has in Matthew. It contains less material and calls neither the Pharisees nor the lawyers 'blind fools' or 'hypocrites'. Yet the Pharisees are guilty of 'neglecting justice and the love of God'. They are open to presumption before God and men. They are actually guilty of leading others astray by being, as hidden tombs, the source of uncleanness to others (11.42-44). The lawyers share in the misdirection of those they teach and are incapable of perceiving the truth in the preaching of the prophets. They have 'taken away the key of knowledge'; by their teaching they have made both themselves and those for whom they accept responsibility unable to perceive and be responsive to the way of God (11.45-52).

All this is indeed severe but, unlike Matthew 23 where it is directed to the crowds and to the disciples *about* the Pharisees (Mt. 23.1), it is addressed to them directly and to the lawyers when Jesus is at meal in a Pharisee's house. It is therefore not a final denunciation of them which assumes that a break has occurred and that dialogue is impossible, but remains open to them. It is less a final assessment than an intermediate response which is made moreover to a particular incident. The Pharisee who has invited Jesus is astonished because Jesus does not actually conform to a custom that might have been expected of one who, by accepting an invitation to a meal, acknowledged some unity with the host, and who was himself a teacher of Israel. It is the

1. See below, pp. 198-99.

assumption of the necessity to fulfil the tradition's requirements and the attempt to impose this on Jesus which brings the denunciation. The outlook which accepted the necessity to impose the tradition on others and which failed to recognize the radicality inherent in Jesus' message and actions becomes the reason for the hostility which Luke has Jesus express. It is made in response to a specific incident and its hostility is directed to a particular facet of Pharisaic outlook, to those attitudes which in practice stopped them from responding to Jesus, the validity of whose message was in fact at least partially realized by them and issued in some measure of response to him.

Jesus' outburst however seems to result less in a change of heart on the part of the Pharisees than in an increasing hostility by them (11.53-54). Opposition is growing, brought about by the Pharisees' inability to respond to him. That inability is, Luke suggests, ultimately brought about by 'hypocrisy' (12.1). In Mark and Matthew, the leaven of the Pharisees is their seeking after a sign (Mk 8.11-15; Mt. 16.1-6). In Luke, the leaven is something more pervasive and generally characteristic of them. Though he may have been encouraged to use hypocrisy at this point by his closeness to that which gave rise to the repeated description of them as 'hypocrites' in the Matthaean version, Luke uses it to make an attack which is directed less at them as people than at the attitude which seems to be generated by their tradition. Something in that tradition produces an attitude which, by being all pervasive, dominates them, stifles their growth and makes them unable to be open to that which deep down they seem to recognise as good. That attitude Luke characterizes as 'hypocrisy'. He warns his disciples to 'beware of the leaven of the Pharisees which is hypocrisy' (12.1). What he means by that may be defined by the following verse which suggests 'being outwardly one thing and inwardly another'.[1] In that case Luke is saying that the insincerity of the Pharisees has taken them over and vitiated what is good in their tradition; it has engulfed them and destroyed their integrity. This would be in keeping with the attack on them in 11.42-44 and would fit with other critical passages such as 16.14 and 7.30. The light which was theirs has been overcome by their basic pride which has taken them over and stopped them from moving forward. Yet, by warning the disciples against the same leaven, Jesus is presented as accounting for that attitude even when he condemns it. Luke's is a less hostile attitude than that which enables

1. Ziesler, 'Pharisees', p. 152.

Matthew repeatedly to call them hypocrites. They are seen to be taken over, to have fallen victim to something so that its presence explains them and actually allows recognition of what is basically good in them. They are a warning and a tragedy.

Luke's reference to the Pharisees, however, becomes the introduction to a discourse which takes up the whole of ch. 12 and which is set against the urgency of the times and the need for faithfulness. Verses 2 and 3, when taken together, talk about the future openness of the proclamation of Jesus and his work which contrasts with the present hiddenness. The life of the disciples is envisaged as a lead into the full revelation at the parousia (12.35-40). It seems that vv. 4-12 are set against the back cloth of opposition which v. 1 suggests is spearheaded by the Pharisees. Hypocrisy elsewhere in Luke has a suggestion of inability to see clearly while maintaining one's ability to do so (6.42). It is compounded by an unwillingness to respond to the eschatological signs of the times (12.56) and to recognize the significance therefore of the presence of Jesus (13.15). It is a distorted vision which fails to discern the eschatological situation and it does so because of a self-satisfaction which leaves no room for a future fulfilment and which is indifferent to others. The inability of the Pharisees to acknowledge that for which they are supposed to be looking stops them from seeing the eschatological action of God when it appears in Jesus, and therefore causes them to be the spearhead of the resistance to the mission (12.1-11). The disciples are warned of succumbing to the same blindness which would stop them also from responding to the eschatological activity of the Holy Spirit (12.8-12). In Mk 3.29 and Mt. 12.31-32, blasphemy against the Holy Spirit is the denying of the Spirit as the source of Jesus' healing activity and is declared in Matthew to have been committed by Pharisees and in Mark by scribes. Luke, however, by having it in the context of Christian post-Pentecostal witness to Jesus, takes the charge away from the Pharisees and makes it one that is actually a possibility to be laid against Christians. This whole section allows that what has happened to the Pharisees through their hypocrisy is a real possibility for Christians for whom its danger will be all the greater since for them it involves denial of the Spirit. All this actually makes the Pharisees closer to the Christian disciples and, even as it in a sense seeks to explain their attitude while condemning it, nevertheless leaves the door to them less than completely shut and actually accentuates the element of tragedy which is to be found in the attack upon them.[1]

Luke's handling of these two parts of the tradition about Jesus and the Pharisees suggests an outlook which, though not entirely straightforward, is at least relatively clear. Jesus is not presented as being in total opposition to the Pharisees. There is not an inevitable rift between them; their tradition does not necessarily make them into opponents of him. Nevertheless, they are in the main either unwilling or unable to allow their tradition to move them forward into a response to him. There is something in their use of the tradition which actually holds them back. And so Jesus is highly critical of them and of their inability to allow the tradition to move them forward. If that inability is characterized as 'hypocrisy', what causes it is shown clearly in Luke's distinctive episodes in which he unfolds his own understanding of what he would term a tragedy.

The first of these episodes is that which presents Jesus at a meal with Simon the Pharisee, and the intrusion of a woman who was a sinner (7.36-50). Much discussion has taken place about Luke's understanding of the significance of the woman's action.[2] Is her love the mark of her repentance so that it is seen as the result of her forgiveness, or is it simply a response to Jesus, so becoming the reason for her forgiveness, even, as it is sometimes expressed, the condition of it? Condition it is unlikely to be, for Luke's whole emphasis is upon the initiative of Jesus, upon the move out to sinners, upon the acceptance of them as the unconditional act of God. On the other hand, Luke is interested in repentance and seems at times to want to underplay the radicality of that unconditional acceptance. So he expounds the Markan account of the radicality of Jesus' call into 'I have not come to call the righteous, but sinners to repentance' (5.32; cf. Mk 2.17). It would not therefore be out of keeping for Luke to understand the woman's love as arising out of her forgiveness by Jesus. So Marshall can actually suggest the likelihood of an earlier meeting between her and Jesus.[3] Yet, though such an understanding cannot easily be ruled out from Luke's thinking for it would again fit his outlook as this is expressed in his understanding of Jesus' parables of the lost sheep and the lost coin—'There is joy before the angels of

1. The element of tragedy is pointed out and developed by R.C. Tannehill, *Israel in Luke–Acts: A Tragic Story*, *JBL* 104 (1985), pp. 69-85.

2. See the discussion and bibliography in Nolland, *Luke*, pp. 349-60.

3. *Luke*, p. 313.

God over one sinner who repents' (15.7, 10)—it is unlikely to be how he understands the significance of the episode.

Such an interpretation of Luke overplays the determining influence of the parable of the two creditors (7.41-42). The theme of the parable however is wider than an application to this particular incident. It points rather to a principle to be seen in the response to the whole ministry of Jesus and to the preaching about him in the early church. As Luke especially pictures it, that ministry is seen in a proclamation of release and renewal (4.16-30) and it will naturally and inevitably appeal to those who see the need of, and are actually longing for, that release. Those who are not burdened, not hemmed in by forces outside themselves, whether they be of sin or of human disdain and oppression, will not meet that proclamation with the same response. The woman has found her release, her hope in Jesus, his presence and his proclamation. Jesus' eating and drinking with tax collectors and sinners has symbolically been of itself the point of release, of hope, of acceptance. Her response has been love, a spontaneous overflowing of her natural humanity caught up into something greater. It is response to grace, to a gracious, moving proclamation in Jesus, and in that response she seals her effective incorporation into the proclamation. So really, her love as Luke sees it here is neither the condition nor the result of Jesus' forgiveness of her sins. Both terms make the action more neatly developed in more clearly defined stages than in fact it is.[1] Verse 47 sums up the whole process as it is written, not merely in the light of the actual historical moment of some particular relationship, but as it expresses Luke's whole understanding of the outgoing outreach of Jesus' ministry culminating in the inclusion of lawless Gentiles, coupled with the failure of the Jewish nation as a whole to respond to him. If the parable is pressed as determining the sequence of events, then it can only mean that Simon himself has already been forgiven. If that is so, it must have been apart from Jesus, for his response to him, though friendly, is still highly suspicious ('If this man were a prophet…') and is certainly far from acknowledging and finding God's eschatological action in him.

The episode is focused on its contrast between Simon and the unknown woman. She, through her love in a response to Jesus' outreach, finds faith and so forgiveness, a relationship. Simon does not find faith: he does not enter into a real relationship. He cannot bring

1. Tannehill, *Luke*, p. 118.

himself to respond to Jesus' proclamation. The parable suggests that this is primarily because he sees no need. His relationship to God is not totally denied but, though he has need to be forgiven little, he cannot move forward and find that forgiveness in Jesus. He is not open to God's forgiveness and to God's call. So, the Pharisees refused the call and the baptism of John (7.29). They refused to be challenged by his call to repentance in the face of God's coming eschatological act. Equally perversely, they refused the open acceptance of Jesus. They turned their backs upon his freedom and, instead, categorized him as 'a glutton and a drunkard, a friend of tax collectors and sinners' (7.34). They did not see the need to move forward; they saw no challenge; they were therefore not open to God's eschatological approach and they refused to see that approach as calling for an open response of universal application. The wonder of the guests—'Who then is this who even forgives sins?'—demands an answer. The tragedy is that Simon and so many of his companions were unable to make it a positive one.

Luke expresses much the same understanding in his inclusion of the parable of the Pharisees and the tax collector (18.9-14). He makes his position clear by his introduction to the parable in v. 9 and by the conclusion in v. 14. The parable itself is to be understood in the light of these two verses. Verse 14 is clear; there is to be a reversal of status. The one who supposes himself to be righteous will be humbled and be revealed as in fact not being so; the one who claims nothing for himself will, on the other hand, receive all. That is the faith that the Son of man wants to find when he appears on earth (18.8). The one who refuses to abandon the riches in which he ultimately trusts to follow Jesus will find great difficulty in entering the kingdom of God (18.24).

What though in this context is the Pharisee's weakness? It is his being of those who 'trusted in themselves that they were righteous and despised others' (18.9). Jeremias sees this as a contrasting attitude to that expressed in the Pauline doctrine of justification by faith as that is usually understood.[1] But is Luke here implying that it means a confidence in himself rather than in God, as Jeremias maintains? This then would make the Pharisee's thanksgiving to God little more than a caricature. But there is nothing to suggest that Luke sees any hint of

1. J. Jeremias, *The Parables of Jesus* (London: SCM Press, 2nd edn, 1963), pp. 139-44.

irony, indeed of bitter irony as it would have to be if Jeremias is right, at this point. The thanksgiving of the Pharisee is genuine.[1] If his prayer were presented as being of itself either hypocritical or God-excluding, then the conclusion that the tax collector rather than the Pharisee went away justified would hardly be surprising. But the parable, as so often, expresses its message in something of a shock. The Pharisee's fault was simply his conviction that he was righteous—that he had no further need. It was his failure to see that more was required, and that more was on offer. It was his presumption, his satisfaction, his sense of being (under God) in control. He was convinced that he was in a right relationship with God, and it was just that conviction which put a barrier between himself and the God who was represented by Jesus.

But, of course, there was a further reason, and that was his contemptuous treatment of his fellow human beings. The Pharisee stood and prayed apart by himself (18.11).[2] His confidence in a special relationship with God, even his full pursuit of what he felt was his privilege of fulfilling obligations to God in response to God's gracious initiative, put him apart from others. His catalogue of virtues was not meant as an attempt to manipulate God; it can be understood as a genuine expression of response to what was seen as God's grace. But his confidence excluded him from oneness with others, and in that isolation excluded him from the sense of need to assert the priority of

1. Evans, *Luke*, p. 643, 'This is not to be regarded as hypocritical, even if exaggerated in its exclusiveness. It is an extension of the thanksgiving of Israel for its election by God from among the nations (Deut. 26.18) to cover the distinction within Israel between those who cared supremely for the divine law in its greatest possible application, and those who cared little or nothing'. Evans sees it as reflecting something of the spirit of Ps. 26; it permeates that of Ps. 119, for example vv. 49-72, and expresses the strengths but also the weaknesses of such an outlook which does encourage complacency and self-satisfaction. This is the minus side of a plus situation. Neale, *Sinners*, pp. 166-78 accepts the Lukan picture as a caricature rather than a historical reality. 'The "historical" Pharisees have not been in evidence so far in the gospel of Luke and this remains true with regard to this parable'. Neale's attempt to see a different outlook between the prayer of Luke's Pharisee and that represented by the rabbinic piety gemara is simply obtained by approaching the two prayers with different presuppositions.

2. Marshall, *Luke*, p. 679, 'The Pharisee, taking his stand, prayed'. Evans, *Luke*, p. 643, 'His prayer has the character of an internal monologue', may be right, though this seems somewhat harsh.

grace and to look for the fulfilment of what his present state could only represent a part. His confidence led him to a satisfaction which failed to make him open to God's redemption when it appeared in Jesus, and it failed to enable him to be caught up in the universality of grace which Jesus brought.[1] And so, in spite of the Pharisee's piety which should have led him to Jesus, and because of his wilful exclusion of others from God's concern as it was expressed in Jesus, it was the tax collector who was justified; the Pharisee himself was not. This again is tragedy. It is a response of surprise, of acceptance of an inevitable, inescapable fact, rather than a positive rejection of the Pharisee and his kind. He had misread God and Jesus, and his faith had not prepared him for this eschatological time.[2]

Luke's final story of Jesus at a table of a Pharisee is in 14.1-24. Tannehill suggests that this has something of a climactic character about it, and that may well be so.[3] In many ways, though, it is less final than the events of 11.37-52 and it certainly has no account of hostility to equal that of 11.53-54. Yet it does mark the end of any real dealings with the Pharisees. After this, there is only hostility on their part so that they 'murmur against him' (15.2), 'scoff at him' (16.14) and complain against the disciples' praise of Jesus (19.39). Against them, Jesus tells the parables of ch. 15, he calls them an 'abomination in the sight of God' because they 'justify themselves before men' (16.15), speaks disparagingly in the parable of the Pharisee and the tax collector (18.14), and says that their reaction at

1. F.W. Danker, *Jesus and the New Age: A Commentary on St Luke's Gospel* (Philadelphia: Fortress Press, 1988), p. 297, 'This particular Pharisee is to be numbered among those who have a habit of being right in the wrong way, and his prayer soon deteriorates'. He becomes a reflection of Israel's sad misapplication and misunderstanding of her election. We can heed Tannehill's warning (*Luke*, p. 172) that 'we should be very cautious about reading Luke's portrait of scribes and Pharisees as historical records of groups which existed at the time of Jesus'. Nevertheless, in our attempts to do more justice to them than is done in the NT as a whole, we should neither overplay that anti-Semitism nor so forget the weakness that is inherent in all religion, as to make historical Pharisaism whiter than white. The weaknesses which are discerned by him in Pharisaism are actually seen by him as potential, and more than partly realised dangers for his Christian contemporaries. For him the Pharisees are not only a tragedy but also a tragic warning.

2. It is their failure to recognise the eschatological situation brought about by Jesus which is the cause of Luke's complaint against them.

3. *Luke*, pp. 182-84.

his entry into Jerusalem is profoundly alien from the religious tradition for which that city stands (19.40).

All this seems to be in keeping with the climax of our episode in 14.24: 'For I tell you that none of those men who were invited shall taste of my supper'. Yet this rejection saying may be as much demanded by its context as by a determined attitude of rejection of the Pharisees. It is part of the parable rather than a dominical comment upon the significance of the parable. The wider setting of this episode is one of strong eschatological urgency. The disciples themselves are not entirely apart from that attitude which the parable ascribes to the Pharisees (12.39-40). Yet the disciples largely will respond while the Pharisees by and large will not for they will refuse to see the urgency of the eschatological situation.[1]

At this point some of the Pharisees seem well-disposed to Jesus (13.31), but they will not actually acknowledge him for what he is. All this takes place as Jesus is on his way to his exaltation at Jerusalem. To the enquirer, he proclaims the challenge and the demand of the hour: 'Strive to enter by the narrow door; for many, I tell you, will seek to enter and will not be able' (13.24). All need to repent (13.1-5), it is the eleventh hour (13.9). If that hour is missed, it will be no good saying, 'We ate and drank in your presence, and you taught in our streets' (13.27). The response must be now.

It is in that context that Jesus' final meal with the Pharisees takes place. 14.1 reflects a genuine invitation, and there is no need to suggest total hostility on the Pharisees' part. Suggestions that the man with dropsy was a 'plant' go way beyond what Luke actually says.[2] Yet 'they watch him' and, in view of 6.7 and 20.20 this must convey suspicion, even opposition. But Luke does not spell out this significance as he does in 6.7, and his telling of the healing incident and the implications of the parable do not suggest overriding antagonism on their part at this point. The episode is one rather of wary dealings, of failure to respond, of hesitancy rather than total rejection.

1. We have noted throughout that Luke has a pro-Jewish and thus a pro-Pharisee stance as well as an anti-one. He remains positive to them. Their rejection of Jesus brings rejection upon them but not one that is stronger than that promised to Christians who fall. All this comes out of Luke's desire to explain why the Pharisees, who could have been expected to respond, did not. Disappointed hopes and unfulfilled expectations control Luke's story.

2. Marshall, *Luke*, p. 578; Fitzmyer, *Luke*, p. 104.

Yet trouble is anticipated; it is an uneasy peace because, as before, Jesus will not be contained within either their conventions or their expectations.

The point of conflict is provided by the presence of the man with dropsy. It focuses upon Jesus' questions and their answers, but the significance of these is not easily determined. Is it a hostile worsting of them? Is it a perverse hostility on their part or is it an embarrassed silence brought about by an inner acknowledgment of the way he follows but which cannot be voiced by them because it would move them beyond the point at which they were stuck? Do they reject the implications of Jesus' reasonings, or are they just unable to acknowledge that which deep down they can assent to? Earlier episodes are clearer. At 6.6 they were 'filled with fury'. Assent to Jesus' question was ruled out, for its legitimacy was far from obvious since it was based on what to them was a doubtful assumption. At 13.15 Jesus had shown the ruler of the synagogue's objection to be virtually frivolous; he was a hypocrite and the Lord had worsted him. Now in ch. 14, however, the situation is far less clear. 'Is it lawful to heal on the sabbath or not?' They are silent. They would not commit themselves. A negative response would have been understandable, but they do not give it. Their silence suggests, if not assent, than at least acquiescence.[1] And so Jesus heals. They cannot forbid him for they recognize the correctness of the act. But then Jesus asks a second question: 'Which of you having a son or an ox that has fallen into a well will not immediately pull him out on a sabbath day?' This question seems to go beyond the surface one of legal interpretation. It points rather to the natural response to a crisis situation where legal niceties are laid aside and the Law which made for love of God and neighbour is caught up to result in a spontaneous action brought about by that love which the Law was concerned to nurture. Crisis situations demand crisis actions. But they could not reply to Jesus' questions. The reason is that it would have meant recognizing the eschatological crisis which Jesus' coming had brought to them. And this they were unable to do. They could not move forward into God's new age.[2]

1. Fitzmyer, *Luke*. 'But to be silent is to agree (especially when legal matters are the issue)'.

2. C.H. Talbert, *Reading Luke*, p. 197: 'The effect of the argument is to expose the callousness of the Pharisees who have an appearance of being religious (keeping the sabbath) but are unconcerned about people in need'. This however is to

So Luke in three sections explains what is holding them back (14.7-24). Their meal is an anticipation of the messianic banquet in the kingdom of God. But as an anticipation it is flawed; the real anticipation is in a meal-unity with Jesus. And why could they not have that unity with him? First, because they chose the chief places as their right. They believed that they were acceptable, but, in an anticipation of the parable of the tax collector and the Pharisee, they are told that they are not. Their confidence actually disqualifies them, for it represents a misunderstanding of the God whose banquet they wish to share. Secondly, their meal was inadequate as an anticipation because it was limited in its scope. The poor, the maimed, the lame and the blind will have a place in the messianic banquet and, unless theirs now includes them, there will be no place for Pharisees alongside those who will come. And thirdly, Luke places at this point his version of the parable of the rejected invitation (14.15-24). He introduces it with an exclamation of one of the guests: 'Blessed is he who shall eat bread in the kingdom of God'. This is a pious response and expresses a genuine hope. The trouble is, though, that it represents a total inability to understand what Jesus has been saying. It puts forward a confidence that those who are at table really are anticipating the eschatological meal. At most it pays only lip service to what Jesus has been asserting, namely, that the meal as it is is not a true anticipation of the kingdom.[1] But it is unlikely even to be doing that; Jesus' teaching has been bypassed—the guest has in no way begun to comprehend the significance of Jesus. So the parable again presses the point of urgency of the hour, the radicality of Jesus' proclamation, and the danger of complacency. The invited guests fail to acknowledge the urgency of the invitation and so presume upon their relationship with the householder that they believe that a refusal by them will not itself bring it to an end. Their complacency is born out of a failure to understand both the true nature of the relationship and also the character of the householder. Misunderstanding leads to presumption which in turn leads to complacency and a failure to be sensitive to the urgency occasioned by a crisis.[2]

see the incident in sociological rather than theological terms.

1. It seems unlikely that the response takes on board the significance of Jesus' first two parables.

2. For the understanding that it is presumption rather than rejection which forms the basis of the guests' excuses, see p. 285.

The guests at the Pharisee's meal have indeed been invited; they are potentially within the covenantal people of God. But they are in grave danger of failing to respond to the invitation when it comes in a form they do not expect and at a time when its urgency is clouded from them by other concerns. They cannot see its radicality. They are presuming upon their relationship with the master. So they do not respond when the call actually comes and, by their lack of response, they exclude themselves, for others will come in. The time is now and the anticipation of the final banquet cannot wait. Their failure to respond is blameworthy and none of the refusers will be allowed in. They are excluded. The master's exclusion of his invited guests witnesses to the reality of the urgency of the present time.

So with the conclusion of the parable of the rejected invitation we see perhaps the climax of Luke's description of the lack of real relationship between Jesus and the Pharisees. In spite of their background, in spite of the Law, in spite of their response to it, and in spite of their basic goodness, they did not respond to Jesus and so they were outside the anticipation of the eschatological banquet which, first, Jesus' ministry and, later, the meals of the church were reflecting. They were actually placing themselves outside of the kingdom by not seeing its presence in Jesus. They continued to ask for signs showing its presence and its coming when, in actual fact, these signs were around them to make it in the midst of them—the healings, the preaching, the coming in of the outcast, the community around Jesus, and the freedom experienced by many as the result of him and his ministry (17.20-21).

That basically according to Luke was their weakness: it was a failure to respond to the urgency of the hour for which their tradition should have prepared them. That tradition should have made them ready to respond to Jesus so that they should have passed through it to see its anticipatory and wider purpose. But they had got stuck in it. It had assumed a definitive, final role rather than a limited, partial one. The Law and their tradition were not of ultimate significance for Luke, for they were not those things which defined and determined the sphere and the nature of the people of God. They should have been caught up in something greater, but the Pharisees as a whole failed to allow it to happen. They saw their tradition, and through it the interpretation of the Law, as something more permanent. Jesus himself did not demand an abandoning of the tradition, but what he did require was a putting of it into its more limited role. It was not to determine his way nor was it to define the response of those whom he brought into the community. The woman who was a sinner was not required to keep the Law; Jesus himself was not subject to sabbath rules; they were not ignored, they were rather caught up in something bigger but in a way that was not actually inconsistent with their true meaning.

The Pharisees are attacked for their hypocrisy, for a blindness in failing to see the true significance of their tradition especially when that tradition is bathed in the clear light of the Lord himself. Chapter 11 becomes an attack upon their attitude to the tradition rather than upon the tradition itself. They should have seen the true nature of the tradition for the tradition itself actually makes that clear. In some way, however, the tradition has a built-in bias to lead them into an attitude of hypocrisy, but the Lord shows how it can be taken up and used to be a pointer to the love and the justice that God requires (11.2). The sabbath itself is affirmed when it is seen as a means of deepening love to God and man (14.1-6). Jesus is able to share in the sabbath meals of a Pharisee. But if Law and tradition impede mercy, concern and openness, then they must go. They have no built-in sanctity and they are retained only if they can be pointers to him who brings God's eschatological fullness.

What for Luke stopped the Pharisee from being caught up in Jesus, for whom the Law and the tradition had been a preparation, was their sense of having arrived, their failure to see what they had as leading them into God's eschatological time. When Jesus arrived proclaiming and anticipating that time, they remained within the old for they felt it to be good (5.39). They, as the Pharisee of the parable, were confident of their present status (18.9-14); that confidence had led them to choose the best seats as fitting for them. Like the invited guests of the parable, their feeling of security in their position led them ultimately into presumption so that when Jesus came taking up their tradition, pointing it to its logical conclusion, opening it to all, they refused to respond because they failed to see either the validity of the messenger or the challenge of the proclamation that the time is now.

Their sense of arrival led them to exclude those who could not share in their outlook or keep their understanding. Jesus on the other hand proclaimed an unrestricted invitation and accepted (at least as a basis) a response, the validity of which was not to be judged according to their understanding. It was their restricting the bounds of God's people, which came out of their sense of having arrived, that was so blameworthy as far as Luke was concerned. The Pharisee of the parable treated the tax collector with contempt, Simon dismissed the woman who was a sinner, Jesus' eating with tax collectors and sinners was condemned, they themselves saw no need to invite the poor, the maimed and the blind to their anticipations of the eschatological banquet. They put bounds around the people of God which were determined by their own understanding as that sprang from their confidence that they were included and that their inclusion determined the conditions for the inclusion of others.

This led them into attitudes which Luke exposes ruthlessly. Basically, this attitude is one of pride. They are lovers of riches (16.14), of men's good opinion or at least of men's external signs of respect (11.43). They are exclusive in their confidence (11.37), and contemptuous of those who do not measure up to their standards (18.11). They justify themselves before men (16.14), and ultimately justify themselves before God (10.29). So Luke's portrait of them is harsh, but nevertheless through it all runs the theme of disappointed hopes. Jesus remains in dialogue with the Pharisees and though, as we have seen, there is something of a developing break, that break is never complete for some of them do become Christians (Acts 15.5). But the movement as a whole does not, and the two groups in the end go their separate ways. We have often spoken of tragedy in Luke's picture. That element is clear in Luke's final meal story for it is preceded by the warning of the friendly Pharisees and by Jesus' lament over Jerusalem (13.31-35). The final encounter with the Pharisees at the entry into Jerusalem, where they are less friendly and represent rather those who refuse to acknowledge the legitimacy of the disciples' welcome, again is close to the account of the Lord's tears over the city (19.39-44). They will not share in the actual passion of Jesus, but neither will they acknowledge him. Their lack of acknowledgment is ultimately not to be distinguished from rejection, and, by Luke's time, that will have become obvious.

How are we to account for Luke's portrait of the Pharisees? It is in part, of course, controlled by the tradition that has been handed down to him. Nevertheless, within that overall tradition his portrait has been given distinctive lines. His is less hostile than that found in Mark for it has a less sharply defined antagonism.[1] It is much less so than

1. Ziesler, 'Pharisees', p. 153.

Matthew's; Luke's attack on them in 11.37-52, though it cannot be seen as anything other than an attack, is less vitriolic than that found in Matthew 23. His own picture contains no such sweeping denunciations of them as is found in Mt. 5.20, 21.45 and 27.62.

J.T. Sanders thinks that Luke's picture of the Pharisees is really a portrait of the Jewish Christians of his time. He writes: 'Luke has gone to considerable lengths to define the Pharisaic opposition to Jesus, over and against Mark and Matthew, as being limited to questions of Halakah or Torah interpretation'.[1] Yet, this is to narrow unduly the Lukan meal scenes and to ignore completely Luke's attacks on the Pharisees as lovers of money, as delighting in the approval of men, as seekers after the chief seats, and as excluders of others. It ignores the eschatological setting of the meals and the deeper aspects of the sabbath healing discussions. The Pharisees are Jews rather than Jewish Christians and it is this deeper aspect of their failure to acknowledge the Lord to whom their tradition should have pointed them, which provides the nub of Luke's argument and the focus around which all else revolves. Luke's portrait of the Pharisees is not to be accounted for by seeing it as reflecting the internal tensions of the church of his day. Luke's Christian Pharisees in Acts 15 are refuted completely by the action of the 'apostles, and the elders, with the whole church' (Acts 15.22) and the later description of the many thousands among the Jews who believe and who are 'all zealous for the law' (21.20) does not imply a continuing group against which Luke reacts. He is able to picture Paul himself as a good Jew, a responsible Pharisee, and one who is able to accommodate himself to the Law. Such a picture of his hero is hardly likely to have emerged if Luke was engaged in tension with Jewish Christians of his time. If Luke's purpose was to present Jewish Christians to whom he was hostile in the guise of non-Christian Pharisees, something much more like Matthew's portrait of them would have been more fitting.

But does Luke's picture reflect some argument with his Jewish contemporaries?[2] This would certainly seem to be true of Matthew's

1. Sanders, *The Jews in Luke–Acts*, p. 91.

2. Beck sees Luke's picture of the Pharisees as controlled by his contemporary situation, *Character*, p. 130. However, we believe that it is controlled rather by the past in an attempt to explain why Israel of the past refused. Luke's picture points to the past rather than to the present. As Beck himself says, p. 206, in Luke, 'lack of specific detail points away from a close encounter of the kind reflected in Matthew'.

picture of Jesus' dealings with them. There, they are presented as persecutors of 'prophets, wise men and scribes' whom Jesus will send to them (Mt. 23.34). They are contemporaries to be reckoned with while there is a great contrast between their practice and that of Matthew's church (Mt. 23.2-3). Matthew's church is actually to learn by reacting to, indeed against, the Pharisees and their teaching. His great denunciation is not made directly to them but to 'the crowds and his disciples' about them (Mt. 23.10). They actually represent and catch up in themselves Jerusalem 'who kills the prophets and stones those who are sent' (23.37). Denunciation of the Pharisees widens out into the rejection of Jerusalem as a whole. Luke, however, does not see the Pharisees as characterizing the opposition to Jesus. At the Beelzebul episode, whereas in Mk 3.22 it is the scribes who accuse him and in Mt. 12.22-24 it is the Pharisees who not only accuse him but actually contradict the legitimate wonderings of 'the people', in Lk. 11.14-15 the accusers are simply 'some of them', presumably of the people who have marvelled. Luke presents a divided people and the hostility is not always spearheaded by the Pharisees. Matthew seems to present them as the supreme opponents who are actually in opposition to his church and whose attitude is represented as one which is wrong and against which his church reacts. His church measures itself by their standards and actually squares up against them.

In Luke, however, this is not so. They are not contemporized as they are in Matthew. Though he tells his stories in the light of the experience, not only of the early church, but of the church which is nearer to and runs into the church of his own times, he nevertheless sets dealings with Jesus in the period of past time. His is a description from the perspective of history. Chapter 11 of Luke lacks the contemporaneity and the immediacy of Matthew's ch. 23. Matthew's missionary discourse refers back to Mt. 9.34 which is introduced at this point so that the missionary discourse itself can have application to the Pharisees who are seen as spearheading the attack on the missionaries of Matthew's church (Mt. 10.24-25). This links up with his accusations against the Pharisees in Mt. 23.34 and, by its use of ideas from Mk 13.9, makes the Pharisees the real opponents of the Christians after the resurrection. For Luke, this is not so. They do not represent Jewish hostility as such, and in Acts of course they appear as friendly to the Christian proclamation (Acts 5.34; 23.9).

Luke sees them, not as representatives of any contemporary

group—though there was no doubt Pharisaic activity in his time—but as figures primarily of the past, as representatives of that group who by their piety, their zeal, their covenantal seriousness, and their response to Israel's election should have been those who would have been expected to respond to Jesus to see the Law and prophecy taken up and fulfilled in him. The tragedy is that they had not, that though they had a natural affinity with Jesus and with the proclamation about him, they had been unable to take on board the newness within the continuity that the coming of Jesus meant. Luke's answer could not be that of Paul, the answer of seeing the old as superseded by the newness of Christ. His thought of resurrection demanded more continuity than did Paul's proclamation of the cross. But he knew that the move from the old to the new, though logical, did demand a leap forward. A radical challenge came to Simon in the demand to accept the woman who was a sinner with the openness, which to the Pharisee could only be laxity, with which Jesus received her. But, as the sabbath conversations show, Luke believed that the Law itself, rightly understood, followed, and entered into, led into the response which Jesus made. The Pharisees actually in their hearts perceived this. The tradition prepared them for it. But they held back. They could not move forward in the way that God, in both Jesus and their tradition, demanded. So they stayed still, confident in themselves, retreating from the eschatological newness that Jesus brought, and so were forced to turn against him whom they should have acknowledged. The Pharisees refused the eschatological action of God in Jesus and continued to look for something else (16.14-15, 17.20-21). They trusted in themselves rather than moving forward into the response required by Jesus: 'We are unworthy servants; we have only done what was our duty' (17.10). The explanation, as far as Luke could see, could only be that of a perversity born out of a failure to understand what they themselves professed. So the climax of the parable of Dives and Lazarus is Abraham's reply to the rich man (one who like the Pharisees loved money [16.14]): 'If they do not hear Moses and the prophets, neither will they be convinced if someone should rise from the dead' (16.31).

Chapter 9

THE LAW

A discussion of Luke's understanding of the Pharisees has brought us to a partial treatment of his attitude to the Law, and it is to a fuller unfolding of this that I now turn. A way into his thinking on this subject can be found through a consideration of the Synoptic accounts of the sabbath cornfield episode (Lk. 5.1-5; cf. Mk 2.23-28; Mt. 12.1-8). Mark's distinctive but somewhat clumsy description of the disciples' action, which talks of the making of a path and says nothing about the reason for so doing, emphasizes the enormity of the deed. The disciples really are working on the sabbath day. The reply of Jesus is strong; David broke the Law when he felt it necessary to do so: 'The sabbath was made for man, not man for the sabbath'.[1] If that is true, man has some freedom over the sabbath and that means further that the Son of Man is actually the sabbath's Lord. Man is not subject to the sabbath and those who are one with the Son of Man are free from its regulations. The sabbath has virtually come to an end.

Matthew's approach is very different. It is the disciples' hunger rather than any passing whim which causes them to sit loose to the Law's demand. Since Matthew has nothing paralleling Mark's disparaging reference to the sabbath, he gives no grounds for criticism of it as an institution. The significance for his disciples is rather redefined by Jesus who as messiah has authority to do this. Nevertheless, the manner in which he does so is in line with the Old Testament responses. As Son of David, he follows in the manner of

1. Though M.D. Hooker (*The Gospel according to St Mark* [BNTC; London: A. & C. Black, 1991], p. 104) points out that Jesus' position as it is here presented is 'not entirely revolutionary' and that rabbinic tradition would not necessarily have opposed it. Nevertheless, the fact that both Matthew and Luke omitted it suggests that they interpreted it more radically. Mark's introduction to the episode suggests that a more frontal attack upon the sabbath was in his mind.

David; as the one whose coming means that God is with us, he acts in a way consonant with that of the servants of the temple, the earlier symbol of God's dwelling among men; and as the fulfilment of prophetic expectations, he carries forward the prophetic outlook. Jesus' interpretation of the Law is authoritative by reason of his messiahship, but it is also justified by its being at one with the outlook of the Law's own authentic interpreters. Jesus' response becomes an explicit attack upon the Pharisaic manner of keeping the Law and their attitude to it.

Luke like Matthew and Mark answers the complaints of the Pharisees from a christological perspective: 'The Son of man is Lord of the sabbath'. The case however is not argued as it is in their Gospels. On the one hand, he does not share Matthew's concern to justify Jesus' action by stressing its conformity with those of the servants of the old covenant. Though Jesus as Son of David is the fulfilment of the old, he is not actually constrained by dialogue with it. On the other hand, he does not justify the action by basing it upon the critical evaluation of the sabbath which is found in Mark. The sabbath is not decried but is simply reduced in status as it gives way before its Lord who acts towards it with an ease which, though perhaps consonant with the Law's innermost meaning (though this is not made obvious at this point) nevertheless is unconstrained by the significance given to it in the Old Testament. It no longer has a part in determining the actual character of the dispensation introduced by Jesus. It is not belittled, but it is downgraded.

Luke's story does not enshrine Matthew's continuing concern with the sabbath, but neither does it have Mark's denigrating of it. Rather, it acknowledges it but in a manner which removes its covenantal value to the sphere of history to make any continuing observance of it of limited significance amounting to something near irrelevance.

Luke has no incident parallel to that contained in Mk 7.1-23 and Mt. 15.1-20. As an event in the life of Jesus, it would have been relevant to any church where table fellowship was a live issue. That Luke does not include it, adapted in some way to make it conform to that point of view expressed through the Cornelius episode, suggests yet again that table fellowship was not a point of dispute in the church to which he was writing. Mark's version, which includes his own radical comment upon a stark saying of Jesus—'There is nothing outside a man which by going into him can defile him' (Mk 7.15,

19)—could be relevant to such a controversy. Matthew on the other hand, by his different form of Jesus' saying (15.11) and by having him restrict the implications of the parable to the validity of the tradition of the elders, moves the incident out of any possible relevance to internal church disputes.

Neither Matthew nor Luke sees this incident in the light of table fellowship rules needed to define the purity of the covenantal community. Luke, as we have seen from his handling of the conversion of Cornelius, does not envisage the Law as having any continuing relevance on this issue. The apostolic decree, though based on Mosaic laws, is accepted by him only as a witness to the character of the Jewish part of that people. The people as a whole respects the decree as a witness to God's action in history without in any way endowing it with continuing covenantal significance. Matthew, on the other hand, continues to give to the Law a validity in defining the sphere and holiness of the community. Mt. 15.20 becomes an attack, not upon the Law but upon the traditions of the elders. Had his church known of the apostolic decree, he could have interpreted it only as a particular instance of an attitude which saw the Law as having some redefined but nevertheless continuing importance for the Christian community. It remained authoritative for the whole community in helping both to define its boundaries and to enable its holiness. One entered a community which was marked by an attitude to the Jewish Law which went beyond respect to accept that it exerted an authority which was acknowledged even when parts of it seemed to be denied (Mt. 5.17-20). Moreover, movement away from its demands had to be justified by being seen as a direct result of the life and teaching of him who, as Jewish messiah, was its final, authoritative interpreter (Mt. 5.1). Matthew's church denied, not the continuing significance of the Law for the community based on Jesus, but that approach to it which, by refusing his messiahship, rejected the church's stance for one which found its authority in the Law itself and in the traditional, non-messianic use of it (Mt. 5.21-48; 7.29; 9.15; 12.12).

Matthew's report of Jesus' answer to the Pharisaic question about divorce avoids Mark's clear criticism of the Law while acknowledging that it awaits a definitive explanation of its true meaning (Mt. 19.3-9; Mk 10.2-9). Whereas Mark sees Jesus' total prohibition of divorce as being a return to the stance of the Genesis revelation that the Law denied, the Matthaean version discusses the question of divorce in terms of the relation of the Genesis expression of the divine ideal to the reality of the human condition. Moses made concessions to human weakness which, though not ideal, were made necessary by that reality. Jesus as messiah reverts to a full response to the Genesis revelation by laying down a more perfect standard which Moses acknowledged but could not himself demand. The Matthaean exception clause in fact keeps the dominical command in dialogue with the Law's attitude, but to the exclusion of the rabbinic approach. By allowing divorce for πορνεία it does not break away from the Law's principles but tightens the Mosaic outlook. Matthew's concern for the 'higher righteousness' is maintained, and this is shown to be an expression of that outlook by which the Law itself was motivated.

Jesus' summary of the Law in its Markan form (Mk 12.25-34) concludes its command to love with the saying, 'There is no other commandment greater than these', thereby suggesting that the commandments as a whole do not necessarily further love but that they may in fact actually work against it. Matthew's version (22.34-40) does not have this saying but climaxes the episode with 'On these two commandments hang all the law and the prophets'. What could seem a criticism of the Law is replaced by a saying which sees it in its entirety as enabling and freeing love. Its commandments are still to be observed for they both define and release a way of love so that Jesus' criticism of the Pharisees is that they have allowed the niceties of their tradition to work to the neglect of the weightier matters of the Law—justice, mercy, and faith (Mt. 23.23). Luke's parallel to this last verse has no reference to the need to keep the Law and to its enabling of these higher virtues. The virtues are mentioned, but he is silent on the part of the Law in assisting them (11.42). Luke accepts of course that the Law can indeed encourage love, justice and mercy for, in his version of a lawyer's approach to Jesus, the lawyer is quite capable of seeing its commands as commending and forwarding the love of God and mankind. The Law itself is subjected to no criticism (10.25-27). Nevertheless, it has a built-in weakness which is revealed in the lawyer's desire to justify himself by determining for himself the limits of its definition of neighbour. He himself is not actually criticized, for he represents the result of a system which by its regulations inevitably restricts the spontaneity and outreach of the love it seeks to engender. Luke knows that the Law's weakness was its partiality and therefore its inevitable inculcation of superiority. The lawyer represents the best of Judaism but he becomes the victim of a particular concept of holiness and of a convenantal understanding which the Law made inevitable. He is told to act in the manner of a Samaritan helping a Jew.[1] The command could be fulfilled only in that radical questioning of Jewish covenantal presuppositions which Luke expresses in the significance he assigns to the Cornelius episode.

If Luke therefore sees the Law as imposing an inevitable restriction on the love which God demands by reason of its placing a discriminatory barrier around the membership of the covenantal people, he must maintain that its pursuit of love is inevitably flawed by reason of that discrimination. Luke as we have seen does not view it as a universal moral indicator but rather as an expression of that morality which comes from the universal apprehension of God. The chief significance of the Law for him was to be found in its inclusion of men and women within the covenantal community of God where he was one with his people. That significance had been brought to an end by Christ to leave Law as the historical possession of Israel who was the source but only a part of that people centred around Jesus Christ.

Morality was not for him its distinguishing factor and, since its part of acting as the boundary marker of the people of God had gone, the Law was given no continuing role in enabling the holiness of the people of God. Indeed, an ethical concern did not rank high on Luke's agenda. As we shall see below, he defends his understanding against those who view his pinpointing of Jesus' acceptance of the outcast as dangerously antinomian. He is not indifferent to ethics, he recognizes them as the ultimate gauge of the reality of the response to Jesus, but that is not where his emphasis is to be found. That lies rather in the wonder of Jesus' outreach. So he does not share Matthew's concern for the higher righteousness and he does not see the Law, however, interpreted, as a means of achieving this. His sermon on the plain parts company with Matthew's sermon on the mount in that its demand is not a searching for that perfection for which Jesus asks (Mt. 5.48) but for an outlook which expresses mercy (6.36). His beatitudes are a statement of the nature of the covenantal community, of its vocation, rather than, as in Matthew, a description of a stance to be sought after. Sinners are called and accepted as sinners even if the response must issue inevitably in repentance which, however, as we have seen, is the result rather than the condition of acceptance.

1. The significance of this is rarely commented upon.

Inculcation of ethical standards and expression of ethical demands did not loom large in Luke's concerns.[1]

But, as a disciple of Paul, Luke was nevertheless aware of the brittleness of his position. Paul had suffered as much from the not always necessarily deliberate misunderstandings of his followers as from the criticisms of his more conservative opponents. Luke must have been mindful that the picture of Jesus that he was painting did in fact leave him open to the charge of moral indifference—'If this man were a prophet, he would have known who and what sort of woman this is who is touching him' (7.39). It is the discussion around this problem which seems to give the best way in to the interpretation of what is undoubtedly Luke's most difficult passage on the Law, namely, Lk. 16.16-18. Verse 16 points to a break between the period of the Law and the prophets and that of the proclamation of the kingdom of God. It so emphasizes the newness of the period of Jesus as to leave little room for the continuity that overall has such an important place in Luke's writings. Verse 17, however, doubles back on this to give to the Law a permanence and an abiding validity which actually seems to be more stringent than that found anywhere else in Luke–Acts. This is followed by v. 18 which on the surface appears to be selected at random, for it is not obviously the most immediate illustration of the outcome of what the previous verses have been saying. In any case, its relevance to what has gone before is not certain.

It appears to be a contradiction of the Mosaic acknowledgment of divorce and it is as such that Mark accepts it and that Matthew revises it. Wilson, in his recent detailed study of these verses concludes that 'any Christian author or reader after CE 70 who knew the ruling of Moses in Deuteronomy and current Jewish customs would most naturally have understood Lk. 16.18 as a challenge to the one and the practice of the other'.[2] This may be true but, nevertheless, is this how Luke himself would have taken it? That Luke meant it as a challenge

1. Beck (*Character*, p. 2) asks, 'In what ways does Luke expect the Christian disciple to be distinguishable from the best representatives of Jewish or Pagan piety?'. Luke unlike Matthew does not think in terms of a higher righteousness. Those who repent must 'perform deeds worthy of repentance' Acts 26.20. For Luke what is distinctive of a Christian is, first, an ethical outreach which is unbounded in its concern and, secondly, an attitude which acknowledges an ethical response as arising out of grace and so one which issues in humility and understanding. In place of Matthew's call for perfection (Mt. 5.48), Luke has one for mercy (6.36).

2. S.G. Wilson, *Law*, 1983, p. 47.

to current practice may be asserted with confidence. Matthew even has allowed that, and Luke's own accounts of Jesus' controversies with the Pharisees when he was dining with them make this attitude characteristic of Jesus. Whether Luke went further, however, to adopt a near-Markan outlook at this point is much more doubtful.

Of significance is the fact that he does not have the ruling stated in the context of a scribal question about divorce.[1] This means that it is not deliberately either contrasted or compared with specific laws of Moses as it is in Matthew and Mark, with the result that its framework in Luke is less about the Law as regulator than about the Law as setting and maintaining a divine standard. It therefore becomes less a question about rules than about an underlying attitude to divorce and remarriage. As such, the Law, however interpreted, was bound to be understood as a check upon easy sexual irresponsibility. As Luke uses the saying, it picks up the Law's underlying intention (as Jesus does so often in the third Gospel) to go to its logical conclusion which is to declare divorce and remarriage as having the status of adultery. Luke's different context means that his understanding of the saying is to be seen as a taking up and completing what was implicit, if latent, in the Law's overall stance.

If this is true, what is Luke really saying in these three verses? Has he any coherent attitude? Wilson thinks that he has not, but that these verses simply serve to show that 'Luke did not intend to offer a consistent view of the Law here or elsewhere'. What we have here are 'three disparate sayings linked by a common theme but not by a consistent approach to it'.[2] This, however, is surely a counsel of despair. Taken as such, it is hard to see how Lk. 16.18 is linked to the preceding verses by even anything so tenuous as a common theme. Since it is wholly unlikely that these verses were already linked,[3] and since Luke is in any case no slavish collector and follower of his sources, it seems more likely that he saw them as linked, not so much

1. Evans, *Luke*, pp. 609-10.

2. Wilson, *Law*, p. 51.

3. Evans, pp. 605-606. Marshall, *Luke* (pp. 626ff.) seems to accept H. Schürmann's point of view (*Traditionsgeschichtliche Untersuchungen zu den synoptichsen Evangelien* [Dusseldorf: Patmos, 1968], pp. 126-36), that Luke was using verses that were already joined. He argues that 'it is almost impossible to ascribe the change in them to Luke' at v. 18. We, however, argue that there is a development in these verses and that, taken together, they form a unity which is at one with Luke's own ideas.

by a common theme, as by a development of a single idea.

As a whole they contribute to the expression of his understanding of the place of the Law in the Christian dispensation. Consistency of outlook can be suggested by seeing these verses, first as an expression of the viewpoint which we have seen developed in Luke–Acts as a whole and, secondly, by seeing them within the context of this section of Luke's travel narrative.

If I have been right in my understanding of Luke's overall perspective, this has centred very much on his idea of Christianity as the fulfilment of Judaism in such a way as to see an overriding continuity between the old and the new. Christianity is seen in terms of the Old Testament history and expectations. Nevertheless, he is aware of the newness of the Christian dispensation in its universality and in its consequent waiving of Mosaic regulations for its Gentile members. The continuity is in fact stretched, if not to breaking point, then at least to redefine and reshape much of the old which is to be caught up in the new. Of this, the Law was the focus and difficulty. Jesus did bring a new attitude to the Law: in him there was expressed a freedom, a release, from its restrictions which nevertheless went, not against the true purpose of the Law, but which caught this up and carried it forward to its inner meaning. So within the overall continuity of his understanding of the relation of Christianity to Judaism, there is nevertheless a discontinuity. Verse 16 expresses that clearly. There is a newness in the preaching of the kingdom. Everyone now presses into it. The entry to the sphere of the kingdom is open to all; that is its glory. Nevertheless, that very glory, that very universality puts strains upon the message of the kingdom so that in someway the proclamation of the kingdom, even the kingdom itself, is under siege. It is being strained, being subject to distortion, on account of the very universality and freedom which are of its essence. That which is essential to it, nevertheless has inherent dangers for the freedom of the message can be abused to become licence. The old, though giving way to the new, can be forgotten and abandoned altogether. Verse 17, therefore, puts constraints upon that freedom. The old must not be dismissed as outmoded. It must be caught up in the new and that means that the Law is not to be set aside, to be dismissed as of no consequence, as bringing nothing into the new age. Freedom from its rules must not be interpreted as licence to reject its outlook, it points to the means of love of God and neighbour. Verse 18 is then seen as an illustration of this requirement. The new age does not allow for the loosening of the Law as the expression of the principle of love of God and of neighbour; Jesus has not abandoned its demands as they contribute to this principle. Luke sees his prohibition of divorce as an intensification of the Law rather than its contradiction. Though the saying is framed in Markan terms, its evaluation of the Mosaic command is rather as Matthew understood it, as a tightening of the Mosaic outlook.

More difficult to understand is why Luke chooses to illustrate his attitude to the Law by a saying about divorce for it does not seem to form the most obvious illustration of his principle. Yet it does seem to have been an important issue for large sections of the early church in the light of the enthusiasms engendered by the expectations of a parousia.[1] The words of the Lord had to be applied to for authoritative teaching upon what was obviously a controversial issue. Again, these words were open to varieties of interpretation as the forms of Mark and Matthew bear witness. Their form and the thought behind them were live issues in Luke's time.[2] Luke presents one form, and points to the thinking behind his understanding of it. But, for him at any rate, as it is presented in its immediate setting and as it reflects his overall thinking, it stands as witness to the influence of the Mosaic Law upon the attitudes and teaching of Jesus.

But these verses also form part of this section of Luke's travel narrative. Awareness of this will help, not only to draw out their significance, but also to explain why Luke has actually included them at this point. The travel narrative seems often to be strung together very loosely and, as such, has become almost the graveyard of those who would hope to follow the development of Luke's thinking in this part of his Gospel. Yet there are signs of clear sectionalisation of the overall travel narrative and it is well to look for these in the interpretation of the individual episodes. The section in which 16.16-18 stands begins with an introduction in 15.1-2, 'Now the tax collectors and sinners were all drawing near to hear him. And the Pharisees and scribes murmured saying, 'This man receives sinners and eats with them'. Jesus is no longer at a meal with Pharisees (14.1-24). That section has ended in a break with them. Jesus' anticipation of the

1. 1 Corinthians 7.

2. It is likely that Luke was written within very few years of Matthew. That both dealt, though in very different ways, with Mark's teaching on divorce, suggests that it remained a live issue at that time.

kingdom of God is found in his relationship with tax collectors and sinners. Nevertheless, it is still about fellowship in that anticipation of the kingdom. The shepherd and the woman of the parables both call together friends and neighbours to join in a celebration (15.6, 9). The prodigal's father sets up a meal (15.23). The outcasts are the ones who come and join in with Jesus; the Pharisees stand, as it were, outside to watch and complain. To them Jesus addresses his parables of the lost sheep, the lost coin and the lost son. The message is clear. The eschatological banquet is anticipated in the presence of him. Will the Pharisees in the person of the elder son accept this, change their attitude, and come in?

But, as we have seen, Luke though stressing the openness of the invitation and though avoiding the moralizing of Matthew, as that is seen in the parable of the man without the wedding garment (Mt. 22.11-14), nevertheless is anxious to show that the outreach of Jesus does not entail any antinomianism. Though he says little about ethics as such, he does show that response to Jesus issues in a change of heart. Levi leaves all to follow Jesus (5.27, 28), even though this is somewhat contradicted by his later ability to set up a banquet for him (5.29). Women from whom he had cast out demons provided for the little community 'out of their means' (8.3). The rich ruler was not willing to make such a show of concern (18.25). Zacchaeus, on the other hand, was willing to do precisely that (19.8). Those who responded to Jesus did actually distribute their superfluity to those who had need. This was fundamental to Luke's understanding. In the young post-Easter community this was a sine qua non for inclusion within the people of God. Failure to do so would result in nothing less than complete exclusion (Acts 5.1-11): it amounted to keeping something of the 'devoted thing' to oneself (Josh. 7.1).

It is therefore wholly in keeping with this outlook that Luke should justify Jesus' acceptance of the tax collectors and sinners by pointing to the need for them to use their money aright. He now (16.1) turns from the Pharisees to the disciples. These must include the tax collectors for it is noticeable that Luke does not include anything in his Gospel which is directed to them alone. We do not know his distinctive message to them. Whatever the original application of the parable of the dishonest steward (16.1-9), Luke sees its immediate point in the right use of possessions and in the assurance that this will be acceptable to the heavenly powers (16.9). Riches make for obligations. They bring greater dangers, but they also bring great opportunities. This may seem a little like justification by works; but it is really quite other than that.[1] The rich man acknowledges the crisis when it is presented to him. The tax collectors respond to Jesus' call. The challenge of the hour demands some mark of their response, and that is to be found in a caring use of their possessions and an honest pursuit of their profession. John the Baptist had told them to 'Collect no more than is appointed of you' (3.13). Jesus goes further to command honesty, but also to assert the principle that 'You cannot serve God and mammon' (16.13).

The Pharisees, however, 'scoff at' Jesus' teaching. They are lovers of money themselves and this encourages them to deride the hope that the tax collectors will respond to Jesus' requirements. Their attitude has not changed from that recorded in 15.1. So Luke has Jesus address them again to justify Jesus' attitude and to point out the futility of their response. It is a new age. The kingdom of God is now preached and it is marked by a contrast to the preaching under the Law and the prophets (16.16). It is for all—that is its abiding mark. Everyone is entering it—with joy, with haste and with enthusiasm. But that very enthusiasm has a danger, for it is capable of distorting the message if it does not result in a change of heart. For the Law is not done away so that there becomes a free for all. The old is not simply blotted out by an enthusiasm which puts no demands through action to serve God in and through love of fellow human beings. So v. 17 expresses a valuing of the old and a positive response to the Pharisaic outlook. The Law still expresses claims that are taken up in Christ. The promise of the new does not destroy the points in the old. Verse 18 gives the prohibition of divorce as a relevant illustration of this at this point. If the tax collectors are to be faced with a demand for the right use of money, the sinners are equally to be faced with the real condemnation of adultery.

The Pharisees, however, are unlikely to recognise the legitimacy of all this. They are still insensitive to the absolute necessity to be aware of the outreach of God's call and openness to others. The rich man did not recognize the need to include the outcast who wished even to be fed 'with what fell from the rich man's table' (16.21). He found himself excluded from the heavenly banquet even while Lazarus was

1. Luke emphasizes the initiative of God and the response of humankind. It is not, to use E.P. Sanders' terms, a question of 'getting in' but of 'staying in'.

included. The Law should have prepared him for this openness and it had not. More though, response to Moses and the prophets should have prepared them for Jesus, his teaching and his resurrection (16.27-31). But it had not because their response to it was imperfect. Yet again, Luke points to the fact that the Pharisees and their companions had gone astray, that they were incapable of responding to Jesus' eschatological call because they had mistaken and become unresponsive to that which they claimed to profess. They had not understood the real message of the Law and the prophets (16.31).

Chapter 10

CHRISTIANS AND JEWS

We have seen that Luke maintains that Jesus is not entirely unresponsive to the Pharisees. His strong criticism of them always stops short from developing into continuing hostility so that even though there is a growing straining of relationships, it is not said to degenerate into a complete break. Hostile though they may be at the entry into Jerusalem, Jesus does not engage in antipathetic discussion with them at this final stage in his ministry and, unlike Matthew and Mark, scribes[1] do not mock him at the cross. Luke's outlook at this point is distinctive.

Again, Luke is distinctive about Jesus' (and therefore the disciples') attitude to the Law. Christians are not under the Law as such but it is not brought to an end in the way that it is in Mark, for Jesus is not described as being actually critical of it. It is taken up by him into something greater which does not negate it but subsumes it under the principles of love of God and of neighbour and disallows by this any limitations it may seemingly place upon the breadth of God's new action in Jesus. By his actions and teachings, Jesus points to its true significance and value.

For Luke, however, the Christian way is not determined by the Law nor is it decided in dialogue with it. There is nothing in Luke which parallels Matthew's 'higher righteousness' as that is worked out in

1. The relationship between scribes and Pharisees in Luke is not clear. He appears to recognize some difference at Lk. 11.37-54 and Acts 23.9 though they are closely related groups, cf. Lk. 5.17. In Jerusalem he distinguishes between them for, in place of Mk 12.13 he has a group of 'scribes and chief priests', 20.19. This grouping also appears at 20.1, 22.2, 22.66, 23.10 where the scribes seem, not to be standing for the Pharisees, but to be taking the place of them. For Luke, scribes seem to be a wider group than the Pharisees, almost the professionals in various different parties.

response to a particular application of the Law and its precepts. In Luke, the Law is bypassed; it is no longer seen as being of great significance as a pointer to the will of God. Jewish Christians will continue to keep it as both Paul and Jesus (after a fashion) did, but they will sit light to it without however denying it. Outside the confines of Judaism, zeal for the Law will have to be tempered by the fact that Christian Jews will enter into table fellowship with uncircumcised Gentiles in a way that is plainly inimical to any rigorous upholding of the Law. Table fellowship is not merely casual meetings or an accommodation to living among Gentiles, but is a fundamental expression of the beliefs of the Christian community and is seen as an anticipation of the meals in the kingdom of God. The apostolic decree is accepted not as expressing some authoritative interpretation of some part of Mosaic legislation for the new age, but as apostolic witness to the Jewish Christians' allegiance to that from which they came and of which they remain a part, and as an acknowledgment on the part of the Gentile Christians of the roots of that into which they have been incorporated.

There is then in Luke something of a lightness of touch towards the Law as this is compared with Matthew on the one hand and with Paul and Mark on the other. If he clings to the fundamentals that he learned from Paul, that the Law no longer defines the people of God and that the day to day business of living is not any longer controlled by attention to its requirements since these have been caught up and deepened in Jesus, he nevertheless mellows rigor in a sensitivity born of a greater appreciation of the continuity between Jesus and the Old Testament dispensation. If he shares an understanding of this latter point with Matthew, to see the Christian dispensation as the fulfilment of the Old Testament prophecies and as one with the Old Testament means of salvation, he nevertheless is entirely apart from Matthew who sees the Law and its outlook as exerting a continuing control upon the way the Christian dispensation is understood. Christians for Matthew are the right observers of the Law as they follow the way of the messiah who himself interpreted its teachings and propounded a way in which its obligations were to be correctly pursued. In Matthew the Christian way is the legitimate way of pursuing the Law and, since it is the way the Jewish messiah unfolded, it declares the illegitimacy of any alternative. Hence the strong attack upon the Pharisees and scribes. There is an exclusiveness about Matthew's propagation of

Jesus' antitheses. Ways are contrasted and conflict is inescapable. Christians and Jews are now inevitably and at every point laying claim to the same ground. There is no no-man's land in between. The territory must belong either to the one or to the other.[1]

Luke's Gospel by its less intense attitude to the Law does not contain within itself the makings of a virulent antagonism to those who practise it in some other way. Of course Luke's proclamation of Jesus as messiah includes a value judgment upon those who reject him. Inevitably, they must be 'cut off from the people' (Acts 3.23). But this is presented as a warning. It does not have the unconditional proclamation of exclusion as in Matthew where the right observance of the Law is seen as in some way still defining the bounds of the people of God. For Matthew, the rigidity and barrier of the Law is still there. Inevitably in Matthew it is a case of 'them' or 'us' in a way that is not present in Luke. All Luke completely reacts against is any attempt to impose the Law or a particular understanding of it upon others.

Luke therefore has a less clearly defined division between Jesus and the people of Israel as a whole than does Matthew.[2] Something of the differences between the attitudes of the two evangelists can be seen in the way they handle the stories of Jesus prior to the actual beginning of his ministry (Mt. 1.1–4.16; Lk. 1.1–4.13). These include the infancy narratives which serve as prologues to their respective works, their records of John the Baptist, and the stories of Jesus' temptation. These reveal the presuppositions behind their accounts of Jesus' ministry and represent their understanding of the nature of the messiah's coming to his people. In Luke, Jesus as messiah is fundamentally one with his people Israel even though his birth in a stable witnesses to the indifference of, or rejection by, the majority. In Matthew on the other hand, he stands as messiah, though of Israel, in a manner that is ultimately over and against her.

The character of their genealogies is different (Mt. 1.1-17; Lk. 3.23-38). Matthew follows the Old Testament pattern, for instance, those found in Genesis 10–11 and 1 Chronicles 1 and 9. It is essentially a legitimation of Jesus by way of his being shown to be of

1. R.T. France, *Matthew* (TNTC; Leicester: Inter-Varsity Press; Michigan: Eerdmans, 1985), pp. 50-54.

2. U. Luz, *Matthew 1–7: A Commentary* (trans. W.C. Linss; Edinburgh: T. & T. Clark, 1989), p. 89. In Matthew 'the chasm between the community and the synagogue was already too deep for a dialogue to take place'.

the true line of David and Abraham. It expresses the accomplishment of the divine plan and presents him as the fulfilment of Israel's history, as the climax of her life and the focus of her covenantal call. Like the Old Testament genealogies, its legitimating aim contains within itself an apologetic purpose.[1] Like them, its emphasis on right qualification, on focusing the divine activity in Israel upon its climax, entails an exclusiveness of outlook for it means that other lines of claimed activity are declared to be void or at least secondary. The inclusion of four women, by its irregularity, points to a dramatic shift in the continuity of God's action to lead to Jesus. God's people is inevitably narrowed down to him so that those who are not with him no longer have a share in Israel itself. The annunciation narrative makes this clear as it witnesses to Joseph of Jesus who will save 'his people from their sins' (Mt. 1.21). This allusion to Ps. 130.8 replaces 'Israel', which is the Psalm's object of salvation, with 'his people'. The 'people' is thus identified as being apart from Israel in a way that it is not in Luke's infancy narratives. There, in Lk. 1.71, the salvation that Jesus brings is to God's people Israel—'Blessed be the Lord God of Israel, for he has visited and redeemed his people'. In Matthew this is not so, for there is from the beginning a separation of Jesus from Israel. Joseph, as a vital part of the genealogical link, is alone mentioned as 'a just man', living according to the purposes of the Law. Elsewhere, Herod 'and all Jerusalem with him' are troubled. 'All the chief priests and scribes of the people' know the Scriptures but instead of leading them to Jesus, and in contrast to the actions of the wise men, the Scripture leads them only to give the information to Herod which will enable him to set out upon the destruction of the messiah.[2] Here again the contrast with Luke is striking. There, though Jesus is born as an outcast, ignored by the Jewish people as a whole, representatives of other Jewish outcasts, engaged in the same work as David, respond to him. Jewish piety has enabled both him and the proclamation of his missions. Elizabeth and Zechariah are said to be 'righteous before God, walking in all the commandments of the Lord blameless' (1.6). John leaps in the womb before Jesus. Mary is described as

1. See M.D. Johnson, *The Purpose of the Biblical Genealogies with Special Reference to the Setting of the Genealogies of Jesus* (SNTSMS, 8; Cambridge: Cambridge University Press, 1969); Davies and Allison, *Matthew*, p. 188.

2. R.E. Brown, *The Birth of the Messiah: A Commentary on the Infancy Narratives in Matthew and Luke* (New York: Doubleday, 1979), p. 182.

fulfilling all the obligations of the Law (2.39). Simeon is 'righteous and devout' (2.25) and Anna is a temple devotee (2.38). The true in Israel are not played down in Luke's infancy narratives in the way they are in Matthew's. The hymns point to the taking out of Israel a people for God's name (1.17, 54-55, 68-69; 2.32, 34).

Matthew's story of Jesus' coming out at his baptism and temptation again present Jesus as true Israel in contrast to Israel after the flesh (Mt. 3.17). Joseph and Mary do not return to Bethlehem, for Herod's action enabled by the Jewish leaders has turned that place from one of covenantal renewal to one of rejection. Instead, they go to Galilee and it is from there, Galilee of the Gentiles (Mt. 4.15) that he goes to his messianic anointing and it is there that he begins his ministry. Jesus goes to the Jordan to be baptized by John, but his baptism is dissociated from that of the people (Mt. 3.13-17). He sees his messianic anointing and the crowds hear the divine approval. Jesus, as the 'beloved son', takes the place of Israel in the divine sonship (Mt. 2.15). The baptism points less to Jesus' nature, which is fully explained in the revelation to Joseph, than to his revelation as son and as messiah of the Jewish people. Through him, sonship is now to be defined. The baptism is followed immediately by the temptation (Mt. 4.1-11) which in Matthew, as contrasted with both Mark and Luke, is a single event occurring at the end of the period of fasting. That period has been a preparation for the actual testing of God's son. Like Israel of old, he is under considerable distress. The three temptations in Matthew's Gospel are built around three quotations which are found in reverse order from the original in Deuteronomy. The contrast with Israel is strong, for whereas Israel failed to respond to God and worshipped instead those who were not gods, Jesus remains obedient. His sonship is accepted and confirmed. Angels are now ministering to him to acknowledge his sonship in a way that Israel was not to.[1]

Luke's story, on the other hand, lacks this narrowing down of God's purpose, of the divine sonship to Jesus and does not set him apart from Israel in the way that Matthew's does. The genealogy introduces, not Jesus' birth, but his temptation and follows immediately after the baptism of Jesus. The baptismal narrative has associated him with the baptism of 'all the people' (3.21-22) and he is thus

1. T.L. Donaldson, *Jesus on the Mountain: A Study in Matthaean Theology* (JSNTSup, 8; Sheffield: JSOT Press, 1985), pp. 91-92, 203.

identified with them in a way that Matthew seems deliberately to obscure. As in Matthew, the anointing of sonship occurs at a distance from the baptism itself. The anointing is a messianic declaration of sonship. It is an objective event, but its significance is given, not to others as in Matthew, but to Jesus himself.

Jesus' sonship is not a replacement of Israel's. His is to be a ministry to the people (3.15), a coming of the Christ to his own in judgment and in salvation in the way foretold by both Simeon and John (1.34-35; 3.16-17). There will be division, but it is a division within Israel. John's message in Luke is a warning to the people and a message is given which will enable their response to the messiah. In Matthew on the other hand it is a proclamation of doom upon the people's leaders (Mt. 3.7-12).[1]

It is at this point that Luke places his genealogy. The placing is not significant, for his infancy narratives have left little room for it to be placed appropriately earlier. What is significant, however, is the way Luke works it in from Jesus backwards to Abraham and ultimately to Adam himself who is called 'son of God' (3.23-38). Jesus is one with mankind; his sonship has implications not only for all Israel but for all mankind. Adam remains Son of God and those born out of him retain something of that sonship. Jesus is seen to be restoring the potentiality that is in Israel and in mankind as a whole. Luke's is not a narrowing down of God's action, it is not a stripping down of those who are in the sphere of relationship to God, but a widening out of the sphere of Jesus' saving work to give it a universal significance which is based on his essential identification with 'the people' and with mankind at large.[2]

The three temptations are not the once-for-all overcoming of Satan's power, the once-for-all establishment of the reality of his sonship that they are in Mark and Matthew. Their reordering means that the reversal of Israel's pattern of temptation is no longer evident. They illustrate rather than contain the whole of the event, for in Luke, unlike Matthew but like Mark, the temptation takes place over forty days. The devil does not come at the end of that period for he has been with him all the time. When the devil leaves, angels are not said

1. Davies and Allison (*Matthew*, p. 302) ask whether Matthew could have envisaged his 'chief villains' the Pharisees submitting to John's baptism and suggest that the text can be read as meaning that they came only for 'critical observation'.

2. Though see Evans, *Luke*, p. 253.

to come to minister to him and to witness to his triumph. Unlike Mark, again, they are not with him all the time (Mk 1.12-13). There is no conclusion in Luke. The battle is not completed, for the devil leaves him only 'until an opportune time'. Jesus' way of obedience is the way of restoring the obedience of mankind, of enabling the sons of Abraham and the sons of Adam as a whole to be renewed in that divine sonship which is potentially theirs. As it will later be for disciples, the contest is an ongoing one. Luke will later have the disciples 'daily' take up the cross and pray for a 'daily' drawing upon the heavenly bread.

Both Luke and Matthew have Jesus in relationship with the crowds who are distinguished from the disciples on the one hand and from the Jewish religious leaders on the other. It is sometimes suggested that Matthew sees the crowds as disciples so as to make them transparent to his own contemporary church members.[1] This seems unlikely for though they are sometimes associated with the disciples (Mt. 7.28; 23.1) they are usually distinguished from them (5.1; 13.36; 24.1). But the fact that they have been so understood suggests that Matthew gives them a positive role. They, as opposed to the leaders from whom they are distinguished, are not incorrigible (9.35-38). Nevertheless, there is in Matthew something of a developing break between them and Jesus.

At the end of the sermon on the mount the crowds, who have been listening in to the teaching, are reported as being 'astonished at his teaching' (7.28). There is an ambiguity in this reaction. At 13.54 the astonishment of the people 'in his own country' quickly turns to unbelief; the astonishment of the disciples at 19.25 has to be countered by Jesus' further teaching. It expresses a reaction which on further reflection can cause the initial response to take opposing attitudes: it can turn either to acceptance or to hostility. In ch. 13 the crowds are contrasted with the disciples who are those who 'know the secrets of the kingdom of Heaven', who 'see' and who 'hear'. The crowds have not been given the knowledge of the secrets; they 'see' but they do 'not see', they 'hear' but do 'not hear'. From them, even what they have will be taken away (Mt. 13.10-17). The crowds are left without understanding in contrast to the disciples who, when Jesus asks 'Have you understood all this?' and they reply, 'Yes' are not said to be

1. P.S. Minear, 'The Disciples and the Crowds in the Gospel of Matthew', *ATR* Supplementary Series, 3 (1974), pp. 28-44.

mistaken. Their understanding is true. They need Jesus' explanations but they do in fact get them and so Peter is enabled to enunciate his correct response to his Lord (16.12, 17). In Jerusalem, the crowds at first seem to play a more responsive role. 'Most of the crowd' welcome him with their garments and branches from the trees (Mt. 21.8). They shout the greeting and to the city's question as to the nature of the new arrival they proclaim, 'This is the prophet, Jesus, from Nazareth of Galilee' (v. 11). Later in the same chapter, Matthew notes that when the religious leaders try to arrest Jesus, they are held back because 'they feared the multitudes because they held him to be a prophet' (Mt. 21.46). Yet the crowds soon turn against him. Before Pilate, the crowd, offered the release of Jesus, is persuaded to 'to ask for Barabbas and destroy Jesus'. They all shout determinedly for Jesus' crucifixion. Pilate washes his hands 'before the crowd' saying 'See to it yourselves' and 'all the people' respond 'His blood be on us and on our children' (Mt. 27.15, 20, 23, 24, 25). What has happened to cause such a change? Kingsbury attempts to reduce the nature of the about-turn by pointing out that, at v. 25, Matthew uses the term λαός rather than ὄχλος. He writes that though 'it would be contrary to the text to say that Matthew's use of λαός reveals a desire to spare the crowds per se from the responsibility for the blood of Jesus', nevertheless, 'Matthew employs this term to show that it was not the hysterical masses who were responsible for the blood of Jesus, but Judaism in its official capacity as the chosen people of God'.[1]

That it is Judaism as such which denies Jesus is quite true, but the point surely is that at this stage, the crowd, which before had been open, partially responsive, and perhaps even on the way to accepting Jesus, at the crucial point opts rather for the chief priests and elders and links up with them in their rejection of their messiah. They have chosen to be part of remaining, rejecting Israel. They have made their choice and taken their stand. By opting to be included among the people they have rejected the new people. Earlier, they had accepted Jesus as a prophet and had prevented their leaders from following the way of the wicked tenants (Mt. 21.46), but acceptance of him as a prophet was not enough. Their assessment of him at the entry as 'the prophet, Jesus from Nazareth of Galilee' (v. 11) had to be carried

1. J.D. Kingsbury, *The Parables of Jesus in Matthew 13* (London: SPCK, 1969), p. 26.

further. They had to learn that his cleansing of the temple (Mt. 21.13) and his take-over of it (vv. 14-16) signified more, that he was the son (vv. 37-38), and that he was both theirs and David's Lord (Mt. 22.45). In ch. 23, Jesus addresses both the disciples and the crowds against the Pharisees but the conclusion suggests that the crowds will desert him, that they will line up with their leaders to have Jerusalem reject him and in turn be alienated from him until the time when they can say, 'Blessed is the one who comes in the name of the Lord' and mean it, for they will then see him in his parousia glory.

In the body of Luke's Gospel there seems to be little difference in the attitude to the crowds from that taken by Matthew's Gospel. Though Matthew's picture of John the Baptist's hostility to the leaders of Judaism is transferred to the multitudes (3.7-17), they are not wholly rejected as is the case in Matthew's presentation. The multitudes stand open to receive instruction (3.10) and it is thereby suggested that least potentially some of them will be included with the wheat. Yet Peter's confession is made in contrast to the partial responses of 'the crowds' (9.18). When they press upon Jesus to 'hear the word of God', they are nevertheless kept apart from Peter and the disciples who are presented with the real significance of Jesus (5.1-11). In the sermon, Jesus addresses his disciples in the presence of the crowds who, as in Matthew, are in the position of those who overhear (6.20; 7.1). At Nain, both the disciples and the 'great crowd' who went with him share in a response which brings true glory to God as they respond to Jesus' deed: 'God has visited his people' (7.11-17). But, as in Matthew, the crowds are set apart from the disciples by the parables where Luke is closer to Mark in seeing God as deliberately closing their eyes and ears (8.4-10).

In the journey narrative there is some hostility between them and Jesus. Some of the crowd (rather than the religious leaders of Mark and Matthew) oppose Jesus by suggesting that he casts out demons by Beelzebul (11.14-23) and others test him by asking for a sign. But their attitude is not said to constitute blasphemy against the Spirit as it is in both Mark and Matthew, and Luke retains that for apostasy on the part of Christians (12.8-12). Luke rather reminds the crowds that they must come to a decision for 'He who is not with me is against me, and he who does not gather with me scatters' (11.23). What is required of them is that they should 'hear the word of God and keep it' (11.28). This same need to be aware of the reality of the hour is put before them in the parable of the rich fool (12.13-21). Later in the same chapter, the multitudes are called hypocrites because they fail to acknowledge the seriousness of the hour. They are in dire need of repentance, for Jesus comes bringing the eschatological call of God (12.54-59). Only a few are to be saved and that means that great exertions are required. The onlookers will not make that exertion and so will fail to enter the eschatological banquet. Their claim to affinity with Jesus, to having followed alongside him, will be no good unless it issues in commitment and surrender (13.22-30).

So the crowds for Luke at this stage are not hostile even though there is a hostile element among them. Neither however are they committed. They remain open to Jesus, recognizing him and listening to him, but overall unwilling actually to decide for him. As the journey proceeds they fall into the background. They continue to follow him but will not make the act of commitment that his presence requires (14.25-36). They have to choose to become effective salt. If they will not, then their saltness is irremediably lost and they are fit only to be thrown away (14.35). Near Jericho, the crowds would have kept the blind beggar silent (18.35-43), but, when they see him healed, 'all the people gave praise to God'.

As Jerusalem is reached the crowd is removed from attention which is directed more to Jesus, the disciples and his opponents. The narrative is coming to the point of climax and of decision. Nothing is said of the response of the crowds at the entry. Attention then is focused rather on 'the whole multitude of the disciples' and on the response of the Pharisees in the crowd. The crowd is seemingly at this point neither responsive nor hostile, though they remain open to Jesus for he teaches the people daily in the temple (19.47) and it is they as in Matthew who keep him safe from the leaders 'for all the people hung on his words' (19.48; cf. 20.19, 26). As in Matthew the crowds are not yet decided for whom they will ultimately stand; they have not yet closed their minds to Jesus. Until the passion narrative begins, they are still open to him: 'And every day he was teaching in the temple but at night he went out and lodged on the mount called Olivet. And early in the morning all the people came to him in the temple to hear him' (21.37-38). They seem to be on his side (21.38). Luke's repeated assertion of this point which is made much less obviously and consistently by Matthew, is seen to contrast their overall attitude with that which they are going to assert so violently before Pilate. They do not appear again until they are suddenly included among those who are addressed by Pilate with his first declaration of Jesus' innocence (23.4). At this point they are every bit as responsible as are Matthew's crowd for the death of Jesus. In fact, in Luke their responsibility is greater for, unlike Mk 15.11 and Mt. 27.20, their enmity is not something stirred up by the Jewish leaders but is rather entered upon deliberately and assertively by themselves. It is a calculated act by the whole people (23.18). Their part in the execution is more positive for, whereas in Mt. 27.26 when Pilate 'delivered him to be crucified', it is the soldiers of the governor who take him over, Luke uses the strongest irony to have Jesus handed over to the Jews who are actually seen as crucifying him, 'Pilate released the man who had been thrown into prison for insurrection and murder, whom they asked for; but Jesus he delivered up to their will' (23.25). The Romans disappear from the scene and the ones who lead Jesus away and then crucify him are the Jewish people.

Nevertheless, alongside this accentuating of the Jewish part, Luke exhibits an outlook which sees it as something less than full-grown perversity. He pictures it as an inevitable unfolding of something greater. All are caught up in the activity of Satan who has gained a hold, not only over Judas but even over the disciples as a whole (22.3, 31-34). To those who come against him Jesus says 'This is your hour and the power of darkness' (22.53). All are pawns on the stage of the drama of God's eschatological battle with Satan. The human beings are in the grip of outside forces which make their part something which is ultimately beyond their control. The disciples are bidden to 'rise and pray that you may not enter into temptation' (22.46). Yet Jesus' previous warnings (22.31-34) and their own sleeping, even though it is in Luke 'for sorrow', make it clear that they will in fact enter into its depths. There is little they can do to resist its stranglehold; the patent absurdity of the two swords is enough to make the token demonstration that is required (22.38).

Again, all is determined by God, 'for the Son of man goes as it has been determined' (22.22). This emphasis upon the detailed fulfilment of Scripture is fundamental for Luke and is repeated at v. 37. In the speeches of Acts, though the whole Jewish people is indicted for the crucifixion (Acts 2.22; 3.14), guilt is mitigated by the fact that their part is itself gathered up into the plan of God and is seen as the fulfilment of Scripture: it all takes place according to the 'definite plan and foreknowledge of God'. Even their lack of understanding is actually caught up in, and so in a sense brought about by, the prophecies which it fulfils (Acts 13.27). In that speech their ignorance of the prophets is blameworthy and their rejection of Jesus has little by way of extenuating circumstances. But even then, they had to 'fulfil all that was written of him' (Acts 13.29)—they are not the masters of their fate. This is brought out even more clearly in the earlier Jerusalem speech where ignorance is put forward as an excuse for their acts (Acts 3.17). Complete culpability comes only after the resurrection when God demonstrates his choice of Jesus. By the time of the death of Stephen (Acts 7.59) ignorance which on the cross is forgiven (23.34) has degenerated into sin. But, at the time of the crucifixion, that point has not been reached and Jesus' plea for forgiveness as Luke records it stands in sharp contrast to Matthew's outlook as this is seen in the cold, calculating responsibility for the sin of Jesus' death which is acknowledged by his crowd (Mt. 27.25).

Luke's passion scene has about it an element of tragedy that is not found in Matthew's. As he is led away to be crucified, there nevertheless follows 'a great multitude of the people, and of women who bewailed and lamented him' (23.26-31). If the people are still alien, Jesus addresses the women, the pious representatives of Israel, as true daughters of Jerusalem, as those who represent a true understanding of Israel's inheritance. Israel is now divided. Her leaders are hostile, the true lament, and the people are ambivalent. 'The people stood by watching' (23.35). At the death of Jesus, it is the Gentile who responds. The multitudes are not able to share that response. Nevertheless, whereas in Matthew, those who passed by derided him (Mt. 27.39), in Luke, and in contrast to the rulers who scoff, 'the people stood by watching' (23.35), and, when all is over, they return home 'beating their breasts' (23.48). They have not actually rejected their Lord, perplexed and undecided though they may be. Jerusalem as a whole has not deserted her inheritance but awaits the proclamation. Israel has already become a divided people and as such she will remain in Acts.

But, of course, by the time Luke and Matthew wrote, Israel as a whole had rejected her Lord. Matthew 10 makes it clear that the mission to her has been largely unsuccessful and it is unlikely that any change of heart will occur before the parousia.[1] The book of Acts, for

1. Davies and Allison, *Matthew*, pp. 191-92.

all Luke's pointing out that some Jews do respond, announces the failure of the proclamation among Israel as a nation. For both, the Jews are an unbelieving majority, apart from the Christian community which is now distinct and driven out of the synagogue by Jewish hostility. Christians are alienated from them and an object of dislike to them.

How do Luke and Matthew respond to this situation? How do their narratives reflect their understanding of the significance of the Jewish refusal? How do they see the relation of the new to the old? Are Christians for them the new Israel or the renewed Israel? There is indeed a difference in these two understandings, for the former implies a rejection of the Jewish people and a takeover of their former privileged status by the Christian community, while the latter understanding leaves the door, if not open, then at least ajar so that Israel is not seen to be entirely cut off from the covenantal promises of God. Some indeed have seen our evangelists as going further from Israel than either of these categories suggests to think rather of the Christian community as non-Israel where a radical discontinuity is envisaged between the time of Israel and the time of the church which is consciously set out in contrast to the old.[1] This, however, remains very dubious for either Luke or Matthew. Luke, for all his emphasis upon the fact that the Law however interpreted no longer defines the Christian community, understands that community as the fulfilment of Old Testament expectations. Israel is renewed at Pentecost and the Gentile incorporation fulfils a pattern expressed in the prophets (Acts 15.16-18). Jesus is set out in terms of the Old Testament agents of God's activity and the presentation of the Spirit is controlled by Old Testament ideas. Likewise in Matthew, the Law has a continuing validity and Jesus is presented as the Old Testament messiah. The fulfilment quotations are not only culled from their settings to fit Jesus (Mt. 2.23), they actually control the picture of Jesus that is built up (Mt. 21.5). It is true that in Matthew there is less control by the Old Testament on the way the overall presentation of the Christian dispensation is described. Gaston, for instance, maintains that in the first Gospel 'the connection is completely and only Christological'.[2] This, however, seems to do less than justice to Matthew's understanding of

1. L. Gaston, 'The Messiah of Israel as Teacher of the Gentiles', *Int* 29 (1975), pp. 25-40.

2. Gaston, 'Messiah'.

the significance of the Law in the Christian community and to his understanding of the cross as the eschatological time of the extension of the mission to the Gentiles.

But if we are justified in excluding the understanding of the Christian community in terms of non-Israel in both Matthew and Luke, what is the understanding of each and how are they to be related? It seems that Matthew believes the church to be the New Israel, and that she is the replacement of the old to the old's exclusion. If that outlook is expressed decisively at 21.43, we have seen that the genealogy, Jerusalem's rejection of the infant Jesus, made all the more stark by the Magi's acknowledgment of him, and the baptism and temptation scenes all work to the exclusion of Israel when she remains unlinked to her Lord. The people's response at the trial before Pilate, and the cross itself suggest a self-exclusion from the sphere of God's community. The aeons change at the death and resurrection of Jesus and, though the exalted Lord's commission does not exclude them from his concern, ch. 10 shows that it will meet with but little response. Jesus takes over from Moses, the church from the people of Israel, henceforth Israel after the flesh is now 'the Jews' apart from the Israel of God (Mt. 28.15).[1]

Matthew's understanding is summed up in the way he presents the story of the centurion's servant (Mt. 8.5-13). The emphasis rests upon the incorporation of the Gentiles but adds, quite unnecessarily unless he wanted to draw attention to the point, that in contrast 'the sons of the kingdom will be thrown into outer darkness'. The rejection of the Jews here is total and unconditional and it parallels Matthew's exclusion saying in 21.43. Luke's version of the story (7.1-10) does not have the saying about inclusion and exclusion. Emphasis rests upon the faith of the centurion, 'I tell you not even in Israel have I found such faith'. His faith is certainly greater than Israel's but it is told to emphasize the Gentile's unusual and unexpected faith rather than, as in Matthew, to pinpoint Israel's failure. Luke's version has the healing take place in response to the request of Jewish elders. He is included in a healing because of his attitude to the Jewish people and their acceptance of him. Israel is not chided.

Luke does have Matthew's reference to inclusion and exclusion at 13.28-29 where however his version differs from Matthew's. Whereas

1. J.P. Meier, *The Vision of Matthew: Christ, Church and Morality in the First Gospel* (New York: Paulist Press, 1979).

in Matthew, the context shows it to be about Israel–Gentile contrasts, in Luke this is not so but it is concerned rather with the urgency of the hour and the need to respond. Membership of Israel cannot be assumed to lead into participation in the kingdom. Israel presumes upon her relationship, for the criterion for entry is not a share in old Israel but response to Jesus. Those who do not respond will be excluded. They will be denied a sharing of the kingdom with Abraham, Isaac and Jacob and all the prophets. Their surprise will be all the greater when they see the fathers of Israel joined not necessarily by themselves, but by men from north, south, east and west.

Egelkraut has argued that Luke has here intensified the hostility that is seen in Matthew's version of the saying. He maintains that it is 'much more radical than in the Matthaean parallel. The coming of the Gentiles is preceded by Israel's rejection. Israel's condemnation leads to the salvation of the Gentiles. Israel's salvation becomes theirs'.[1] This, however, is to go further than Luke himself. Luke does not say that the exclusion of the Jews is a necessary pre-condition for the inclusion of the Gentiles; he does not even say that they are taking the place of the Jews. It is rather Matthew who has the alternative, Jews or Gentiles, Israel after the flesh or new Israel. In Luke, on the other hand, the contrast is rather between the true in Israel, represented by Abraham and Israel's leaders, and the false Israel who at the climax of her history refuses Jesus. When the kingdom comes, the true will be included and the false will not because they refused Jesus and so refused to enter into their historical fulfilment. It will then be no good claiming a natural identity with him, for that undoubted benefit of the Jewish people as a whole will have been cancelled out by their perversity. The disobedient in Israel will be separated from their own people, and the reality of that exclusion will be made all the more poignant by the inclusion of others whose natural state had not made them the obvious recipients of that eschatological inheritance. Luke here, unlike Matthew, does not see a Gentile takeover. His is rather a challenge to Israel. It is not a transfer-situation, whereas Matthew's is. Luke's God remains open to Israel even though those in Israel who refuse Jesus are themselves refused.

1. H.L. Egelkraut, *Jesus' Mission to Jerusalem: A Redaction Critical Study of the Travel Narrative in the Gospel of Luke, Lk. 9.51–19.48* (Europäische Hochschülschriften, Reihe 23, Theologie 80; Frankfurt: Peter Lang; Bern: Herbert Lang, 1976).

Luke's understanding of the attitude of God to Israel in the light of the coming of Jesus is set out in his account of the rejection at Nazareth which for him is, as is usually acknowledged, given programmatic significance (4.16-30). Just what that significance is, however, is more problematical. Overall, it presents two possible interpretations, namely, that it is to be understood either as a declaration of God's rejection of Israel in the appearing of Jesus or as an expression of Luke's attempt to justify the situation brought about by Jewish rejection of him. Decision between these two possibilities has to be made in the light of which it it is felt best accounts for a narrative which is not easily unpacked.[1] Jeremias, it is true, has offered a third possible interpretation which mellows the harshness of the first of our possibilities without moving over into the more positive assertions of our second. For him, the reaction of the audience to Jesus is presented as hostile from the outset. Verse 22, so far from expressing admiration of Jesus and acknowledgment of his authority witnesses to the hearers' refusal of him and to their rejection of his message. The offence in the proclamation was Jesus' refusal to complete the sentence of Isa. 61.2 which speaks of the 'day of vengeance of our God'. Jesus, by omitting this, was placing himself above the prophetic message and so was to be seen as refashioning the expectations of what God's coming would entail. Jeremias therefore has Luke proclaim a rejection of the Jews by Jesus in response to their rejection of him. Jesus does not set out to announce a transfer of status from Jews to Gentiles, but, when the Jews rejected his widening of the sphere of God's concern, his response is a rejection of them and an announcement of a turning to the Gentiles.[2]

Such an outlook, though it makes Jesus' response in vv. 23-27 more easily understood and certainly more acceptable as a programmatic utterance, nevertheless appears to do less than justice to Luke's

1. See, for instance, discussion in Brawley, *Luke–Acts and the Jews*, pp. 6-27; B. Chilton, 'Announcement in Nazara: An Analysis of Luke 4.16-30', in R.T. France and D. Wenham (eds.), *Gospel Perspectives*, II (Sheffield: JSOT Press, 1981), pp. 147-72; J.A. Sanders, 'From Isaiah 61 to Luke 4' in J. Neusner (ed.), *Christianity, Judaism and other Greco–Roman Cults*, I (Leiden: Brill, 1975), pp. 144-55; Sanders, *Jews*, pp. 164-68; R.C. Tannehill, 'The Mission of Jesus According to Luke 4.16-30, in J. Eltester (ed.), *Jesus in Nazareth* (BZNW, 40; Berlin: de Gruyter, 1972), pp. 51-75.

2. J. Jeremias, *Jesus' Promise to the Nations* (trans. S.H. Hooke; SBT, 24, London: SCM Press, 1958), pp. 44-45.

thought. It is not likely that Luke meant the audience's response to Jesus in v. 22 to be understood as an unfavourable one. His use of μαρτυρέω in Acts 10.22, 43; 22.12 expresses a favourable rather than an unfavourable response and this makes it unlikely that the dative here is one of disadvantage. Again, though Luke's use of θαυμάζω at Lk. 20.26 can contain within itself an element of hostility, this is not its primary emphasis, and elsewhere at 2.18, 33; 9.43 it is has not any ambiguity but expresses wholly positive reaction.[1]

The second part of Luke's sermon is in response, not to hostility, but to approval. That approval, however, is inadequate. Though 'is not this Joseph's son?' is meant approvingly, it is of course a totally unsatisfactory evaluation of Jesus. The reply contains within itself the seeds of conflict brought about by a lack of openness on their part and a claim to authority on his. Nevertheless, it is Jesus himself who takes the initiative and thus turns a favourable response and one which could at least have been built upon into one which was inevitably hostile and furious. What does Luke see him as doing?

J.T. Sanders interprets Luke's concern as exclusivistic. It was 'to show how God's will was carried out in the Jewish rejection of salvation and the consequent Gentile mission'.[2] With the appearing of Jesus, salvation was now to go to the Gentiles and not to the Jews. The references to Elijah and Elisha showed that this was begun even in the prophets; Jesus was bringing a pattern to a head. He was marking the shift in aeons. Now, what was anticipated and proclaimed in the prophets is being realized in the person of Jesus. His coming seals the rejection which continuing Jewish hostility to the word of God has produced. Luke then envisages the appearing of Jesus to bring about the divine rejection of Israel and the transfer of the covenant to the Gentiles.

Such an interpretation does justice to the Jewish change of mood

1. Bertram, *TDNT* 3, pp. 37-40 notes that θαυμάξω in Luke refers to something that is not yet developed as a proper belief. This, of course, is true but it expresses nevertheless a positive, even if as here a partial reaction rather than a hostile one. Nolland, *Luke*, p. 199, though saying that the force of 'Isn't this Joseph's son' cannot be clearly determined, nevertheless believes that it expresses an objection to Jesus claims. Taken with θαυμάξω, however, it would seem that it expresses a partial but inadequate response.

2. *Jews*, p. 168.

from wondering, if hesitant, approval to open unambiguous hostility. It does justice to Jesus' initiative and to his challenging attitude, to his use of the Elijah/Elisha illustrations of seeming exclusiveness, to the active even if ultimately ineffective fury of the people, and to Jesus' withdrawal from them. Nevertheless, it fails to account for a number of points in the episode.

The harshness of the interpretation seems to run counter to the tone of the Isaiah quotation which is the episode's controlling factor and which is part of an exultant proclamation of the coming of God to his people to bring freedom, release and restoration. The Scripture used by Jesus maintains the re-establishment of a relationship. Luke omits the reference to judgment and rejection for it is not even a call to repentance. The emphasis rather is upon the gracious approach of God, upon the divine initiative and, however much that must include a response and even a re-examination of the people's presuppositions, the whole point is contained in the exuberant announcement of God's freeing activity. As a proclamation of rejection it is inconceivable, for such a nuance would belie and negate that upon which it is based. Its message is not to be found in exclusiveness.

Undoubtedly, the hardest part of the speech to unravel is its references to Elijah and Elisha, and it is upon these that the negative evaluations of Israel's place must be based. Here seems to be the justification for an exclusivist interpretation of the speech. The prophets did not answer Israel's needs and went instead to Gentiles, and Jesus will do the same. But are Elijah and Elisha to be understood as rejecting Israel? Elijah it is true fought against Israel as she then was, but the fight was to recall her to God; it was to restore her covenantal commitment, to make her once more responsive to God. That call meant a reshaping of her as the remnant that remained true had to find expression in a new monarchy and a reshaped people. But Elijah was essentially the restorer of Israel and it was as such that the expectations of his reappearing pictured him. 'He will turn the hearts of the fathers to their children, and the hearts of children to their fathers' (Mal. 4.6). 'Elijah does come first to restore all things' (Mk 9.12). Luke himself bears witness to this understanding when the angelic visit to Zechariah says of John,

> And he will turn many of the sons of Israel to the Lord their God. And he will go before him in the spirit and power of Elijah to turn the hearts of the

> fathers to the children, and the disobedient to the wisdom of the just, to make ready for the Lord a people prepared (1.16-17).

Luke did not see Elijah as turning his back upon Israel in order to undertake concern for the Gentiles. He was rather rejected by Israel as she then was. Israel did not respond to him, and at home his work could have been accounted a failure. His ministry to Gentiles was not entered into because he had rejected Israel but because, as part of his outgoing concern, it was all that was really open to him. The reference points to the wonder of Israel's rejection of Jesus, to the marvel of her lack of response rather than to God's rejection of her. Jesus' ministry actually follows the paths of those of Elijah and Elisha who were nevertheless continuing prophets to Israel. They had a continuing concern for her; and so it was with Jesus. Lack of success at home and a concern with Gentiles did not disqualify him as a prophet of Israel and it did not entail a turning away from her.[1]

The conclusion of the episode is not a rejection of Israel as it must be seen to be if Sanders' interpretation of the story is to be accepted. Jesus is rejected by his people; they set out to destroy him; he however turns upon them to stop their intention from being realized and so to pass through them to go on his way. As Fitzmyer remarks, 'This is the first occurrence of the significant verb πορεύεσθαι in the Gospel proper'.[2] It is found at highly significant points in Luke's writings to express a movement forward in the accomplishment of Jesus' mission to be achieved in the events culminating at Jerusalem. It occurs at the powerful verse which introduces the journey to Jerusalem (9.51), characterizes his determined movement towards his goal (9.57), is found in Jesus' own summary of the divine plan (13.33), keeps the movement towards Jerusalem to the fore (17.11), and points to the fulfilment of the divine will (22.22). At the conclusion of the Nazareth episode it bears witness, not to Jesus' rejection of his people, but to the fact that the rejection of him by them can neither thwart nor deny the divine purpose which is to achieve that lordship which is to be bestowed upon him when he will be established as Israel's Christ. Jewish rejection can neither thwart nor deny that fact. This, rather than the rejection of the Jews by Jesus, marks the conclusion of the episode as Luke tells it.

1. Brawley, *Jews*, p. 26, 'Elijah and Elisha function to show how Jesus stands in line with other prophets who failed to find acceptance among their own people'.

2. *Luke*, p. 539.

Luke's telling of the story does not find its significance in Jesus' rejection of the Jews but in their rejection of him. It is that which the climax emphasizes but it does so in such a way as to maintain that that rejection neither stops nor disproves Jesus' messiahship which the baptism has announced, the overcoming of temptation established, and which Jesus' ministry of compassion, as proclaimed in the Isaiah programme, will effect. Luke's purpose in the Nazareth story as a whole is to show that Jewish rejection does not mean that all this is brought to nothing. He will account for the rejection by saying that it is virtually inevitable and that it is in keeping with earlier prophetic careers.

Jesus proclaims God's action in himself in a wide-ranging ministry of release, of fulfilment of needs, and of overthrow of oppressing powers. His hearers witness to him and to the gracious announcement which he makes. It is a response of acceptance and expectation. They say, 'Is not this Joseph's son?'. Of itself, this is not meant by Luke as a critical response. They are not offended by his beginnings for the response remains one of pride in his local origins. Nevertheless, it does contain within itself the makings of conflict for, in claiming Jesus for themselves, they are both confining him within the terms of their own expectations and are making claims upon him. It is this that Jesus takes up with his use of the proverb, 'Physician heal thyself'. Jesus' work at Capernaum is known by them. They rejoice in it, provided that they themselves become at least equal sharers in his bounty. They expect this and assume their place in the salvation that he offers.

Jesus however knows that it is not as simple as that. 'No prophet is acceptable in his own country'. Why? Their earlier comment gives the answer. 'Is not this Joseph's son?' points to familiarity, to presumption. They are making Jesus conform to their expectations. And the truth is that he does not, that indeed he cannot. His gift of freedom needs a change of heart. The salvation he brings demands a reassessment of their understanding, of their presuming upon their covenantal place with God and their certainty of inclusion. Their preconceived ideas will allow neither for that newness for themselves nor for the openness to others that Jesus brings and without which he can do nothing. 'No prophet is acceptable in his own country' is Luke's comment upon the tragedy arising out of Jewish rejection of that which was really theirs but which their natural ties with him stopped them from finding.

That according to Luke was why the Jews failed to respond to Jesus. They would not accept the radicality that he and his message contained. They would not be judged by him. Lk. 4.25-27 become a comment on the situation. Jesus' failure with his people, his lack of success with them, the contrast emphasized by the relative successes among the Gentiles, might be seen as a disqualification for the claims that he made for himself and that others made on his behalf. Luke sets out to show that this is not so. Elijah had little success among his own people. Elisha healed Gentiles to the seeming neglect of Jews. Lack of visible success among their own people and a concern with outsiders did not disqualify them as prophets to and of Israel; concern with Gentiles did not take the place of ultimate concern with Jews. Neither the inclusion of the Gentiles nor Jesus' denial by Israel could deny Jesus' claim upon Israel. He stood before her to widen her horizons and to cause her to rethink her relationship with God. But Nazareth could not enter upon such a rethink. Challenge was seen as condemnation so that an inclusive proclamation could not be tolerated. His kinsfolk could only vent their wrath upon him, but that could neither deny his message nor stop his entry upon his universal lordship. Nor indeed, as the Elijah and Elisha references suggest, could it mean that his concern with Israel was necessarily at an end.

Luke's narrative becomes an explanation of Jewish rejection of Jesus which it sees, not as the result of divine rejection of her, not even as issuing in that, but as the inevitable if tragic failure brought about by her presuming upon her relationship with God and her unwillingness to move forward into God's new age. If this is how it accounts for the Jewish rejection of Jesus, it justifies the relative failure of Jesus and of Christianity with Israel by seeing it as in keeping with earlier relationships of the prophets with their own people. In this way, Luke's story of the Nazareth rejection is distinctive, not only in its context, but also in its outlook from those of Mark and Matthew. Mark records Jesus' failure with his own people—'And he could do no mighty works there'—without attempting to justify or explain it. 'And he marvelled because of their unbelief' (Mk 6.1-6). It arises out of their unwillingness to accept one of their own number, but no attempt is made to understand this. 'They are offended at him'. The event leaves Jesus perplexed but it does not occasion a rejection of them by him. Matthew's version however envisages just that. The hostility of the crowd is accentuated—'Where did this man get all this?'—and issues in a rejection of them by Jesus—'And he did no mighty works there because of their unbelief' (Mt. 13.53-58). Matthew and Mark have distinctive approaches to the episode as a comment upon the relationship of Jesus and so of Christianity to the people of Israel. Mark's is an attitude of wonder at the rejection. Matthew does not attempt to explain that wonder but rather emphasizes Jewish perversity which issues in their rejection by Jesus. Luke in this is closer to Mark than he is to Matthew. Jewish perversity is, though blameworthy, understandable, and Jesus himself does not apportion blame. Luke explains the refusal and, being able to explain it, is able to go beyond Mark's amazement without resolving it in Matthew's hostility.[1]

Luke's Nazareth episode, therefore, becomes not a rejection of the Jewish people by God through Jesus, but rather an attempt to understand and to counter the problems raised by the Jewish rejection of him. Their refusal of him does not negate the claims made by his followers on his behalf for it follows a scriptural pattern and is compensated for by the inclusion of the Gentiles which it actually seems to further. The fact of the rejection of Jesus by the Jews remains a cause of wonder, but it has about it an inevitability born of Jewish presumption, of their feeling of having arrived, of having virtually some claim upon God, and it is this which is for Luke his major complaint against the people of Israel as a whole.

Jesus leaves Nazareth to go on his predestined way which will lead him to Jerusalem as the determined place of his death and exaltation. Distinctive to Luke is the long travel narrative (9.51–19.48), and it is in this section of his Gospel where Luke's alleged hostility to the Jews is usually said to be focused. So Egelkraut, in a comprehensive study of this section, has seen both its form and its contents determined by the motive of the rejection of the Jewish people. Jesus sets out in 9.51 on a journey which announces the judgment of Israel, her exclusion from the covenant, and the transfer of the status that had been hers to the Gentiles.

> In the travel narrative, Luke wants to write an account of how Israel rejected the kingdom which was offered to it, how it came that judgement befell it, and how it came that its place in God's economy was taken by

1. R.H. Gundry, *Matthew: A Commentary on his Literary and Theological Art* (Grand Rapids: Eerdmans, 1982), pp. 282-84.

others. He writes from a point when God's special dealings with Israel are over.[1]

Such an understanding of the travel narrative, however, encounters an immediate and recurring difficulty—there is no point in Luke–Acts where Luke obviously makes this transfer clear, for there is no point in the two volumes as a whole where the door is said to have been shut against Israel. The best case for such a point can be made on behalf of Paul's response to the Jews at Rome, but we have nevertheless already seen that that episode does not have the climactic status that such an interpretation has to give it. It just will not bear that weight. Elsewhere, in the two volume work, there is not any one point which announces such a change of aeons. Egelkraut himself has some ambiguity here. The travel narrative is announced as a journey of hostile intent. There is no intensification of hostility and 'when (Jesus) finally reaches Jerusalem it is almost like an anti-climax'. Yet he maintains that Luke 'wants to show how Jesus called Israel to repentance'. So Egelkraut struggles to allow for a final contest in Jerusalem, even though his earlier statements have left little room for either appeal or response. 'All the conflict and hostility should not hide the fact that this is supposed to be the hour of grace for Israel, the hour of its peace 19.14 and salvation 19.9'. But 'Jerusalem's doom and that of Israel both as a nation and as the people of God are sealed with Jesus' entry into Jerusalem'. Nevertheless, 'The proclamation of the gospel in Acts to the Jews of Jerusalem is, notwithstanding, a bona fide appeal to each individual to "save yourselves from this crooked generation"'.[2]

There is some confusion in Egelkraut's thesis. His difficulties are really two, namely, a difficulty in focusing the point of exclusion which he believes is fundamentally proclaimed throughout the narrative, and that in making real allowance for the appeal and the grace that he allows is still to be found in it. And the fact is that the travel narrative as a whole and the Lukan account of the events in Jerusalem are not so uniformly and unconditionally hostile as Egelkraut asserts. Jesus comes to claim his own, to make his definitive appeal to the people. That claim is rejected. It issues in a condemnation of those who reject, but not in a rejection of the people as a whole. However stern the warnings, however harsh the judgment on those who should

1. Egelkraut, *Mission*, pp. 195-96.
2. *Mission*, pp. 206-207, 194, 133.

have known better, Israel as a whole is not rejected for Luke tells of those within Israel who do accept,[1] he portrays Jesus' response as one of grief rather than outright hostility, and he keeps the way open for a continuing appeal to the people.

Luke introduces the travel narrative with a sombre statement of Jesus' determination to go to Jerusalem (9.51). It is, however, primarily a declaration of the testing of Jesus rather than one of a judgmental sifting of Jerusalem.[2] Though it bears some affinity to prophetic oracles of doom (Jer. 21.10; Ezek. 6.2; 21.7) these do not control Luke's use which is related rather to the Suffering Servant passage of Isa. 50.7. The emphasis rests upon Jesus' determined movement toward his sufferings in Jerusalem which will enable his exaltation in his ascension to heaven.[3] Such an emphasis has already been given to the Jerusalem reference by the conversation with Moses and Elijah at the transfiguration (9.30-31). The determination of Jesus, the hardening of his countenance, is to be accounted for by his resolve to enter upon the way of suffering...rather than in any movement against Jerusalem. The object of τὸ πρόσωπον ἐστήρισεν is an undertaking of a journey, the following of a determined way for himself. It focuses upon, not a message that he will proclaim or enact, but upon his own path of suffering. πορεύομαι, εἰς in Luke does not have a connotation of hostility but simply one of fulfilling a predetermined path (4.37, 42). This is particularly noticeable in 9.56 where Jesus moves to another Samaritan village when he has already received rejection from a similar one and where he has deliberately forbidden a hostile response to such a rejection. The whole movement of this introductory verse is controlled by its contribution to the accomplishment of Jesus' being received up, by his progression to his exaltation. It is true that this is to be enabled by means of rejection and crucifixion but these are caught up in the ascension which is the ultimate goal and towards which the whole journey points. The focus

1. Egelkraut, *Mission*, p. 206 emphasizes that the parable of the fig tree is directed against all Israel. But 13.1-5, though emphasizing the urgency of the hour does not suggest that all will not respond.

2. Danker, *New Age*, p. 208; Evans, *Luke*, p. 436. *Contra* Maddox, *Purpose*, p. 47; Egelkraut, *Mission*, pp. 79-81.

3. 9.51 includes suffering, death and resurrection which find their climax in the ascension. M.C. Parsons, *The Departure of Jesus in Luke–Acts: The Ascension Narratives in Context* (JSNTSup, 21; Sheffield: JSOT Press, 1987), pp. 128-32.

is upon Jesus rather than upon Jerusalem as such, and the framework of the narrative is controlled by this end.

Two verses later, Luke says that the Samaritans refused Jesus 'because his face was set toward Jerusalem' (9.53). Jerusalem is thereby presented as the object of his concern rather than of his hostility for it remains unlikely that Samaritans could have been represented as being against his intention if that had been a hostile one. He goes to Jerusalem rather to bring Jewish history to its fulfilment which is to entail nevertheless the fact that he is to be rejected by the ones he comes to redeem. J.T. Sanders has contrasted Jesus' refusal of his own people at Nazareth.[1] This however is to introduce a false contrast for Jesus turns against neither the Samaritan village nor Nazareth but rather moves on from both to go forward to his destiny at Jerusalem.

Jesus' journey meets with a divided response. Near its beginning occurs the mission of the seventy which, though it may in part anticipate the post-ascension Gentile mission,[2] is more likely to be concerned with the mission to the Jews which in Matthew's Gospel is contained in Jesus' address to the twelve (Mt. 10.1-42). Luke however does not see the twelve as a continuing body but as a group which gives definition and meaning to the Christian community as renewed Israel. They themselves stand as witnesses to the nature of the new community rather than, as in Matthew, as the instigators of the universal mission. Their place is Jerusalem from which they set out periodically to link the mission to her and to which they return. The Lukan form of the commission to them (23.48-49; Acts 1.8) is other than Matthew's missionary commission (Mt. 28.19-20). Wherever the mission takes place they act as witnesses to the church of the significance of what has occurred.[3] As Israel of old witnessed to the nature of Jahweh by receiving his prophecies and watching them enacted, so the twelve witness to the nature of God's action in Jesus by receiving his understanding of the events that have occurred around him as the fulfilment of all that the Old Testament expected (Isa. 43.10, 12; 44.8). So for Luke the seventy represent the continuing mission to

1. *Jews*, pp. 143-44, 'To put the matter as bluntly and plainly as possible, no charge is made against the Samaritans who reject Jesus'. But, on our understanding, no charge is made against Nazareth either.

2. Talbert, *Reading Luke*, pp. 116-17.

3. Tannehill, *Acts*, p. 141.

Israel.[1] That mission meets a divided response. Sanders has emphasized the woe of Jesus addressed to Chorazin and Bethsaida which he sees as 'proving the principle set out in the Nazareth synagogue sermon that God's salvation was always intended for Gentiles and not for Jews',[2] but he can make this the point of the episode only by his favourite device of separating out the speech from the narrative. Such a plainly illegitimate way of treating Luke's work, however, points only to the wrongness of the conclusion. Luke is harsh upon the refusing Jews. Of that there can be no doubt. Those who reject will at the parousia receive condemnation (10.14; 13.27-28; 19.27). But that is a different matter from rejecting the Jewish people in toto or from saying that salvation has been removed from them. Egelkraut, again in order to stress failure among the Jews, understands Jesus' response to the seventy as a checking of their enthusiasm and an emphasis instead upon Israel's failure to respond.[3] But Jesus' vision of Satan's fall points rather to the reality of the establishment of God's heavenly rule by means of the overthrow of demons in the mission, and his prayer of rejoicing acknowledges a response on the part of some. The mission it is true is not wholly successful, but it is not a total failure and, as it witnesses to a divided response, it reminds the reader that all is not wholly dark in Israel. Jesus can call the disciples blessed for they are witnesses of God's eschatological action in her (10.23-24).

Jesus' progress causes a division within Israel. There is in fact a concentration of passages which speak of the harsh treatment of those who reject, for Jesus' coming causes a crisis which results in a judgment of those who refuse to respond to it. It is now the hour of visitation (19.44) and, though this points back to the song of Zechariah with its assertion that in Jesus God 'has visited and redeemed his people' (1.68), the failure of the vast majority to respond means that the positive redemption has been over-shadowed by the judgment which is the other side of the single divine movement. Tannehill, indeed, contrasts these two references to say that 'the great expectations aroused at the beginning contribute to the tragic effect of this turn in the plot, for we feel the loss more keenly in contrast to the great hopes'.[4] This change

1. Evans, *Luke*, pp. 444-45.
2. *Jews*, p. 181.
3. *Mission*, pp. 142-53.
4. Tannehill, 'Israel in Luke–Acts: A Tragic Story', *JBL* 104 (1985), pp. 69-85.

of expectations in the light of the reality of the Jewish rejection of Jesus can only be accounted for by expressing the wickedness of the generation which rejected him. They should have been expected to acknowledge him for, in Luke in particular, he comes in fulfilment of Old Testament expectations and as the Lord who is one with the pattern of her history. He was no unexpected messiah and therefore the rejection of him must be seen as wholly perverse.[1] Punishment must come upon this evil generation (11.29-32, 50-55; 13.22-30; 14.24). Nevertheless, Luke never regards the perversity as completely irredeemable. They are no better than those they would count as wicked. 'Unless you repent you will all likewise perish' (13.5). But the dice is not yet finally cast. Whereas Mark and Matthew have the cursing of the fig tree, Luke has a parable of delay, of constraint, of hope retained. There is still a chance (13.1-9) even though it is the last hour.[2]

Because Luke of course knows that Jerusalem has fallen and that the vast majority of Israel has remained unresponsive to the Christian proclamation, his Gospel contains strong references to the destruction of Jerusalem which he sees as arising out of the Jewish rejection of Jesus. The result of her perfidy has issued in an overwhelming disaster which, as Tannehill points out, is seen to embrace all the people.[3] The tree has now been cut down. Yet, two things in Luke are distinctive here and make for a softening of the divine attitude to Israel. He emphasizes the Lord's witness to the coming event as a tragedy born out of the inevitability of Jewish perversity, and he distances the divine activity from the actual events of AD 70. These stop him from presenting these events as the outcome of the divine rejection of Israel.

In a scene unique to him (19.41-44) Luke has Jesus weep over Jerusalem as he enters the city to anticipate her rejection of him and his way of peace and to see its result in her choosing a way that will

1. L. Grollenberg, *Unexpected Messiah* (London: SCM Press, 1987).

2. Sanders (*Jews*, p. 190) notes that it is not clear to what the postponement refers and thinks that it is probably to the end of Acts. Yet as we have seen, the end of Acts does not mark the end of the possibility of repentance. It cannot be the fall of Jerusalem because the sights of this verse are on a wider area. The emphasis may therefore rest upon the delay representing for Luke's contemporaries the urgency of the present. The 'all' expresses an urgent warning rather than an actually realised event.

3. Tannehill, *Acts*, pp. 54-55.

lead to destruction. As Tannehill emphasizes, 'Jesus' mood while viewing the city is one of tragic pathos, not of vengeful anger'.[1] Her destruction arises out of the inevitability of her rejection of his way of openness to follow one of self-determination born out of presumption caused by her self-confidence in her divine choice. This, as of old, will cause her to put confidence in her own ability to survive in her own reading of her place in God's covenant rather than in a trust and a response to him. There is an inevitability about the nemesis that will ensue (19.41-44).

It would of course be wrong to make Luke too modern and to see him as differentiating between what God wills and what he allows. His God was no remote spectator of events; he is involved in Pilate's massacre and in the fall of a tower (13.1-5). Yet there is a distancing of his involvement. His is something less than a direct activity. Natural happenings are caught up in his workings, but Luke does not say that he directly brings everything about. In the Nazareth episode, the Jewish rejection of Jesus is caught up in the divine overall control, but it is explained as arising out of their perversity in such a way as to avoid making God responsible for that rejection. The same balance is seen in Luke's attempt to understand the Jewish part in the crucifixion of Jesus. They are guilty and they are blameworthy yet they are caught up in something greater as they contribute to the accomplishing of the divine purpose and to the fulfilling of the expectations of Scripture (Acts 2.23; 3.17-18). There is therefore still a plea for forgiveness and a putting forward of extenuating circumstances.

In keeping with this, Luke distances God's direct activity in the circumstances surrounding the fall of Jerusalem. Another of his peculiar stories, that of Jesus and the lamenting women of Jerusalem (23.26-31) may indeed be 'a prophetic judgment oracle in form',[2] but it points to the actions of men rather than to those of God. Though the proverbial saying—'If they do this when the wood is green, what will happen when it is dry?'—is sometimes referred to as God's action, this is unlikely.[3] Luke does not see God's direct initiative in the crucifixion of Jesus to view it in itself as a divine requirement, or as something which in itself satisfies some divine necessity. He, of the

1. *Luke*, p. 160.

2. J.H. Neyrey, 'Address to the Women of Jerusalem', *NTS* 29 (1983), pp. 74-86.

3. J. Schneider, *TDNT*, V, p. 38.

New Testament writers as a whole is furthest from any understanding of the cross in sacrificial, substitutionary or penal terms. For him, the death is not a divine requirement but a necessary means to a universal exaltation. It may not be for him the unhappy accident that is sometimes proposed for his evaluation of it, but it has no value for him in itself for it is never in Luke separated out to become the focal point of God's saving plan. Jesus' saying to the women therefore is actually critical both of those who brought about his own crucifixion and of those who will cause the sufferings to Jerusalem. It points to his undeserved suffering and to the enormity of the sufferings which will engulf both innocent and guilty in Jerusalem. Again the element of tragedy is present and it is of such a kind as to make it inevitable that God's immediacy is distanced as the cause of both events. Human beings are those who are being criticized.[1]

The place where Luke seems to bring the fall of Jerusalem most fully within the orbit of God's activity is in the eschatological discourse at 21.22. The destruction of the city by foreign armies is to take place in the 'days of vengeance, to fulfil all that is written' (cf. 1 Kgs 9.9: The Lord has brought all this evil upon them'). The idea of fulfilment seems to put it firmly within the divine plan so that, as Marshall expresses it, 'Prophetic language increases the idea of divine judgment'.[2] Yet even here there are indications that Luke is again distancing God's direct hand in the event. In the first place, he has removed it from the end-time and, while this is primarily because he is looking back on the event in history, it nevertheless has the result of weakening the emphasis upon God's direct intention in the event. He has nothing like Mk 13.20/Mt. 24.22 which speaks of the direct overwhelming control of God. While the omission of such an idea, if he knew of it, is sometimes accounted for on the grounds of his wanting to point to the drastic, extended judgment of God which made him avoid any suggestion of God's restraining hand,[3] it is unlikely that

1. It may have a wider dimension to include all, human and superhuman figures, who together make this time that of the 'power of darkness'. As we have seen, Luke portrays the cross against the backcloth of a cosmic order to point to the totality of the power of evil which, unleashed here, is also to be seen in the fall of Jerusalem and the disasters surrounding this. Luke still sees the power of Satan as active even after the ascension, though that event has guaranteed his ultimate downfall.

2. Marshall, *Luke*, p. 773.

3. Fitzmyer, *Luke*, p. 1347.

Luke would have accentuated God's destruction of Jerusalem without calling out some mark of tragedy and pity (13.34; 19.41; 23.28). It seems rather that it finds no place in Luke's account of the destruction of Jerusalem because it implies a greater, more immediate and eschatological hand of God in the event than he wishes to express.

In the second place, Luke links his account of the fall of Jerusalem to the persecutions which will befall the disciples, and, by his use of 'before all this' in 21.12 separates both the persecution and the horrors of Jerusalem from the events of the end-time in a way that Mark and Matthew do not. Mt. 24.14, 15, and 29 take up both the persecution and the fall into the direct orbit of the end as part of the eschatological timetable decreed and effected by God. Luke, however, does not. Lk. 21.25 picks up vv. 10 and 11 and, by including vv. 12-24 as not unrelated but nevertheless not linked events to the End, sees them as part of preliminary history where God's reign is hidden and where his effective power over the earth is limited. Luke more than the other Gospels sees this world as an effective battleground between God and Satan who will not be finally destroyed until the parousia (Acts 2.35).

In the third place, the fall of Jerusalem marks for Luke a part of the 'times of the Gentiles' (21.24). These times will not be completed until the parousia. I shall argue later that fulfilment of these times is to witness a resurgence of Jerusalem,[1] that her destruction does not have the last word, but that it is part of that period which the parousia will bring to an end with the revival of Israel and the restoration of Jerusalem. There is something provisional about Jerusalem's destruction.

Tannehill has pointed out that the judgment falls upon the city as a whole, upon leaders and people, upon both the guilty and the innocent.[2] The early speeches in Acts lay the blame for the death of Jesus equally upon all as they indict Jerusalem as a whole (Acts 2.23; 3.13; 13.27). Acts 2.40 exhorts the people of Jerusalem to 'save yourselves from this crooked generation'. Many however do respond. The future lies with them and James can later tell Paul of many thousands of believers in Jerusalem (21.21). It is not suggested that Jerusalem's rejection of Paul brought that situation to an end. The destruction of Jerusalem therefore embraces the innocent as well as the guilty; it will

1. See below, pp. 240-43; cf. 106-107.
2. *Acts*, pp. 54.55

include the descendants of the weeping women as well as of the jeering leaders. It would be hard for Luke to see the hand of God fully in control of that event, because for him by the end of Acts there is in Jerusalem a well-established Christian community which focuses and controls the universal community centred upon it and which remains basically at one in outlook with the continuing adherents of Judaism. This for Luke again compounds the tragedy of Jerusalem.

Luke then does not see God as having rejected Israel and he does not envisage a takeover of Israel's position by others. He is not in fact anti-Semitic. He is indeed harsh with those who reject Jesus, and it is hard to see how he could be otherwise for his whole theological understanding of Jesus' place in the history of Israel and of God's dealings with her make him emphasize that Jesus is the logical outcome of that history and the fulfilment of prophetic expectations. His Jesus is no unexpected messiah. Those who reject him therefore have no real excuse. Yet, Luke continues to make excuses. On the cross Jesus cries, 'Father forgive them for they know not what they do' (23.34). In the Pentecost speech, though there is a strong need for repentance, they are described as being in the grip of something outside themselves, for all happened 'according to the plan and foreknowledge of God' (Acts 2.23). In the temple, their ignorance is said to have contributed to God's purposes (Acts 3.17-18). At Antioch, their ignorance of both Jesus and the prophecies are blameworthy, yet again it is said to have enabled the fulfilling of those prophecies (Acts 13.27). Their refusal of the Christian proclamation of the resurrection is more blameworthy for Stephen categorizes it as a sin (Acts 7.60). This though is still in accordance with prophecy and at Rome it is said to be in accordance with their attitude throughout their history (Acts 28.26-27). It does not necessarily signal the end of God's dealings with them. It is therefore significant that Luke has a different understanding of the sin against the Holy Spirit (12.8-12) from that found in Mk 3.22-27 and Mt. 12.24-29. In those Gospels the charge is made in connection with the Beelzebul episode so that in Mark it becomes a sin of denying Jesus' empowerment by the Spirit, and in Matthew one of speaking against the Christian proclamation. Luke, however, does not have the saying in this context but in connection with Jesus' comments upon the witness of the disciples. The sin against the Holy Spirit becomes one therefore of apostasy.

Luke's parable of the pounds (19.11-27) is frequently understood as an expression of his hostile attitude to the Jewish people.[1] When it is, anti-Judaism is usually seen to be focused at two points, namely the Lukan introduction (v. 11) and the allegorical element within the larger parable (vv. 14, 27). As more generally understood, the introduction is seen as a Lukan attempt to counter disappointments brought about by the non-arrival of the parousia, either by moving attention away from its apocalyptic framework or by pointing out that Jesus himself allowed for a delay before its coming.[2] Jesus is thus seen as being used to warn Luke's contemporaries not to be deflected from the pursuit of Christian discipleship either by misplaced enthusiasms or by misguided disappointments.

Those on the other hand who see Luke's introductory verse as an expression of Luke's belief that the kingdom is no longer open to the Jewish people as a whole point rather to the parable's reinterpretation, not of the timing of the appearing of the kingdom, but of the kingdom's nature and of the personages of its recipients. Luke has the Lord address the disciples who, in spite of his earlier teaching on the way to Jerusalem, still expect the kingdom to be one that is centred on Jerusalem and established over Israel. Luke's readers have become, as it were, stuck with the understanding of the kingdom as it was expressed for instance in Gabriel's proclamation at the annunciation (1.32-33), and so needed yet further teaching to lead them to see that, by the time Jesus entered Jerusalem, the die had been cast to seal Israel's rejection of her Lord in his rejection of her. The kingdom was not being established either then or later in Jerusalem for Israel had been bypassed. The disciples had to learn this. The citizens had rejected their king. The allegorical verses show how, when Jesus entered his kingdom at the exaltation, his fellow Jews rejected the proclamation about him so that when he returned in his kingly power having received his kingdom, their doom would be sealed in his rejection of them. If the parable within a parable speaks of rejection by the king because of their rejection of him, the introduction to the whole sums up the relationship of Jesus to the Jews and sees the entry into Jerusalem itself as actually focusing the whole story of that

1. J.T. Sanders, 'The Parable of the Pounds and Lukan Anti-Semitism', *TS* 42 (1981), pp. 660-68.

2. Fitzmyer, *Luke*, pp. 1228-29.

relationship to think of the refusal of the kingdom to the Jews as not only foreseen by God but actually determined by him.

Such an interpretation however has a number of problems. The nobleman is a fellow citizen of those who rejected him; he is not alien to them. His servants therefore who are to share his rule are to be thought of, not as Gentiles, but also as fellow citizens. They share in the rule of the twelve over Israel which is promised to them at the Last Supper (22.28-30). Those who are slain are not the fellow-citizens as a whole for the judgment does not exclude the whole people from his rule. What happens is a division, terrible in itself but not a rejection of all. It does not have about it that feeling of totality which is found for instance in the Matthaean parable of the rejected invitation where the result of rejection is said to be that the king 'was angry, and sent his troops and destroyed those murderers and burned their city' (Mt. 22.7). As in Lk. 14.24 the Lord's fury is centred upon a more limited number. This is true also of Luke's parable of the wicked tenants (20.9-18). Though it does not spare those who are to be punished but rather heightens the drastic nature of the retribution (v. 18), it nevertheless does not contain the blanket condemnation that is found at Mt. 21.43. A group is not rejected as a whole; the rejection is more directed at those within the group who merit it.

The Lukan ascension narrative as this is found in Acts 1 gives little support to the idea that the parable of the pounds speaks of the demise of the kingdom to Israel for, not only do the eleven appear to have totally misunderstood its message if that were its meaning, but Jesus' answer to them does not spell out such an implication as it must have done if their question—'Lord, will you at this time restore the kingdom to Israel?'—was totally misconceived (Acts 1.6-8). Jesus does not deny the validity of their expectation; what he refashions is not its truth but the timing of its happening. Again, when on the journey to Emmaus, and the two disciples say 'We had hoped that he was the one to redeem Israel', the risen Jesus does not deny that hope but confirms it by pointing out that the career of Jesus did not disqualify him from mesiahship, but rather fulfilled scriptural expectations and so showed that he was the Christ who would in fact redeem Israel as the Scriptures foretold (24.21, 25-26).[1] The redemption of Israel is

1. Here we would dissociate ourselves from the position taken by Moessner (see Introduction, p. 27 n. 3) where he believes Gabriel's proclamation to express an attitude to the Kingdom which is alien from Luke's own. There is nothing in Luke–

not excluded from the work of Christ but is rather essential to it, for, at Acts 3.20-21, in the initial post-Pentecostal appeal to Jerusalem to acknowledge God's servant who was 'sent to you first, to bless you' as 'sons of the prophets and of the covenant which God gave to your fathers' (Acts 3.25-26), it is the work of Jesus as Christ 'to establish all that God spoke by the mouth of his holy prophets from of old'. That future coming is an object of Jerusalem's hope, certainly not for her fear.

Luke's Jesus has three clear opportunities to say that the kingdom is not for Israel, but the fact is that he does not make use of them. When the Pharisees ask him when the kingdom of God was coming, with the clear implication that they were to see it as a hope, Jesus does not deny the reality of that hope (17.20). When at the entry to Jerusalem 'they' expected the redemption of Israel, they are not told that their hope was wrong (19.11-27) and when at the ascension the eleven express their conviction of a positive hope for Israel, the Lord does not deny that conviction. It is the timing which is open to question not their beliefs through which they will witness to him. As far as Luke is concerned, the twelve do not waiver in their conviction which had it been false would have made their preaching about him futile.

Acts as a whole to suggest that Luke entirely redirected the Jewish hope to which he gives such prominence.

Chapter 11

The Kingdom of God

If Luke and Matthew share a common concern in their efforts to relate the Christian community and its beliefs to the disbeliefs of their Jewish neighbours and in their seeking after some sort of self-definition for that community brought into being by the whole work of God in Christ, they also share in a further concern to come to terms with the delay of the parousia and so to form some positive evaluation of the continuing existence of the Christian community. Both Luke and Matthew have been understood as exponents of salvation history. That there is some truth in this is seen in the fact that, as compared with Mark, or indeed with John, they seek to give positive value to the past and to the present as they are envisaged as moving forward into the parousia and as they are seen as times of opportunity for the testing and witness, not only of individuals, but also of the Christian community as a whole.

A three-stage approach to salvation history in Matthew's Gospel does not, however, carry conviction since it appears to mark too great a break in his understanding between the time of Jesus and that of the church. More evident is the differentiation between the time of Israel and the time of Jesus. God is now active in a person rather than through a place, and Jesus, rather than continuing Israel now represents the manner of God's activity in the world. Israel's Scriptures point to Jesus who, as the messiah of Israel, responds in obedience where Israel as a people failed (Mt. 4.1-11). The covenantal community has now passed into those who are founded on him (Mt. 5.1). Jesus' coming represents a new stage in salvation history which leaves Israel after the flesh aside and rejected (Mt. 21.43). With his coming there is indeed a disjuncture. The Scriptures point to him rather than to the community brought into being through him.

There is little to be said, however, for separating the period of Jesus from that of the church and for seeing the inauguration of a new time through his death and resurrection.[1] The way Matthew presents the cross and resurrection seems to arise from a concern with Christology rather than with one arising out of salvation history (Mt. 28.16-18). Jesus is now established and revealed as the universal Lord of life and death. It is his vindication and glorification since he is now installed effectively as Son of God. The Gentile mission anticipated in his ministry (Mt. 8.11) and pointed to in the prologue (Mt. 2.11) can now be effectively undertaken, but the mission to the Jews is not thereby brought to an end. The mission of the twelve points to a Jewish mission beyond the resurrection which it anticipates and sums up (Mt. 10.23). No new attitude to the Law appears at this point since Jesus has already commended its continuing authority, at least as it was interpreted by him, and his last command gives this an abiding validity (Mt. 28.20). Again, though the cross and resurrection effect the glorification of Jesus, Matthew reflects that glorification throughout the ministry which carries it back to the point of naming where Jesus becomes 'God with us' (Mt. 1.23). Matthew's Christology is throughout an exalted one where the Son of David already exhibits the marks of the glorified Lord.[2] Matthew moves already in the direction of John. As an introduction to the Passion narrative, he alone among the Synoptics has Jesus say, 'You know that after two days the Passover is coming, and the Son of man will be delivered up to be crucified' (26.1) for his Jesus is really already in control. The meeting of Caiaphas and the Jewish leaders is thereby given a Lordly sanction. He knows of Judas's plans (26.25) and meets him (26.50), and even now he could appeal for the overwhelming support of angels (26.53).

But this outlook has permeated Matthew's Gospel so that, on the one hand, his portrait is consistently more reverential than that found in Mark,[3] and, on the other, he does not have that preliminary, preparatory and partial atmosphere found in Luke's picture of Jesus' movement towards a goal (12.50). The true address to him in his lifetime is that which comes naturally to Matthew's church, 'You are the Christ,

1. J.D. Kingsbury, *Matthew, Structure, Christology, Kingdom* (Philadelphia: Fortress Press, 1975).

2. G. Bornkamm, G. Barth and J.H. Held, *Tradition and Interpretation in Matthew* (trans. P. Scott; Philadelphia: Westminster Press, 1963).

3. H. Benedict Green, *The Gospel according to Matthew* (New Clarendon Bible; Oxford: Oxford University Press, 1975), p. 4.

the Son of the living God' (Mt. 16.16),[1] while on earth he takes on the character of the embodiment of Wisdom (Mt. 11.25-26). Even Matthew's missionary charge to the twelve addresses the church in his own day since, though placed in the past and having a past dimension, it takes on a contemporaeneity as it accounts for the church's failure among the Jews and sets it within the expectations of the church's Lord (Mt. 10.16-23). Israel's priority includes priority in blame and in punishment. Jesus' call to humility becomes a direct address to Matthew's own day (Mt. 18.1-35).

Matthew does little to separate off the period of Jesus from that of the church. There must, of course, be differences between the two times because between them there occurs the resurrection and glorification of the Lord, but Matthew has actually mellowed the differences to make the Son of David one with the church's Lord and to enable him to address it directly across the ages. Matthew does not in fact operate with the period of the church as an independent category, so that Kingsbury's understanding of him as working rather with two periods, the time of Israel and the time of the earthly exalted Jesus does in fact do more justice to the evangelist's Christology.[2] While Strecker, as an exponent of the three-stage pattern of salvation history in Matthew, has been criticized for looking at that Gospel through Lukan spectacles and for being over-influenced by Conzelmann's analysis of Luke, Conzelmann's own approach to the third Gospel has not gone unchallenged in such a way as to call in question the manner of his division of Luke's scheme into three succeeding periods in time.[3] Certainly, Luke's work does not allow for water-tight compartmentalisation into three distinct periods of salvation history. Such compartmentalisation flounders on the placing of John the Baptist and his relation to the period of Jesus on the one hand, and, on the other, on the determining point where that period comes to an end. More serious is the question whether such an understanding does justice to the Lukan presentation of the work of Jesus as a whole.

Luke's work does not really lend itself to a theory of salvation history which advocates a clear demarcation between three succeeding periods. Conzelmann's separation of Jesus from the period of Israel appears to rely too much on a reading of Luke which is controlled by

1. Green, *Matthew*, p. 151.
2. J.D. Kingsbury, *Matthew*.
3. See above, pp. 18-26.

a particular interpretation of Lk. 16.16 and which is made at the expense of any contrary message which the infancy narratives might be seeming to proclaim. Minear's oft-quoted comment on Conzelmann's use of 16.16—'Rarely has a scholar placed so much weight on so dubious an interpretation of so difficult a logion'[1]—is certainly justified. Not merely does it rely upon a particular interpretation of μέχρι to use it in an inclusive sense, but it also ignores the close connection of that verse with what follows and which gives some modifying value to it. μέχρι is not used elsewhere in Luke–Acts. In the New Testament it is found in both an inclusive and an exclusive sense so that this does not determine Luke's use here. Elsewhere though, in spite of the separation between John and Jesus in the baptismal episodes where, given Luke alone one would not know that Jesus had actually been baptized by John, the two are not clearly divided. The infancy narratives do not allow for such a separation. Fitzmyer sees John as a transitional figure. He redefines Conzelmann to let the point of demarcation be the baptism of John.[2] This however is again difficult for it too fails to give value to Luke's assertion that both John and Jesus represent, though to different degrees, the revival of the Spirit's activity. But, leaving this point aside, does 16.16 really allow for a separation between the period of Israel and that of the Christian dispensation? I have argued that it must be interpreted within its context. Certainly, in the light of v. 17, it becomes less of a demarcation than Conzelmann maintains. Law is carried over within the period of the proclamation of the kingdom. John straddles both periods, but more to the point, he bears witness to the link between the two, to the taking up of the one into the other. Verses 16 and 17 together, buttressed by v. 18, allow for continuity between Jesus and the so-called period of Israel rather than for a caesura between the two. John is the greatest of the prophets, the culmination of Israel's prophetic heritage but, as the one who is filled with the Spirit from the womb, he acknowledges Jesus who is actually conceived by the Spirit. In the context of the witness of the true in Israel and of their inspiration by the Spirit, he points to Jesus not as introducing a new period but as bringing in the eschatological consummation of Israel. He, as possessor of the Spirit, is brought into that eschatological

1. P.S. Minear, 'Luke's Use of the Birth Stories', in *Studies in Luke–Acts*, p. 122.

2. *Luke*, p. 185.

renewal which, outside the infancy narratives, must actually await the eschatological Pentecostal outpouring dependent upon the exaltation of Jesus.

John does not actually belong to the period of Israel in the way Conzelmann suggests nor does he straddle the two periods in the way that Fitzmyer maintains. Luke's conception of him is actually greater than either of these understandings allows. He rather unites Jesus to Israel and becomes the means whereby Israel's history is caught up in Jesus and the faithful to be carried forward to find its eschatological fulfilment in the events of Jesus' ἔξοδος at Jerusalem. Pentecost is the eschatological renewal of Israel and she is now summoned to acknowledge its happening.

The infancy narratives in Luke form the prologue to the two volumes to proclaim Israel's fulfilment in Jesus. In him, God 'has visited and redeemed his people' (1.68) so that in him is realized 'the mercy promised to our forefathers' (1.54-55) and his 'holy covenant is remembered' (1.72). Though the magnificat proclaims divisions, its ending suggests that these are within Israel and do not negate the fact that God 'has helped his servant Israel, in remembrance of his mercy, as he spoke to our fathers, to Abraham and to his posterity for ever' (1.54-55). With all this acknowledged, John can wait in the wilderness for 'the day of his manifestation to Israel' (1.80), when he will be introduced as a part of the eschatological event which will embrace both Israel and Rome herself (3.1-3).

Unlike Matthew, of course, Luke does not have John preach the drawing near of the kingdom and so share in the message both of the Lord and of the disciples (Mt. 3.2). His role is solely to point to the Lord himself. But this does not thereby place a caesura between him and the time of Jesus. Jesus in Luke points to himself as the bringer of the eschatological redemption of God (4.18-19), and the twelve go 'preaching the gospel and healing everywhere' (9.6). According to Luke, John does preach 'a baptism of repentance for the forgiveness of sins' (3.7). At Lk. 24.47 the risen Lord points to universal preaching of 'repentance and forgiveness of sins' in the power of his name. John's proclamation comes very close to this. The difference of course is in the baptism. Acts 2.38 characterizes that in the name of Jesus as being for repentance and 'for the forgiveness of sins'. Its promise now, however, is that 'you shall receive the gift of the Holy Spirit' thereby effecting an incorporation into the eschatological people of God. John's baptism of course could not effect it (3.16; Acts 19.4-6) for that could be achieved only after the Lord's exaltation. Yet, with that necessary, indeed essential limitation, John is brought into the closest possible relationship with the Lord as in some way bringing Israel's pre-messianic history to a climax and enabling it to be carried forward to its fulfilment in Jesus. Followers of his in Acts 19.1-7 are nevertheless called 'disciples'. So, though both Acts 10.37 and 13.24 set John before the proclamation of the word, the qualification for him who is to make up the number of the twelve is to have been a witness of Jesus 'beginning from the baptism of John' (Acts 1.22). John straddles pre-messianic Israel and Israel responding to her messiah as in Luke's scheme he units Israel to her Lord and witnesses, not to the end of the period of Israel and its demise in the period of Jesus, but to Israel's fulfilment in her Lord. He does in fact witness to Luke's scheme as contemplating, not two periods, but one as he presents Jesus as the fulfilment of Israel's history, as the making present of her expectations, and as antitype to the Old Testament saving types in prophets, lawgivers and priests. To him the faithful in Israel will respond to find through him that possession of the Spirit to which the prophets pointed (Acts 2.16-21).

Luke then—and in this he appears to be unlike Matthew—does not separate the period of Israel from that of Jesus who, in his Gospel, remains very much one with Israel and who is recognized by the faithful among the people. But does he separate the period of Jesus from that of the church? If he were to do this he would again be unlike Matthew. If he does, the demarcation of such a period would seem to be best found in the Ascension, the double narrating of which could point to such a change in aeons. In the Gospel, it marks the end of the 'life' of Jesus, looking back to it as the presence of salvation in our midst, while in Acts it begins the period of the church which comes out of it and which is thereby seen nevertheless to have continuity with the life and teaching of Jesus.[1]

But again, is this really the significance of this event as Luke himself understands it? In the Gospel, Luke presents the life of Jesus as moving forward inexorably and determinedly towards this event. His ordering of the temptations of Jesus (4.1-13) finds its climax in a temptation to reverse dramatically the divinely ordained way of

1. P.A. van Stempvoort, 'The Interpretation of the Ascension in Luke and Acts', *NTS* 5 (1959), pp. 30-42.

effecting Jesus' Lordship; the attempts of the people of Nazareth to throw him down from the heights cannot stop his progression to the real heights (4.29-30). At the transfiguration, Moses and Elijah talk of the accomplishment of his 'exodus' at Jerusalem (9.31), and the whole journey to the holy city is a progression towards his ἀναλημψις (9.51). The Ascension is not for Luke one event which brings the earthly life of Jesus to an end, but is rather the fulfilment of the whole; that which takes up, completes, and carries forward the whole to enable it to become contemporary with the church of all seasons. It vindicates the life and the significance of the universal mission to which Luke points through his narrative in Acts. It is the declaration that 'God has made him Lord and Christ, this Jesus whom you crucified' (Acts 2.38) as it expresses a value judgment upon what Luke has recorded in his two volumes and as it points back to the hopes expressed in the first two chapters of his Gospel. It marks, not the close of one period and the beginning of another, but the culmination of the first upon which it expresses a value judgment and which it carries over into the second which it then unfolds as supporting and justifying its claims.[1] Through it, Jesus' life is left, not as something of the past, but is brought into the present as it makes Jesus contemporary with Stephen, with Paul and with Luke's readers. The life of the church as recorded in Acts proceeds from the event which enthroned Jesus, not in the sense that it describes a sequence of events moved forward by an impetus given in the past, but as a series pointing to its source in the present reality of a contemporary, exalted Christ, and moving out from him as in the manner of spokes from a wheel's hub. Conzelmann himself acknowledges that 'the fact that redemption history falls into certain clear divisions does not mean that the community of believers has no living encounter with Christ in the present and that it has instead merely a historically mediated knowledge of his past and future ministry'.[2] They are drawn into a present relationship in a community which depends not merely upon the past of its Lord for making it ever new and for moving it forward into his future. The works in Jerusalem and baptism itself, which also is 'in the name of Jesus' (Acts 2.38), Stephen's witness and death, the call of Paul, the conversion of Cornelius, the apostolic decree, the move into Europe,

1. This is made more certain by the recent insistence upon the post-ascension activity of Jesus in Acts.

2. *Theology*, p. 36.

and the enabling of Paul's witness at Rome all take place at the direct instigation of the Lord himself or of the Spirit poured out by him. Luke's use of the concept of the name and his references to the personal activity of the Spirit (Acts 13.2; 15.28) witness to his understanding of the present as the time of the eschatological activity of the exalted Lord and so actually break through the constraints placed upon his understanding of the indwelling corporate Christ caused by the expression of his beliefs in terms controlled by Old Testament concepts.

For the life of Jesus in Luke is always moving forward to its future so that the time of Jesus' ministry has about it a permeating, controlling atmosphere of incompletion, of moving forward into something greater. It is of the nature of a prelude to the realization of its reality and completion. Jesus is possessed of the Spirit in himself as he is commissioned at his baptism and confirmed by his temptation (3.22; 4.1). He fulfils the expectations of Isaiah 61. Nevertheless, outside the infancy narratives and the references to post-Pentecostal times (11.13; 12.10; 12.12) Luke is restrained in his references to the Spirit. Jesus is anointed by the Spirit as the prophet of the endtime so that he can in himself 'rejoice in the Holy Spirit' (10.21). But Luke is careful to keep the activity of the Spirit confined to Jesus' eschatological status. It is not yet the age of the Spirit so Jesus' healings are enabled, not by the Spirit as in Matthew, but by the 'finger of God' (11.20). In Acts, the 'mighty works and wonders' witness to Jesus' empowering not by the Spirit, but by God (Acts 2.22). Jesus does not act in his own right and in his eschatological fulness until he has been exalted to the right hand of God (Acts 4.11-12).

So, in Luke, Jesus is always on the way. Satan is being defeated in the ministry (11.20-23; 13.16) but the real victory will be by means of the cross and resurrection, witnessed at the ascension (Acts 2.34-35). Samaritans will not receive him because his ministry is as yet only preparatory in nature (10.52-53). The present points forward to the future for, just as the disciples must be ready for their future (12.40-43), so Jesus himself is 'constrained' until his baptism, by way of death and exaltation, is accomplished (12.49-50). He goes on his way 'today and tomorrow' until 'on the third day' he finishes his course. The present moves on into the future which accomplishes that for which the present is merely a necessary prelude (13.31-34). In this passage, Luke is already looking beyond the time of Jesus when

Jerusalem is unable to welcome him at his entry to the eschatological fulfilment when she will (13.35). He does not really become her or anybody else's Lord until his glorification.

Conzelmann writes: 'The time of salvation has come about in history, as a period of time which, although it determines the present, is now over and finished'. He justifies this immediately on the basis of Lk. 22.35-36 which, he says, 'distinguishes between the period of Jesus and the present in order to bring out their individual character'.[1] While this verse does indeed differentiate between the time of the mission of the seventy during the ministry of Jesus and the events surrounding the Passion, it announces the arrival of a new stage which marks the completion of that to which the ministry has pointed and one when the true eschatological battle is to take place. The time of preparation is at an end; the ultimate period is beginning. This suggests that it is the time which is beginning now which is the time of fulfilment, for it includes the crucifixion, resurrection and ascension, and, for Luke, these cannot be seen as something less than the enablers of the time of salvation. Contrary to Conzelmann, therefore, the time of salvation is not 'over and finished'. As has often been remarked, the time of Jesus' ministry is not an ideal Satan-free period.[2] It is preliminary to the conflict, one of moving forward to it, one of preparation for it. The eschatological time is now beginning with the events that are to take place in Jerusalem. The ascension rather than the cross is for Luke the actual redemptive event, for it marks the ultimate victory over Satan, enables the establishment of the eschatological community to make Jesus a universal, timeless Lord who draws people into the sphere of the kingdom of God which is now established as a certainty and reality by means of these eschatological events in Jerusalem.

But that does not mean that the time of Jesus, preparatory though it is, is in Luke's scheme left behind. Though historically separated from the present, it is not theologically reduced. Through it, Jesus addresses the disciples who are Luke's contemporaries as their living Lord. The preparatory nature of the period of the ministry is recognised by Moule who understands Luke as making the 'resurrection the

1. *Theology*, p. 36.

2. S. Brown, *Apostasy and Perseverance in the Theology of Luke* (*AnBib*, 36; Rome: Pontifical Biblical Institute, 1969).

Christological watershed dividing the gospel from Acts'.[1] One should not go on to assert however that this means that Luke was not informing the whole with his understanding of Jesus' present status as Lord of the Christian community. Luke's is in itself no historical reconstruction. Men address him as κύριε and the close relation of this to Luke's own use of κύριος means that the former is to be interpreted in terms of the latter. So, for instance, when Peter, in response to the parable of the watchful servants asks, 'Lord, are you telling this parable for us or for all?' Luke's response is 'And the Lord said...' and then he goes on to recount a further parable which is plainly directed to Luke's readers (12.35-48).[2] Past and present are distinguished but not separated. Luke rather superimposes the present over the past but in such a way that the past is given a value in its own right as it is seen as an unrepeatable, but nevertheless preliminary period which enabled the present Lordship of Jesus to become a reality.

Conzelmann would thus seem to be correct when he maintains that Luke 'defines the narrative as the historical foundation which is added as a secondary factor to the kerygma'.[3] However, it would not seem right to draw from this the conclusion that the kerygma and the narrative are thereby separated. 'Separation' is too strong a word, for the narrative remains in fact the vehicle of the kerygma which is actually proclaimed by means of it even as it is justified by it. So the events of the narrative as a whole point forward, as we have seen, to the kerygmatic proclamation of the sufferings, resurrection and exaltation of the Son which together enable his installation as Lord. Equally, while he uses the narrative as a witness to the past to explain both the growing rejection of Jesus by the Jews and the distancing of the parousia from the time of Jesus, Luke nevertheless uses the past dimension as a spring board to enable the exalted Lord to address the present of Luke's contemporaries.[4] The mission of the seventy

1. C.F.D. Moule, 'The Christology of Acts' in *Studies in Luke–Acts*, p. 165, *contra* Conzelmann, *Theology*, p. 179.

2. See *Christ the Lord*, pp. 49-50.

3. *Theology*, p. 170.

4. It is always, however, an address which meets Luke's contemporaries by way of its setting either in the life of Jesus or in that of the early church. Luke remains conscious of the difference between past and present and he addresses the present indirectly by way of the past. See also Tannehill, *Acts*, p. 34. 'It is dangerous to assume that Peter, for all practical purposes, steps outside his narrative context and preaches the gospel directly to the narrator's situation'.

becomes a continuing mission to Israel and is followed by an address to Luke's contemporaries (10.22-24). If the parable of the Good Samaritan is primarily explanatory of the reason for the Jewish failure to respond to Jesus, it is followed by the Martha–Mary story which takes up the same reasoning and applies it directly to Jesus' church (10.38-42). The failure of the Pharisees to be alert to the eschatological situation becomes the entry into a direct exhortation to eschatological urgency addressed to Luke's readers (11.37-52; 12.1-48). Challenges to the Pharisees and scribes, again directed at the past failure, become the spring board for addresses to the disciples to be alert to the urgency of the new situation (16.1-13). The parable of the Pharisee and the tax collector, again explaining a situation with its roots in the past, is taken up into the need to receive the kingdom of God like a child (18.15-17).

Luke's narrative does in fact move forward on two levels as it both speaks of a situation in the past which it sees as a basis for and justification of events in the history of the Christian community and in the career of its Lord, and also speaks to the present as it proclaims that Lord and exhorts those who have been drawn into his community by means of an indirect address of the exalted one. Past and present are interwoven, identifiable yet not capable of separation, for the past has actually been caught up in the present as the whole is illustrated by the reality of its living Lord. Luke's is kerygmatic history where the story of the past is used in the service of the present which alone fulfils it and gives it permanency. Luke's assertion that his Gospel is the story of what Jesus 'began to do and to teach' must be given its full value.[1]

1. Haenchen, *Acts*, ad hoc denies this and Conzelmann (*Acts*, p. 3) says 'ἄρχεσθαι "to begin" is weakened to a kind of helping verb'. Yet in the sonorous terms of the prologue to Acts which points back to and concludes the significance of the prologue of Luke, it seems almost certain that Luke gives the verb a much stronger significance. This is suggested by the manner in which he uses ἄρχεσθαι in his two volumes. It does not always have a strong force, for example, Lk. 3.8 and Acts 11.15. Yet at other times it emphasizes a significant sequence of events and points to a careful ordering, e.g. Lk. 3.23, Acts 11.4. It is used to point to an actual sequence of events in which the beginning is so emphasized as to enable it to become the basis for the other happenings which are actually linked to it. The beginning both enables and points to the end. So, Acts 1.22 points to the beginning of Jesus' ministry in that of John; the complaint of the multitudes before Pilate sees the ministry in Jerusalem as the climax of what started in Galilee, Lk. 23.5. The risen Jesus sees the

So the time of salvation is not in the past but in the present. The 'today' of Jesus' Nazareth speech (4.21) is not exhausted in the past of Jesus. It finds it beginnings in that point but these are carried over into the whole eschatological event to include the present of Luke's contemporaries.[1] Luke's general outlook on the unity of the time of Jesus and the time of the church which takes up the period of Jesus and incorporates it, indeed fulfils it, in the period of the church, makes this inevitable. As having programmatic significance, the Nazareth episode has the events of Jerusalem in its sights and the historical events of the speech are extended to include not merely the rejection of Jesus in his lifetime but also the Jewish rejection of the proclamation about him and the inclusion of the Gentiles. But, more even than these two points, the quotation from Isaiah has itself a built-in future aspect. The prophet is sent to preach and to proclaim the coming of a future event. Jesus becomes the eschatological prophet of whom the prophet in Israel was a prefigurement and type. Jesus is the true Spirit-filled prophet, for he is in himself fully part of the eschatological event.[2]

As the eschatological prophet, he announces a coming act of God for he points forward to a future coming of the release of God's people. As he is enabled to do this by the Spirit, the time of that release becomes the age of the outpouring of the Spirit of which his miracles are an anticipation but which are as yet only pointers to the complete fulfilment (7.21-23; 11.20; cf. 10.18). Jesus fulfils the prophetic expectations, not merely by his present ministry, but more significantly by his present preaching and enabling of the future direct redemptive activity of the Lord. Its fulfilment is therefore not

universal mission as proceeding from and enabled by the witness in Jerusalem, 24.47, and justifies his own career by scriptural witness which began with Moses and is continued through all the prophets, 24.27. In the light of this usage, ἤρξατο in Acts 1.1 must be given a deeper significance than either Haenchen or Conzelmann allow.

1. *Christ the Lord*, pp. 41, 47.

2. Jesus is seen as the fulfilment of the prophet's preaching. His is the real preaching of eschatological urgency and he points forward to the future which fulfils the prophet's hopes. He is actually the anti-type to the prophet rather than to the prophet's expectation. Like that of the prophet, Jesus' message focuses on the future.

exhausted by the ministry which rather anticipates and preludes the full redemptive activity of God.[1]

But does the actual fact of Acts mean that the eschatological dimension of the early church's existence and of its expectations is thereby reduced if not actually submerged completely? Does the existence of Acts entail a belief in ongoing history so that the parousia is abandoned as the determining factor of the church's life which is now made to come to terms with the world and its continuing history? Conzelmann maintains in effect that it does. The church is now under attack but its hope cannot be in an early parousia but in its picture of the kingdom and in the anticipation of that brought to it through its memory of its presence in the life of Jesus and the earliest chapter of the church's life. 'Luke recognises the uniqueness of the events of that time, and his picture of the early church is not meant to harmonize with the present, but stands in contrast'. The church is now 'the ecclesia pressa during which the virtue of patience is required'.[2]

Conzelmann's understanding of Acts as picturing an 'ecclesia pressa' is a welcome corrective of that widely-held view which sees it as a triumphalist presentation of the Christian mission, but it is one, nevertheless, which, unless it can be infused with a realistic but vital hope, makes for an inevitable loss of the eschatological dimension of early Christianity. Christianity then becomes a question of holding on to the possession of a memory of Jesus which informs a picture of the kingdom which will one day be attained. The present is then related effectively neither to the past of that memory nor to the future of the picture. The presence of the Spirit becomes, not a part of the eschatological experience, but a substitute for it.

However, the existence of Acts does not in itself mean the necessary abandonment of an early expectation of the end nor does it entail an inevitable evacuation of the eschatological dimension from the present. Acts is in fact not offered as a first chapter of an ongoing church history which is thereby meant to edify the church in its continuing mission.[3] It is rather an explanation of the situation in

1. C. Westermann, *Isaiah 40–66* (trans. D.M.G. Stalker; London: SCM Press, 1969), pp. 364-67.

2. *Theology*, pp. 14, 207-13. Cf. P. Vielhauer, 'Paulinism', p. 47, 'How uneschatologically Luke thinks is apparent not only from the content, but from the fact of Acts'.

3. Kee, *Christian Origins*, p. 107: 'The important unfinished business in this

which the church finds itself in the present and one which by justifying that situation with regard to Jewish rejection of the gospel and the resulting predominantly Gentile constituency of the church can counter the loss of nerve brought about by the continuing delay of the End and can thereby give to the Christian community some self-identity and hope. Luke's explanation does not rest however at the level of the historical but becomes one that is predominantly theological to counter the theological perplexities which the historical situation has produced. The infancy narratives place the whole work firmly within the sphere of theological kerygma as Jesus is proclaimed as the hope of Israel and the restorer of God's covenantal promises to her. Gentiles are included within the sphere of that hope but it is nevertheless made clear that they do not take Israel's place as the primary object of God's concern. The non-fulfilment of the hope becomes the primary theological problem for Luke. The story of the ascension in Acts takes the form of an acknowledgment of the perplexity felt by Luke's contemporaries. The apostles' question—'Lord, will you at this time restore the kingdom to Israel?'—echoes their continuing concern which is met by a hope, a promise and a commission. Knowledge of times and seasons is not theirs to know, but they will receive the Spirit which becomes a guarantee of the fulfilment of their expectations. Their universal witness will point to the reality of the fulfilment of their expectations which rests ultimately upon the glorification of Jesus in the present and which can therefore expect a future manifestation of that glory (Acts 1.6-11). In Acts the account of the ascension has that programmatic significance which is given to the gospel by the rejection at Nazareth. The pattern of that rejection is worked out systematically until it climaxes and leaves Paul at Rome. The two volumes buttress the faith of Luke's

situation is for the witness of the new community to press forward. Still to be accomplished in the contemporary life of the church is the divine intention... "I have set you to be a light for the Gentiles, that you may bring salvation to the uttermost parts of the earth"'. Kee forgets Luke's belief in a near parousia, his concept of witness and the fact that the climax of the book is the preaching of Paul at Rome. Luke is interested in Paul and in the fact that his career can actually be seen as a fulfilment of the Lord's promise. The church at large is not exhorted to engage in witness and missionary activity, and this dimension is singularly lacking in Paul's address to the Ephesian elders which is a defence of Paul rather than a programme for his successors. Luke does not envisage an ongoing mission: it is rather what has already happened that concerns him.

readers by countering the disappointment of the actual historical facts through enabling these to be seen nevertheless as witnessing to the Lordship of Christ.

As he sums this up in the preface to Acts (Acts 1.1-5), Luke sees the time between the resurrection and the ascension as one of explanation and justification. Jesus shows himself alive 'by many proofs'. The resurrection is the lynch-pin of Luke's argument and this no doubt made him include the most crassly materialistic of all the resurrection stories (24.26-43). Equally important, however, was the teaching about the kingdom which, by justifying events around the resurrection, enabled that event itself to be believed in. The resurrection and the sufferings are the fulfilment of Scripture (24.44-46). In this, Luke is one with the outlook of his predecessors. He, however, goes further than they by including within his understanding of the fulfilment of Scripture both the universal preaching and the manner of its accomplishment (24.46-47). The twelve are not the actual accomplishers of the mission. Their place is to give it theological significance, to enable it to be seen as the renewal of Israel and the fulfilment of her eschatological hopes (24.48).[1] They are to enable the universal witness, as it has actually been achieved, to be given an eschatological dimension and to be seen both as the fulfilment of scriptural expectations and also as the actualization of the promises of Israel's Lord. It is as this, that Luke recounts his story in Acts in the manner of the Deuteronomic histories of old.[2] The sufferings of Jesus seem to deny his messiahship

1. Tannehill, *Acts*, pp. 102-103.

2. *Christ the Lord*, pp. 176-77. D.L. Bock (*Proclamation from Prophecy and Pattern: Lucan Old Testament Christology* [JSNTSup, 12; Sheffield: JSOT Press, 1987], p. 35) acknowledges my use in *Christ the Lord* of the Gentile mission's success as supporting the belief in Jesus as Lord but questions 'whether the success of universal mission declares Jesus to be Lord as much as it was the realisation of Jesus' Lordship which helped create the climate for Gentile mission (Acts 10.34-43). Luke is seen to be writing descriptively rather than defensively. One wonders, however, whether this motif should be stated in the form: the success of the Gentile mission showed the Lordship of Jesus. Could it not be the exact reverse for Luke? Could it be that for Luke the key-point is that it is the Lordship that demands and guarantees the Gentile mission' (p. 34). While Bock's pattern could be seen as the outcome of Luke's scheme of promise and fulfilment, the problem of such an outlook is the realization that runs deep in Luke's thinking and which wrestles with the fact that how things actually turned out did not really fulfil OT expectations. Luke has to struggle hard to make his case that that part of the OT expectations has already

and the subsequent history of the mission would seem to go against his Lordship. Gentiles come in, though the nations as a whole and Rome in particular remain at best ambivalent and often hostile. The Jews overall have turned their backs on the proclamation. Luke's time is one of 'ecclesia pressa', and the open manifestation of Lordship promised in the expected parousia has not been fulfilled. Jesus remains a hidden Messiah. Luke's contemporaries, like the apostles of old, must often have stood gazing up into heaven in perplexity (Acts 1.9, 11). Luke's narrative in Acts is to counter that perplexity as he attempts to enable his contemporaries to see a positive realization of their hopes in the present and so to look for their open realization in the future which comes out of the present acknowledgment of him as Lord and Christ. If the first volume shows that Jesus' career does not disqualify him from messiahship, his second justifies the church's faith in it by showing that 'times of refreshing' have indeed come 'from the presence of the Lord' and that they can now wait expectantly for the 'Christ appointed for you', for the preliminaries have been fulfilled and the way is clear for 'the time of establishing all that God spake by the mouth of his holy prophets from of old' (Acts 3.19-21).[1]

The fact of Acts therefore does not mean that Luke has necessarily abandoned belief in an early parousia, for his writing of a second volume as a sequel to his Jesus story does not inevitably imply a 'distinctive view of the imminence of the kingdom'.[2] On the contrary, his story of the past means that the hope grounded on that past could as well have been a hope in an early parousia as in the continuation of the world and of history. He ends with a story of a fulfilment of a promise, for the gospel had been proclaimed to the end of the earth. The nations as represented by the Roman power have had a gospel proclaimed to them, and those destined for salvation have been linked to the renewed Israel centred upon the twelve. Paul, as the apostle to the Gentiles, has been one with the twelve to link up his converts to them and to the community built upon them. His death is of little

been fulfilled. The Gentiles have to be used as a make-weight to the refusal of the Jews. Luke has to struggle hard to show that the career of Jesus did in reality meet OT hopes. These Scriptures proclaimed the mission as part of the Messiah's activity but it needs the risen Lord and the influence of the Spirit to make the claim believable. The mission awaits the confirmation of the parousia.

1. *Christ the Lord*, pp. 119-24.
2. Fitzmyer, *Luke*, p. 234.

importance, for it is his work, climaxing in Rome as the fulfilment of promise which is of ultimate concern for Luke. If Paul himself had an eschatological perspective from which he viewed his activity among the nations, Luke shares in that perspective to see it in terms of Old Testament prophecy and fulfilment.[1] The conclusion of Luke's two volumes enshrines an eschatological hope which is in every way as strong as that contained in the ending of Mark's Gospel. Both, open-endedly, seek to strengthen the parousia hope in their readers. For Mark, his readers will see Jesus in glory in the Gentile world.[2] Luke, buttressing a faith that could well have been threatened by the failure of the realization of that hope, can look at the founding of the community in order to see the hand of God in it and to keep alive, even to rekindle, a faith which subsequent history might seem to call into question. Paul in Rome, in spite of his impending death, can continue 'preaching about the kingdom of God and teaching about the Lord Jesus Christ quite openly and unhindered' (Acts 28.31). Luke has written his story, not to encourage further missionary preaching or to strengthen readers grown weak in the proclamation of the gospel, but to rekindle confidence in the faith in which they believe and to assure them that the parousia remained a living hope.

For Luke sees the parousia hope as a necessary part of a Christian's belief in Jesus. All is not well in the present, and its partialities need to be balanced by a promise of an impending future, one that does indeed impinge upon the present to give it realism, perspective and confidence. Luke's distinctive parousia discourse (17.20–18.8) is concerned not merely to give perspective to the Pharisees' failure to read the signs of the present, but to maintain that the present finds a climax in a parousia which will be real and complete, showing the futility of all that has been put forward as substitute for it, and to make it clear that the parousia actually impinges as a fact upon the present.[3] Its purpose is here said to be, not judgment but vindication and, while judgment can be given a present reference even though the event which embodies it is left for an indefinite future, vindication cannot so easily be thus accommodated. Luke sets out the Lord's teaching to the effect

1. *Christ the Lord*, pp. 116-44.

2. D. Nineham, *The Gospel of St Mark* (Pelican Gospel Commentaries; Harmondsworth: Penguin Books, 1963), pp. 445-47.

3. This causes Luke to emphasize both a parousia and the delay in its arrival.

that 'they ought always to pray and not lose heart' and he concludes by promising them action issuing in a speedy vindication. His aim is to deepen faith, indeed perhaps rather to stop its dilution if not disappearance (18.8) and he cannot do this by promising some future, though distant, intervention. Nothing less than a promise of something impinging fully upon the present will fit the bill. Likewise, in his version of the Synoptic apocalypse (21.5-36), Luke again counteracts false substitutes and allows for a delay between the time of Jesus and that of the parousia (21.9-9).[1] In contrast to such substitutes, the End will be ushered in by natural and supernatural calamities which none can mistake (21.10-11, 25-26). These will lead into the coming of the Son of man (21.27). It is on these events and their outcome that Luke puts his emphasis. He does not have the Markan reference to the gathering together of the elect at the coming of the Son of Man (Mk 13.27), but instead has a distinctive verse which brings both the natural/supernatural calamities and the coming itself within the immediate purview of his readers as they are put forward as compelling, vital and relevant events which impinge upon them. 'Now when these things begin to take place, look up and raise up your heads, because your redemption draws near' (21.28). The kingdom of God is near in a temporal as well as a spatial sense for he now includes all these events within the experience of 'this generation' of Luke's contemporaries. They will undergo distress at its appearing and will be in danger of dissipation while they wait. So they are to be warned, even as they wait in hope, to 'watch at all times, praying that you may have strength to escape all these things that will take place, and to stand before the Son of Man' (21.36). Once more, the taking up of the urgency of the warning into the promise of the reason for the coming means a direct impinging upon the outlook of Luke's contemporaries as the parousia becomes an immediate hope for them.

The hope is not exhausted in an individual parousia though Jesus is already in glory and Stephen's spirit can be commended to him as he witnesses to Stephen's message and receives him into his heavenly kingdom (Acts 7.56, 59).[2] It is 'through many tribulations' in this life that we are enabled to 'enter the kingdom of God' which finds its

1. R.J. Hiers, 'The Problem of the Delay of the Parousia in Luke–Acts', *NTS* 20 (1973–74), pp. 145-55.

2. C.K. Barrett, 'Stephen and the Son of Man' in *Apophoreta: Festschrift für Ernst Haenchen* (BZNW, 30; Berlin: Alfred Töpelmann, 1963), pp. 31-38.

present reality in the heavenly realm (Acts 14.22). So the seventy can proclaim that 'the kingdom of God has come near' in a spatial as well as a temporal sense to those who refuse the message even as they proclaim the inclusion of those who accept the message within its embrace (10.9, 11-12). Nevertheless, the kingdom of Christ which is established as a present reality in the heavenly realm (22.28-30) awaits its revelation on earth (22.16-18). Christians can enter that kingdom at death but the hope is realized fully only when it is revealed on earth, and it is that event which Luke offers as the climax of the hope when its fulness will be established. The preaching of the kingdom has this two-fold dimension. The Lukan beatitudes express a strong sense of present promise of a future reality (6.20-23). The kingdom is already guaranteed to the poor though its rewards remain for the future. The rich are already outside its promise though the judgment awaits a future realization (6.24-26). The prayer of the disciples is for the coming of the kingdom in the future and for a daily living out of its power meanwhile in the present (11.2-3).[1] Prayer therefore becomes important in Luke for the lives of both Jesus and his disciples as through it they are enabled to receive the Holy Spirit poured out in power upon them by their heavenly Lord (11.13). So they live out of the power of the kingdom in the present and anticipate its revelation in the future as they 'devote themselves to the apostles' teaching and fellowship, to the breaking of bread and the prayers' (Acts 2.42).

All that, however, is neither the climax of the kingdom nor the ultimate hope for the Christian. Some of Luke's readers 'will not taste of death before they see the kingdom of God' (9.27).[2] It will be realized fully and openly and they will enter it not at their own death, but when it is revealed at the parousia, for 'this generation will not pass away until all has taken place' (21.32). Most first-generation Christians have by the time Luke wrote entered the kingdom at their death, and Luke can even assume that the majority of his readers will follow this course, but some will not because the parousia remains the climax of their hope and the guarantee of the kingdom's reality. Jesus' own resurrection has guaranteed the resurrection of those who follow him and the defeat of the ruler of this world is assured (Acts 2.34, 35 quoting Ps. 110.1).

For Luke is actually the least individualistic and the most widely

1. *Christ the Lord*, pp. 161-66.
2. *Christ the Lord*, pp. 21-23.

embracing of the three Synoptic evangelists. Hope is not exhausted by the present but looks for its fulfilment to the future as the time of 'establishing all that God spake by the mouth of his holy prophets from of old' (Acts 3.21). We have already seen that that which is to be established includes the restoration of Israel. The parousia becomes for Luke, not primarily a time of judgment, though judgment is included and is inevitable (10.14; 13.28; 14.24), but a time of fulfilment and hope. It is the point of revelation to Israel and of the establishment of the divine rule which Jesus' meals with his followers, with his critics and with the outcasts have anticipated. Satan's defeat begun in Jesus (10.18) and continued in the apostolic preaching (Acts 26.18) will be revealed after the final *peirasmos* (Lk. 21.25-26) when men will be restored as sons of God (3.38). The people of God will be re-established in its fulness, and relationship with God will be found in membership of it.

The parousia then retains its place in Luke's expectations, and belief in its nearness continues to exercise a controlling influence over his understanding of the nature of the work of God in Christ and of the nature of the Christian hope. Luke has in fact included an element of delay in his reporting of the Lord's words about it (12.38-40; 18.1; 19.11; 21.9, 12) but this is to be accounted for, not by a belief on the part of Luke in an extended future, but by the fact of a past which has already occurred. Luke has to account for a delay that has already taken place with its accompanying strains upon faith and its encouragement of false, and inevitably limited, substitute hopes. Luke denies the reality of such substitutes and says that the Lord himself countered expectations of an immediate return. Instead, as an immediate expectation, he offered the gift of the Spirit and, as a promise, he announced a universal preaching 'in his name to all nations, beginning from Jerusalem' (24.37). What is distinctive to Luke is his moving of the emphasis away from the parousia, as it is found for instance in Mark, to place it upon the present Lordship of Christ as Luke saw that established at the ascension. The burden of proof becomes, not the parousia, but the ascension.[1] So, before the high priest Jesus' witness to himself rests, not upon a vindication climaxing in a future event, but upon the immediate exaltation of himself to the right hand of God (22.69). It will not be seen (cf. Mk 14.62; Mt. 26.64) by the high

1. E. Franklin, 'The Ascension and the Eschatology of Luke–Acts', *SJT* 23 (1970), pp. 191ff.

priest but it will nevertheless be real enough as Jesus' kingdom is established in the present. The transfiguration in Luke becomes a momentary glimpse of the glory of Christ established at his exaltation rather than at the parousia (9.27; cf. Mk 9.1)[1] for the powerful event has already taken place so that what remains for the future proceeds inevitably from the ascension as its outcome.

The parousia, though the ultimate hope, is not that upon which the burden of proof must rest. That for Luke is found in the ascension. His work witnesses to his belief in that and justifies it both by his account of the earthly life of the Lord and by his story of the establishment of the universal witness under the inspiration and power of the Holy Spirit poured out by the exalted Lord. It nevertheless entails a belief in a parousia which impinges directly in its promise upon Luke's generation. It is no appendage but an inevitable and necessary conclusion to Luke's kerygma, for he knows that this world as it now is and the life of Christians within it cannot contain the reality of the effective Lordship of Christ that he believes must be established. It is here where the chief differences between him and Matthew are to be found.

There is in fact little real difference between Matthew and Luke in their expectations about the timing of the parousia as this is related to the time of Jesus. Both allow for an extended period between the time of Jesus and that of their contemporaries and in each case this is accounted for simply by the fact that they are both writing at some distance from the time of Jesus. Luke's parable of the pounds is told to counter the beliefs of Jesus' contemporaries in an immediate parousia (19.11-27), while Matthew's parable of the talents emphasizes that the master returns only 'after a long time' (Mt. 25.19). The element of delay which is so apparent in Matthew's extended ending to the apocalyptic discourse (Mt. 24.45–25.46) is paralleled by the whole tone of Luke's first call to watchfulness on the part of the disciples (12.22-53): 'You also must be ready: for the Son of man is coming at an unexpected hour' (v. 40). Both discussions extend the warning found at the end of the Markan apocalypse (Mk 13.32-37) and counter the slackness caused by the delay that is there warned against.

Nevertheless, as we have seen, Luke does not expect a long period between his own time and the parousia. Acts does not entail a belief

1. J.G. Davies, 'The Prefigurement of the Ascension in the Third Gospel', *JTS* NS 3 (1952), pp. 229-33.

in a continuing mission but rather records how the Old Testament expectations of the end time can be seen actually to have been fulfilled. There is in fact little in Luke's Gospel to suggest that he himself or the church to which he was writing had a continuing lively missionary concern. A parousia was expected soon and its coming did not wait upon an ongoing mission; its arrival is not said to depend upon a successful outcome of a continuing enterprise. Luke's apocalyptic discourse has nothing like Mk 13.10—'And the gospel must first be preached to all nations'—or Mt. 24.14—'And this gospel of the kingdom will be preached throughout the whole world, as a testimony to all nations; and then the end will come'. Lk. 21.13 does indeed talk of persecution as providing an opportunity for witness—'This will be a time for you to bear testimony'—but it speaks less positively of this as a part in the divine redemptive plan and says nothing about it as a necessary prelude to the End. Luke does not see the universal mission as leading directly into the End in the way that Matthew and, though less obviously, Mark do. It does, as we have seen, have eschatological significance but that is to be found primarily in its past accomplishment rather than in any necessity laid upon the present or the future to work for its accomplishment. Luke's concern with witness to all nations is less one of continuing missionary zeal than a justification of the missionary situation and an attempt to see it as fulfilling scriptural promises and so giving credibility to the church's claims.[1] While Acts 26.23 maintains that the messiahship of Jesus means suffering, resurrection and a proclamation of 'light both to the people and to the Gentiles', Luke's definitive statement of the risen Lord (24.46-48) suggests that his primary concern is to show that the universal mission is to be understood as a witness to the truth of the church's claims about that messiahship. The story of Acts is unfolded, not as one of describing the result of the messiahship of Jesus but as one of justifying belief in that messiahship. It is a theological justification of the church's beliefs about Jesus showing that his whole career, on earth and in heaven, can be seen as the legitimate fulfilment of Old Testament expectations. The sufferings were a problem but they could be justified from scripture. The universal witness was required by that same scripture and Luke shows that what has happened can legitimately be seen as fulfilling those requirements. As it is expressed in the prophecy of Isaiah, 'The Lord has bared his holy arm before the

1. *Christ the Lord*, pp. 119-24.

eyes of all the nations; and all the ends of the earth shall see the salvation of our God' (Isa. 52.10). The twelve are 'witnesses of these things' (24.48). Like the Israel of old (Isa. 43.10, 12; 44.8) they are interpreters of the events to draw out their meaning and, by their existence, to point to the nature of the community and to the significance of its life and being.[1] They witness both to the facts and to the significance of the facts—the sufferings, resurrection, ascension and of the events that have proceeded from them. They are not here 'sent out'[2] but their task is rather to bring meaning to the events that happen. In Acts 1.8 their witness is to 'the end of the earth', but, again, it centres in the meaning they are to give to the mission rather than in a missionary task laid upon them. Luke does not assign a missionary task to them; they may in fact have undertaken such, but Luke himself does not record it for the last that is heard of them is their action through Peter at the apostolic council. Peter, it is true, is instrumental in bringing in the Gentiles without circumcision, but Luke recounts this episode for its significance rather than as a part of a continuing apostolic missionary activity. Luke recounts the choosing of the twelve in the context of his sermon on the plain, that is as their part in the establishing of the nature of the new community, rather than as in Matthew (10.1-4), in the context of a missionary enterprise.

Matthew's last scene (28.16-20) means that his Gospel is actually more open-ended in its missionary concern than is Luke's work. The Lord's presence is with his church 'to the close of the age'. In the light of Matthew's apocalyptic discourse (Mt. 14.14) it suggests a continuing missionary activity until the parousia. Yet, we have seen that Matthew has little hope for missionary success among the Jews and, in the rest of his Gospel, there is little outgoing concern for the Gentiles. Matthew's church is now virtually a third race which sees itself not only as distinct from unfaithful Israel, but also from unbelieving Gentiles (Mt. 18.17; 21.43). Faith will be found among both Jews and Gentiles but there is little optimism of a continuing outreach to them. Matthew's allegory of the last judgment (Mt. 25.31-36) may show a more positive attitude to outsiders in that its reference to the little ones may refer back to 10.40-42 and so express hope for those who have done Christians service. More likely though, in its context of warnings to those within the Christian community (24.3–25.46), it

1. *Christ the Lord*, pp. 95-99.
2. Marshall, *Luke*, pp. 903-907.

refers back to the little ones of 18.10-14 and so becomes a further warning about Christians' treatment of fellow Christians. Matthew overall has the outlook of a gathered church which sees salvation restricted not only to those who come in but to those who respond in a particular way. So Matthew's Gospel thinks only in terms of inclusion of individuals. Some Jews will still come in right until the parousia (Mt. 10.27), and testimony before Gentiles will still bear fruit until then (Mt. 24.14),[1] but the hopes of the final scene have in fact been realized in the present, and the concern of the current times is less one of missionary activity than of a confident, and therefore a rigorous, waiting for the parousia in an assurance that the Lord dwells in their midst. Nevertheless, though a Matthaean concern with the parousia as a present fact cannot be ruled out, it is less vital than in Luke and its impingement has constantly to be asserted in a warning about behaviour. Whereas in Matthew, the parousia remains primarily as a threat, for Luke, though the threatening aspect is not denied, it is advocated primarily as a promise and as an object of hope and longing.

So, while Luke's is a picture of an 'ecclesia pressa', where confidence lies in a belief about its hidden Lord and in a reversal of that hiddenness in the near future, Matthew's is rather one of a church whose confidence is derived from its own present situation which, it believes, witnesses to the presence of its exalted Lord in its midst (Mt. 27.16-20). The two Gospels therefore relate their own present to the presence of the kingdom in very different ways. Compared with Mark, they both place an emphasis upon the kingdom in the present, and for neither of them does its establishment in power wait for some future, dramatic event (Mk. 9.1).[2] So both of them see the works of Jesus as witnessing to the pressing in of the kingdom upon the present (Mt. 12.28; Lk. 11.20); the kingdom is now ἔφθασεν ἐφ'ὑμᾶς. It is already an established reality. Nevertheless, they do not understand its presence in identical ways. Matthew's reference to the Spirit associates the present closely with the presence of the kingdom. Luke's pointer to the activity of the 'finger of God' distances the kingdom from the earthly arena. God works from heaven as he did of old (Exod. 19.3; Isa. 6.1). Jesus himself is one with the kingdom (Lk. 1.32-33; 4.18-19) but the eschatological sphere itself is not actually manifest on

1. Donaldson, *Mountain*, pp. 166-68.
2. Hooker, *Mark*, pp. 211-12.

earth.[1] Something of the same outlook occurs in the difficult passages about the kingdom under siege (Mt. 11.12; Lk. 16.16). In Matthew, the kingdom is said to be under attack by men in the present who do violence to it. In Luke the kingdom is being proclaimed and it is primarily the message about it, man's understanding of its nature, which is the subject of violence. It is the picture of the kingdom rather than the kingdom itself which is being distorted. In Matthew, the proclamation 'The kingdom of God has come near' (Mt. 10.7; 10.9, 11) is one of an event to come, a promise of something appearing in the hearers' midst. In Luke, it is otherwise. It is a proclamation of something that has already happened. In the mission of the seventy, those who respond are told that it has drawn near to them—they are now living within its sphere as it hovers over them. Those who reject the preaching are nevertheless told that it has drawn near, that it is locally near to them, though the significant omission in their case of ἐφ' ὑμάς means that they are not living out of its embrace.[2]

A passage which is not easy to unravel is that where, in answer to the Pharisees' question when the kingdom of God was coming, Jesus describes it as 'not coming with signs to be observed; nor will they say, "Lo, here it is" or "There" for behold, the kingdom of God is in the midst of you' (17.20-21).[3] Set within the wider context of Lk. 17.5–18.8, it is directed to that section's teaching about faith which is seen to require both response (17.7-10) and discernment (17.11-19). The Pharisees are seen to have neither, for their question is said to be based upon false presuppositions so that their understanding of the kingdom's nature is wholly misguided. Their question could be understood as one of genuine perplexity; more likely though it is thought of as arising out of scepticism. They, like the nine lepers, are unable to see signs of the kingdom in Jesus and, instead, they require pointers in external, visible events of which the significance can be clearly discerned. Such marks of obvious presence however will not be available, for to seek them is to mistake the real nature of the kingdom which Jesus makes possible. The present reality of the kingdom is not to be discerned in compelling, undeniable events: it is of a different nature from that. Again, men will not be able to objectify it as being 'here' or 'there' for it cannot be either

1. See above, pp. 16-18.
2. Marshall, *Luke*, p. 423.
3. Sanders and Davies, *Gospels*, p. 296.

localized in a place or encapsulated in an earthly entity. On the contrary, it is ἐντὸς ὑμῶν. Though of itself, this could point to the kingdom's manifestation in the present in a series of events, the presence of a community, or in the activity of the Spirit, and, if it had appeared alone as the answer to the question, such an immanent application could not have been ruled out, nevertheless the fact that its meaning is controlled by the denial that the kingdom exhibits quantifiable signs or is seen in a localised manifestation, suggests that such an understanding is unlikely. Its reality rather is transcendent, present in the heavenly sphere, witnessed to by signs which can in fact be gainsaid, and found in the present in an other-worldly realm. Earlier, Jesus had pointed to his healings as witnesses to the present reality of the kingdom, but they are pointers to it rather than being themselves included in it, for what gives them significance is not their fact but the nature of the one who performs them. He himself alone is the one within the kingdom as he anticipates the final victory of his exaltation (12.20). Here, in ch. 17, Luke, having pointed to the kingdom's transcendence, nevertheless goes on to give the disciples, as opposed to the Pharisees, a hope of its future, early manifestation at the coming of the Son of Man.[1] They must not allow the kingdom's present otherness to lead them into seeking false substitutes for, or artificial guarantees of, its full manifestation which will be realized at the coming of the Son of Man (17.22–18.8).

Such an understanding has sometimes been viewed as attributing a near-Platonic outlook to Luke.[2] The truth though is otherwise, for such thinking remains within the realm of apocalyptic. In his study of the eschatology of Hebrews, C.K. Barrett maintains that emphasis upon the heavenly dimension is itself the outcome of the epistle's eschatology:

> By means of this terminology it is possible to impress upon believers the nearness of the invisible world without insisting on the nearness of the parousia. The author of Hebrews did believe that the parousia was near (Heb. 10.25) but lays no stress upon this conviction.[3]

1. *Christ the Lord*, pp. 16-21.
2. This was expressed in some reviews of *Christ the Lord*.
3. C.K. Barrett, 'The Eschatology of the Epistle to the Hebrews', in D. Daube and W.D. Davies (eds.), *The Background of the New Testament and its Eschatology: Studies in Honour of C.H. Dodd* (Cambridge: Cambridge University Press, 1956), pp. 363-93.

Luke in fact, as we have seen, retains an emphasis upon the future but the guarantee of that future, the ground indeed of confidence in it, is in the present, even though unseen, reality of the enthronement of Christ in heaven and in the consequent establishment of the kingdom of God in that sphere. Believers live in the present out of its power as they wait for its full revelation on earth. Of apocalyptic in general Rowland states,

> Apocalyptic may have contained eschatological teaching, but the point cannot be denied that its hope for the future on a horizontal plane is always matched by the conviction that on a vertical plane these hopes already in some sense existed with God and could be ascertained by the visionary fortunate enough to enter God's presence and receive his information.[1]

Luke presents the earthly Jesus as just such a visionary when, in the light of the seventy's report on their mission, he says, 'I saw Satan fall like lightning from heaven... Nevertheless, do not rejoice in this, that the spirits are subject to you, but rejoice that your names are written in heaven' (10.18, 20). Luke's readers, sharing in the vision of Jesus and of the privileged leaders of the early church can have a confidence in the future which is derived from their certainties about the present. As Barrett expresses it, 'The significant fact is the breaking into this world of the heavenly world, and to know what is now in heaven is in consequence almost the same as knowing what will be on earth'.[2]

Luke's understanding of the 'ecclesia pressa' therefore stands in contrast to the outlook of Matthew's Gospel which has much more confidence in the present life of the church as it is seen as the sphere of the present, authoritative Lord. We have already discussed Luke's picture of the extension of the church in Acts to dismiss that accusation of triumphalism which is so frequently made about him.[3] Luke bangs the drum because he has to, because he needs to show that the actual progress of the mission can bear the interpretation he puts upon it. But the present is not pictured as one in which either the Christian community or the individual within that community has arrived. His church must still pray, earnestly and without abandonment, for the coming of the kingdom (11.2-4; 18.1) and the Lord's Prayer is seen in the third Gospel as oriented wholly around that end.

1. C. Rowland, *The Open Heaven* (London: SPCK, 1982), p. 357.
2. 'Eschatology', *SJT* 6 (1953), pp. 136-55, 225-43 (138-39).
3. See above, pp. 122-26.

In Matthew, the Lord's Prayer is part of general instruction to the disciples which inculcates a relationship to the Law and a life in the community that are both centred in ethics arising out of a right approach to God (5.1-10; 6.1-18). Its petitions to God are to be related to, and the effectiveness defined by, the petitioner's relationship to other people (6.14-15). Luke's setting on the other hand is not one of general instruction in a discipleship measured largely in ethical terms, but is rather one about the nature of the kingdom and of the need of perseverance before its coming. In contrast to Matthew, the element of conditionality is not provided by dealings with others, but by trust in God. It is persistence in prayer (11.5-13) which looks for the presence of the Holy Spirit which is then seen as a gift to the community to enable perseverance in the light of disappointments and persistence in the response to the word of God (11.28). The presence of the Spirit enables disciples to discern the reality of the kingdom of God out of which they live and to continue steadfast in the continuing struggle with the hostile powers (11.24-27; Acts 4.23-31). Times of *peirasmos* bring a falling away from that constancy (8.13) resulting in a falsification of the Spirit's significance and an exclusion from the community (Acts 5.4-5). Blasphemy against the Holy Spirit is the refusal to respond to the Spirit's empowering of witness to Jesus (12.8-12).

The Lukan Lord's Prayer is therefore a prayer of the community living out of the presence of the kingdom but also in the face of earthly trials and disappointments. It becomes a much more specific prayer than its Matthaean counterpart and its significance is wholly eschatological. The kingdom is not realized on earth in such a way that its presence can be seen as an anticipation of its final state, and so his version does not relate the petition for the coming of the kingdom to the extension of the doing of God's will on earth. Luke therefore emphasizes the reality of daily discipleship. The situation is such that the need of a daily taking up of the cross (9.23) can be met only by a petition for a daily living out of the power of the eschatological kingdom. *Peirasmos* in Luke is more awful than it is in Matthew. He does not mellow its starkness with the first Gospel's 'but deliver us from evil' (Mt. 6.13). Matthew (like Mark) in the Gethsemane episode sees the disciples' sleeping as their falling into temptation (Mt. 26.41). Luke gives a greater significance to *peirasmos*. Jesus' first statement, 'Pray that you may not enter into temptation' is not occasioned by their falling asleep (22.40) and it is repeated after the sleep. The sleep becomes only a pointer to something much greater and, in the light of his saying of Jesus at the supper about Satan's request to 'sift' the disciples (22.31-34), suggests a falling into Satan's clutches and a falling away from Jesus. It is therefore that apostasy which expresses the unforgivable sin and which is seen as an anticipation of the final release of evil which will embrace so many before the manifestation of final salvation (8.13).

Life within the Christian community does not for Luke actually embody the life of the kingdom. The community is indeed the eschatological community as it lives its life out of the power of the kingdom and Luke's picture of it in Acts is at pains to make this clear (Acts 2.43-47). But it has not 'arrived' in the way that Matthew, for all his emphasis upon the judgment of the parousia, understands it. Luke understands the church as living out of the kingdom rather than as anticipating it in the Matthaean manner. It is not a community boasting in the direct presence of its Lord in its midst (Mt. 28.20) but is conscious that just as its Lord was constrained on earth (12.50), so its goal is beyond the present with which it cannot rest secure. It is by way of many trials that the kingdom is to be entered (Acts 14.22) for the present remains in some way a contrast to, rather than an anticipation of, the kingdom.

Matthew's church was conscious that in its leader, Peter, it had received the 'keys of the kingdom' (Mt. 16.19). Luke's Peter has had a full manifestation of the Lord's glory (5.8) and he had not fallen in the way that Matthew pictures him as doing (Mt. 16.23). He stumbles it is true, but 'when he has turned' he is to strengthen his brethren (22.32). Nevertheless, he does not actually reach the heights assigned to him by Matthew. Though in Luke he is the first to receive a vision of the risen Lord (23.34), the apostles collectively have to receive new understanding rather than to be instructed to go on teaching in the way that they have already received from Jesus (24.44-49). There is actually less givenness in what they are to proclaim, for the implications of Jesus' Lordship have to be worked out in response to the Spirit's promptings (Acts 15.1-29). Luke, for all the idealization of his picture of the early church, is aware that the implications of the kerygma deriving from the exaltation of Jesus were not as clear-cut as Matthew's Gospel suggests, and his understanding of the last meeting between James and Paul (Acts 21.18-25) is one of less certainty than

Matthew's Gospel allows. If Luke's Peter does not rise to the heights of authority that Matthew's Gospel gives him he does not fall so sharply. He is less a man of contrasts than both Matthew and Paul seem to present him. If Matthew's Gospel seems to claim him as a proponent of that point of view which prevailed at Antioch after the rebuke of James (Gal. 2.12), and to glory in that reversal of weakness, Luke would seem to claim him more for a view that saw his withdrawal from table fellowship as weakness and to move him in a Pauline direction (Acts 15.6-11).[1] But Luke's understanding of the outcome derives from his perception of the church as less confident than Matthew's outlook suggests, as rather that of a pilgrim church wrestling with a number of perplexities in the light of its understanding of a heavenly Lordship of its master which as yet awaited a confident realization on earth.

1. See below, pp. 383-85.

Chapter 12

CHRISTOLOGY

Both Luke's perception of the nature of the Christian life as it is lived out in the present and his understanding of Jesus in terms controlled by Old Testament concepts made for a Christology which is very different from that found in Matthew. Jesus does not indwell his church, for neither the Old Testament framework of Luke's Christology nor his understanding of the Christian way would make for such a confident view of the present life in the Christian community.

This less exalted view of the present of the Christian community is reflected in his use of ἐκκλησία. He uses the term frequently in Acts though the vast majority of instances refer to the local church. At 20.28 it bears a universal significance though too much should not be made of this as evidence of Luke's own understanding for, in that farewell speech to the Ephesian elders, Luke is consciously seeking to assert Paul's own outlook and this he does in the speech as a whole with no little success. Luke shows himself to be aware of the wider use of the term when at Acts 9.31 he talks of 'the church throughout all Judaea and Galilee and Samaria' and at 15.22 tells how it 'seemed good to the apostles and the elders, with the whole church...' Nevertheless he does not really make this outlook his own since for him the church, though being the sphere of the covenantal people of God in which salvation and a relationship with God are realized through incorporation into the people of God, is nevertheless a very human body seeking to live out of the kingdom as it strives to respond to the promptings of the Spirit which interpret the mind of the ascended Lord. Though, as we have seen, Luke sees the covenantal community as the means of enabling salvation to be found by the individual as he is incorporated into the pilgrim people of God, he does not confer upon the church an exalted or quasi-mystical status such as is given to it by Paul when he sees it as the body of Christ or by Matthew when he views it as the sphere of the indwelling Lord. Luke's view of the community is more pedestrian as he presents it rather as living out of the presence of the kingdom which nevertheless remains apart from it and as receiving more indirect guidance from its Lord as this is mediated primarily by the Holy Spirit. The Lord himself does not indwell the community but privileged recipients of his favour have to be alerted by voices, visions and dreams from him when at special points the veiledness of the Lord can be removed. Chief among these for Luke, of course, was Paul's experience on the Damascus road. Yet even here, the significance of the experience had to be mediated either by Ananias or by a further special vision (Acts 9.15; 22.21). Though before Agrippa the initial encounter is given an abiding status (Acts 26.16-18), elsewhere, Paul has to advance by way either of the authority of the community or of special revelation. He is not pictured as the disciple of an indwelling Lord. His own discipleship is not described by Luke in terms which measure up to that estimate of Lord-disciple relationship pointed to by the voice from heaven, 'Saul, Saul, why do you persecute me?' (Acts 9.4; 22.7; 26.14). Such an understanding does not enter into Luke's thinking as a whole. For him the relationship between Lord and disciple remains an external one.[1] He does not have an understanding of a corporate Christ indwelling either the individual or the community. His Christ remains in heaven even though Luke starts to do justice to the wider Christian experience by his use of the concept of the name. That he does so in this way witnesses to the strength of the control exercised over his thinking of the experience of the work of God in Christ in terms dominated by an Old Testament control.

Luke is often understood as being controlled largely by the idea of promise and fulfilment, and this no doubt provides a useful entry into his thinking. Yet such a control over his writing must be understood as more than a seeking to establish proof from prophecy.[2] Luke does indeed use the concept of promise and fulfilment to demonstrate that Jesus is the Christ, and I have argued that his purpose in Acts is actually to present the story of such part of the early church that he records as witnessing to the fulfilment of Old Testament expectations and so as powerful support for his claim that Jesus' Lordship does

1. This is really what distinguishes him from Paul and John and what in actual fact therefore puts him apart from Matthew's final scene.

2. See the discussion in Bock, *Proclamation*, pp. 261-79.

indeed do justice to the Old Testament expectations. It can therefore be accepted by those whose hopes were fashioned by the instruments of the old covenant. Nevertheless, Luke's use of the Old Testament is dictated by more than apologetic or polemical concerns. It arises rather out of Luke's fundamental outlook which sees Jesus as one with the Old Testament and as the fulfilment of Israel's history. His coming does not introduce a new era, nor does it declare the inadequacy of God's earlier work in Israel. Rather, it completes it by bringing Israel's hopes to fruition and by extending God's sway effectively to include the Gentiles. So Jesus is one both with Old Testament history and with the earlier instruments of God's saving work. Typology, Israel's expectations, the nature of her history, and the fundamental Old Testament understanding of the manner of God's activity therefore came together to control the way in which Luke presents the person of Jesus and the nature of his work. While on the surface Matthew appears to be the Synoptic evangelist paying most service to the Old Testament and its prophecies, this is in fact a misjudgment of the actual situation.[1] Typology after the infancy narratives is notoriously difficult to uncover in the first Evangelist's presentation of Jesus. That outlook which sees a new Pentateuch in Matthew is difficult to substantiate and Jesus on the mountain gives his law more as messiah than as antitype to Moses.[2] John the Baptist rather than Jesus is portrayed in terms occasioned by the Old Testament portrait of Elijah. Even in the infancy narratives, Jesus is better understood as the antitype of Israel than of Moses. In Luke, however, it is otherwise. Jesus is the climactic, the eschatological prophet. Prophets of old were inspired to make their proclamation by the action of the Spirit: John the Baptist as the greatest of that line is filled with the Spirit from the womb; Jesus as the eschatological inaugurator is actually conceived by the Spirit for his being is itself witness to and part of God's final eschatological activity. Yet the Spirit is essentially functional. Jesus is portrayed in terms derived from the biblical presentations of Moses, Elijah, Elisha the servant of Isaiah, and the Isaianic herald of the new age. He is one with these even as, being their fulfilment, he is greater than they. It is not until his exaltation that he actually transcends their

1. Matthew's appeal to the Old Testament is not determinative for his christological explanation as it is for Luke.

2. Davies and Allison, *Matthew*, p. 423, 'Any alleged comparison with Moses is dwarfed by the ways in which Mosaic categories are transcended'.

categories. Yet even then, he does not break free from Old Testament control. In accordance with the outlook of the Psalms, he is installed as Son and he is enthroned as the Lord who sits at God's right hand (Pss. 2.7; 110.1). His sway is universalized as Gentiles enter into its sphere. What is now an established heavenly realm is reflected on earth as men acknowledge his rule. But Satan's rule, though decisively broken, is not yet finally destroyed. Men as they respond to the proclamation, move from the sphere of darkness into the light (Acts 26.18). *Peirasmos* remains a present reality (11.4) and the final trial is awaited as a prelude to the complete revelation of the glory that is already the Son's (22.27) even though the cloud still hides even what to the eyes of faith it proclaims (Acts 1.6-11).

Jesus in Luke–Acts, though not an absent Lord, is a hidden one whose present activity and nearness have to be argued for. Disciple and Lord remain apart from each other, addressing each other but from a distance. Jesus can encourage by his example so that the disciple follows him in the way and like him by the way of suffering passes into the heavenly sphere (Lk. 13.32-33; Acts 14.22). There is truth in that view which sees Luke as portraying Jesus' death in martyr terms to encourage the imitation of him in the Christian's daily life, for Jesus is one with both his Old Testament predecessors and his Christian followers.[1] The fulfilment of earlier messengers of God, he is the *archegos* of those who come after him (Acts 5.31). He can guide by example, intervene with visions, appear from heaven, and give a mouth by which opponents of Christians will be confounded. But he cannot indwell his disciples. Instead, they are brought within the sphere of his present either by the action of the Spirit or through the Old Testament concept of 'the name'. Luke's understanding of Jesus in Old Testament terms and his thought of the present kingdom as otherworldly mean that there is no room in his thinking for an immediate indwelling of Lord and disciple. For his is a Christology 'from below', where Jesus is wholly subordinate to the Father whose agent he is. His person is described almost entirely in functional terms.[2] For all the value derived from such an Old Testament

1. B.E. Beck, '*Imitatio Christi* and the Lucan Passion Narrative', in W. Horbury and B. McNeil (eds.), *Suffering and Martyrdom in the New Testament* (Cambridge: Cambridge University Press, 1981), pp. 28-47.

2. This runs counter to D.L. Bock's estimate that for Luke, Jesus 'is Lord in the fullest possible sense' (p. 270) and his assertion that Luke's Christology 'breaks

understanding of the person of Jesus, Luke's emphasis upon continuity and his seeing Jesus in terms of oneness with the old does, nevertheless, put a constraint upon him to mean that his presentation of Jesus while giving witness to his outreach in terms perhaps unsurpassed in the New Testament nevertheless is unable to reflect the total impact of the early Christian experience of life in him.

new ground in equating Jesus' status with that of God by means of the application of the title Lord to Jesus' (p. 187). 'Jesus', he maintains, 'performs God's task and holds his status' (p. 225). He concludes that 'all descriptions of Luke's Christology as "adoptionistic" fall short of the truth' (p. 237). 'Adoptionistic' is indeed an unhelpful way of characterizing Luke's Christology for it continues to suggest something more ontological than Luke allows. His Christology is functional. Bock's assertion that 'by the time Peter gets through the citation of Ps. 110 and speaks of Jesus as Lord and Messiah, it is clear that Jesus is κύριος in the same way that God is, because he sits at God's right hand doing his work' is precisely to forget the different status that the psalm gives to its two Lords. To be at God's right hand is to exercise authority on behalf of God, but it is a delegated authority nevertheless and in no way expresses identity of status. To claim for Luke 'identification' between God and Jesus is to forget Luke's OT control and its typological significance. Joel 2.32—'whoever calls on the name of the Lord shall be saved'—is taken up in Peter's appeal to be baptized 'in the name of Jesus'. This is the way, however, that the 'Lord our God' calls men and women to himself. Through Jesus they are brought into the people of God. Jesus may rule over that kingdom, but it is nevertheless God's kingdom (Lk. 22.28-30). Jesus is the κύριος of that people, the one by whom they are united to God, but it is God himself rather than Jesus to whom they have been united. Jesus stands on the human side rather than the divine. Stephen prays to Jesus as the one who gathers together the people of God which is linked to him. But here, the function of Jesus as the κύριος, is clear, and the parallel between the martyrdoms of the κύριος and the disciple is explicit. But the prayer of the community as a whole is made to the Lord God, not to Jesus, and his activity, exercised through Jesus, sustains them (Acts 4.23-31). This prayer represents the fundamental stance of Luke and the later speeches do not advance beyond its pattern.

Part III

LUKE'S USE OF MATTHEW

Chapter 13

POSSIBILITIES AND PRESUPPOSITIONS

It is now some thirty years since S. Petrie, in an often referred to article, wrote that 'For those who retain the hypothesis, "Q" is only what they choose to make it'. He talked of the 'vagaries' of Q, of its 'nebulosity' and complained of 'the subjectivity and arbitrariness in its reconstruction'.[1] Q remains a hypothetical source. The primary reason for postulating its existence is a belief that Luke could not have taken at least the bulk of the material that is common to him and Matthew out of Matthew to produce what we now have in his Gospel. It would have entailed too great a re-ordering of Matthew's material: it would have meant too great a revision of both his incidents and his sayings. It would have served to produce something which seems in large parts at any rate inferior to the original. So Q is regarded as necessary. What is seen as Luke's method, and the value that is placed upon his final work make it inevitable.[2]

Such an outlook which necessitates a belief in Q, however, gives rise to one constant problem. The material that is common to Matthew and Luke and out of which Q is culled is, in fact, not all that 'common'. If there are passages such as Mt. 7.7-11/Lk. 11.9-13, Mt. 11.25-27/Lk. 10.21-24 and Mt. 23.37-39/Lk. 13.34-35 where the identity of wording is such as to suggest a direct use of some common source, at other times the relationship appears far less obvious. What are we, for instance, to make of the different forms of the Lord's Prayer (Mt. 6.9-18; Lk. 11.2-4), of the beatitudes (Mt. 5.1-11;

1. S. Petrie, 'Q Is Only What You Make It', *NT* 13 (1959), pp. 217ff.

2. Typical is W.G. Kümmel's comment, *Introduction to the New Testament* (rev. edn trans. H.C. Kee; London: SCM Press, 1975), p. 64, 'What could possibly have motivated Luke, for example, to shorten Matthew's sermon on the mount, placing part of it in his sermon on the plain, dividing up other parts among various other chapters of his Gospel, and letting the rest drop out of sight?'

Lk. 6.20-23), of the story of the centurion's servant (Mt. 8.5-13; Lk. 7.1-10), of the parables of the talents and of the pounds (Mt. 25.14-30; Lk. 19.12-28)? How are these passages in Matthew and Luke related to each other and how are the differences to be accounted for? What has been altered, by whom, and when? Vincent Taylor, writing about the variation in the closeness of agreements, spoke of the need to determine the causes 'of this perplexing phenomenon'.[1] Belief in the existence of Q requires an assumption that the evangelists are primarily compilers, perhaps collectors, often tidiers-up, pickers and choosers of material through which their own ideas can be expressed, rather than radical revisers using material before them as spring-boards to be refashioned so that they, and more importantly their readers, can land where the evangelist wants himself and them to be. By its very nature, belief in Q must reduce the activity of the evangelist to a minimum.

When the upholders of Q do admit an individual role to the evangelists, it is more often than not Matthew who is allowed to be the more adventurous of the two.[2] There seems to be a reluctance to allow for this on the part of Luke. In part, this seems a response to the way his preface is understood as expressing an intention of objectivity, a searching for reliable sources, and a concern for accuracy. In part it arises out of the categorizing of Luke as primarily a historian, as seeing his two volumes controlled by historical concerns and expressing a historical method. A third factor is that evaluation of his theology as being more primitive than that expressed in Matthew. Yet, as we have seen, the preface is not so easily subjected to historical interests but gives full place to a theological concern.[3] The way Luke handles his history suggests a theological rather than an archaeological outlook. Luke's faithfulness to his sources cannot assert that overriding control that some would see in his handling of what was before him.

1. V. Taylor, *The Gospels: A Short Introduction* (9th edn; London: Epworth Press, 1960), pp. 22-23.

2. G.N. Stanton, *The Gospels and Jesus* (Oxford: Oxford University Press, 1989), p. 89, 'Most scholars accept that on the whole Luke has retained the order and content of Q more fully than Matthew, so reconstructions of Q are usually based on Luke'.

3. See above, pp. 169-70.

A recent assertion that 'in general Luke appears to give more sayings in the original form than does Matthew'[1] needs to be subjected to very careful scrutiny. While its outlook may be supported, say, in the evangelists' different versions of the Lord's Prayer and of the beatitudes, where Matthew's can be seen as a community document expanding the sources in the light of community reflection and shaping them in response to the needs of the church so that the Lord addresses the present situation directly, it is less easy to support its approach and so to minimize Luke's creativity at other points. What is one to say, for instance, of the different versions of the healing of the centurion's servant (Mt. 8.5-13; Lk. 7.1-10)? Here the vocabulary seems to reflect a Lukan usage which suggests at least a free handling of any source. The presence of σπουδαίως, ἤμελλεν τελευτᾶν, μακρὰν, τασσόμενος, στραφεὶς, ὑγιαίνοντα all seem to reflect Luke's hand. Both Luke and Matthew could be seen as expanders of their source. What though of the condemnatory verses which Matthew has in 8.10-12 and which are found in another form at Lk. 13.28-29? It is sometimes suggested that these verses could have been in Matthew's form of Q,[2] but this is to bring in a hypothetical 'extra', the only reason for which seems to be the reluctance to admit the evangelists' freedom in their use of sources. Matthew could, of course, have added it from a detached Q pericope which Luke has retained elsewhere. Equally, however, Luke could have omitted it at this point because its harsh attitude to the Jews did not fit the significance of the story as he wanted to unfold it. His understanding of Jesus' statement 'Not even in Israel have I found such faith' praises the Gentile without necessarily implying criticism of the Jews. After all, the Jews in his version of the story have not been faithless but faithful: there is no hint of inadequacy in their response to Jesus. The Gentile is just super-faithful! Luke could well be the omitter of material to use it at a different point and in a manner which tones down the original version's hostility to the Jews. If it is asked why he did not use it in this way at this point, the answer must be that even its toned-down criticism was not suitable to his reshaping of the incident.

But has he in fact reshaped the incident? Some have maintained that

1. R.S. Stein, *The Synoptic Problem: An Introduction* (Leicester: Inter-Varsity Press, 1988), p. 103.

2. A.H. McNeile, *The Gospel according to Matthew* (London: Macmillan, 1915), p. 103.

the extra 'Jewish' material was already in Luke's source by suggesting either that his source differed from Matthew's or that Matthew has abbreviated Q.[1] But if the latter is the case, why should Matthew have omitted the detail of the Jewish initiative? He is, of course, hostile to the Jews and he has already shown this in his infancy narratives. But these serve as something of a prologue to his Gospel. He does indeed include a harsh prediction by Jesus in 8.10-12 which reflects Matthew's situation at the time of writing. But most of the collection of miracles in chs. 8–9 are directed to Israel so that, in spite of Pharisaic opposition, 'the crowd marvelled saying "Never was anything like this seen in Israel"'. Jesus goes around Israel preaching and teaching and 'when he saw the crowds, he had compassion on them, because they were harrassed and helpless, like sheep without a shepherd' (9.36). There seems no reason therefore for Matthew to have made an earlier source harsher by omitting the approach of the Jews, even if it represented one on the part of the Jewish leaders to whom Matthew was particularly harsh. Appeal to his well-known tendency to abbreviation seems to pay scant respect to his theological intentions and concerns. Much more likely is the possibility that Luke at this point has added the detail of the approach of the Jews. Marshall, in his concern to keep to a minimum Luke's creative handling of his material, says, 'The linguistic evidence slightly favours the case for Lukan insertion, but it is hard to see why Luke should have altered the story to such an extent without some bias in his sources'.[2] This however is to fail to acknowledge that the story thus shaped fits Luke's theology perfectly. Jesus goes first to the Jews, a nucleus of them do respond, from their response is made possible an incorporation of Gentiles into the people of God, and ultimately Gentile faith far outshines that of Israel herself. It is hard to see how the creative hand of Luke could be denied at this point.

In discussions of the parable of the rejected invitation (Mt. 22.1-14; Lk. 14.15-24), there is again the tendency to play down the possibility of Lukan redactional activity. Marshall suggests that the basic form of the parable can be recovered and that, when it is, it is 'found to

1. R.T. France, *Matthew*, p. 154; 'Matthew typically omits this detail as not essential to the story, and represents him as approaching Jesus directly in the first instance. The racial element in the confrontation is thus more emphatic in Matthew's version'.

2. *Luke*, p. 278.

be very close the Lukan form'.[1] Others have suggested that the differences between the two forms have come about prior to their inclusion in the Gospels.[2] Where it is allowed, redactional activity is mainly found in Matthew. So Gundry writes, 'From the standpoint of an assumption that Matthew found the present parable in a setting and form similar to Luke's, his revisions accord with his manner as seen in other passages'.[3] It has been suggested that Matthew reduced the double invitation of outsiders to one and that signs of this are to be seen in his earlier double approach to those originally invited.[4] The parable does, of course, reflect Matthew's idea of the present existence of the kingdom in his church, his anti-Jewish polemic, the historical situation of his own day, and does fit comfortably into the outlook seen in the group of parables found together in this strategic place in his work. The additional section could well be from him, an allegorization of his expectations for his church as these are reflected in other passages (Mt. 13.36-43, 47-50). Yet, if the double invitation of outsiders were in Matthew's source, it remains difficult to see why he should have reduced its implications. Its omission might have added to the anti-Jewish polemic by playing down any Jewish response and limiting it to complete outsiders, but this is to forget the Jewishness of the twelve and of Matthew's Gospel as a whole and to exclude Jews from any community constituted on the basis of Matthew's final scene (Mt. 28.16-20).

What though of the possibility that Luke derived this parable from a form like that given in Matthew 22? The ultimate double invitation would certainly fit his understanding of the inclusion of both Jews and Gentiles. The altering of the setting of the parable from that of a royal wedding feast to one of a less unique banquet is to be accounted for by its setting in Luke's Gospel. It is found in the context of Jesus' participation in a meal with a ruler of the Pharisees, and therefore its suggestion of a banquet makes a more immediate link with that than would Matthew's wedding feast. The eschatological setting is not diminished but rather enhanced by the fellow-guest's exclamation, 'Blessed is he who should eat bread in the kingdom of God'. Luke sees

1. *Luke*, p. 584.

2. E.P. Sanders and M. Davies, *Studying the Synoptic Gospels* (London: SCM Press, 1989), p. 64.

3. *Matthew*, p. 432.

4. Michaelis, *TDNT*, V, p. 108.

Jesus' meals as strong anticipations of the eschatological banquet, but for him Jesus does not fully become king until the ascension. His telling of the parable is such that it is meant to include the situation of Jesus' ministry as well as that of the post-Pentecostal church. It explains the Jewish rejection of Jesus' initial approach as well as their rejection of the kerygma.

As we have seen, Luke is less harsh in his attitude to the Jews than is Matthew, and this is what could have caused his alterations to the Matthaean form of the parable. In his version, the excuses bear some relation to the exemptions of Deut. 20.5-7. While Linnemann's understanding of them as expressions of delay rather than of complete refusal seems unlikely in itself,[1] they represent presumption upon the relationship with the host rather than a direct refusal of him. It is the failure to see the urgency of the hour and the compulsiveness of the invitation that is blameworthy. The reaction of the host, though strong, is not a wholesale and unlimited destruction but an exclusion of those whose failure in understanding led to a self-exclusion even though it was actually effected by others. It reflects very much the outlook of the Lukan version of the Matthaean form of Jesus' response to the centurion (Lk. 13.25-28; Mt. 8.11-13).

Different versions of a parable incorporated independently by the two evangelists into their particular works remain unlikely, for what is found in both Matthew and Luke fits comfortably into the outlook of those Gospels as a whole.[2] The possibility remains that both Matthew and Luke used their common source freely to come up with what we now have in their respective Gospels. Equally however, it is possible that one evangelist revised a form that is found in the other's work. If this is the case, it is in fact easier to account for a Lukan revision of a Matthaean form than it is to suggest how Matthew could have derived his from a form similar to that found in Luke. For that, the double invitation to outsiders remains a problem.

In the parables of the talents and of the pounds (Mt. 25.14-30; Lk. 19.11-27), the differences are of course much greater. Though basically they both make the same point of the need for watchfulness in an eschatological situation, they have different numbers of servants

1. E. Linnemann, *Parables of Jesus*, p. 89.

2. Though we must be aware of Hooker's warning (*Mark*, p. 4), that we may in fact be bringing in our own ideas rather than those coming naturally out of the evangelist's work.

who are entrusted with different amounts, while Luke has an allegorical insertion within the parable itself. Marshall plays down the possibility of redactional activity on the part of the evangelists. It would, he says, be 'remarkable' if they had both engaged in such at this point.[1] More likely, he suggests, is that they worked on different recensions of Q which had been influenced in their different ways by the somewhat inconsequential but vividly creative art of popular storytelling. Yet it remains more likely that there was more determined creative activity on the part of the evangelists than such an approach allows. Matthew could have taken his three servants out of Luke's ten, for the third evangelist deals effectively only with three, and for Matthew to have talked of ten would have seemed unduly stereotyped in view of his having just used a parable about ten maidens. He could have varied the amount of the gifts entrusted to the servants to reflect the varied statuses and abilities of the different groups within his community. It is obvious that there were tensions within that community and it is likely that here he wished to exhort the less privileged. They too had their responsibilities. The greater value of the gifts fits in with Matthew's thinking big: he thereby makes a didactic point about the value of what has been entrusted to the Christian community. The warning of 'weeping and gnashing of teeth' fits his overall style.[2] Would he though have omitted the allegory within the parable proper? Its seeming anti-Jewishness and the wrath of the king would have fitted what he portrays elsewhere (Mt. 22.7). It would not have contributed directly to his main concerns in this chapter, but it certainly would not have distracted from them. It would have led into the thinking seen in the allegory of the sheep and the goats even if the intention of this latter story had been restricted in its threat of judgment to Matthew's own church. If its setting were wider (as it is usually understood) and its message related to the attitude of outsiders to Matthew's church, then the allegory of Luke's additional section in the parable of the pounds would have been wholly appropriate.[3]

On the other hand, the allegory within the parable could well have

1. *Luke*, p. 701.

2. M.D. Goulder, *Luke, A New Paradigm* (JSNTSup, 20; Sheffield; JSOT Press, 1989), p. 12.

3. J.C. Fenton, *Saint Matthew* (Pelican Gospel Commentaries; Harmondsworth: Penguin Books, 1963), pp. 400-401.

been a Lukan addition. Luke's setting for the parable is one designed to let it counteract disappointments caused by the delay of the kingdom's appearing and by the rejection of the Christian proclamation on the part of the Jews. Luke is meeting the problem of causes rather than dealing merely with the symptoms of inertia and lack of enthusiasm. Delay and rejection go together. The master of Matthew 25 becomes Jesus himself in his historical career, the Lord who goes to receive a kingdom and to return with authority which he will demonstrate to friend and foe alike. The Lukan servants all receive the same amount because they are all in the same condition of standing poised for eschatological urgency. They become ten because they represent, not particular individuals but the whole community. The sum they receive is more realistically aligned to the ambivalent situation of Christian discipleship as Luke perceives it. Luke does not elsewhere have 'talents'; Matthew does (Mt. 18.24). On the other hand, Matthew does not have 'pounds' which occurs in the New Testament only in Luke. The parenthesis of v. 25—'And they said to him, "Lord, he has ten pounds"'—presents something of a difficulty. Luke is certainly not on the side of the rich, and so the element of seeming injustice is real to him. Nevertheless, the situation of the continuing church reveals the truth that those who have faith arising out of a discernment of the eschatological urgency of the hour do in fact receive more, while those whose sense of urgency flags quickly lose even what faith they have (19.26; 18.8).

The possibility of Luke's creative activity cannot be denied at these three points. It is at least potentially as realistic as that more willingly allowed to Matthew and, in fact, it seems easier to account for his creative handling of something like a Matthaean form than it is to explain Matthew's supposed handling of a form similar to that found in Luke. The other possibility that accounts for the differences by suggesting a long-term development issuing in different forms used conservatively by the two evangelists cannot be ruled out, but it nevertheless has to rely on postulating a rather haphazard development of tradition and the existence of various sources which when taken over and handled very conservatively by the evangelists happen to fit the theology which Matthew and Luke, each in their very different ways, express. Their handling of these sources of necessity then has to be understood as much more restricted than is their use of Mark where allowance has to be made for their creativity.

It is here that belief in Q as a source of Luke almost of necessity demands postulating something like the proto-Luke theory if the hypothesis upon which Q is built, namely Luke's conservative handling of his sources, is to be upheld. The proto-Luke theory is needed to sustain the belief, first that Luke handled Mark conservatively and therefore could be expected to show the same constraints in his dealings with any other sources that came his way, and, secondly, that the unity of outlook found in Luke is derived from an extended source controlling the theology of the Gospel that was finally produced. Proto-Luke allows belief in Luke's conservative handling of both the shape and contents of Mark and so is almost an inevitable hypothesis to enable Luke to be viewed as a collector of material which he handled consistently in a restrained manner. For, as Caird wrote in his defence of proto-Luke, 'the Markan hypothesis involves the corollary that Luke used wide editorial freedom in rewriting his sources'.[1] But can belief in Proto-Luke be sustained? Proto-Luke is often said to have accounted for the following sections of the completed Gospel: 3.1–4.30; 5.1-11; 6.20–8.3; 9.51–18.14; 19.1-27, and the passion and resurrection narratives.[2] There is a certain consistency about the material thus extracted, for unity is given to it by a Jerusalem orientation with Jesus moving to the goal of his ascension here. He becomes the Second Adam, the universal renewer by way of the restoration of Israel. The temptations climax with that to jump from the pinnacle of the temple. Nazareth's rejection furthers his progress, 6.20–8.3 allows for the ministry in Galilee which that episode demands, and 9.51 introduces the journey to Jerusalem. The parable of the Pharisee and the tax collector is followed by the story of Zacchaeus and the parable of the pounds which leads straight into the narrative of the last supper and to that of the passion and resurrection.

All that, however, is quite another thing from suggesting that it is this material which provides the outline for the completed Gospel and that it was into this that Markan blocks were fitted. Of itself, it is a somewhat unstructured, inconsequential narrative which, even allowing for the possibility that it was not intended to be a final work and that some of its episodes may have been replaced by Markan equivalents or near-equivalents, does not make for a developing and

1. G.B. Caird, *Saint Luke* (Pelican Gospel Commentaries; Harmondsworth: Penguin Books, 1963), p. 23.

2. *Luke*, pp. 23-27.

explained story. The Nazareth episode has no previous narrative to justify the speech's reference to Capernaum, the call of Simon allows for no kind of earlier contact with Jesus which would form a basis for the request to use his boat as a floating pulpit, no gathering of disciples precedes the giving of the sermon on the plain, there is no account of any appointing of the twelve which could serve as a justification of Jesus' promise to them at the last supper (22.28-43), the journey to Jerusalem with its sonorous entry at 9.51 is given no rationale of the kind provided by the Lukan distinctive addition to the transfiguration story (9.30-31) and which it demands, and the events in Jerusalem are left without any real reason such as is given them by Luke's use of the Markan predictions. Without the material derived from Mark, it lacks a real skeletal framework capable of sustaining either a reasoned discourse or an unfolding narrative of the kind demanded by the presuppositions behind proto-Luke.

The rejection at Nazareth is perhaps the decisive episode in coming to any decision about proto-Luke (4.16-30).[1] Its lack of any real justification for the speech's reference to a previous ministry in Capernaum means that it is unlikely to have been part of any extended narrative of the kind required by the proponents of proto-Luke. Its positioning is theologically rather than biographically controlled and its place as the first real incident in Jesus' ministry is accounted for by Luke's use of it as an alternative opening declaration to that which he would have found in Mk 1.14-15. In keeping with his later alteration of Mk 1.38, he redefines Mark's 'gospel of God' in such a way as to turn its future thrust into a justification of the nature and significance of Jesus' ministry so as to make that ministry witness to the reality of the future act of God to which it points.[2] The Old Testament quotation becomes the vehicle of Luke's own christological stance as this is revealed in the kerygmatic speeches of Acts 2.23 and 10.38. Luke's is a conscious reshaping of the Markan declaration and emphasis.

If Mark's Gospel suggests a christological declaration at this point, Luke's own overriding concern with the Jewish rejection will have been responsible for his placing a justificatory speech in the mouth of Jesus. He shares such a concern at this point in the narrative with Matthew who also makes Jesus leave Nazareth to dwell in Capernaum which becomes the centre of a Galilean ministry which itself

1. *Luke*, p. 23.
2. See above, pp. 17-18.

anticipates and enshrines a Gentile outreach (Mt. 4.12-17). Matthew's problems are the same as Luke's even though his manner of solving them is completely different.

If I may for the moment anticipate my later suggestions, it seems that Luke could actually have been influenced by Matthew to make that Gospel the reason for his extended narrative and be the basis for both the Capernaum reference and his unusual use of Ναζαρά (4.16; cf. Mt. 4.13). His use of βιβλίον in place of his more usual βίβλος (4.17, 20; cf. 3.4; 20.42; Acts 7.42) is then to be explained by the fact, not that he is using a source, but because he is here referring to the scroll itself rather than to the contents of the prophecy. Jn 20.30 has a parallel usage and the same distinction between the book and its contents is made by Rev. 1.17 as compared with Rev. 3.5; 20.15.

If unusual vocabulary does not necessarily point to the use of some unidentified source or sources, the contents of the speech can be accounted for by viewing it as an exposition of Luke's own concerns. The speech is seen to express a consistent and logically developed point of view once it is read, not as Luke's factual description of an event in Jesus' ministry, but as his giving to that event a definitive character which encapsulates his understanding both of the significance of the ministry as a whole and of the events leading up to and including those of his own time. In Mark, the hearers move from wonder to a hostility which is occasioned by Jesus' origins among them. Just why this should be is not explained and Jesus is left marvelling at their unbelief. Luke's narrative is an attempt to explain this unbelief, to see Jesus himself as actually accounting for it, and to embrace it within the scheme of God's wider purposes. It is in fact a response to Mark and it is this basis which shapes it as a whole, determines its parts, and even makes for the rough edges that are sometimes seen in it. The Markan narrative exerts some constraint over Luke's story telling as he battles to resolve the perplexities to which Mark gives expression.

Luke's handling of Mark's version of Jesus' rejection at Nazareth means that his divergencies from the order of that Gospel do not necessarily imply the use of another source which he is thought to be following in preference to that provided by the second Gospel, but suggests rather the possibility that they are thematically and theologically motivated. Luke could not leave the rejection at Nazareth in its Markan position which implied weakness, failure, withdrawal and separation. By giving it a programmatic position and by explaining this in the sermon, he tones down its negative outlook to enable its failure to be caught up into the divine purposes and so to justify that which Mark simply acknowledges with incredulity.

Other Lukan divergences from Mark's order express a similar theological control. That his account of the call of Peter (5.1-11) is based upon Mark seems clear from the fact that no real purpose is served by the inclusion of the other three disciples. They are simply there. The narrative moves between the plural and the singular in such a way as to allow the spotlight to fall upon Peter alone but to do so in a manner which does justice to the tradition of Mark who states that the others were called at the same time. The reason for such a highlighting of Peter seems to be the part he is to be assigned in Acts and the not uncontested movement out into the Gentile world that he inaugurates. Luke makes the incident into more than the call which Mark describes to enable it to become a point of disclosure by Jesus and of discernment and comprehension on the part of the apostle. Peter who has already been with Jesus is now given an insight which outstrips that of his fellows and which actually equals what in Acts is to be given to Paul. His is a discernment which is to be worked out in the process of his later actions and in the deepening understanding of its significance.

In Mark, the parable of the mustard seed is used as part of his explanation of the 'secret of the kingdom' which is contained in the contrast between its present hiddenness and future revelation (Mk 4.21-32). Luke however has not used his Markan source to make this point but has systematically transformed it into a section about hearing the word of God (8.4-25).[1] The parable of the mustard seed does not fit such a message so he transfers it to a later point in his Gospel (13.10-21). As a comment upon that event, it witnesses, not to the contrast between the past and future of the kingdom, but to its reality in the present as the healing accomplishes its part in Jesus' defeat of Satan and enables people such as the woman to come within its embrace. Nevertheless, he has not abandoned Mark, for 13.18-19a suggests the influence of Mk 4.30-31 and differences from Mark betray, not another source, but Luke's rewriting to enable him to express its significance as he sees it. By use of the aorist ἐγένετο εἰς δένδρον in place of the present tense found in both Mark and

1. W.C. Robinson, 'On Preaching the Word of God', *Studies in Luke–Acts*, pp. 131-38.

Matthew, he points to the reality of something which has already happened in Jesus. Luke is looking back to a past enabling of a present reality. The kingdom already exists, and the Christian community lives out of its power like birds nestling in the branches of a tree.

A further transposition of the Markan order is found in Luke's account of the anointing of Jesus (7.36-50; cf. Mk 14.3-9) where, however, the differences between the stories in the two Gospels are of such a kind as to make Luke's dependence upon another source seem a distinct possibility. Nevertheless there are strong links with the Markan account. Fitzmyer, for instance, notes some seven points in which Mark and Luke agree. He allows some evidence of conflation in that Luke does not name the Pharisee at the beginning of the episode but only later calls him 'Simon'.[1] These considerations could, in fact, point to a free handling of the Markan episode on the part of Luke who rewrote the story in order to make it relevant to his concern with both Pharisees and sinners. The host becomes 'one of the Pharisees' in order to link the scene with Luke's previous episode which contrasts Pharisees and tax-collectors. Luke now introduces this story in order to bring sinners into that contrast. Since Jesus in his Gospel eats either with disciples, with sinners and tax collectors, or with Pharisees; it is appropriate that Simon should become a Pharisee. The woman anoints Jesus' feet because this serves as a much more appropriate expression of simple love than does Mark's royal anointing of the head.

Do these considerations suggest that Luke could have built up his episode from Mark? They could if an adequate reason can be found for his wanting not to have included the Markan episode where it is and as it stands in the second Gospel. Mark's is the first episode in his passion narrative and the significance of the event for him is contained in Jesus' own explanation, 'She has anointed beforehand my body for the burial'. The episode contributes to the unrelieved starkness of Mark's narrative as Jesus enters into the depths of death. Anointing is the final acknowledgment of death, the witness of its reality, the last vain attempt to delay the dissolution of the body. For Luke, however, it is precisely this corruption of death from which God protects Jesus. The women spend much time in preparing spices, just as in John Nicodemus engages in absurd extravagance. Irony is present in both Gospels, for God raised Jesus. In the early speeches of Acts, Luke expresses the Old Testament witness to the resurrection of Jesus

1. *Luke*, p. 685.

in words of Ps. 16.10, 'Thou wilt not let thy Holy One see corruption' (Acts 2.27; 13.35). Anointing of Jesus' body in death was unnecessary, not required, and actually wrong, for preservation of the Lord from corruption depended, not on the vain acts of men and women, but upon the powerful vindication of God.

There is every reason therefore for Luke to have avoided Mark's episode, but he takes over its themes of contrasting attitudes and of outgoing love to use it powerfully to explain the outlook of the Pharisees as he builds up his explanation of the reasons for their rejection of one who should have been theirs. Again, no source other than Mark is required, and Luke is seen as one who is open to a drastic re-ordering of the Markan incidents whenever theological considerations make it desirable.

If all this speaks against Jeremias's verdict that Luke is 'the enemy of rearrangement',[1] it also puts a large question mark against the belief that he keeps his sources separate. The story of the rejection at Nazareth and the parable of the mustard seed show that this is not so for they reveal Luke as clearly keeping his eyes on more than one source, while the Nazareth episode, the call of Peter, and the anointing of Jesus show him introducing episodes from one source into a context provided by another. Luke does indeed have 'blocks' but they are far less self-contained and exclusive of material derived from elsewhere than is often suggested.[2]

Most important of all, these episodes show (and their number could of course be multiplied) that Luke handled his Markan source with very great freedom, not merely in his selectivity, but also in his free re-writing when theological considerations made it desirable. If there seems to be little real evidence of proto-Luke in the body of the Gospel, we have to allow that even there, when theological considerations made it necessary, Luke has in fact re-written Mark very freely indeed.

If this is true of Luke's handling of Mark in the body of the Gospel, it is even more likely to have happened in his taking over of Mark's passion narrative for here the differences in outlook between the two evangelists appear in their most concentrated form. If, as Caird accepts, in the passion narrative 'out of a total of 163 verses, there are

1. J. Jeremias, *The Eucharistic Words of Jesus* (London: SCM Press, 1966) p. 161.

2. See, for instance, the over confident diagram in Taylor, *Gospels*, p. 37.

87 verses which have some counterpart in Mark, but only 20 in which it is the sort of verbal similarity which is usually regarded as evidence of dependence' and if there are 'no less than twelve transpositions of Mark's order',[1] this witnesses only to the fact that the concentrated kerygmatic and theological concerns which are inevitably expressed in any narrative of the passion are different for Luke from those which he found in his source. The body of the Gospel shows that he was no slave to his sources, and his passion narrative does no more than confirm this. If Luke appears to use Mark more freely in the passion narrative than he does in the body of the Gospel, this is merely because the concentration of the multiplicity of concerns in this crucial episode makes such a difference necessary.

For Luke expresses ideas which are very different from Mark's. For Mark, the crucifixion of Jesus was less of a problem than an opportunity to enable the Christian proclamation to meet the reality of the situation out of which he was writing. Jesus on the cross was the basis of the proclamation, and the reality of the depths of the cross was alone capable of enabling both the glory that was to come out of it and the future it ensured for his readers. For Mark no less than John, and though expressed in a very different way, the cross was essentially the glory of Jesus, the point of God's action. For Luke however it was otherwise, for the cross was but the climax of the sequence of events of suffering that moved forward to the glory that was no longer intimately connected to it. Luke's risen Jesus is not recognized by the wounds of the crucifixion. His crucifixion scene is therefore wholly other than Mark's. Even in his death Jesus is open to the outsider as he has characteristically been throughout the ministry, and he passes through death to await the reversal in the resurrection and so to enter into his present glory thereby becoming the means of salvation for all who respond to the story about him. The heavenly realm is now a reality for him, and so the farewell meal with its discourse emphasizes this eschatological dimension to make its continuation in the early church's breaking of bread become both a sharing with his presence and an anticipation of the heavenly banquet which is promised thereby. The twelve are assigned places of honour as exercisers of judgment in the heavenly kingdom. They are given eschatological significance and the realities of their post-ascension life are to be lived out in the light of that (22.14-38). Peter stumbles rather than falls and

1. Caird, *Luke*, p. 25.

so the account of the denial is gentler to allow him to remain within sight of the captive Lord who is then able to bestow a searching but restorative look (22.61-62).

The leaders of the Jews do not take part in the mockery of Jesus for, perverse though they are—and Luke does not hide their perversity—they are not degraded for, they are doing 'whatsoever (God's) hand and (God's) plan had predestined to take place (Acts 4.28). Now is the time of trial (22.46) when Satan's power is unleashed (22.3), when the reality of the eschatological tribulation is entered into (22.35-38), when it results in the Lord's death, but when God's victory is made possible.

The Jewish trial is in the morning only, partly to regularize the proceedings, partly to bathe Peter's fall in a gentler light, and partly to tidy up Mark's narrative which, by portraying the night session as an unofficial gathering (Mk 14.53), has reserved the council's official consultation for the morning. Luke tells a story of Jewish perversity, for the nation in its official leaders deliberately turns its back on one who should have been recognized as Christ. He therefore remakes Mark's scene to give it the status of an official repudiation. They are closed to the truth (22.68) not because they do not recognize it, but because they refuse to acknowledge what they recognize. 22.70 is both a recognition and a denial of its implications. 'Christ' leads into 'Son of God', not as equivalents as Conzelmann maintains[1] nor as un-Lukan distinctions as Catchpole suggests,[2] but as a Lukan exposition of disclosure, recognition and rejection. At Lk. 4.41 the demons discern that Jesus is the Christ but the response which gives adequate expression to the significance of this function is that Jesus is 'Son of God'. 'Christ' does not exhaust his significance but has to be taken up and universalised in terms of Divine sonship. Paul at Damascus, preaching that Jesus fulfils the function of the Christ again proclaims him as 'Son of God' (Acts 11.19-22). The annunciation to Mary describes Jesus' function as Christ but both begins and ends with his acknowledgment as 'Son of God'. So Luke at the trial changes the context and divides up the manner of the high priest's assault upon Jesus (cf. Mk 14.61) to make it an official, climactic, determined rejection of him.[3] No charge

1. *Luke*, p. 84.

2. D.R. Catchpole, *The Trial of Jesus* (Leiden: Brill, 1971), pp. 274-78.

3. 'Jesus' appearance before the Sanhedrin, which in Luke loses any appearance of a trial that may have been left to it in Mark, is a stark attack upon him', *Christ the*

regarding the temple is made, partly because Luke has no complaint against the temple so that Jesus cleanses it, takes it over, rather than rejects it, and partly because he can transfer such a charge to the trial of Stephen and then bring Lord and disciple more closely together.

Since no reason is given in Mark for Pilate's abrupt and decisive question of Jesus, 'Are you the king of the Jews?', Luke supplies one in such a way as to point to the dishonesty of the charge and the perversity of the Jews in making it. He does in fact seem to be magnifying the hostility to bring the nation into the refusal of the Christ. Jerusalem as a whole rejects Jesus at this point and it is to the Jews that Pilate hands Jesus over for execution. All however is built up upon the Markan outline, and the one unexplained intrusion, the trial before Herod, is to be accounted for both by Luke's urge to link the trials of Jesus and Paul and by his understanding of it all in terms of Psalm 2 (Acts 4.25-28). Luke however does not give the last word to perversity for, although the people as a whole is implicated, there is also a group which laments. The people follow Jesus to his crucifixion but, already moving beyond the perversity they showed before Pilate, they dissociate themselves from the hostility of the rulers at the cross, and are open to be moved into the beating of their breasts at Jesus' death (23.13, 18, 23, 27, 35, 48). Meanwhile, the lamenting women act as the representatives of the true daughters of Zion. We have already seen reasons for the Lukan rewriting of the Markan picture of the crucifixion. Other sources are not required, for Luke's story of the cross is made to continue Jesus' outreach, his obedience and his confidence. Mark's form of the Gentile centurion's response is revised to include it within that servant dimension that is so clear in Luke's overall presentation of Jesus.[1]

Luke's story then, both in the passion narrative and in the Gospel as a whole is built upon that of Mark which determines it overall and with which there is a constant dialogue. Proto-Luke is not merely an unnecessary hypothesis, it is a mistaken one in that it fails to give a true account of the manner of Luke's writing and results in an evaluation of his Gospel which is at variance with its true significance. Luke's is a thorough revision of Mark's work. His re-arrangement of Mark's order in the body of his Gospel may have been less than that undertaken by Matthew who consistently shows a propensity to collect

Lord, pp. 92-93. Official Jewry rejects her Lord.

1. *Christ the Lord*, pp. 61-64.

together material that is often scattered in his sources. Luke does not go in for this, but this is precisely because he is influenced by Mark's journey scheme which Matthew's large blocks of material have obscured. But he does nevertheless move Mark around when it is necessary in order to further his own ideas. His freedom comes out most clearly in the passion narrative but it has been revealed in such significant episodes as the Nazareth rejection and the call of Peter. He has rewritten Mark freely when it suited him, and this rewriting has been just as thorough as his theological reworking required. Luke is no slave to his sources. His use of Mark shows selectivity, re-arrangement, thorough revision, and theological re-interpretation. We cannot avoid the implications pointed out by Caird, but must of necessity accept that Luke did in reality 'use wide editorial freedom in rewriting his sources'.

Luke handles Mark freely and with a creativity which is in fact greater than that shown by Matthew. This has important implications for our understanding of what is likely to have happened at those points where Luke and Matthew have material that is obviously related and where Mark is not the common source. We can no longer approach such material from a position which is biased in favour of the originality of the Lukan version and we have earlier in fact shown reasons for suggesting that a number of these narratives make more sense when the creativity which can be seen as accounting for the differences is assigned to Luke rather than to the author of, or the tradition behind, the first Gospel.

But can we go further than this to suggest that Luke actually used the first Gospel? Is Q in fact disposable? Is the freedom with which Luke handled Mark of such a kind as to make credible that further freedom which he would have had to employ on the first Gospel if he did in fact use it?

Before that possibility can be considered, however, it is necessary first to assess the significance of the agreements of Matthew and Luke against Mark, for these at least raise the question whether one of these Gospels was actually used by the other. Major agreements between Luke and Matthew against Mark are found in their stories of the ministry of John the Baptist, the temptation of Jesus, the Beelzebul controversy, and the parable of the mustard seed.[1] To make the

1. R.T. Simpson, 'The Major Agreements of Matthew and Luke against Mark', *NTS* (1965), pp. 273ff.

possibility of Luke's use of Matthew at these points into a probability requires an explanation first of his uncharacteristic decision to follow Matthew here rather than Mark, and, secondly, of the actual manner of his using Matthew if in fact that was what he was doing.

Matthew's description of John's ministry is fuller than that found in Mark (Mt. 3.1-12; Mk 1.1-8; Lk. 3.1-18) and so serves as a better basis for Luke's own version which is fuller still. More important, Matthew contains an account of John's preaching of repentance which Luke, by shifting it away from Pharisees and Sadducees in the direction of the crowds as a whole, is able to make into an instance of prophetic preparation for the coming of the messiah. Israel as a whole must not presume upon her sonship in Abraham but must bring forth fruits worthy of repentance. The true in Israel—'all the people' (v. 21)—are baptized and Luke takes this opportunity of adding a notice of John's sociological teaching which, alongside the general principle addressed to the crowds as a whole, contains special instructions to the outcasts and more especially to the tax collectors who are baptized by him and actually thereby take upon themselves the obligation not to increase their riches by means of exploitation. Tax collectors are not without response and Jesus' later acceptance of them is itself built upon this Johannine imperative.[1] So, later at 7.29, Luke again points to the baptism of all the people including tax collectors and takes up the Matthaean suggestion (3.7) that Pharisees rejected John and so rejected Jesus also. Mark's narrative had nothing like this which would serve as a basis for this Lukan concern. It was important for him to express such a concern in the cause both of linking the community of Jesus with Judaism and also of defending the point that Jesus' outreach was not ethically indifferent even if it was not ethically controlled. The ethical demands upon tax collectors was made by John, and Jesus could be understood as building upon that in his many warnings against the dangers of riches.

Matthew's fuller narrative enabled Luke to express all this; nevertheless he did not leave Mark aside but actually used him as his control at certain significant points. Following Mark, he had John come 'preaching a baptism of repentance with a view to forgiveness of sins' (3.3; cf. Mk 1.4). Like Mark therefore, but unlike Matthew, he did not have John actually proclaim the kingdom (Mt. 3.2). He also followed Mark in his adoption of that Gospel's formula for introducing the

1. See above, pp. 203-209.

Isaiah quotation. He omits the Markan/Matthaean description of John as Elijah redevivus but he did this systematically in the body of his Gospel in order to present Jesus himself as the antitype of Elijah.[1] The Markan/Matthaean setting for John (Mk 1.5-6; Mt. 3.5-6) was transferred to the introduction of Luke's story which itself became the opening declaration of that systematic unfolding which his preface had announced.

Luke takes over Matthew's form of the narrative of the temptation of Jesus, not merely again because it is fuller than Mark's, but because, whereas Mark's is pictured in terms of an initial battle with Satan,[2] Matthew's concentrates on the obedience of Jesus which establishes his sonship. Luke's concept of Jesus' journey to his exaltation at Jerusalem emphasizes this obedience at a number of significant points (4.43; 6.12; 9.22, 32, 35, 51; 12.49-50; 13.32; 22.28, 42-44). He reverses the order of the last two temptations in order to point to the contrast between a self-assertive open demonstration of Lordship and that which actually happened at the ascension which the last episode of his Gospel describes.[3] The ministry of angels is omitted because the series of temptations represents but the beginning of Satan's attack. Victory is not yet achieved as it is in both Mark and Matthew but awaits the final resolution through the events of the suffering which culminates in the cross. Jesus is going in the right direction, but his sonship is not yet guaranteed.

Luke however is again influenced by Mark to picture the temptation as lasting over the period of forty days rather than to present Matthew's single determinative event (Lk. 4.2; Mt. 4.2-3; Mk 1.12). Even here, where Matthew is most completely followed, the Markan Gospel remains as a background control.

In Mk 3.20-30, the Beelzebul episode is portrayed as part of a series of controversy stories, and Matthew has something of the same setting (Mt. 12.24-29). Luke, however, has removed it from this context to make it part of a section on prayer for the coming of the kingdom and for the present gift of the Holy Spirit as a sign of its reality (11.1-13). Jesus' casting out of demons is also a sign of the kingdom's presence (11.20) and of its hovering over the Lord's activity in the world.

1. *Christ the Lord*, pp. 67-69.

2. Hooker, *Mark*, pp. 48-52.

3. E. Franklin, 'The Ascension and the Eschatology of Luke–Acts', *SJT* 23 (1970), pp. 191ff.

Since Mark has no actual reference to the presence of the kingdom,[1] Luke of necessity follows Matthew. Nevertheless, he alters him to replace that Gospel's reference to Jesus' empowering by the Spirit with one of empowerment by 'the finger of God'. This is often seen as odd in view of Luke's interest in the Holy Spirit and more especially in the light of his reference to the Spirit at 11.13.[2] However, since Luke does not see the disciples as empowered by the Spirit until after the Pentecostal outpouring, that verse must refer to the period of the church rather than to the time of Jesus' ministry. Though Luke sees that ministry as empowered by Jesus' initial anointing by the Spirit (4.18), he does not say that the healings are Spirit-enabled. In Acts 2.22, Jesus is proclaimed as 'a man attested with mighty works and wonders and signs which God did through him' and even when Jesus is proclaimed as Spirit-filled, the reason for his good deeds is seen, not because of his possession of the Spirit, but in the fact that 'God was with him' (10.38). The activity of the Spirit in the world is not demonstrated until after Pentecost but, even then, miracles are enabled by the name of Jesus rather than by the Spirit. Luke therefore at 11.20 seems to be using Moses typology (Exod. 8.19; Deut. 9.10) in a manner which is in accordance with his overall understanding of the nature and means of Jesus' healing works.

Luke has his own version of the parable of the overcoming of the strong man (11.21-23; Mt. 12.29; Mk 3.27). Suggestions that this represents the form contained in his and Matthew's source and that Matthew left this in favour of the Markan version seems less persuasive than the position that Luke rewrote Matthew.[3] Why Matthew would have found Luke's version unattractive is not easy to imagine. Its heightening of the present eschatological activity would have been sympathetic to his understanding, it does more justice to the earlier imagery that Jesus uses, and it is more immediately suitable to Jesus' conclusion. It is easier to see it as Luke's rewriting in the service of

1. Compare Mk 3.20-27 with Mt. 12.25-29 and Lk. 11.17-22.

2. Though see Evans, *Luke*, p. 492, where though he notes that it is generally asserted that it is unlikely that Luke changed 'spirit' into 'finger', he himself says, 'But this is not absolutely certain. For all its frequency in L–A "the Spirit" is nowhere associated with healing or exorcism (except perhaps 4.18ff.). For the agency in healing Luke tends to use OT terms'.

3. F.G. Downing, 'Towards the Rehabilitation of Q', *NTS* 11 (1965), pp. 169-81.

emphasis, for its biblical imagery (Isa. 49.24; 53.12) is a fitting vehicle for the eschatological battle by which he pictures Jesus' movement to his ascension.

Again, it is easy to see why he has omitted the Matthaean/Markan understanding of blasphemy against the Holy Spirit (Mt. 12.31-32; Mk 3.28-29) for, unlike both Mark and Matthew, he does not have Jesus' healings as Spirit-directed. Matthew has altered the Markan version in order in part to differentiate between the time of Jesus and that of the outpouring of the Spirit, but perhaps more especially in the light of v. 28, to emphasize the rejection of the Pharisees. Luke, who is more favourably disposed to the Jews, transfers the blasphemy against the Spirit to a later part of his Gospel to use it in an episode referring, not to those hostile to the Gospel, but of those who might be tempted to apostatize and to deny the Spirit-witness in them (12.1-12). The passage as a whole is best understood as a Lukan adaptation of a Matthaean development of the Markan source.

Much the same is to be said of Luke's version of the parable of the mustard seed (13.18-19). We have already seen why he omitted it from his use of Mark for he was not concerned with that evangelist's contrast between the present and the future. Instead, he takes it over from Matthew where it is also joined to the parable of the leaven (Mt. 13.31-33; Mk 4.30-32) to use it in a section which talks of the gathering of many into the kingdom of God and the rejection at its future realization of those who should have been included but who denied Jesus. The woman with the spirit of infirmity represents those who are open to the release brought about by the defeat of Satan in Jesus' ministry. As such, she is already within the embrace of the kingdom and anticipates her inclusion in that banquet which will be denied those who presume upon their place. From Matthew 13 he takes over in a modified way the thought of the present reality of the kingdom. Even though he rejects Mark's contrast between the littleness of the present and the greatness of the future, because for him the kingdom is already real though transcendent, he is not uninfluenced by Mark for his introduction is worked in the Markan form.

These major agreements of Matthew and Luke against Mark are best explained in terms of Luke's free revision of Matthew's adaptation of Mark. Luke appears to have known both Mark and Matthew, to have followed Matthew at these points because what he was saying and the way he was saying it had something of importance to offer to the expression of his own understanding and which was not found in Mark's version of these incidents. They represent a conscious departure of Luke from his Markan primary source but, nevertheless, even here the overall primary authority of that source was not denied, and Matthew's narratives were actually altered in the light of Mark's versions. Such a view of the relationship between the three Gospels at these points allows consistency of outlook to Luke in that it does not deny the primacy of the authority that he gave to Mark over Matthew. These incidents were in general distinctive, not in the sense of contrasting with Mark, but in that of contributing to that new outlook which the passing of time and the changing situation of the church made necessary. They are more of the nature of being useful than of being of a high degree of significance.

The minor agreements also suggest the probability that Luke knew Matthew for, as Sanders maintains, they 'have always constituted the Achilles' heel of the two-source hypothesis'.[1] Even when allowance is made for possible chance agreements, assimilations and textual corruptions, there remains a hard core of agreements which is not so easily dismissed.[2] It is, of course, possible that Matthew and Luke

1. Sanders and Davies, p. 67.

2. Goulder, *New Paradigm*, p. 50. A case for the minor agreements' pointing to Luke's use of Matthew has recently been strongly urged by R.H. Gundry, 'Matthaean Foreign Bodies in Agreements of Luke with Matthew against Mark: Evidence that Luke used Matthew', in F. van Segbroeck, *et al.* (eds.), *The Four Gospels* (3 vols., BETL, 100; Leuven: Peeters, 1992), II, pp. 1467-95. He notes (p. 1468) 'Its essential point consists in the Matthaean and un- or even anti-Lucan character of these particular agreements. They do not fit Luke's redactional purpose in the pericope at hand'. They occur because Luke is actually following Matthew carelessly. While Gundry's advocacy of Luke's use of Matthew and his recognition that the minor agreements point strongly to this are to be welcomed, his acceptance of Luke as a somewhat careless follower of Matthew runs counter to our argument for his theological consistency and care. So, for instance, at the call of the twelve, Mt. 10.2 and Lk. 6.14 agree against Mk 3.16-18 in that they both omit Mark's 'that they might be with him'. Gundry maintains that Luke has powerful reasons for keeping this phrase and, in view of Luke's declared qualification for the replacement of Judas, Acts 1.21-22, he appears to have a point. Nevertheless, it is not strong because he ignores the context in which Luke places the call, namely the sermon on the plain where for him the twelve are primarily witnesses to the nature of the people of God there constituted. This for Luke is their distinctiveness and they are in fact only one part of those who during the ministry are with Jesus (Lk. 8.1-3). As T.A. Friedrichsen says ('The Matthew–Luke Agreements against Mark', in

independently used a form of Mark which at points was different from canonical Mark.[1] Here, at any rate, the bringing in of hypothetical forms and versions—a move which on the whole should be rigorously controlled—is made superficially more attractive by the difficulty inherent in the alternative. If Luke used Matthew at these points to alter, add to, or extract from the Markan version, it is hard to see why he did not do this more widely to include Matthaean additions like those found, say, at Caesarea–Philippi and at the crucifixion. If he knew Matthew, he followed him in the minor agreements at a number of relatively insignificant points and in the major agreements for a number of more important narratives, but remained uninfluenced by him at some of his more significant additions. It suggests a fairly careful perusal of Matthew's Gospel combined with a firm (but not necessarily easily comprehended) discrimination in its use.

Nevertheless, a number of points suggest hesitation about the introduction of some form of non-canonical Mark. Matthew and Luke seem sometimes to be following an 'improved' Mark, hence the suggestion of deutero-Mark, and at others an inferior Mark, giving rise to suggestions of proto-Mark. A single Mark containing both improvements and inferior characteristics is no harder to believe in of course, than to think of Matthew's using our Mark in this way to make both seeming improving and retrograde alterations. It merely shows the subjectivity of our use of terms like 'improvements' and 'inferior versions'—perhaps it would be wiser just to remain with 'differences'! But once we cease to categorize differences in terms reflecting our presuppositions, a Lukan use of Matthew at these points makes much more sense. So, Matthew omits Mk 2.27 from his version of the

F. Neirynck [ed.], *L'Evangile de Luc* [BETL, 32; Leuven: 1989], pp. 335-91 [369]), 'A more sound methodology requires that possible independent Lucan reasons for the minor agreements first be carefully studied before coming to the conclusion Gundry favours.' Luke's is a much more sensitive handling of Matthew than Gundry maintains and it is therefore likely to have been much more thorough and more theologically controlled than he allows. His suggestion that Luke's use of Matthew was only as some kind of 'overlay' to his final work actually underplays the influence of the first Gospel upon the third and does less than justice to Luke's methodology. Why Luke used it at these points in preference to Mark if he, as Gundry's historian, recognized the midrashic character of Matthew is hard, if not impossible to understand. Gundry's Luke is inconsistent in general and in part incompetent.

1. Sanders and Davies, *Studying the Synoptic Gospels*, pp. 73-75.

cornfield incident, not because he is using a proto-Mark, but because its negative down-grading of the sabbath is unacceptable to him. His Jesus does not belittle the law. Luke chooses to follow him and to omit Mark's evaluation of the sabbath because his Jesus, though sitting loose to the law, does not devalue it even when he sees it superseded in himself. Both Matthew and Luke approach the issue from a christological perspective as opposed to Mark's controversial and legal concern. Again, both Matthew and Luke omit γονυπετήσας when it is found at Mk 10.17. It is sometimes objected that they are unlikely to have reduced Mark's christological witness,[1] and so proto-Mark is proposed as the source of their narrative. Matthew, however, could well have done just that. Though using γονυπετῶν at 17.14, he has replaced its use at Mk 1.40 by προσεκύνει which is more characteristic of him. For him, however, both represent what Matthew sees as a true acknowledgment of Jesus for in both instances the supplicant addresses Jesus as κύριε. Here, however, such a recognition is denied and the man is represented rather as something of a failed disciple. His is but a limited surrender; hence the omission of γονυπετήσας for it is just too positive. Luke sees the point and follows Matthew in the omission.

Of some importance is the minor agreement in the passion narrative where both Matthew and Luke focus the summons to prophecy in the challenge to tell who struck Jesus (Mt. 26.26; Lk. 22.64; cf. Mk 14.65).[2] Perhaps it is easier here to justify a different form of Mark as the common source, yet it is by no means obvious that such a hypothesis is required. Mark, after the Sanhedrin's condemnation of Jesus, has them derisively reject the claim that they have perceived in his answer to the high priest. A grand gesture on their part is called for. Matthew here lacks the insight on Mark's christological intricacy but instead sets out to increase the sheer wilful hostility of the Jewish leaders. Their perversity is more ignominious and less on a grand scale. Surprisingly, he omits Mark's reference to their blindfolding of Jesus, but he knows that it has happened for he is following Mark's narrative. So, in that knowledge and with his less grand aim, he focuses the Markan taunt in the jibe to recognize which one of his tormenters has actually done the striking. As Matthew writes, it is a wholly understandable revision of Mark. Luke, on the other hand, has

1. Sanders and Davies, *Studying the Synoptic Gospels*, p. 98.
2. Goulder, *New Paradigm*, pp. 6-9, 750.

the mockery before the conviction. Mark's grand irony therefore would be wholly out of place and in any case the mockery is undertaken by custodians rather than by the Jewish leaders themselves. He does have Jesus blindfolded, and the Matthaean form of the taunt is therefore increased in appropriateness.

These instances of minor agreements suggest that they are to be accounted for, not by the introduction of hypothetical forms of the Markan Gospel but by Luke's following of Matthew's rewriting of the Markan source, and it is likely that the minor agreements as a whole respond to such an approach. Neither Matthew nor Luke were slavish followers of Mark, and alternative versions of Mark which they were deemed to have used in a highly conservative manner should be introduced to explain these agreements only when it is impossible to discern logical reasoning behind the possible changes made to canonical Mark.

A second reason for doubting the existence of other versions of Mark as sources for the first and third evangelists at a number of points in their Gospels is the pervasive character of the minor agreements. It is not just a question of alterations, additions and omissions consisting of a number of words and phrases. There is in fact a wider, more diffuse, but nevertheless telling link between the two Gospels at a number of points and in distinction from the parallel narratives in Mark. So, in their stories of the transfiguration (Mk 9.2-13; Mt. 17.1-13; Lk. 9.28-36), both Matthew and Luke point to the change in Jesus' face, both omit Mark's reference to the fuller's professionalism, and reverse Mark's order of naming the two visitors. They both deal with the Markan evaluation of Peter's answer, Matthew by omission and Luke by a subtle twist in Mark's phraseology. Both report the coming of the cloud while Peter was speaking and so take a more positive view of his reply, and both change the positioning of Mark's reference to Peter's fear in such a way that the Markan fright is changed into awe.

These agreements could, of course, be the result of independent revisions of the Markan form. Matthew and Luke might both have been influenced by Moses typology, and they might both have been tidying up Mark. Their common dealing with Mark's comment on Peter's response, however, is less easily understood as independent working, as is their common reordering of Mark's reference to the disciples' fear. Luke, it is true, does not follow Matthew in having

Jesus meet and remove the apprehension, but this is accounted for by the realization that his community stands half way between the attitudes reflected in the other two Gospels, neither sharing fully in the lostness apparent in Mark nor in the confidence reflected in Matthew.

Overall, there seem to be just too many points of contact for Luke and Matthew independently to have been altering Mark. Again, the differences from canonical Mark are too pervading for them to be accounted for on the supposition that some other form of Mark was being used. Such a Mark would have been so different from our Mark as to be virtually a rewrite rather than a revision of him at these points. The relationship between the three is rather to be explained by the suggestion that Matthew revised Mark and that Luke, though using Mark as his primary source, rewrote that in the light of what in Matthew seemed to him as improvements upon Mark.

Much the same can be said in the light of the minor agreements in the accounts of the trial of Jesus before the Sanhedrin (Mt. 26.57-75; Mk 14.53-72; Lk. 22.54-71). Some of these could be accepted as fortuitous improvements upon Mark. So at Mt. 26.58 and Lk. 22.24 they both have the imperfect where Mark has the aorist. Even the fact that they both use 'Son of God' in place of Mark's 'Son of the Blessed' may be no more than coincidence. On the other hand, Luke's form of the interrogation seems to have been influenced by Matthew's version of Mark. Both have the demand that Jesus should tell them whether he is the Christ rather than rest content with Mark's simple direct question. Luke's reply, 'If I tell you...' picks up the Matthaean form of the answer and emphasizes the perversity that Matthew, by his version of their question and Jesus' answer already makes clear. Mark's direct version of Jesus' answer becomes σὺ εἶπας in Mt. 26.64 and ὑμεῖς λέγετε ὅτι ἐγώ εἰμι in Lk. 22.70. Both Matthew and Luke suggest that the Jews' understanding of messiahship needs deepening, Matthew by the addition of in πλὴν v. 64 and Luke by his construction resulting in a second question. Both add a reference to an imminent glorification—Matthew by the addition of ἀπ 'ἄρτι in v. 64, Luke by his use of ἀπὸ τοῦ νῦν (v. 69)—but Luke, by his omission of the second part of the Danielic reference, alters the significance that Matthew sees in its expected manner of achievement.

Again, if they were following a Mark different from canonical Mark, it would have presented a very different narrative with the emphasis placed upon Jewish perversity rather than on that

Christology which seems to be at the heart of canonical Mark's telling of the story. All this therefore suggests that it is more likely that Luke revised Mark with one eye on Matthew, at least at certain points, than that they were both following a Mark which differed significantly from our canonical Gospel. Luke used Mark as his primary source but, in his rewriting of it, in his drastic revision to make it a vehicle for the service of his community at a later date and in very different circumstances, he used Matthew—who had in some sense done the same sort of thing, facing perhaps many of the same problems but often presenting very different answers—as in some way contributing to the final form of the Markan narratives as he wished to tell them.

Such a conclusion, however, raises in an acute form the problem presented by the fact that—in a large number of incidents—Luke, if he knew Matthew as well as Mark, nevertheless omits some highly significant Matthaean additions to the original Markan narratives.[1] We have already noticed one of the most obvious of these, Luke's non-inclusion of the Lord's promise and commissioning of Peter at the time of the apostle's witnessing to the person of Jesus (Mt. 16.18). Other significant non-interpolations occur at the pericope on divorce (16.18; cf. Mt. 19.9), at the baptismal encounter between John and Jesus (3.21-22; cf. Mt. 3.14-15), in the cornfield episode (6.1-5; cf. Mt. 12.5-7), at the entry into Jerusalem (19.37-44; cf. Mt. 21.10-11), at the trial before Pilate (23.1-25,; cf. Mt. 27.24), and at the death of Jesus (23.47-49; cf. Mt. 27.51.2). Is it likely that, knowing Matthew, he would deliberately have omitted these additions which are often found in passages where he seems actually to have points in common

1. It is clear how influential the argument based on this fact is, though many of the conclusions drawn from it are supported by little more than hunches or suppositions. So Kümmel, *Introduction*, p. 64, 'Is it conceivable that Luke would have taken over none of Matthew's additions to the text of Mark?' But Luke does take over additions (for example, narratives of the Baptist and the temptation) when it suits him. Little attention is given to the fact that he might have had very good reasons for not taking many of the Matthaean additions to Mark. What seems so sensible to us, as being obvious improvements on Mark, may not at all have appeared in this guise to Luke. Here subjectivity takes over. It is to the fore in Stanton's question (*The Gospels and Jesus*, p. 88), when he asks, 'Why did Luke find Matthew so unattractive, when in almost all other parts of early Christianity it became the favourite gospel?' But would Paul have found Matthew attractive if he had known it? The answer is by no means obvious, and if it could be guessed at, it would almost certainly be 'No'.

with Matthew over and against Mark? So, at the recognition by Peter, both Matthew and Luke expand Peter's reply and the form given by Luke seems to reflect, even as it turns aside from, that found in Matthew. In both Matthew and Luke the disciples are ordered not to tell anyone that Jesus is the Christ. While Matthew has this explicitly as the contents of Jesus' charge, this is unnecessary for Luke since, because the charge and the confession are not separated by Jesus' promise to Peter, his command 'to tell no one this' is a direct reference to Peter's response. Mark at this point is less direct.

Nevertheless, it is just the really significant Matthaean addition in the Lord's promise to Peter that Luke must have deliberately omitted if he were aware of Matthew at this point. For Matthew, this is undoubtedly one of those places where he legitimates the teaching and practice of his church. If it is taken up and re-applied at Mt. 18.18, it also looks forward to the Lord's final command to his church (28.18-20) and back to the sermon on the mount which becomes its ideal. It is true that Matthew's Peter is rebuked as in Mark. Nevertheless, in Matthew, v. 21 introduces a new stage in which the teaching on suffering appears. The teaching on suffering is no longer seen as an actual part of the Caesarea–Philippi revelation; it is not intimately connected as an integral part of the messiahship in the way that it is in both Mark and Luke. That messiahship is rather seen as a backcloth in the light of which the suffering is to be understood. So, when the rebuke of Peter appears, it is reported as something of a separate incident. It means, not that Peter's whole idea of messiahship is wrong as Mark implies, but rather that Peter has not yet taken that extra dimension on board.

Matthew could of course have omitted the rebuke altogether as Luke was to do. But Matthew is aware of Peter's failings. He has become something of a founding figure to Matthew's church, but he was known to have denied the Lord and, since there is no mention of a resurrection appearance to Peter in Matthew's Gospel, it seems that Peter as Matthew's church claimed him was known to have fallen after the resurrection as well as before it. The rigorism of Matthew's Gospel represents that of a Peter who would have been rebuked by Paul at Antioch (Gal. 2.14). Matthew's Peter is drawn back into the sphere of the activity of James, and he witnesses to a Christ whose church is still in some form of dialogue with a law however revised in the light of the messiah's interpretation of it.

Such would seem to be implied by the Lord's promise to Peter. Luke however has a very different understanding of that disciple. For him, Peter is Paulinized in a way that is unlikely to have been acceptable to Matthew's community and which is almost certainly less than correct historically. Luke's Peter has no problem at all over the matter of eating with Gentiles and the agonizing over the law that such a question actually raised.[1] He would go beyond James' requirements as they are expressed in the apostolic decree. True, he accepts them as does Luke's Paul, but he, like the Paul of Acts, regards them as a concession to strict Jewish–Christian susceptibilities. So Luke plays down the weaknesses of Peter to omit the Lord's rebuke at Caesarea–Philippi and to make his denial a stumbling rather than a falling into Satan's πειρασρός (Lk. 22.32). Nevertheless, he does not wish to introduce Matthew's praise of Peter into the Markan version of Caesarea–Philippi. Mark would not have accepted Peter in that way—as a co-author of that outlook advocated by the apostolic decree—and Luke could not adopt a Peter whose status was contained in a legal-type stringency of ethical interpretation designed on the one hand to retain a role for the Jewish Law and on the other to put question marks against that Pauline freedom which was so basic to Luke. So he declines to include the Matthaean addition and instead goes on his way to present a Peter whose greatness is found in his insight rather than in a conscious way of life.

Other Lukan non-interpolations from Matthew are to be understood in this way, as conscious distancings from Matthaean stances at particular points. So the Matthaean exception clause is avoided because it is seen, not as a concession, but as a movement in the direction of rigorism, of legalism, which the Markan Lord rejects and which Paul spurns (1 Cor. 7.10). Matthew's additions to the narrative of the death of Christ (27.51-54) are not followed because Luke does not see that as the eschatological turning point which occurs rather at the ascension. His John does not recognize Jesus at the latter's baptism for, though the babe in the infancy narratives does, that episode has the character common to Luke's first two chapters, namely that of prologue significance which encapsulates and sums up the totality of the

1. Luke's Peter would certainly not have withdrawn at the request of James who indeed, in Luke, would not actually have made such a request. Peter could not have done though he would not have been indifferent to the need to carry the Jerusalem church with him.

person's place in Luke's understanding. His John does not proclaim the kingdom. The episode in Lk. 7.18-35 has something of the character of a revelatory discourse which moves John into a new style of understanding rather than as in Matthew having John actually renege on his earlier insight. At his telling of the cornfield episode Luke does not follow Matthew in his introduction of priestly and prophetic justification of Jesus' action, because he has a Lord who is not related to the Law in the way that Matthew is. He does not follow Matthew at the entry into Jerusalem because his witness is limited as in Mark to that of the disciples rather than to the crowds in general, and he does not include the episode of Pilate's washing his hands for that is intimately connected with the Jewish self-curse which, as we have seen, would have been so contrary to Luke's thought.

All in all, therefore, the Lukan refusal of significant Matthaean additions to the Markan narrative in no way works against the hypothesis that Luke knew Matthew and used him as one of his sources. What it does do, however, is to point to the nature of that use, to emphasize its selectivity, and even to disclose a critical light in which Luke viewed that Gospel and its handling of Mark. Mark's Gospel is so very definitely his primary source. Matthew remains supplementary, but the significant Lukan departures from its handling of Mark show that Luke is uneasy with some of its most characteristic attitudes. His omission of a large number of Matthaean additions to Mark shows that he parts company with the first Gospel's attitude to the Jews and to the Law, that he revises its understanding of the place of John the Baptist and his relation to the kingdom, that he sees the disciples' witness as being centred in the exaltation of Jesus which happens, not by way of the cross and resurrection but at the ascension, and that he does not find the essence of discipleship in the obedient response to a church's ethical instructions. Luke's understanding of the Christian witness is in reality very distinct from that found in Matthew.

The underlying reason in fact for many of the Lukan omissions of Matthew's additions to Mark comes out of those very real differences we have earlier noted between Matthew and Luke, differences which are of such a kind and which present such an overall divergence of outlook as to suggest that Luke basically approved of neither the way Matthew resolved the historical difficulties encountered by his church nor the basic theological outlook which resulted from such a resolution. Our reading of Luke's preface, with its underlying hesitancy about his predecessors in the field, suggests that while he regarded Mark's Gospel as a witness which merited great respect but which the passing of time made inadequate as a basis for commending continuing belief in Jesus in the light of new circumstances and changed problems, he found Matthew's attempt to meet the need posed by those very circumstances and problems inadequate, if not downright wrongheaded, in its resulting attitude to Law, to the Jews, and in its eschatological interpretation of the present times. If Mark was inadequate and needed updating, Luke recognized Matthew as such an updating of Mark but one which in fact was misguided.

Orchard and Goulder both believe that Luke's differences from Matthew are caused by the fact that he was writing for Gentile Christians whereas Matthew was concerned with a more Jewish–Christian community.[1] Such a view, however, is not easily upheld. Some have suggested a Gentile–Christian provenance for Matthew[2] while others have linked Luke firmly to a community of Jewish Christians and God-fearers.[3] My earlier discussion of the two Gospels suggested in fact that there was unlikely to have been a very great difference—if any at all—in the ethnic situations of the two communities linked, albeit in different ways, to them. Both were mixed. Both had a basis in a predominantly Jewish–Christian grouping but both were moving into that area where that was ceasing to be the dominant influence which was in fact fast becoming primarily a Gentile one.

Luke's dissatisfaction with Matthew went much deeper than Goulder and Orchard suggest and it was this which made him subordinate Matthew's updating of Mark to his own. In my earlier sections I suggested the causes of this dissatisfaction. Luke, I maintained, was strongly influenced by and was indebted to Paul's view of the Law, however much he may have bathed it in a different light. Matthew who stood in this respect at the other end of the spectrum from Paul would therefore have been uncongenial to him. That evangelist's hostility is mellowed in a reaction which acknowledges the tragedy

1. Goulder, *New Paradigm*, pp. 22-23; B. Orchard and H. Riley, *The Order of the Synoptics: Why Three Synoptic Gospels*? (Macon, GA: Mercer University Press, 1987), pp. 248-50.

2. G. Strecker, *Der Weg der Gerechtigkeit* (Göttingen: Vandenhoeck & Ruprecht, 1962); J.P. Meier, *Law and History in Matthew's Gospel* (Rome: Biblical Institute Press, 1976).

3. Esler, *Community*.

involved in the historical reality of the Jewish rejection both of Jesus and of the Christian proclamation about him. Here also my assessment has been very different from that made by Goulder who maintains that 'Luke's gospel is best thought of as being developed in the 80s, after the break with Judaism became final (6.22 and Acts *passim*): Matthew in the 70s, while there was yet hope (5.11; 10.23; 17.17, etc.)'.[1] Rather, I have suggested that the situation (as opposed to the response) is much the same in both Gospels. The break has virtually happened: the actual hope of Israel's coming in within the period of history is giving place to a realism which accepts that she will not. That this is no new thing is suggested by Paul's own outlook and by the Markan turning away from Israel to the Gentile sphere. No change in situation between Matthew and Luke can be posited from the Gospels' texts. What can be affirmed, however, is a change in the response to that situation and this is in a direction opposite in fact from that proposed by Goulder. Whereas Matthew has accepted the situation and envisages the church as doing something of a takeover from the Jewish covenantal community, Luke neither accepts nor enters into it. He tries to explain it, but throughout sees it as nothing other than a tragedy. Whereas in Matthew there is but one place where hope can be suggested for the Jewish people (23.39), Luke leaves that future open and makes room for a future eschatologically realized recognition as Israel responds to her true Lord.

Again, all this means that Luke sees eschatology as being less realized in the present than does Matthew and he therefore accepts the parousia as having a positive role. It retains the aspect of hope in a way that Matthew's emphasis upon its judgmental role does not. Luke is more ambivalent and thus more realistic about the realities of discipleship in the present. It is 'through many tribulations' that we enter the kingdom of God (Acts 14.22). His Jesus does not therefore indwell the church as he does in Matthew and the church is less directly related to the kingdom. His Christology is a less exalted one as he retains a certain distinction between past and present and distinguishes between, though without separating, the historical Jesus from the exalted Lord.

If it was the two former points—concerning the Law and the Jewish people—which caused Luke to react against the Matthaean interpretation of the Christian proclamation, the latter points also

1. *Paradigm*, pp. 352-53.

encouraged him to reshape Matthew's outlook. His Gospel is to be seen as a development from, and as a re-application amounting to a revision of, the insights and message of Mark and as a redirection of much of the outlook of Matthew. It is no longer as it was in the days of Paul, a struggle for survival, a question of fighting for the integrity of the Gospel. The main battle has been fought and won and it is now a question of different emphases and of different applications of the proclamation in the light of differing, and inevitably partial, insights into the significance of Jesus. But that Luke felt the Matthaean response to be misguided and that he struggled to reinterpret it in the light of his own particular understanding of the Pauline gospel there can be little doubt.

He would therefore, both by necessity and design, handle Matthew's Gospel in a way that was other than his handling of Mark. Mark was his primary source and, theologically, he had few complaints against it. True, he reshaped that Gospel's attitude to the Law to make Jesus, though free from its requirements, more positive towards it, but this proved no difficulty for him because he had already done the same kind of thing for his hero Paul. Eschatology presented more of a problem, for time had gone on and the expectations of the Markan proclamation had not been realized. But Luke was not shaped in the Conzelmann mould and what he did was, not to deny the future eschatological dimension nor the emphasis that both Mark and Paul had placed upon it, but to distance it from the actual time of Jesus and, while retaining the hope of its imminence as impinging upon the present, to shift its Markan importance, as being the burden of proof for the correctness of the proclamation's claims about Jesus, away from it to the ascension, to the bestowal of the Spirit which proceeded from it, and to the actuality of the universal mission undertaken in the Spirit's power. So Mark was reinterpreted to meet new situations brought about by the passing of time.

Nevertheless, his was a radically free treatment of a respected source. Much was omitted if it failed to further his picture of Jesus as the fulfilment of Israel's history and of the scriptural expectations regarding its culmination. However, the vast majority of its positive insights were developed and its concept of one, single, dramatic journey to Jerusalem was built upon to make it the overriding structure of Luke's Gospel, but to do so in a way that enhanced the continuity which it seemed to challenge but with the implications of which, however, it seemed not to be greatly concerned. Its passion narrative was freely rewritten to maintain that continuity, to present the cross as but the climaxing of the suffering way of Jesus which enabled the resurrection and ascension, and to take more account of the Jewish and Roman parts in bringing it about. In this latter concern, he remained apart from Matthew's outlook even though he used that Gospel's questions to come to very different answers.

So he engaged upon a thorough revision of Mark to enable his story to express his own understanding built up in dialogue with it. As his primary source, Mark was in fact the informer, or at least the deepener, of many of his own insights. But that his own Gospel was nevertheless a very free handling of what he respected is clear.

With Matthew it was otherwise. Luke had most likely lived for some time with Mark and its approach was on the whole congenial to him even if it did not ask all the questions with which he was now concerned. Matthew, on the other hand, was a recent find, and there is much to be said for the view that the immediate occasion for the writing of Luke's Gospel was the publication or (if the relationship is less immediate) the discovery of that work. That it was asking questions that were of overwhelming concern to Luke is clear.

However, Luke basically did not like what he saw as Matthew's answers, for they represented a tradition which had diverged forcefully from that expressed by his hero Paul. Luke had for too long been an admirer of the Jewish tradition for him to deny its essential validity in enabling its adherents to find its fulfilment in one who was Israel's Lord. That the outsiders had now been included only added to the tragedy of the insiders' refusal, but their inheritance could not be totally gainsaid by their wilfulness and Luke remained convinced of God's future act of restoration. Nevertheless, that outsiders were now sharers in the covenantal people meant that the Law which had actually made them outsiders was no longer seen as having any part in defining the people of God. Revered still by Jewish Christians as that which had brought them to where they now were, and respected by Gentile Christians as what had enabled the universal Christ to be, it nevertheless took on a new status, not as an archaic hangover it is true, but rather as a witness both to that from which they came and also to what they now were.

But if Luke could not rest content with the exclusion of Israel as a whole, he equally could not accept the present as an anticipation of the kingdom of God. He lived mindful of the weakness of the community and of its threatened nature. Seeing it as an 'ecclesia pressa', he was unable to share Matthew's confidence in it as an expression of the present earthly reality of the kingdom. His eschatology, arising out of the present, made him closer to Mark's outlook, and his wide sympathies made him unable to share Matthew's near self-satisfaction.

So his use of Matthew was other than his use of Mark. Mark was primary, Matthew was secondary: Mark was respected, Matthew was regarded with more than a little suspicion. Time had made Mark inadequate, but Matthew had not come to take its place. Luke does in fact conflate Mark and Matthew, but it is not that kind of conflation occasioned by the use of two equally valued, or at least two equally influential, sources. It is not just a priority given to Mark because he is an old friend. On the contrary, Mark is his primary source. Matthew is a well-used source, but it is a much less influential one; it is, in reality, a much less respected one.

Chapter 14

MATTHEW'S DISCOURSES

One of the areas in which Luke's suggested knowledge of Matthew has been questioned is that of the Matthaean discourses. Why, it is asked, should Luke, if he knew them, break them up in the way that he does? Streeter, many years ago, thought that no single source could be behind Matthew and Luke at these points. 'On the contrary', he wrote, 'it appears that sermons in Matthew and Luke can be derived from a single written source only if we postulate an almost incredible amount of editorial freedom in rewriting parts of the original'.[1] Such a view often leads into an evaluation of the results. So R.H. Stein writes,

> The Sermon on the Mount ranks as one of the greatest works of literature ever written... Why would Luke, who was by no means an inept writer, choose to break up this masterpiece and scatter its material in a far less artistic fashion throughout his Gospel?[2]

If Streeter approaches the writings of Matthew and Luke from a perspective which underplays the distinctive role of the evangelist as he brings his work to bear upon a particular situation with its immediate needs, Stein judges their works from a viewpoint reflecting modern criteria rather than those of the first century. We may indeed see Matthew's sermon on the mount as a masterpiece, though this in itself is to ignore some of the difficulties that have been discerned in it. As A.E. Harvey has recently noted, 'For the greater part of the history of the church the sermon on the mount (seen as the quintessence of the teaching of Jesus) has been a *problem*'.[3] When it is approached, less as direct teaching of Jesus than as Matthew's particular presentation of

1. B.H. Streeter, *The Four Gospels* (London: Macmillan, 1924), p. 250.
2. Stein, *Synoptic Problem*, p. 96.
3. A.E. Harvey, *Strenuous Commands* (London: SCM Press; Philadelphia: Trinity Press International, 1990), p. 22.

that teaching, the problem is actually intensified for Matthew's sermon represents a response, the emphasis of which is occasioned less by a timeless understanding of the teaching of Jesus than by particular questions, if not the actual controversies, which were part and parcel of the situation of the church of his day. It is far from being a dispassionate summary of that higher righteousness which Matthew discerns as being at the heart of Jesus' teaching, but is itself determined by these issues to such an extent that it is in part controlled by the circumstances out of which he is writing and to which he addresses his work. The demand is for perfection and, while this in general comes out of the evangelist's understanding of the church as the anticipation of the kingdom, its actual nuance is in fact determined both by his polemical concern to buttress his attacks upon his Jewish contemporaries, while deflecting their criticisms of the stance of his church towards the Law which both parties claim as their own, and also by his dislike of the outlook of some of his fellow Christians, both within and without his local church, which appears to him to downplay ethics in its concern with the grace of God seen in Jesus Christ. It is by no means clear that Matthew's contemporaries would have valued his sermon with that awe accorded it by some of its modern exponents.

That Luke should have treated it with such respect is unlikely for he would not have approved of its outlook on contemporary Judaism, would not have appreciated its concern with a right and careful attitude towards the Jewish Law, and would no doubt have been suspicious of its attack upon those who failed to measure up to its standard of righteousness. Luke, as we have seen, did not have a compelling concern with morality for he did not see the Christian ethic as distinctive. He was rather concerned to express the wonder of the grace of God exhibited in the response of the outsiders to the message of Jesus. In this, his stance was a Pauline one. Like the apostle, he was not indifferent to ethics and we have seen his concern to combat the charge of antinomianism. Nevertheless, an ethical rigor did not lay at the heart of his understanding of Christianity. Davies and Allison remind us that suggestions that Mt. 5.19 refers to Paul 'remain far outside the bounds of certainty'.[1] Nevertheless, they allow it as a possibility and Luke could hardly have failed to see its relevance to the teaching of the apostle, at least as it seemed to some who could not enter sympathetically into its stance and, perhaps even more likely,

1. *Matthew*, p. 497.

into the attitudes of some of the apostle's more enthusiastic followers. That Matthew's criticisms contained in ch. 7 expressed a polemic against those who took a line other than his own is highly likely and they could be addressed, less to out and out antinomians, than to those in his church who followed what he would regard as a dangerous freedom in ethical questions. In other words, they could be addressed to those who took a line not unlike Luke's own, and Luke's quite deliberate re-directing of the Matthaean emphasis would therefore be wholly understandable.

Ulrich Luz in his short survey of the history of the interpretation of the sermon on the mount writes,

> The most fruitful thought is that the Matthaean theology can be understood frankly as a classical example of 'sect theology', i.e. as a theological draft of a minority group which was led by Jesus to *its* life-principle of obedience and love. Matthaean theology is basically perfectionistic. It understands grace generally as help in praxis.[1]

Matthew in his sermon sets before his community a standard which they must attain and which will itself determine, not merely their membership of the community in the present, but also their entry into the future kingdom of heaven.

Luke's sermon on the other hand approaches these teachings of Jesus from a different direction. The polemic of Matthew is omitted for his collection of teaching is neither to distinguish the community in its ethical stance from that of its Jewish neighbours, nor is it to place a particular concept of righteousness, centred on respect for ethical demands, before them. Christopher Evans heads his commentary on Luke's sermon on the plain 'The life of the Israel of God', and he maintains that it 'may be argued that it is an abbreviated form of Matthew's deliberately limited to the two themes of love and true discipleship'.[2] Matthew in fact puts before his readers a standard that they are to achieve, a definitive set of observances that they are to follow, a new law which they are to have constantly before them, the requirements of which they are to strive to fulfil. Luke's sermon is equally demanding but its presupposition is mercy rather than perfection. What it does is to recall his community to its true nature, to set before its members the vision of what they are, to summon them to

1. Luz, *Matthew 1–7*, p. 219.
2. Evans, *Luke*, pp. 322, 326-27.

respond to God's call. It is of course a challenge, but whereas Matthew's is to ethical striving, Luke's is one to respond to the initiative of love in an acceptance of the true nature of what they as a community are meant to be. It is not a question of mutually exclusive attitudes, but it is certainly one of differing emphases, of alternative stances, and of different approaches to the nature of the response demanded by acceptance of Jesus as Christ and Lord.

Luke's sermon on the plain therefore serves a very different purpose from that of Matthew's sermon on the mount. Both Matthew and Luke have Jesus address the disciples directly with the crowds as more than overhearers, but nevertheless as a wider, secondary, uncommitted audience. Luke, however, has the additional—and for him the determinative—factor in the distinctive grouping of the twelve; the sermon follows immediately after the choosing of the twelve from out of the ranks of the disciples. The twelve do not cease to be disciples, but are now named as apostles (6.12-16). As the replacement of Judas by Matthias immediately before the Pentecostal outpouring of the Spirit makes clear (Acts 1.15-23), the twelve became the witness to the community of its nature as the faithful within Israel, the call to acknowledge its status, and the summons to see itself as eschatologically renewed Israel.

So in Luke, Jesus 'lifted up his eyes on his disciples' (6.20) to proclaim the nature of the community thus brought into being and to give it its foundation charter. The Lukan beatitudes actually define who the disciples are in the context of Israel's hopes and expectations. They act as a direct address to the disciples who become the poor, the hungry, the mourners and the hated, the outsiders within Israel who were nevertheless proclaimed as those who would receive God's vindication. The point for Luke is that all the disciples are addressed as the poor who are already entering into the sphere of the kingdom. The other three beatitudes are then addressed to subgroupings within the overall definition, to those whose situation will actually be reversed in the future. Luke knew perfectly well of course that not all the disciples were sociologically poor. Levi was quite capable of giving a great banquet for Jesus and his friends (5.29), Zachaeus gave a promise regarding only half of his goods (19.8), the disciples were encouraged 'to make friends for yourselves by means of unrighteous mammon' (16.8), and the women who accompanied Jesus and the twelve 'provided for them out of their means' (8.3). But they have taken over the attitude of the biblical poor, of those who were waiting for their vindication and were open to the promise of God's redemption.

It is the note of eschatological redemption that Luke emphasizes. It is there of course already in Matthew but what is more peripheral in the first Gospel becomes completely central in the third. Luke emphasizes the future eschatological banquet in the kingdom of God and sees the present as the promise of inclusion in that. His beatitudes therefore stand within the Old Testament and apocalyptic tradition of reversal. Luke's church awaits the future redemption with hope and expectation (21.28). His community which reflects that future as it lives out of the power of the Spirit waits for its vindication. As J.O. York has recently established, reversal plays a large part in the thinking of Luke and it becomes explicit here in the beatitudes and in the woes.[1]

The form of both the beatitudes and the woes shows how dominant is the theme of eschatological reversal for Luke at this point. The reversal is between two contrasting groups in the present and their contrasting fates in the future. The recipients of the woes are also addressed in the second person but are nevertheless contrasted with 'you who hear' (6.27).[2] They are addressed directly but nevertheless as part of the 'great multitude of people' who come to listen to Jesus (6.17) and of 'the people' who overheard his teaching of the disciples (7.1).

Luke's beatitudes are different from Matthew's because they perform a different function from his. The second person address and the material characteristics of those addressed contrast with Matthew's third-person approach and with the spiritual qualities he enumerates. Matthew describes the kind of life to which a disciple should aspire; Luke on the other hand presents the real significance, the true nature, of his community and promises a future vindication for those who are in it.

If we are right in this interpretation of Luke's beatitudes, there is nothing to suggest that he could not have taken them over from Matthew. His sermon becomes the foundation charter of the community now brought into being, hence the second person address which may in part have been suggested by the last of Matthew's promises.

1. J.O. York, *The Last Shall be First: The Rhetoric of Reversal in Luke* (JSNTSup, 46; Sheffield: JSOT Press, 1991).

2. *Last*, pp. 57-58.

His beatitudes announce the establishment of the eschatological community such as he was going on to describe in the beginning of Acts and convey the promise of its future vindication. He was thus brought into that area of reversal which sustained Old Testament hopes and apocalyptic expectations and it was this reversal-promise which determined both what he extracted from Matthew's list and also his addition of the woes. From Matthew he selected what was appropriate for this theme. Like Matthew, his first beatitude brings the blessings of the future into the present out of which the future grows (6.20), and like his it is inclusive of the whole. The list is restricted to the poor, hungry, weepers and the hated for they are descriptions of the community as it is rather than characteristics to be achieved, and they allow for that reversal which Matthew's other categories do not. Luke's fourth beatitude allows for no direct reversal, but it has a double place in Matthew and reflects the conditions of both Luke's and Matthew's churches. Its second person address may well have influenced Luke's form of the whole.

Luke's beatitudes then may well have been taken over from Matthew and altered to reflect the fact that Luke himself was giving, not spiritual qualities to be striven after, but a statement of the nature of the Christian community, and a promise to it. It is characterized as the poor, and includes within itself those who weep, hunger and are hated. But, despised by many, it is the fulfilment of the Old Testament expectations of those who are to be vindicated by God and, if the beatitudes state the reality and express the hope, the sermon as a whole then goes on to summons the community as to its true stance.

So Luke's sermon on the plain serves a very different purpose from that of Matthew's sermon on the mount. Whereas in Matthew the sermon becomes something of a compendium of the Christian life, or at least of that part of it which was relevant to the evangelist's community as it faced the problem of self-definition in relation to the 'synagogue across the street', Luke's sermon avoids such breadth of purpose to concentrate on a much more limited aspect of the life of the Christian community. All reference to Jesus' teaching as it is related to that contained in the Law is omitted for, as we have seen, it was no part of Luke's purpose to unfold it in these terms. The Law as such had no continuing claim upon the Christian community, and Luke was not at variance with the local Jewish community over its interpretation.

But it was in precisely the question of the Law that Matthew's sermon seemed to exhibit polemical concerns. The highly conservative statement of principle in Mt. 5.17-20 is one which counteracted the outlook that Luke had learned from Paul, and it would certainly have represented for him an attack upon Paul's position. This polemical aspect continues throughout the sermon and has a large role in determining its outlook. In part it is directed against Jewish religious activity and in part against Gentile religiosity. Matthew's hostility leads into a concerted attack upon other Christian groups and it is this which forms the climax to the sermon. Few who seek to enter life will do so for the gate is narrow (Mt. 7.13): many false prophets will arise and will produce bad fruit which is to be understood as a less than Matthaean moral outlook (7.15-20). Many who claim to follow Christ will not be acceptable to him (7.21-23) and those who do not meet the standards of the sermon will fall at the judgment if not earlier (7.24-27). Here the tone is clearly polemical and it actually expresses hostility towards an attitude which is represented in part at any rate in Luke's Gospel for his is a story of wide outreach and generous acceptance and as such it represents an outlook which runs counter to Matthew's own emphasis.

Luke does of course end his sermon as does Matthew with the parable of the two householders and his form is not in any way less challenging than its Matthaean counterpart. It is equally demanding, but the object of its criticism is different. In Matthew it is the failure to live up to the ethical and religious standards that the sermon has propounded. Luke's version of the sermon on the other hand puts forward no such wide-ranging considerations for its contents really centre around a love expressed in mercy, a lack of judgment, and a humility that is realistic about one's own imperfections. Those who by the use of the parable are declared unacceptable are those who do not live in this way. They may call Jesus 'Lord' but if their discipleship, if their Christian way of life, is not directed by this outlook, then their works, their law, their merits, even their attitude of measuring up to an inner response to what they see as the way of the Lord will be of no avail.

Luke's form of the sermon is best understood as a conscious reaction against that found in Matthew. It omits what its own understanding deems unacceptable. Its transfers occur because Luke's is not a compendium of the Christian life. Its inclusions take Matthew's sayings and re-direct their aims and polemic. So he alters a large number of Matthew's statements. Love of enemies is taken out of the field of comparison with the Law (7.32-35); the Matthaean demand for perfection (5.48) becomes one for mercy in imitation of the Father's mercy (6.38). This leads into the command to be non-judgmental, into the Matthaean form of which is inserted the parable of the blind man leading the blind with its direct application in the saying that 'A disciple is not above his teacher, but every one when he is fully taught will be as his teacher' (6.40). Judgmental attitudes arising out of an exclusiveness and an intolerant interpretation of the Christian dispensation go against the attitude of the teacher himself. 6.43-45 reverses the outlook of the Matthaean original (Mt. 7.15-17) which makes good works the test of a prophet's genuineness and thus results in the narrowing of the acceptable, to concentrate instead upon a looking for good fruit where it is to be found. Discernment there must be, but the attitude of the discerner takes on a different, more positive stance. So they are all reminded of their inadequacy. 'Why do you call me, Lord, Lord, and do not do what I tell you? (6.46). Again, it is not a question, as it is in Mt. 7.21, of dividing the sheep from the goats. It is a common failure to measure up to the love, mercy and non-judgmental attitude which the Lukan Lord is commending. The concluding parable becomes a warning for all.

So, the Lukan sermon can be seen as an extraction from the Matthaean to suit its place in his narrative as the foundation charter of the community that Jesus called into being and as a direct response to that attitude demanded of the community and assigned to Jesus by the Matthaean sermon on the mount. Luke has in fact adapted the sermon according to his own understanding and to his purpose in writing his Gospel. As such it reveals a reaction to the ideas and outlook presented in Matthew 5–7.

There are of course two other discourses in Matthew which, as they stand, are not found in Mark and which might have been expected to have been seen in some form in Luke, namely the Matthaean missionary discourse (Mt. 10.1-42), and that on church behaviour (Mt. 18.1-31).[1] Luke does in fact deal with the missionary discourse in a way which is not unlike that in which he deals with the sermon on the

1. H.B. Green, 'The Credibility of Luke's Transformation of Matthew', in C.M. Tuckett (ed.), *Synoptic Studies: The Ampleforth Conferences of 1982 and 1983* (JSNTSup, 7; Sheffield: JSOT Press, 1984), pp. 131-56 (134-36).

mount, by including some parts relevant to his purpose in a not dissimilar discourse, by moving other parts to different but relevant contexts in his Gospel, and by omitting altogether such passages as are inimical to his purpose. He takes over Mark's sending out of the twelve with but minor alterations, the chief being his addition of 9.2 which brings in a reference to preaching which, though possibly derived from Mk 3.14, 15, is by its mention of the kingdom of God and to healing, perhaps more likely to have been influenced by Matthew's version in 10.7. Though close to Mark's charge in its inclusions, he is nevertheless in agreement with Matthew's disallowing of a staff. So, even here, though relying on Mark, he is not uninfluenced by Matthew though it is in his account of the sending out of the seventy that his main use of Matthew 10 is to be found.

It would, of, course have been possible for him to have omitted the Matthaean discourse altogether, but Mark and Matthew both suggest that their charges have some significance as addresses to the evangelist's contemporaries. If this is true of Mk 6.7ff. with its mention of sending out in pairs, it is even more true of Matthew 10 where the twelve are in a sense contemporarized to represent at least the official leadership of Matthew's own church, however much that leadership was democratized.[1] For Luke, however, the twelve are neither a representative nor a continuing group: they are rather a one-off demonstration of the source and significance of the church's life.[2] The continuing life of the church, seen here in its missionary aspect needs to have another group to represent it and through which it could be addressed. Hence Luke's introduction of the seventy with its Mosaic precedent and world-wide significance. For the episode of the seventy he uses Matthew, and the address to them takes over a number of verses from Matthew's discourse. References to the labourers and the harvest come from Mt. 9.37-38, and the stance of the missionaries is derived from Mt. 10.7-16. This is supplemented by Matthew's later reference to Capernaum and Bethsaida which is found in Mt. 11.21-24 and which is suggested by a reference to Sodom and Gomorrah in Matthew's actual discourse (10.15). This passage is followed by Christ's thanksgiving to the father in Mt. 11.25-27 and so forms a fitting climax to Luke's episode at 10.21-22. He omits the Matthaean conclusion (Mt. 11.28-30) because its picture of Jesus as

1. Brown and Meier, *Antioch and Rome*, pp. 70-71.
2. *Christ the Lord*, pp. 95-99.

the embodiment of Wisdom is inimical to his understanding of him as a prophetic figure inspired by Wisdom and Spirit.

At this stage he omits the Matthaean references to persecution which are paralleled in Lk. 21.12-17, the exhortations to watchfulness and the threat of divisions which are found in his first eschatological discourse at 12.2-7, 51-53, and the passage about the taking up of the cross (Mt. 10.38) which he uses at 14.26-27 where it will form part of the equivalent of Matthew's addition to the parable of the rejected invitation. The result is to make the Lord's commission of the seventy much more focused and to present it as a parallel to the missionary charge to the twelve. And it is this which his control by Mark would suggest. Luke will have plenty to say in Luke–Acts about the mission's negative side, but this must be seen in the light of its positive significance which he will point to in the rest of his work as a whole. It is to this overall vision that Luke's account of the sending out of the seventy is directed, namely the significance of the worldwide mission in its witness to the nearness of the kingdom. So Luke 10 is made to express the message of Luke–Acts as a whole and it is in the light of this significance that the sufferings and disappointments of the present time must be measured.[1]

Luke's omission of Matthew's church discourse as this is found in Mt. 18.1-25 is not difficult to understand. Its first nine verses are largely found in Mk 9.33-48 and Luke takes over as much of this as he wants. Matthew adds little of significance to the Markan passages but, by his making them into part of a single, extended discourse, has introduced an attitude which expresses the outlook of a closely-integrated and clearly defined community. This would have been alien to Luke's concept of a community which is far less closely bounded than is Matthew's. Apart from the parable of the lost sheep, he basically omits the rest of the discourse. Mt. 18.15 and 21 have something in common with Lk. 17.3, 4 which could have been gathered from Matthew and addressed to the disciples as a warning in

1. It is the theological implication of mission, with its successes and failures, which concerns Luke rather than, as Talbert suggests (*Reading Luke*, p. 117), practical instruction and guidance. Luke is taken up with the theological significance rather than the practical considerations. Tannehill (*Luke*, p. 237) 'In spite of the words of threat and condemnation in 10.12-15 which emphasize the rejection that Jesus and his messengers are encountering, the return of the seventy-two is a scene of joy and triumph'.

the light of the telling against the Pharisees of the parable of Dives and Lazarus (16.19-31). He could have taken over the parable of the unmerciful servant, but to have included it at that point would have threatened the eschatological immediacy of the material in chs. 16–17. The eschatological dimension of the quality of forgiveness and its need is rather brought out by Luke at 12.57-59 (cf. Mt. 5.25-26).

The parable of the lost sheep is of course used by Luke as one in his complex of three parables directed against complaints that Jesus was eating with tax collectors and sinners (15.3-7). That section in the third Gospel is controlled by the parable of the prodigal son as Luke now tells it, and his version of the lost sheep, with its extension in that of the lost coin, is fashioned in the light of that parable's outlook. On the other hand, any suggested Matthaean revision of a Lukan form of the parable hardly explains the Matthaean lack of a search 'until he finds it' and the consequent 'when he finds'. Though Matthew might have altered the original to enable an expression of care for the ninety nine which the Lukan form seems to put at risk, the playing down of the demands of the search, which his form of the parable suggests when it is compared with the Lukan version, makes revision on his part unlikely. Whether Luke's setting is controlled by independent, and more historically, accurate information can only remain an open question.

Luke's neglect of the Matthaean additions to the Markan forms of the parables and eschatological discourses (Mt. 13; 25) is accounted for by the fact that he would have distanced himself from the former's close association of the community of disciples with the kingdom of heaven as its anticipation and means of entry, and from the latter's use of the three parables to emphasize the theme of the judgment of the community at the arrival of the parousia. Luke rather sees the kingdom as transcendent, to be manifested at some time in the future to the world and to the church for which it is primarily not an object of warning but of hope.

It is by no means obvious then that later evaluations of Matthew's discourses, and more especially of the sermon on the mount, as masterpieces would have been shared by Luke and his contemporaries. Though the teaching of Jesus may best be appreciated as being in the Wisdom tradition rather than in that of Law, it is not clear that this is how Matthew himself and his church understood it.[1] The sermon on

1. See Harvey, *Strenuous Commands*, p. 316 n.3 above.

the mount interpreted in terms of Jesus' promise to Peter, of the ecclesiastical discourse, and of the risen Lord's commissioning of the disciples suggests rather a legal framework, and the tone of the sermon remains one of polemic rather than one of considered, impartial instruction. Other Matthaean discourses are not without this polemical character and reflect an outlook which in its exclusiveness and rigorism is unlikely to have appealed to Luke. He therefore breaks up these discourses so that Jesus' progressive movement to Jerusalem might not be impaired and he includes such part of the rest of Matthew's teaching as he wishes to take over in the structure of his central section.

Chapter 15

THE CENTRAL SECTION

The really distinctive thing about the third Gospel is of course its central section, and it is this above all which threatens Luke's standing as a careful composer. Even some of the most ardent admirers of Luke's artistry and creativity have to allow that these chapters are not easy to explain, and their actual form remains hard to justify. It is to this section that the belittlers of Luke's reshaping of Matthew are able to go for most of their support. Indeed, it is hard to see how Luke's reputation for being a careful writer can survive some of the estimates of this section which many have found to be a muddle, or at least an uncoordinated mass of ill-defined material. It is not easy to avoid Marshall's conclusion that 'The difficulty of tracing a logical progression through the section may well be due to the nature of the material as it reached Luke'. How can one whose resurrection and infancy narratives have taken on the shape of carefully constructed extended pieces have been satisfied with the central section? Is it after all a question of sources? Must the estimate of Luke as a skilful handler of sources, a careful creator of material, go to be replaced with one of Luke as a slavish follower of sources which provided the ultimate control of his work? Is what this section contains there simply because it is all Luke had to work on? Certainly, this central section must be accounted for if Luke's reputation as an artistic and theologically motivated controller of a carefully constructed narrative is to survive. We shall look at the central section to consider its form, its contents and its order.

Luke casts this central section in the form of a journey (9.51, 57; 10.1) of which the purpose and goal is Jerusalem (9.51; 13.22, 33: 17.11; 18.31; 19.28).[1] Attempts to see this as determined by Luke's

1. See the discussion in D.P. Moessner, *Lord of the Banquet: The Literary and Theological Significance of the Lukan Travel Narrative* (Minneapolis: Fortress Press, 1989), esp. pp. 13-44.

historical concerns are vitiated by the inconsequential nature of the historical and geographical settings.[1] Luke does not appear to be bound by the constraints of realism since not only are geographical notices often vague (e.g. 17.1), but settings seem to be controlled by something other than historical reporting. So, for instance, the Bartimaeus incident is moved (and in the process the name removed) to before the visit to Jericho in order to allow its climactic role to be taken by the Zacchaeus incident which expresses more fully the Lukan understanding and significance of the purpose of Jesus' ministry (19.1-10).

Equally unlikely is the suggestion that the idea for the section was the result of a constraint imposed upon Luke by his sources. Goulder's viewpoint that it was his 'policy with his sources' which 'forced the journey on him at this point' seems to do less than justice to Luke's overall scheme.[2] It is true, of course, that the theme of a journey is suggested by the Markan source for which Luke had so much respect, but belief that an extension of this into a distinctive Lukan feature was determined by his concern to accommodate the many units of material which he has so far omitted from Matthew remains an inadequate explanation for Luke's end product in that it fails to account for the very large number of distinctive Lukan episodes which owe their place to his own intention and, on Goulder's view, to his own creative urge. Luke's journey is much more than a peg on which to hang a mixed array of varied garments so that none should be lost.

More suggestive is that view which sees Luke's concept of a journey as giving, in Tannehill's words, 'a sense of narrative movement and tension to a long section of Luke's gospel that otherwise would become a static collection of teachings'.[3] However, valuable though this idea is, our understanding of what determined the shape and outlook of Luke's narrative as a whole suggests that something more than dramatic and aesthetic concerns were his primary motivation. He is in fact determined primarily by theological considerations as he seeks to put before his readers the truth of the Gospel as he understands it and so to meet the perplexities that they are facing. Luke sets out to buttress his readers' belief that by his resurrection God really has

1. J.W. Wenham, 'Synoptic Independence and the Origin of Luke's Travel Narrative', *NTS* 27 (1987), pp. 507-515.

2. *Paradigm*, p. 458.

3. *Luke*, p. 229.

established Jesus as Lord and Christ (Acts 2.36) and that this belief is not denied but rather established both by the actual career of Jesus and by the universal witness that proceeded from this exaltation.[1]

Luke's description of Jesus' considered journey to Jerusalem is therefore most likely to be under a theological control. It is in fact determined, first by his Christology, secondly by his response to the fact of the rejection of Jesus by Israel as a whole, and thirdly by his understanding of Jesus' gathering of a renewed Israel which is established by his exaltation and by the outpouring of the Spirit.

The form of a journey is determined in the first instance by his Christology, by his envisaging the life of Jesus as a consciously determined movement by him to his ascension which is to mark that point where he enters fully into his role as Christ and Lord. If this is made clear by Luke's addition to the transfiguration narrative where Moses and Elijah speak of his ἐξοδός which he is to accomplish at Jerusalem (Lk. 9.31), the journey to it is announced at significant points in his overall narrative. So, Luke's account of the temptations climaxes with one to jump down from the pinnacle of the temple and so by a visible dramatic act reverse the hidden and secret manner by which God had willed his Christ to be exalted. The reaction at Nazareth prefigures the Jewish attempt to destroy Jesus at the cross, but Jesus' reversal of such intentions and his movement forward to his goal again prefigures his exaltation. He was sent to move forward in a determined progression (4.43) and notices of movement are frequent. The journey itself is pointed to by Luke as a considered advance towards his ἀνάλημψίς (9.57), and Samaritans do nothing to hinder or divert its progress (9.53). Witnesses go before him to prepare the way for his coming (10.1). Jesus himself is constrained until his baptism is accomplished (12.50) and he must go on his way 'today and tomorrow until on the third day [he is] perfected' (13.33). Large crowds travel with him (14.25) and when he enters Jerusalem 'the whole multitude of disciples' acknowledges, not the coming of the kingdom as in Mark (11.10) but the king who is about to bring 'Peace in heaven and glory in the highest' (19.38). Jesus goes on to receive a kingdom and to return (19.12) but the immediate joy, the immediate

1. J.H. Davies, 'The Purpose of the Central Section of St Luke's Gospel', *TU* 87 (1963), pp. 164-69.

result is his exaltation to heaven and the establishment of the reign of God from there.[1]

Luke's understanding of Jesus is one which sees him as the eschatological prophet like Moses (Acts 3.22) who follows the pattern of Moses' rejection (Acts 7.25-29) but who also like him journeys to a mountain and from there enters into his heavenly inheritance. His is a journey to that goal. Mosaic typology plays a large part in Luke. Like Moses, Jesus earlier goes up to a mountain (Lk. 6.12-19; cf. Exod. 19.2-3, 20). On the mountain, his chosen come to him (Exod. 24.9-11). Like Moses he comes down from a mountain to address the people as a whole (Exod. 19.25) and form them into a community. Now he travels with them to their inheritance and his heavenly realm. Elijah had also journeyed to his exaltation and had taken Elisha with him for he was to receive a portion of his spirit. Like the apostles, he was to watch his departing master (Acts 1.9-10; cf. 2 Kgs 1.11-12).

Luke's Christology is one of movement, of a sustained and determined progress towards an exaltation from which and in the power of which a universal mission proceeds. Until then, Jesus is constrained for his role as eschatological prophet is caught up in, and in the process shattered by, his exaltation which makes him Christ and Lord. Luke's is a Christology which is controlled by Old Testament expectations. These, plus his decision to write in a historical dimension, mean that past and present are never entirely assimilated for the past is conceived rather as providing the springboard which enables the present to be. Though Jesus' Lordship is anticipated on earth and though he addresses the future from the past as he already anticipates that Lordship which is to be his in reality only then, Jesus during his ministry is only on the way to that which he is to become. As the risen Christ says of himself, 'Was it not necessary that the Christ should suffer these things, and enter his glory?' (Lk. 24.26). Messiahship and Lordship for Luke are conceived primarily in functional terms. Jesus' is a career, the effective realization of which is focused at the ascension. Before then, his life is constantly moving forward, and afterwards its effective realization is being furthered.

Luke's Jesus therefore is essentially one with Old Testament history and with God's saving activity effected through it (Lk. 1.54-55,

1. This contrasts with Matthew's ending where the exalted Jesus indwells his church (28.18-20).

72-73). In him Israel's history reaches its fulfilment. John the Baptist, so far from being the climax of the period of Israel which gives way before the periods of Jesus and of the church, links Israel to Jesus to find its fulfilment in him. Jesus therefore journeys to Jerusalem to enable Israel's history actually to confront the Jerusalem of his day. He comes as the climax of those who brought Israel face to face with her Lord, but like them he is to meet opposition, hostility, and rejection as contemporary Israel follows in the ways of her ancestors. Moses, Elijah, Samuel and the Suffering Servant all met rejection, and even David's recognition that he looked forward to a future was denied when Solomon's temple was given the significance of finality (Acts 7.47).

In Jesus' journey to Jerusalem the whole of Israel's past, the riddle of her history, is caught up to confront the Jerusalem of his day. So, at the entry, when Pharisees would prevent the acknowledgment of him by his followers, Jesus replies, 'I tell you, if these were silent, the very stones would cry out' (Lk. 19.40). The city recognizes the climax of her history even if her religious leaders are unable to do so.

Luke's second volume will tell of the remaking of Israel and of the coming in alongside her of the Gentile part of this recreated people of God. Acts will describe how this community came to be a true fulfilment of that which prophets of old foresaw (Acts 15.16-18). It was not a ready-made community but one which had to discern its true nature as it responded with understanding to the significance of the presence of the Spirit in its midst. Discernment was a growing and a deepening process as the community pondered on the meaning of Jesus' ministry. The initial outpouring of the Spirit could be understood as witnessing to the exaltation of Jesus, not merely because of his resurrection but because during his ministry he had been seen as a 'man attested by God with deeds of power, wonders, and signs' (Acts 2.22). The coming in of Gentiles is already anticipated in his concern for the outsider (Acts 11.36-38), and above all in the meals which form so much a part of Luke's journey narrative. The apostles are those who witnessed, not merely the resurrection, but all that happened 'during the time that the Lord Jesus went in and out among us' (Acts 1.21). They can therefore become, not merely reliable witnesses of the resurrection, but also articulate witnesses of the significance and meaning of Jesus and of the implications of that life for the nature and stance of the community which rests upon it. Even Paul grounds the defence of his concern with the collection on words of Jesus (Acts 20.35).

The community lives as it embodies the response to the life of Jesus. The young community in Jerusalem reflects his own concern for the poor and his warnings to those who have riches (Acts 4.34) while the lives and deaths of its leading figures reflect the life and death of their Lord. Paul's belief that it is 'through many tribulations that we enter the kingdom of God' (Acts 14.22) carries on the outlook commended by Jesus when he advocated a daily taking up of the cross (Lk. 9.33).

The community therefore consciously reflects upon the life of its Lord and the implications of his teaching. It will constantly return to his ministry to perceive the right stance of its present action: it will faithfully apply the outlook of the Lord to its contemporary situation. The church is aware that it journeys with Jesus, alongside him, as it meets him in the present through dialogue with his past.[1] It was no doubt this apprehension which provided the third motivation for Luke's presentation of this central section of teaching in the form of a journey. Jesus of the past was enabled to address the present. As he journeyed to the point where he would leave the disciples he took them with him on the way to use the journey together as a time of addressing, first the foundation members of the renewed people of God and, through them, those who would follow after them. The 'Lord' who was addressed by Peter and who warned his contemporaries is also 'the Lord' who through that warning addresses all (Lk. 12.22-41).

Moses typology was already important for Luke. We have seen that it provided a pattern for the initial establishment of the community and also one for the 'prophet like Moses' to move forward to his goal. With him went the disciples and, on the way, he was able to instruct them for the future. In the light of this, it was almost inevitable that Luke should see Jesus' teaching on his journey in terms of that which earlier had been given by Moses in Deuteronomy.

Christopher Evans earlier characterized Luke's central section as being controlled by the pattern of Deuteronomy and thus gave force

1. Luke is, as we have seen above in Chapter 12, conscious that Jesus acts in the present but is nevertheless not himself present as he is in Matthew. Jesus is the church's contemporary, but it meets him primarily through its recounting of the past and through participation in the breaking of the bread which for Luke has this predominantly eschatological association.

to that view which saw it as modelled upon the Deuteronomic idea of Moses' address to the people of God as they travelled to their future inheritance in response to him who was travelling to his place in another kingdom.[1] Moessner has more recently built on Evans' insight to make it in one sense less ambitious and in another sense more theologically significant.[2] He sees a more fundamental typology than that contained in the material's sequence to find its significance in the actual form and content of the central section as that expresses Luke's understanding of Jesus as the eschatological prophet like Moses.

Deuteronomy itself instructs those Israelites who are to move into the promised land in the context of an indictment of the generation which came out of Egypt and remained largely disobedient through its inability to discern and to respond to the wonder of what was happening in its midst. The people as a whole rejected Moses who came to them as an instrument of God and in some way their rejection made his own death necessary.[3]

Deuteronomy therefore is a drastic exposure of that weakness which brought disaster to the majority of the generation which witnessed God's saving action, a powerful admonition of those who, having learned from the failures of the vast majority of the people, were to move into the promised land, and an explanation of the relationship of the community to the prophet who was in its midst. This triple function of Deuteronomy is taken over by Luke to determine the nature of the teaching that he expresses by way of the central section of his Gospel. The leaders of Israel are challenged and arraigned in a manner not far removed from that which informs Deuteronomy's address to the contemporaries of Moses. At the same time, those who respond are warned of precisely the same dangers. Martha has to learn the same lesson as that put before the lawyer who desired 'to justify himself' (10.29, 41-42), the disciples are to 'beware of the leaven of the Pharisees, that is their hypocrisy' (12.1-59). They must learn to sit light to the things of this world in a way that the Pharisees

1. C.F. Evans, 'The Central Section of Saint Luke's Gospel', in D.E. Nineham (ed.), *Studies in the Gospels: Essays in Memory of R.H. Lightfoot* (Oxford: Basil Blackwell, 1955), pp. 37-53.

2. See above, p. 328 n.1.

3. There is little to be said however for Moessner's suggestion that portraying Jesus as the 'prophet like Moses' has the significance of giving theological and saving content to the death of Jesus. See above, pp. 77-78.

were unwilling to do (16.1-31). The scepticism of the Pharisees about the drawing near of the kingdom in Jesus is paralleled by the lack of confidence on the part of the disciples about its reality (17.22–18.8). Even the feelings of the Pharisee of the parable are not far removed from the disciples' need to learn that the kingdom can be received only after the manner of a child (18.9-17).

Bo Reicke long ago described the contents of the central section as instruction and discussion.[1] Though 'discussion' is perhaps better termed 'confrontation' or 'accusation' insofar as it represents what is primarily a challenge that is thrown down by Jesus to his contemporaries, a recognition of this double aspect in the journey narrative represents a true evaluation of its significance. The eschatological prophet who is moving forward to his exaltation addresses his contemporaries to upbraid them for their hardness in responding to the saving presence of God which has been enacted among them and, in the light of this, addresses those who do respond to encourage them in the stance that must be theirs as they enter into their eschatological inheritance but as they face the temptations that await them. Hope is tempered by reality and the promise is conditioned by the need for a continuing alertness. As Moessner writes, 'Both for the words of Jesus (that is, context) and for his journey (that is, form) the Moses of the book of Deuteronomy serves as a literary–theological model'.[2]

But if this concentration of Luke upon Jesus as the fulfilment of the prophet like Moses explains both the form and the nature of the contents of this section, is it also of service in explaining the order of its material? Is Evans right to suggest a control exercised by the order of Deuteronomy?[3] There are certainly strong links to be found especially at the beginning of the journey. 10.1-3, 17-20, which talk of a setting out on a journey, reflect the beginning of Deuteronomy (1.1-8, 19; 2.1). The encounter with the self-justifying lawyer points to Deuteronomy 5 and 6, and Jesus' attack on the Pharisees while he is at dinner with them (11.37–12.12) may well reflect Deuteronomy's discussion of clean and unclean at 12.1-6. The episode of the crippled woman and the final description of the journey in the first part of the section (13.22-35) may be suggested by Deuteronomy's rules for

1. B. Reicke, 'Instruction and Discussion in the Travel Narrative', *TU* 73 (1959), pp. 206-16.

2. *Banquet*, p. 285.

3. See the criticisms of J.W. Wenham, 'Synoptic Independence'.

release (15.1-18) and by its regulations for pilgrimage festivals (16.6–17.7). In the second part of the section the sabbath discussion may be related to the legislation of Deuteronomy (17.8-18) and the parable of the great feast to Deuteronomy's regulations of 20.1-9. The parable of the unjust steward at 16.1-8 may reflect the Deuteronomic prohibitions of lending for interest at 23.19-20, that of Dives and Lazarus (16.19-31) Deuteronomy's concern for the weak (Deut. 24.6-22) and that of the Pharisee and the tax collector (18.9-14) Deuteronomy's setting forth of the need for response (Deut. 26.1-19).

Certainly, Deuteronomy does seem to have had some influence over these episodes which are all distinctively Lukan. Luke is relating Jesus' teaching to that of Deuteronomy, even to the point of following a sequence of themes which he has taken from Deuteronomy and which he seems to have fashioned either as a development of, or in reaction to, some of that book's ideas. Nevertheless, in spite of the close Deuteronomic connection, this is not enough to suggest that Deuteronomy of itself exerted the final control over the order of Luke's central section. Material in that section is linked to a Deuteronomic parallel but it is not wholly controlled by it. The closeness of parallelism does not extend throughout the narrative.

For much the same reason, some attempts to find a chiasmus in this section remain less than convincing. It is not easy to include all the material in such a scheme. So Bailey,[1] though he is able to account for some ninety per cent of the material, is nevertheless forced to leave aside such enigmatic but significant passages as Jesus' thanksgiving at the return of the seventy (10.21-24), the verses about the continuing validity of the Law (16.17-18), and the first ten verses of ch. 17. Attempts to bring everything in the narrative within a chiasmic order seem on the other hand to result in postulating contrasting sections which become vague in content and ill-defined in structure. Talbert[2] includes the first piece of Bailey's excluded material within a section extending from 9.57–10.14 and heads it 'Following Jesus'. This, however, does little to give real descriptive value to the material it contains. Indeed, while the designation 'Following Jesus' may serve as the description of the penultimate section of the chiasmic structure (18.35ff.), it remains less than explicit as a description of the mission

1. K. Bailey, *Poet and Peasant and through Peasant Eyes: A Literary–Cultural Approach to the Parables in Luke* (Grand Rapids: Eerdmans, 1983), pp. 79-85.

2. *Reading Luke*, pp. 111-13.

of the seventy. For an alleged chiasmic structure to carry conviction, there is need of a closer link than is described in such general terms.

This is true even of Blomberg's more modest suggestion which finds a chiasmus, not in the section as a whole, but in five pairs of parables which are seen as forming the basis of the section and around which other material is thought to have been structured.[1] Certainly the parables of the good Samaritan and the Pharisee and the tax collector (10.25-37; 18.9-14) do suggest something of an *inclusio*, and a parallel pattern can be seen at at least two other points, those of the importunate claimants (11.5-8; 18.1-8) and those of the girded loins and the dishonest steward (12.13-21; 16.18-31). But the correspondence is nevertheless very general and some similarity is almost inevitable in the light of the small number of themes with which the parables of this section, as the material as a whole, deal. The place of the parable of the dishonest steward could equally well be taken in the above comparison by that of the rich fool (12.13-21). The parable of Dives and Lazarus (16.19-31) hardly parallels that of the rich fool. Their messages, certainly as Luke understood them and most likely in their original use, are different. Again, Blomberg's scheme has to omit one of Luke's original parables in this section, that of the lost coin (15.8-10). That parable is controlled by the parable of the lost son (15.11-32) which contains little parallel (as it must in Blomberg's scheme) with that of the fig tree (13.6-9).

The parables just do not lend themselves to such a close scheme. The relatively small number of themes in the central section makes for inevitable similarities but these are not of such a kind as to suggest any deliberate parallelism either of structure, order or content. Even if the Old Testament background of these parables reveals Luke's hand rather than, as Blomberg maintains, that of some source whether it be found in Jesus' teaching or not, and if, as Sanders suggests, Goulder's estimate of Luke's creativity in this section is best revealed in just these parables, there is not the tightness of parallelism to suggest an intentional chiasmic structure.

Though there does not seem enough parallelism to support the view that chiasmus formed the actual control of Luke's material in this section, that such a suggestion has been made does point to the fact

1. 'Midrash, Chiasmus, and the Outline of Luke's Central Section' in R.T. France and D. Wenham (eds.), *Gospel Perspectives*, 111 (Sheffield: JSOT Press, 1983), pp. 217-61.

that the journey narrative falls into two parts with the conclusion of the first coming at the end of ch. 13.[1] The end of that chapter has brought to a climax an indictment of this generation in general and of Jerusalem in particular set within the context of the Lord's own rejection which nevertheless will make possible that exaltation which will itself serve as a means of enabling his future return to Jerusalem in triumph (13.22-35). The whole is a close parallel to what will happen at the end of the journey when Jesus enters Jerusalem. At both points, the Lord travels with his disciples, faces the rejection by Jewish religious leaders, laments over the city but nevertheless moves forward consciously to his exaltation (18.28-44). Such a close parallelism clearly divides the section into two parts. A further pointer to the separation of the two parts is seen in the fact that whereas the first part has, according to Orchard's synopsis,[2] something like 134 verses which are paralleled in Matthew, the second part has but 32, 14 of which are to be found in the Lukan additional apocalypse of 17.20–18.8. There may be other, more remote parallels with Matthaean material, but the difference in close parallels is striking. Clearly, if Luke were using Matthew in both parts, he was using it in two very different ways.

We have already noted that it is in the second part of the section that the most significant points of contact with Deuteronomy are to be found. Lukan parables in this section seem to reflect knowledge of Deuteronomy. That of the great feast shows knowledge of the Deuteronomic regulations at 20.1-9, the unjust steward of the prohibitions (23.19-20), Dives and Lazarus of its concern for the weak at 24.6-22, and the Pharisee and the tax collector of the requirements of Deut. 26.1-19. These are all peculiar to Luke and could well suggest, not necessarily Lukan total authorship, though this cannot be ruled out for at least some of them, but certainly his free handling of any pre-Lukan material. So here, the great feast could be a rewriting of

1. Talbert makes the break at 13.33 with 13.34-35 the first part of the return chiasmus: Bailey breaks at 13.35 though he finds a chiasmic structure within 13.22-35: Goulder puts the ending of the first half of the narrative at 13.21 for it is here that Luke's full use of Matthew comes to an end. We suggest that the break occurs at 13.35, for this allows the first half to come to some climax which is then paralleled and actually heightened at the entry into Jerusalem.

2. J.B. Orchard, *A Synopsis of the Four Gospels in Greek* (Edinburgh: T. & T. Clark, 1983).

Matthew, just as the parable of the lost sheep could have come from that Gospel. On the other hand, neither the parable of the unjust steward nor that of Dives and Lazarus seems tailor-made to express the use that Luke actually makes of them.[1] Even here, he does not seem to be entirely without some constraint imposed upon him by the existence of sources.

Nevertheless, that Luke's creativity was given free reign in this section seems hard to deny and it is significant that it is much easier to find a logical thread running through this part and controlling its order than it is for the first part of the narrative. The whole has an eschatological excitement focused upon the meals in which Jesus shares and which are used to express judgments upon them as partial anticipations of the future eschatological banquet which is itself fully anticipated at the last supper as Jesus prepares to enter his kingdom.

So ch. 14 points to the failure of the Pharisaic meals as anticipations of the kingdom. If ch. 15 contrasts them with Jesus' own eating and drinking with tax collectors and sinners, it nevertheless is still concerned with the lack of response on the part of the Pharisees. Though the introduction to the immediate section (14.1-6) has pointed both to their failure and to the correctness of Jesus' stance, the (possibly Lukan) addition to the parable of the prodigal son expresses continuing anxiety over the Pharisees and the hope that they will yet come in (15.31-32). The murmurings of the Pharisees are not simply ignored, for ch. 16, though highly critical of them at v. 14, nevertheless takes note of their criticisms to meet them in its insistence that freedom should not degenerate into licence. The rich man's goods must be used rightly and πορνειά is not simply accepted. There must be a response to Jesus which issues in an ethical response (16.13, 18). *Peripateia* is already being proclaimed and this is now made explicit in the parable of Dives and Lazarus (16.19-31). The Pharisees again, however, are not simply rejected. Their denial of Jesus is explained in a very definitely Lukan verse—'If they hear not Moses and the prophets, neither will they be convinced if someone should rise from the dead'—the stance of which is to be repeated by both Stephen and Paul (Acts 6.53; 28.26-27).

Luke is working within a Deuteronomic understanding which means that, while confronting the failure to respond, he is also building upon it to encourage and warn those who become disciples but who

1. See the discussions in Evans, *Luke*, pp. 595-600, 611-16.

are neither free from the temptations which made others fall nor separated out entirely from them.

In ch. 17 he addresses the disciples with a command to faithfulness in the light of the eschatological situation. Once more, disciples are to beware of attitudes which have caused the Pharisees to fall. 16.31 has seen these in a lack of true response both to Moses and to Jesus. The Jewish lepers follow the Law but they nevertheless fail to acknowledge him who is its fulfilment. The Pharisees show their scepticism regarding Jesus, their failure to respond to the eschatological presence in him, by asking when the kingdom is to come. They are oblivious to its signs manifested in him (17.20-21).

Their scepticism has its roots however in that which will cause the disciples to lose confidence and to embark upon false values based upon false hopes (17.22-23). In contrast to both scepticism and loss of hope, the Lord puts before Luke's contemporaries both the certainty of its coming and the necessity for their continuing in faith (18.1-8). It is at this point that Luke rejoins Mark.

This section of the travel narrative has a consistent theme and a reasonably clear development. Nevertheless, every part included in that development is not obvious. Chapter 14 introduces the teaching about the Pharisees' meal with the story of the man with dropsy and it is not clear that this of itself is tailor-made for Luke's purpose. The teaching to the multitudes which follows the parable of the rejected invitation is more suited to its context and could well have been put together by Luke himself from sources and possibly in reaction to Matthew's parable of the rejected guest which, because of its rigid ethical criteria and its possibly anti-Pauline stance, would have been unacceptable to him. Chapters 15 and 16 hold together well though the material of ch. 16 again is not all tailor-made for the occasion.[1] Chapter 17 contains some material (for example, vv. 1-4) that is not immediately relevant to its context. Luke is using sources and it is hard to deny that some of them fit less easily into his theme than do others. Nevertheless, there is a logical development overall and one which suggests ultimate control by Luke.

1. Evans, pp. 581-82, notes the coherence in these chapters. Marshall (*Luke*, pp. 613-14) sees a 'general trend' in ch. 16 even though he says, 'But the unity gives the impression of artificiality'. Tannehill sees little development in the section as a whole. Talbert, p. 153 finds a unity in ch. 16, 'from the concern with possessions that runs through it'. See above, pp. 204-209.

The first half of the journey narrative presents a rather different picture. It is indeed not entirely without order but it is in fact somewhat less easily discerned. It begins with a movement of Jesus and his disciples who journey both with and before him. The response to their witness calls out his own witness to himself. True to the Deuteronomic pattern, this is contrasted with a response of a lawyer who represents Israel as a whole and whose failure is centred in self-justification which stops him from being open to the radical outreach of God (10.25-37). Disciples are warned of the same fatal attitude in the story of Martha and Mary (10.38-42) and this leads naturally into a section on prayer which enshrines a right stance in an eschatological urgency to pray for the coming of the kingdom. That which gives reality to the prayer is the witness to the nearness of the kingdom seen in the activity of Jesus (11.14-23). Disciples, in the light of this, have to be alert (23.26) and blessedness is reserved for those who not only hear the word but who also keep it (27-28). The crowds are condemned because of their absence of vision and their lack of faith (29-36). Such a lack of response is focused on the Pharisees who represent those whose light has become darkness (37-54).

Again following the Deuteronomic pattern, Luke warns the disciples against 'the leaven of the Pharisees' and so encourages them to be alert to the realities of the eschatological situation (12.1-50). That includes teaching which introduces further upbraiding of the multitudes who fail to acknowledge the significance of the times (54-59). Chapter 13 contains the themes of urgency in the face of the reality of Jesus' mission to Jerusalem and indeed in the face of his future return. It warns the rejecting, encourages the responsive, and points forward to Jesus' glorification.

The narrative is less illogical than it at first appears, particularly when it is seen as expressing the threefold outlook of Deuteronomy. Nevertheless, it has not such an easy development as to suggest an ordering by Luke which was not without some form of external constraint. It suggests rather the presence of sources which were not completely pliable to his purpose.

A large part of its contents is paralleled by Matthaean material, and the common order of a significant proportion of this is striking. It is in fact such as to suggest that the overall control of this section is Matthew and that it is the first Gospel which forms both the core of its contents and the control of the order in which the whole is presented.

Luke begins his journey at 9.51. The Moses' typology of the whole and the appearance of the two figures of the old covenant at the transfiguration encourages him to use Elijah typology at this point since this suggests the same eschatological dimension and the same concept of journeying with Jesus. The Samaritans refuse to receive him as did Nazareth at the beginning of the Galilean ministry and in so doing forward his movement towards his goal at Jerusalem. They will be the first outside Israel to hear after the Pentecostal renewal of Israel but Luke's salvation–historical perspective demands that they should not come in as a people until then. Mt. 10.5 has actually suggested this passage but Luke plays down its offensiveness to give a reason both for Jesus' seeming bypassing of them and for their refusal of him. The picture parallels the earlier response at Nazareth.

The mission of the seventy is suggested by Matthew's missionary discourse which is where Jesus instructs his future church on its life in relationship with Israel. It is in fact less of a discourse about the nature of a mission, but goes beyond that given in Mark to address the problems of failure and of the consequent hostility from without and alienation from those with whom one was naturally united. The message of that chapter therefore is of significance for Luke and his community as it too faces the strains of separation and of disappointed hopes.

Like Matthew's mission, that of the seventy is addressed to Israel. As with Matthew's twelve, Luke's seventy are to preach ἤγγικεν ἡ βασιλεία τοῦ θεοῦ. Luke adds ἐφ'ὑμᾶς for those who believe, in accordance with his own understanding of the nature of the kingdom's presence. Mark does not have any such reference to the presence of the kingdom in his story of the twelve. Luke though seemingly following Mark in his sending out of the twelve (9.1-9), does include the concept in his account and this suggests that he is there also influenced by Matthew 10. He uses it again in connection with the sending out of the seventy because at this point Matthew is his primary source.

Though using Matthew, he selects from it for he is not at this time concerned primarily with the problems of either persecution or failure. At this stage, as with the purpose of Acts as a whole, his concern is, though to acknowledge the failure, to point rather to the success which is to be seen as a sign that the kingdom is near. The hostility to the mission cannot be denied so he goes to the next relevant passage in Matthew to enable him to acknowledge that and finds it at Mt. 11.20

from which he takes the attack upon Chorazin, Bethsaida and Capernaum.

He follows this with a suitable verse from Matthew's discourse—10.40—as it points both to the severity of the rejection and the nature of the one who is rejected. But the emphasis remains on the success and its significance is acknowledged at the seventy's return (10.17-20). Here he uses words which in Matthew follow Luke's last passage taken from him (Mt. 11.28-30). These express the unity of the Father and the Son and enable Jesus' expression of thanks to the Father. He does not take over the rest of Matthew's thanksgiving however because its idea of Jesus as the embodiment of Wisdom is alien to Luke. For him, Jesus is inspired by Wisdom as he is by the Spirit, but he is not its personification. That runs counter to Luke's idea of Jesus as the agent of God, one with the prophets, and not of another order from them. At this point he adds 10.23-24 which he takes from Mt. 13.16-17 and which forms a highly appropriate conclusion to the episode of the seventy. These verses also lead into the episode of the self-justifying lawyer. The actual use of this incident at this point may be suggested by the Deuteronomic positioning of the summary of the law, and the earlier reference to the Samaritans makes the parable singularly appropriate. The episode of Martha and Mary makes a fitting climax to the sequence and Mary stands for all who, abandoning self-justification, are able to find their fulfilment in their acceptance of Jesus. That acceptance and its openness to God's final activity through Jesus forms a fitting prelude to teaching on prayer. Though we cannot be certain that Luke's form is an adaptation of the Matthaean Lord's Prayer, for a separate source and even one which occasioned Matthew's form cannot be ruled out, Luke is more likely to have adapted Matthew to concentrate its petitions upon the eschatological situation as he understood it and as he expressed it in the form of his journey narrative. Its form becomes a response to the words of the Lord at the last supper when he covenants a kingdom to his disciples and his prayer rescues Simon from the clutches of Satan (22.28-34). Luke follows the prayer and its accompanying parable with what is a further appropriate section from Matthew's sermon on the mount (Mt. 7.7-11). Matthew's use of 'good things' has an eschatological potential, but Luke makes this actual with his reference to the giving of the Holy Spirit (11.13) and so expresses his typical understanding of the Spirit's eschatological dimension as the anticipation of the final presence of the kingdom.

The last passage taken over by Luke from this section of Matthew was Mt. 11.25-27. What follows that in Matthew has already been used by him in his following of Mark (Mt. 12.1-14) and the next section of Matthew (12.15-21) is a 'formula quotation' passage. We have already seen that these are not favoured by Luke, so its omission causes no surprise. This brings him to Matthew's Beelzebul episode (Mt. 12.22-32). Luke therefore includes this as part of his eschatological teaching, though he omits Mt. 12.31-32 because his understanding of blasphemy against the Holy Spirit is centred in apostasy rather than in Israel's opposition. In place of these verses he adds the section from Mt. 12.43-45 which follows on from the reference to the casting out of demons, even though its actual form is made less appropriate by his having recast Matthew's house imagery into talk about palaces (11.21; cf. Mt. 12.29). Mt. 12.43-45 leads into the episode of Jesus and his mother and his brothers (Mt. 12.46-50). Luke has already taken this over from Mk 3.31-35 at 8.19-21, but his being faced with this episode at this point in Matthew suggests his inclusion of a further reference to Jesus' mother at 11.27-28.

Luke has now arrived at Matthew's parables chapter. He has, however, already made use of Mark's chapter of parables so he has no reason to use much material from it now. He does nevertheless do a little cleaning up. His use of Matthew 12 had not included the episode of Jonah and the Queen of the South. The Jonah reference he takes over and revises to emphasize the lack of response on the part of those who refused to hear the word of God. Since preaching is the point, he omits the reference to the Queen of the South. Jesus anyway, as we have seen, was not for Luke the embodiment of Wisdom, and the use of Matthew's reference to her coming to 'hear the wisdom of Solomon' might have suggested that outlook which he avoids.

The conclusion of Matthew's parables chapter is followed by the story of the death of John the Baptist and the ministry in Gentile territory (Mt. 14.1-15). Luke has already shown his distaste for this by his omission of it when he was following Mark. It leads in Matthew into the story of Jesus' attack upon the tradition of the elders (15.1-20). This is not of itself of interest to Luke who overall does not put weight upon the minutiae of the Law and its surrounding 'hedge'. Nevertheless, the Matthaean material here and the controversy of

Mt. 16.1-12 does bring the Pharisees to the fore and it seems that it is this, as well as the possible Deuteronomic concern with sacrificial regulations (Deut. 12.1-16) which suggests his next episode of controversy with the Pharisees (11.37-54). For this he uses the later and climactic attacks of Matthew 23 while, nevertheless, reducing considerably the hostility found in that chapter.

The Lukan reference to Pharisaic hypocrisy, suggested by the repeated refrain of Matthew 23, is nevertheless fashioned in terms of Mt. 16.5 which is the next, and very near, section of Matthew to discuss the Pharisees. In the light of Mt. 16.1-4, Luke's 'hypocrisy' is to be interpreted in the sense of failure to discern the eschatological situation, a failure brought about by their sense of having already arrived at the fullness of God's action. Luke is actually going to use that passage later (12.54-56) where he will address it to the multitudes as a whole who are unwilling to respond to this eschatological time and where he will actually describe as hypocrisy their failure to 'interpret the present time'.

Luke then, in the light of the warning about Pharisaic hypocrisy, now addresses the multitude and then the disciples in an effort to encourage them to respond actively to the challenge of the hour (12.1–13.9). In doing so, he uses some parts of Matthew's missionary sermon which he has not included at the sending out of the seventy—Mt. 10.26-27; 28.3—and adds the reference to 'blasphemy against the Holy Spirit' which he has not used earlier because of his different understanding of its meaning (11.14-20; cf. Mt. 12.31-32). Both multitudes and disciples need to recognize the true nature of the eschatological situation in which they are involved. The parable of the rich fool follows at this point (12.13-21). Once more, the question of the right attitude to the times is focused upon the need to hold lightly to material possessions. He uses passages taken from a couple of Matthew's sermons: 12.22-31 is taken from the sermon on the mount (Mt. 6.25-33), as is 12.33-34 (Mt. 6.19-21) freely adapted in the light of Luke's emphasis. Mt. 24.43-44 and 25.1-13 form the basis for Luke's passages of warning (12.35-48). He will not later take over the Markan parallel passages (Mk 13.32-37) which will have been the bases for the Matthaean sentiments because his apocalyptic chapter is essentially one about a hope which will bring the calamities to an end (21.28, 36). His warnings are transferred systematically to his passage in ch. 12 for it is here where his teaching about the need to be alive to eschatological exigencies is focused. He knows that the death and resurrection of Jesus are points of division not only within Israel but also within families. So, after pointing to the disciplining of the Lord and his own constraints, he goes on to the constraints upon the disciples. These he speaks of in terms of Mt. 10.34-36 (12.51-53).

But, in keeping with Luke's overall way of changing his audience, he now returns to have the Lord address the multitudes. He uses Mt. 16.1-4 and adapts it freely to his theme. Again, a passage from Matthew's sermon on the mount (5.25-26) is taken up and similarly adapted, though it could have been from some other source which is linked to the episode which he includes at 13.1-5. However gathered, it forms a fitting climax to the section which is brought to a suitable close with the parable of the fig tree (13.6-9).

The last passage which Luke has used from Matthew was Mt. 16.1-4. This in the first Gospel is followed by a Markan section and such material from here as Luke wants has already been used in his following of his Markan source. That has taken him as far as Matthew 18, for he is unlikely to have found Mt. 17.24-27 to his taste. But Matthew 18 is again unlikely as a whole to have appealed to him for it breaks with his eschatological urgency and speaks instead of a settled, closely defined community. He will remember bits of it, but these he will use in very different settings.

At the end of ch. 18 Matthew returns to Mark 10 which Luke is going to take up at his own ch. 18. So it is at this point that Luke's real and thorough gleaning operation from Matthew's Gospel comes to an end. From this point, any use he makes of Matthew becomes significantly less thorough and systematic. It no longer has a controlling influence upon his narrative. And so it is at this point that he brings the first part of his overall section to a climax with the rest of ch. 13 to summarize and in fact climax the theme of eschatological urgency.

Until now, Matthew has provided a large part of the structure of the section. But now his use of that Gospel appears to take on a different perspective.[1] He has taken 12.54-56 out of Mt. 16.1-3 which he has

1. The second part of Luke's central section has less of Matthew and very much more of his own distinctive material. Goulder, however, suggests that Matthew still determines the shape of this part of the narrative (*New Paradigm*, pp. 570-72, 581-83). Luke, he believes, makes use of numerous sayings from Matthew 17–25 which he has earlier omitted, and the order of much of the material is suggested by Luke's

duly interpreted so as to eradicate Matthew's interest in Pharisees and Sadducees and to allow his concern to be directed through the multitudes to Israel as a whole. He adds material which is paralleled in

systematic procedure of following Matthew in a reverse order. This would have resulted in something like a systematic gleaning from a roll read from the end backwards. He finds seven instances of this parallelism of material in a reverse order and argues that 'Their combined impact makes a Lukan policy of reverse gleaning through Matthew 25–16 very probable'.

Does Goulder's suggestion, however, carry conviction? The interrelation between the suggested parallels is convincing in only two, or at best three, instances. Luke's episode of Jesus' attacks on the Pharisees at 14.1-14 might have been suggested by Mt. 23.2, 6, 12 and the parable of the great supper at 14.15-24 by Mt. 22.1-14. The parable of the father and the two sons (15.11-32) could perhaps have been developed out of that in Mt. 21.28-32. Elsewhere however the parallels do not carry conviction. Matthew's reference to a tower in 21.33 is hardly a foundation for, or even a hint of, the Lukan warnings in 14.25-35; Mt. 18.6-21 and 17.20 scarcely suggest Lk. 17.1-10; and Mt. 16.4-28, however much and on this reasoning rather oddly supported by Matthew 24, offers little to point to either the place or the contents of Luke's eschatological section in 17.20–18.8. Goulder himself puts Mt. 18.23-35 in brackets as a parallel to Lk. 16.1-13.

Overall parallelisms have to be stronger than these to carry the weight that Goulder places upon them. But if Luke is as thorough in his gleaning of Matthew as Goulder suggests, then some of his omissions from this part of the first Gospel would seem to make little sense. Why did he not take over the Matthaean parable of the labourers in the vineyard which would have fitted his purposes so admirably, and why did he not make fuller use of the parable of the two debtors which would have lent itself so dramatically to his eschatological message? Luke could easily have altered its setting in the way that he did for the parable of the lost sheep. It seems that his gleaning was less thorough than Goulder would suggest.

Again those passages allegedly derived from Matthew do not seem to have the significance in controlling Luke's order that such a theory would maintain. Is the placing of the contents of Luke 14 for instance controlled by Matthew's material? This might account for the parables but it leaves the incident on which the parables hang, albeit loosely, unexplained (14.1-6). Goulder himself sees this incident of the healing of the man with dropsy as occasioned by the need to give an example of the Pharisaic misdeed of 'binding heavy burdens on men' (11.46). Couched in terms of Mt. 12.9-13, Luke has used this incident already at 10.17 but he now goes back to it again supplying different details and moving its setting to a house. But what does it add to this chapter? The link to 'binding heavy burdens on men' is better accounted for by the incident at 13.10-17. The story of the man with dropsy is in fact superfluous at 14.1-6 either as an illustration of an earlier saying against the Pharisees or as an introduction to the criticisms of them that are made at the meal itself. As actually related to its immediate context it has a built-in redundancy other

Mt. 5.25-26 and then follows that with distinctive material which would seem to come from his own sources. Overall, it remains more likely that the parable of the fig tree, though perhaps developed by Luke so as to express his own theological emphases, is taken by him from a source, or even directly from Old Testament imagery, rather than from the Markan–Matthaean story of the cursing of the fig tree. He follows this with his story of the healing of the crippled woman (13.10-17). It comes out of the parable in that it challenges Israel in the synagogue to acknowledge that that to which the sabbath, rightly understood, pointed is in fact happening in the ministry of Jesus when Satan is being bound as a prelude to his final overthrow.

The rest of ch. 13 expresses this Lukan understanding of the presence of the kingdom as being revealed through Jesus' confrontation with Israel and Jerusalem. The parables of the mustard seed and of the leaven point to the beginning of the kingdom's influence through Jesus, to its nature as being established through his activity, and to its future revelation for all to see. These parables are of course found together in Matthew 13 so it is possible that Luke garnered them from there. If it be asked why only these two, his omission of the others can be explained because they represent the Matthaean understanding of the kingdom as being openly realized in the present of the Christian community, an idea which is, as we have seen, alien to Luke. Luke's form is dependent upon either Matthew or his source rather than upon Mark, yet he is not uninfluenced by the second Gospel. His introduction reflects Mark's perplexity about the kingdom and avoids the Matthaean confidence in its visibility in the present. Yet at the same

than as providing the setting for the meal, as a story with value in itself, and as an illustration of the growing break between Jesus and the Jewish people. It seems to be where it is simply because it came to Luke in some source and was used by him to be the peg which provided both the occasion and the reason for the criticisms at the meal. But it was in fact not tailor-made for the occasion.

This suggests that the control for the order of the material in this section was not provided by Matthew, and also that Luke had more than his Gospel as the source of its contents. The order of this part of the central section seems to be controlled by its themes as these were in part shaped in their exposition by sources which Luke had and which he used alongside his own creative artistry. Just what was the product of more direct sources and what was the result of a free development of very indirect sources must inevitably remain often an open question. But the order of Luke's central section would suggest that both established sources and constructive creativity had a part in bringing the section to its final form.

time, by omitting the contrast between small and great, he avoids Mark's sense of emptiness in the present and his putting all emphasis upon the future. Luke expresses a confidence in something which though hidden in the present is nevertheless real.

Chapter 13 contains some material paralleling Matthew in vv. 18-21, 24 and 28-30 which are found in various parts of the first Gospel. Is Luke here using the first Gospel or is he making use of independent versions, either oral or written? Robert Morgan suggests that at various points Luke is using material which actually served as the source for Matthew's version and suggests that even though Luke knew Matthew's Gospel, 'a weak form of the Q hypothesis may still outweigh the case for dispensing with it altogether'.[1] The simpler hypothesis that Luke derived virtually all his material from Matthew is questioned because in some cases the third Gospel's version looks more primitive and cannot easily be explained as the result of Luke's own thinking and because, particularly but not exclusively in the travel narrative, some of this material seems to have been joined to special Lukan material before Luke himself took it over. Morgan does not in his paper give examples of his thinking but his first point would find support in the Lukan form of the beatitudes and of the Lord's Prayer as well as perhaps in Luke's version of the Beelzebul controversy (11.14-23) and his form of the parable of the mustard seed (13.18-20), while his second point could include his parables of the mustard seed and of the leaven (13.18-21), that chapter's use of the passage referring to the exclusion of some of Jesus' contemporaries from the kingdom and the inclusion of patriarchs and Gentiles (13.28-30), perhaps the parable of the lost sheep (15.3-10) and the three verses linking John, the Law and divorce (16.16-18). In ch. 17, the first four verses do not make for obvious connection with their context and could therefore have come from a collection of sayings already joined in a manner less clearly than would have been expected of Luke himself if he had been responsible for it.

Such possibilities of course cannot be ruled out, for it is unlikely that all oral or even written traditions were included in Mark and Matthew so that none existed independently. Luke and Matthew may have shared in some of these and Luke therefore may have taken over some of them rather than use Matthew at these points. Not all his special material is necessarily his own creation and some available to

1. R. Morgan, in an unpublished paper.

him may have paralleled Matthew's sources. Nevertheless there are few instances, if any at all, where the form actually demands a pre-Lukan source. We have seen that even the beatitudes make good sense as vehicles of Lukan theology adapted from Matthew as their source and that they fit into a sermon which is itself an adequate expression of the Lukan purpose at this point. Again, the Lukan form of the Lord's Prayer expresses Luke's own beliefs and fits comfortably into its context of eschatologically motivated prayer (11.2-4). The Beelzebul passage also fits such a context and its form is an adequate expression of Luke's ideas (11.14-23). Its coming at this point is controlled by Luke's use of Matthew and its form reflects a Lukan revision of his adaptation of Mark. The parable of the mustard seed is again a Lukan adaptation of a Matthaean revision of Mark and, as it stands in Luke (13.18-20), it links the thought of the kingdom, whose presence is witnessed to by the healing of the woman oppressed by Satan, to its future revelation. So Luke at this point brings in the passage about the future inclusion in the kingdom which he had earlier omitted from his version of Matthew's story of the centurion's servant (7.2-10). The eschatological dimension, the references to Jerusalem and her rejection of Jesus, and the thought of Jesus' future revelation are all determined by the climactic nature of this section and its paralleling of the conclusion of the whole narrative at the entry into Jerusalem.

There is little to suggest that Luke was using sources here other than Matthew. He may have been aware of some and we cannot definitely exclude that possibility, but there is actually very little to demand such a course. Luke does have some rough edges which are such as to suggest that not everything was tailor-made for his purpose but his use of Mark shows that he was no slave to his sources and he himself could well have been satisfied with the logic of his ordering of them.

At times his version of a story, a parable or a saying may appear more 'primitive' in that it seems not to have what looks like Matthaean church accretions, as for example in the Lord Prayer, may reflect less hostility to the Jews, for instance in the description of those to be included and excluded at the messianic banquet, or may seem to express a more primitive Christology as in its omission of the Wisdom saying found in Mt. 12.28-29. His version of the parable of the lost sheep may seem to be a better reflection of the situation in the life of

Jesus than is Matthew's version which could express later ecclesiastical concerns. But Luke would have known of the tradition of Jesus' outreach from Mk 2.13-17 and his own background may have caused him to emphasize this aspect in the tradition just as it caused him to deepen Jesus' concern with women, his eating with outsiders, his interest in Samaritans and, in Acts, the inclusion of the Gentiles. If his own concerns made him at times appear more 'primitive' than Matthew, his own beliefs could equally have shaped a number of Matthaean christological statements in this direction, as indeed they could have caused him to alter some of Matthew's views about the Jews, the eschatology of the Lord's Prayer and the descriptions of those who are to be called 'blessed'. Ideas on all these things did not develop in a straight line and it is a fundamental mistake to use what are essentially alien criteria to assume that they did.

What most strongly supports a belief that Luke knew some of Matthew's sources and that he was at a number of points using these rather than Matthew himself, is the fact that, to have gathered all his pieces out of Matthew, would have meant a detailed scavenging from that Gospel and one which occasioned a determined, perhaps repetitive, minute examination of its contents. It seems an unusual exercise, but the number of minor agreements between the two Gospels suggests that Luke was indeed engaged in a thorough examination of Matthew, and this detailed scrutiny is made the more likely by the possibility that he was actually reacting against it. His was a detailed refutation of much of what the first Gospel was proclaiming and it was perhaps this attitude of Luke to Matthew which caused him to engage in his distinctive exercise. Downing has a number of times pointed out that if Luke knew both Mark and Matthew, his manner of using them was idiosyncratic in the extreme. Luke would have been working in a way that was without parallels among his contemporaries. 'Luke', he writes,

> omits any of the close quotations of Mark by Matthew, re-adapts the adaptations, but often cites the unique additions by Matthew to Mark word for word. This is clearly contrary to anything our other first-century sources would lead us to expect... Not only is the material 'unpicked', then, and meticulously, but it is unpicked to allow an unprecedented and barely coherent choice.[1]

1. G. Downing, 'Contemporary Analogies to the Gospels and Acts', in C.M. Tuckett (ed.), *Synoptic Studies*, pp. 61-62.

It may indeed be 'unprecedented' but we have argued that it is by no means 'barely coherent'. Luke is an evangelist with a distinctive message, one which is, in large part at any rate, fashioned in conscious disagreement with one of his sources and which involves a determined reshaping of his other. Luke works with a definite aim in view. It is true of course, as Downing maintains, that 'Purposes can be easily imagined, and supported in detail'. Justification for the method alleged can always be found and the justifier is often in danger of allowing his or her own insights to burgeon so that in the end they do a take-over. But Luke was a creative theologian, a free handler of his sources, a believer with a vision and a proponent of a particular understanding of the significance of the Christian proclamation. The Gospels may not have been unique but they were distinctive, as their authors are seen to be propagators of a strong eschatological belief centred around the exclusiveness of God's action in Jesus. Luke may have shattered the mould created by his contemporaries but in so doing he nevertheless seems to have worked in a tradition which would not have cut him off from a Mark, a Matthew or, indeed, a John.

Chapter 16

INFANCY AND RESURRECTION NARRATIVES

It is frequently suggested that the differences between the infancy narratives of the first and third Gospels are of such an order as to present almost insuperable difficulties to the belief that Luke could have known Matthew.[1] Though they share a number of points, the ways in which even these are expressed are so different as to make it hard to postulate a direct influence, while the material as a whole contains a series of such diverse incidents that harmonization of the two is possible only by postulating a second visit to Bethlehem which would in fact seem to make little sense of the narratives of either of the two evangelists' work as they now stand. Had Luke known Matthew, it would mean not merely that he chose to ignore the greater part of his material, but that he wrote in such a way as to exclude a large part of its contents.

The obvious way to account for such an activity would be to suggest that Luke had sources other than Matthew and that he chose these deliberately to the exclusion of that source provided by the first Gospel. However, suggestions that Luke had such an extended source have little to commend them for they fail to take into account the Lukan style of the first two chapters and the Septuagintal nature of its writing which, though more determined perhaps than in other parts of Luke–Acts, is nevertheless not unrelated to such Septuagintal passages as are found in the earlier half of Acts. These suggest that Luke wrote in such a way in order to express his understanding of the events in terms of biblical fulfilment. As Fitzmyer expresses it, 'The sooner we

1. Brown, *Messiah*; R. Laurentin, *Structure et Theologie de Luc 1–11* (Paris: Gabalda, 1957); Nolland, *Luke*, pp. 22-23. See the survey by R.E. Brown, 'Gospel Infancy Narrative Research from 1976–1986, Part 11, Luke', *CBQ* 48 (1986), pp. 660-80, and his *Biblical Criticism and Church Dogma*, pp. 74-85, 156-61.

reckon with the rather uniform Lukan Greek style in the infancy narrative, the better'.[1]

Was Luke, nevertheless, constrained in some way by sources? Those who think he was, are usually impressed by the existence of some seeming rough edges in the narratives which are explained on the grounds of sources which were not open to complete unification.[2] While supposed Baptist sources or alleged discrepancies between chs. 1 and 2 have not secured a large number of supporters,[3] wider support has been mustered for that view which would suggest some Jewish–Christian or even simply Jewish source material for the canticles of these chapters, more especially for the songs of Zechariah and of Mary (1.46-55, 68-79). It is frequently said that they fit but loosely into their contexts, that they are inappropriate as commentaries upon the actual events with which they are connected, and that they themselves do not really reflect Luke's theology.[4]

These arguments, however, are less than convincing. Certainly it is true that they could be taken out of their contexts without impairing the actual flow of the narratives. But this is made inevitable by their very nature for, unless they are so constructed as to demand a direct response from some character in the scene, they are of necessity capable of such extraction. They are of the nature of commentaries upon the events rather than being actual integral parts of the incidents. They are direct addresses to the reader. But it is just their appropriateness as commentaries upon the events which is questioned. Zechariah's song is seen as being more appropriate to the birth of the messiah than to that of his precursor while the triumphalism and militarism of the magnificat is said to be of little relevance to either the nature of the singer or of him whose coming birth it celebrates.[5]

However, this is to forget the place of the canticles in the biblical development of such songs. The magnificat is fashioned by the song of Hannah (1 Sam. 2.1-10) which, though a commentary upon Hannah's

1. *Luke*, p. 312.

2. Brown, *Birth*, pp. 250-53; Fitzmyer, *Luke*, p. 311; Nolland, *Luke*, p. 22.

3. P. Winter, 'Some Observations on the Language in the Birth and Infancy Stories of the Third Gospel', *NTS* 1 (1954–55), pp. 111-21; 'On Luke and Lukan Stories', *ZNW* (1956), pp. 217-42.

4. See the discussion in S. Farris, *The Hymns of Luke's Infancy Narratives: Their Origin, Meaning and Significance* (JSNTSup, 9; Sheffield: JSOT Press, 1985), pp. 14-30.

5. Farris, *Hymns*, pp. 14-30.

situation, sees it as typical of Yahweh's whole redemptive activity. The immediate situation is, if not ignored, then at least not directly pinpointed as it is caught up in the whole complex of God's saving work to which it points and of which it is seen to be a part. So it is with the song of Mary. Jesus, seen as the climax of God's whole saving activity within Israel, is celebrated as the culmination of all God's redemptive work with her. Mary herself represents the poor, the remnant, the pious in Israel who, as the true believers, await Yahweh's redemption. Mary is faithful Israel and as such is already Christianized. It is right that her song should be sung in response to the greeting of the mother of the Baptist, for John is envisaged by Luke as the restorer of the true in Israel. He is presented as the one who will go before the Lord (and so before his Christ) 'in the spirit and power of Elijah, to make ready for the Lord a people prepared' (1.17). The Baptist is 'filled with the Holy Spirit even from his Mother's womb' (1.15) and as such is already part of that eschatological act of God which is witnessed to by the outpouring of the Spirit. The song of Zechariah therefore is appropriately an acknowledgment of the whole saving act of God through Jesus and of which John himself is a part. John himself has no significance other than as the true response of Israel to Israel's messiah. It is wholly appropriate that the as yet unborn babe should leap in his mother's womb when he is confronted with him as the yet unborn messiah and Lord (1.44). Luke incorporates John fully into the work of God in Christ. This is made clear in the annunciation to Zechariah (1.14-17) and the Benedictus acts as an entirely appropriate expression of that understanding.

The canticles therefore fit the narratives of Luke 1–2 as a whole and play a vital part, not in moving the story forward, but in expressing Luke's understanding of the significance of Jesus and of his place in the history of God's redemptive activity in Israel. This remains essentially true even though some have seen in them a distinctive Christology which is other than Luke's own.[1] The Jewishness of their thought is, however, no argument against composition by Luke for we have seen repeatedly that it is the Old Testament itself which exerts a final control over Luke's Christology to give it its distinctive shape even to the extent of imposing a less than adequate expression of the Christian recognition of the corporate, indwelling Christ. Similarly,

1. D.R. Jones, 'The Background and Character of the Lukan Psalms', *JTS* 19 (1968), pp. 19ff.

the fact that the magnificat and benedictus reflect a particularistic rather than a universalistic outlook does not count against Lukan authorship for again it is the Old Testament eschatological renewal of Israel with an extension of it to include Gentiles which controls his thinking (Acts 15.12, 18).[1] The first essential is the recreation of faithful Israel. Then, and only then, can Christ, his servants, and renewed Israel become 'a light for revelation to the Gentiles' (2.32; Acts 13.47; 26.23). Becoming this, Israel herself will be glorified (2.32).

There is therefore no reason to see anything other than a unified theology throughout Luke's infancy narratives or to understand it as anything other than the theology of Luke himself. The canticles express, not a Jewish–Christian theology of some unidentified group of *anawim*, but that of Luke himself as he perceives the Christian community as the poor in Israel (6.20; Acts 2.43-47), being one with the piety expressed in the Psalms (Pss. 34.6; 40.17; 70.5), and with those who in the Old Testament waited for God's redemption with expectation, openness and detachment from earthly goods in anticipation of God's deliverance. That some have sought without great success to uncover various sources in these narratives witnesses to the success of Luke's own enterprise and to the magnitude of his achievement.

It must nevertheless not be forgotten that the greatest of modern Lukan interpreters, Hans Conzelmann, has questioned such an evaluation of Luke's infancy narratives. He writes that 'The authenticity of these first two chapters is questionable',[2] and maintains that there is expressed in them a theology which is peculiar to them and which fits uneasily if at all into that found in the third Gospel as a whole. So their eschatology is seen to be distinctive in that the Spirit is already outpoured upon a situation where the period of Israel is caught up into the period of salvation; Israel herself is viewed more positively than in Luke–Acts as a whole to be given a continuation with God's covenantal activity which is denied to it in the main body of the work, while the Christology is different in that Jesus is already exalted and given a contemporaneity which is not allowed to him elsewhere.

Yet the overall theology of these chapters is one with that found in the two volumes. Jesus on the journey to Jerusalem is already

1. See above, pp. 52-60.
2. *Theology*, p. 172.

anticipated as the Lord he is becoming; he, and later his followers, are receivers of an outpoured Spirit, and he is understood throughout in terms of Christ and Lord, the one who as God's instrument is exalted to God's right hand. Israel is not left behind, right up to and including the end of Acts, and John the Baptist, in spite of separation in the actual body of the narrative, is viewed as being one with the whole work of God in Christ (Acts 10.37; 13.24-25; 19.2-3). Jesus' ministry can be isolated as the middle of time only by ignoring the significance that Luke gives to the ascension and to the forward thrust that is to be discerned in his unfolding of the ministry of Jesus.

Nevertheless, it remains true that there is a difference between these chapters and the rest of Luke–Acts. This, however, is not a difference in theology but a different perspective arising out of the fact that these two chapters have a different role from that given to the various parts in the rest of the two volumes. They serve, not as the first chapter of an unfolding narrative extending to the end of Acts, but as the prologue to the two volumes. They are the statement which the work as a whole explains and justifies, and as such they make a proclamation much in the same way, though of course not to express the same ideas, as is made by the prologue to the fourth Gospel.[1]

The theology of the infancy narratives is the same theology as that expressed in Luke–Acts as a whole. It is the theology of Luke. Any sources that may have been available to him have been recast so as to become appropriate vehicles for the expression of his own ideas. The style is adopted by Luke as serving the better expression of his understanding. The prologue plays its own distinctive role but in the service of a unified development of Luke's thought.

If therefore it remains unlikely that there were written sources underlying Luke's narrative to place any constraining hand upon the free expression of his own ideas, is it nevertheless more likely that he had a number of traditions upon which to build and which provided, if not a skeleton for his story, then at least a series of points around which his narrative was developed? R.E. Brown has noted some eleven points which Luke's narrative has in common with that of Matthew, and he concludes that

> since it is generally agreed among scholars that Matthew and Luke wrote independently of each other, without knowing the other's work,

1. Conzelmann himself repeatedly refers to them as 'Prologue'.

> agreement between the two infancy narratives would suggest the existence of a common infancy tradition earlier than either evangelist's work.[1]

This alleged 'common tradition' does in fact represent a core tradition forming the main structure of the two narratives for it includes the references to Joseph and Mary, the Davidic descent by way of Joseph, the virginal conception, and the birth at Bethlehem. The heart of this is, of course, the virginal conception for it is this which controls most of the other common features. But is such a 'common tradition' more likely than that which Brown dismisses, namely the dependence of one evangelist upon the other?

Expression of the virginal conception is confined in the New Testament to the infancy narratives of Matthew and Luke. The task force of New Testament scholars investigating the place of Mary in the New Testament writings concluded that they 'found no reference to the virginal conception in the New Testament apart from Matthew and Luke'.[2] Though John has sometimes been seen as witnessing to such a belief in that the Jews who invariably get Jesus wrong, witness to Jesus' sonship from Joseph (6.42), the witness of Philip to Nathanael (1.45) suggests that John did not view it as an inadequate description. The Jewish mistake was not in denying the virginal conception but in refusing to recognize Jesus' divine sonship. His ultimate father was not Joseph but God. If anything, he seems to want to stress the fact that Jesus' parents were known in order to exclude any charge of illegitimacy that might have been made against Jesus (8.41). Again, Mark seems to know no tradition of the virginal conception. Mk 6.3 seems not to express such an idea. Had Matthew understood it thus it remains unlikely that he would have altered it to contain a reference to 'the carpenter's son' (Mt. 13.55). Indeed, it looks as if he acted to avoid any slur that he might have seen in Mark's reporting. While the difference is usually accounted for on the grounds of Matthew's reverential attitude which avoided calling Jesus a carpenter, it is equally (and perhaps more) likely that he was rebutting what he saw as a slur about Jesus' parentage and one to which he felt peculiarly sensitive. That Matthew was sensitive to this attack upon Jesus may well account for the use of the women's names in the genealogy with their accompanying suggestions of irregular unions used and blessed by God. It is

1. *Birth*, pp. 34-35.

2. R.E. Brown, *et al.*, *Mary in the New Testament* (London: Chapman, 1978), p. 289.

not until his use of the Isaiah quotation (Isa. 7.14) at Mt. 1.23 that an unequivocal reference to a virginal conception is found. Stendahl has called Matthew's use of the tradition 'theologically mute'.[1] His emphasis is upon the part of Joseph, a Son of David, in incorporating Jesus into the Davidic line.

Luke, on the other hand, is much clearer about the virginal conception than is Matthew. It is true that in the Nazareth episode he has Jesus referred to as 'Joseph's son' (4.22) but in the light of his explanation in the genealogy (3.23), it is clear how he expects his readers to understand it. The people of Nazareth do not perceive the true significance of what they are saying. Luke in his Gospel tones down considerably the adverse comments of Jesus towards Mary, found both in Mark and (though in a lesser degree) in Matthew (Mk 3.34; Mt. 12.49). Though it is probably too much to say that Luke sees Mary as a disciple at this point, she is not excluded from the Christian family. Luke is distinct among the Gospels. Mark has no virginal conception and no honouring of Mary, Matthew has a virginal conception but no honouring of Mary, John honours Mary but is without a virginal conception. Luke alone has both a wholly positive evaluation of the virginal conception and an honouring of Mary.

There does not in fact seem to be a strong tradition of the virginal conception which caused both Matthew and Luke to write in the ways that they did. Though such a tradition cannot be ruled out, there is no need to assume that it came independently of Matthew to Luke. It is more likely that Luke learned his tradition from Matthew and that he set out to make explicit what was less clearly so in the first Gospel. He centred his narrative on Mary because that would allow the tradition to be made unambiguously clear and because, in accordance with biblical imagery he could let her be the natural embodiment of the faithful in Israel. He used a genealogy through Joseph because he was building on the Matthaean tradition of Davidic incorporation through him. A genealogy was really superfluous but he was constrained by Matthew's example which, because he deemed it unsatisfactory because of the women (to him a slur) and its narrowness, he altered and moved its position to after the baptism where for him it made more sense since, in accordance with Mark, he saw that point as the effective incorporation of Jesus into his divine sonship which

1. K. Stendahl, 'Quis et Unde? An Analysis of Matthew 1–2', in W. Eltester (ed.), *Judentum, Urchristentum: Kirche* (Berlin: Topelmann, 1960), pp. 94-105.

he viewed in Old Testament functional terms. Luke's narratives surrounding Mary and the virginal conception can be satisfactorily explained as a development of Matthew to express ideas suggested by him but which were developed by Luke to become a vehicle for his own insights.

Why though is Luke so different? Why has he used a Matthaean outline to build up a narrative which is not only other than Matthew's but which virtually excludes a large part of that evangelist's narrative and a significant part of the theology which it expresses? Here, we must recall the conclusions of our second section. Luke expresses beliefs which are not only distinctive from those found in the first Gospel but which are expressed, in part at any rate, in contrast to, indeed even in opposition to, a number of those of Matthew. These we saw centred upon different attitudes adopted to Israel, and different understandings therefore of the Christian community's relation to Israel, not of the past, but of the present. Both saw continuity with the past but, whereas for Luke that continuity meant a continuing concern with Israel and an abiding link to her, for Matthew that same sense of continuity resulted in something like a takeover, a passing of the covenant from Israel to the church, and an exclusion of Israel herself from the sphere of God's concern. In both Matthew and Luke the infancy narratives serve as prologues to their respective Gospels, and the proclamation, the theology expressed in narrative form has therefore to be different and in fact mutually exclusive. Matthew's infancy narratives would not have appealed to Luke. His two-volume work demanded other themes, and hence other stories were required to express them. He built upon Matthew but in a manner that was less that of dialogue than of reaction. His narrative centres around Mary[1]. That is suggested by Matthew for it is from him that Luke has taken over the fact of the virginal conception. Matthew's story, however, ignored Mary to be centred upon Joseph in a narrative which expressed hesitance, even uneasiness about Mary's part. Luke counters this to produce a wholly positive, theologically charged, narrative which makes the virginal conception clear beyond any shadow of doubt. That this was not essential to Luke's understanding is made clear by his use of the genealogy through Joseph in connection with the baptism rather than with the birth. The Spirit's activity at the conception did not of itself necessarily involve the virginity of the

1. See the discussion in Brown, *Mary*, pp. 206-208.

mother, but that this was important to Luke is made clear by Mary's prominent, but of itself inconsequential, question to the angel at the time of the annunciation (1.34). The announcement is made to her and not to Joseph, thereby eliminating any remaining hesitations that might arise from the following of Matthew's version.

But if the actual prominence of Mary is suggested by Luke's doubts about the adequacy of the Matthaean narrative, his use of her reaches out beyond her to make her the representative of the pious, the responsive in Israel who were awaiting God's redemption and who were able to find and acknowledge that in Jesus. Mary, as Hannah before her, stands as the embodiment of the true in Israel. Luke was aware of the concept of the 'daughters of Zion'[1] for he uses it of the

1. R.H. Gundry, *Matthew; A Commentary on his Literary and Theological Art* (Grand Rapids: Eerdmans, 1982), in fact reverses our argument to make Matthew's a free rendering of a Lukan-like infancy narrative which both writers found in a greatly extended Q. Luke, as the historian among the evangelists, recognised the historical character of this Q episode and so followed it faithfully. Matthew's as being historically irreconcilable to Luke's is of the character of a midrashic rewriting of Q. So the natural genealogy of the source is transformed into a royal one, the annunciation is transferred to Joseph on the pattern of that to the father of John the Baptist, Gabriel's announcement that Mary has 'found favour with God' becomes the basis for Matthew's assertion that she 'was found to be with child of the Holy Spirit', Dan. 2.2, 10 causes the shepherds to become Gentile magi, their coming is determined by Lk. 2.15-16, their joy by Lk. 2.10, and the star by Lk. 1.78. The return of the shepherds and the family's journey to Jerusalem are altered into a flight from persecution, and the sacrifice in the temple is transformed into the slaughter of the babes (pp. 15, 17, 20, 26, 31, 32, 35, 37).

Apart from the somewhat wooden use of words, it would be possible to account for such changes by supposing that they were caused by just those theological ideas which we believe Luke recognized in Matthew's work and found as not according to his own understanding, namely its basic anti-Jewish stance and its determination to present its community, now fast becoming predominantly Gentile, as doing a takeover from the Jews of their status as the covenantal people of God. Matthew does indeed make for less continuity between the old people and the new, and his story of the temptation presents Jesus as the true son taking the place of the disobedient Israel. He is less favourable to Mary and he could have wanted to omit her willing part in the making of a new people in the service of his understanding of discontinuity. Nevertheless, it is then hard to see why he should have omitted both the universal implications of the census and the pointing to the Jewish rejection implied in the story of the birth in a stable. The journey to Bethlehem and the rejection there would have contributed to his aims. Had he known Luke, it is difficult to see why he should have replaced the story of the shepherds with that of the wise men

women who followed Jesus to his cross (23.28). The angelic salutation to Mary (1.28) recalls Zech. 9.9 and Zeph. 3.14-17. Luke's mention of her at Acts 1.14 in connection with the twelve and others expresses something of the same theme. The episode of Jesus in the temple at the age of twelve (2.41-51), issuing in her 'keeping all these things in her heart', begins that learning, chastening process which Simeon foresaw as a sword piercing her own soul (2.35). Mary in her person represents the true Jewish–Christians who as the true in Israel acknowledge the fulfilment in Jesus of God's covenantal concern.

Goulder makes the annunciation and birth of John the Baptist the controlling scene of Luke's pre-birth narratives.[1] Though this would in some ways account for the developing activity of the Holy Spirit until it climaxes in the Spirit-conception of Jesus, and would give due weight to the influence of the Markan placing of John (Mk 1.1-8), this

rather than keeping the two. On the other hand, it is much easier to understand why Luke should have found no place for the wise men in his theological scheme. Luke more likely replaced Matthew's royal genealogy with one which, while omitting the, to him, offensive references to the women, traced the more humble line of Jesus via David and Abraham, to Adam as more befitting one whose messiahship was established by way of obedience only at his exaltation by a direct act of divine reversal. Jesus himself was for Luke one who fulfilled Mary's acknowledgment that God 'has put down the mighty from their thrones, and exalted those of low degree' (Lk. 1.52).

If these considerations make it more likely that Luke has recast Matthew rather than the reverse, a number of general points give added weight to this position. Luke's presentation of Paul in Acts suggests that he is searching after a theological presentation rather than a strictly historical one: presuppositions biasing the interpreter in favour of his historicity over that of Matthew are in fact misplaced. His handling of Mark is much freer than is Matthew's and we have seen that this is determined more by theological rather than historical considerations. I believe that it is wholly likely that Luke used Matthew's infancy narratives and rewrote them in the light of his own parallel but very different theological concerns. That he did this is a more likely explanation of his working than that he ignored Matthew at this point because he recognized its midrashic nature: 'Just as Luke usually preferred Mark and Q to Matthew, so he usually preferred the other tradition of the nativity to Matthew's version, perhaps because Luke regarded that other tradition as historical, saw unhistorical embellishments in Matthew's version, and did not want to compromise his own historiographical purpose.' To assign a historiographical purpose at this point to Luke seems to go against the tenor of Luke–Acts as a whole. As Meier writes, *JBL* 103 (1984), pp. 425-27, Gundry's 'presuppositions do not fit the data'; cf. the discussion of Gundry's *Matthew* by P.B. Payne in R.T. France and D. Wenham (eds.), *Gospel Perspectives*, III (Sheffield: JSOT Press, 1983), pp. 177-216.

1. *New Paradigm*, pp. 206-208.

as a whole seems unlikely. The overall control is Luke's reading of Matthew and his working to clarify, emphasize, and express his own understanding of the significance of its reporting of Jesus' conception. He then works backwards from that in the light of his own understanding of the activity of God in Jesus as the culmination and fulfilment of his covenantal activity in Israel. John, as the eschatological Elijah, witnesses to Jesus as the culmination of Israel's prophetic line. As this, the Spirit is upon him from the womb (1.15). Though of a highest standing this nevertheless marks him off from Jesus himself who is actually conceived by the Spirit (1.35). Zechariah as the agent of the temple witnesses therefore through his acknowledgment of John to the finality of Jesus even as, after the birth, the true adherents of the temple and the Law respond to him (2.25, 36) at just the point where the parents bring Jesus 'to do for him according to the custom of the law' (2.27).

Prophecy, Law and temple all witness to Jesus and the true adherents of the old covenant are led by them to him. The parallelism of the stories of John and Jesus have led to the birth of John. He now awaits his future role and the way is clear for Luke to concentrate solely upon Jesus. Matthew is of course silent on all this and the way is clear for Luke to develop his narrative as he needs it for an adequate expression of his theology.

Matthew places the birth at Bethlehem in the setting of the coming of the Magi to suggest that it was that city which was home to Joseph and Mary. Luke, in contrast, has a shortish visit occasioned by the census and lasting only long enough for the requirements of the Law to be accomplished in the temple itself. For him, Jesus' home is Nazareth in Galilee; that city is not seen as any recently acquired haven from Jewish animosity. It may represent the periphery of Israel, but it is not a stepping stone to the Gentile world. Rather, it enables something of an ingathering of Israel to be collected in readiness for the Pentecostal outpouring at Jerusalem. Nazareth not Bethlehem, is the home of Jesus and the springboard of his ministry.

So Luke needs to get Mary and Joseph to Bethlehem in order for the birth to take place there. To do so, he uses the universalized and idealized census. Jesus is born when the whole world is on the move, and his birth in the city of David comes about as the result of the divine use of the all powerful but uncomprehending Roman power. His birth takes place in a manger for there was no room for him in the κατάλυμα. Jeremiah had complained of the hiddenness of God's activity: it was as that of one who stayed for a short time in a κατάλυμα (Jer. 14.8). Jesus was even more hidden. The world as a whole passed him by, and Jewry could find no place for him. But Mary and Joseph cared for him and shepherds, as representatives of the outcasts and reminiscent of David, came, summoned by angels as Matthew's visitors were by a star. The visit of the shepherds is no doubt modelled on Matthew's visit of the magi. Luke could not use them, except by making a direct refutation of Matthew's account. He would not have wanted the climaxing of Gentiles to the exclusion of Israel that Matthew's story proclaimed. He might want a Gentile presence, but that could come only as a result of recognition and response on the part of the Jewish faithful. This was suggested in his infancy narratives, but not yet fully accomplished. So Matthew's wise men have to be laid aside, their coming hinted at, and indeed foreseen and determined by Simeon's witness of a gentile response to the light and glory of Israel (2.32).

Luke's infancy narratives can be seen as a determined response to the stories he found in Matthew. Sources underlying Luke are unlikely, and the points he has in common with Matthew are more likely to have been derived by him from that Gospel rather than from any independent tradition. He has reacted to Matthew to produce a coherent narrative which, by recasting what the first Gospel contained, becomes a fine expression of his own theology which he is then to go on to unpack, explain and develop in his two volumes.

The resurrection narratives can be dealt with more briefly.[1] It is usually agreed that Matthew's story of Jesus' Galilean appearance, while it represents a movement out to all nations, is also (in the light of the move there after the return from Egypt 4.12) a movement away from Jerusalem. Though the Jews are included within the summons to a universal preaching, what emerges is a break with the past to express something of a new people in tension with the Jews. Jesus appears as already glorified and it is as such that he indwells his church. The anticipation of the parousia is made with a view to proclaiming the full eschatological sufficiency of the present, and the parousia itself is no longer looked for with longing or anticipated as an early event. Those who are to become disciples are distinguished

1. See my discussion in *How the Critics Can Help* (London: SCM Press, 1981), pp. 126-54.

by their observance of Jesus' teachings which are seen as related to the law through a deepening of its demands and a summary of its decrees in a commitment to love. The community is bounded by baptism in a trinitarian formula.

All this represents an approach which is distinctly other than that found in Luke–Acts. Both Matthew and Luke are of course concerned with the missionary enterprise but, whereas in Matthew this missionary enterprise is represented as primary and ongoing, in Luke the arrival of Paul at Rome is seen as a fulfilment of the Lord's commands. The 'witness' is to the world in much the same way that Paul seems to have understood his missionary enterprise. It seems that the parousia is now awaited.

Luke will replace Matthew's realized eschatological picture of an already glorified Lord with his double account of the ascension which he will represent as the moment when the Lord enters into his glory. It is seen as a withdrawal, gratefully acknowledged in the Gospel in response to the departing Lord's blessing of his followers (24.51-53) but occasioning in Acts an attitude of perplexity and loss (Acts 1.10). The disciples' confidence has to be restored by the outpouring of the Spirit and the universal witness which is enabled by that. Luke's Jesus is withdrawn, a usually hidden though not inactive Lord whose manifestation is awaited with hope (24.52).

So Luke's resurrection narratives reflect the summary that he gives at the beginning of Acts. 'To them he presented himself alive after his passion by many proofs, appearing to them during forty days, and speaking of the kingdom of God' (Acts 1.3). Jesus' teaching is not merely harping back to a definitive content given during the ministry. What Luke offers is proof of Jesus' resurrection (hence the somewhat crass nature of his most materialistic presentation [24.41-43]) and teaching about the nature of the kingdom—the need of Jesus' suffering, his exaltation to and place in heaven, the Spirit's presence as the witness to that and the universal witness as a guarantee of the reality of that presence (24.25-27, 45-49; Acts 1.6-8, 11).

Luke's narrative is of a different hue from that found in Matthew for he presents a different theology by way of it. Matthew's narrative could only have seemed inadequate to him for it appeared to represent a proclamation which was not only wrongly focused but which failed to answer the questions that Luke and his readers were asking. His Jesus is less present in his church and Luke meets the problem of

Jewish rejection with different answers. The Lord's command to remain in Jerusalem, which counters not merely Matthew but also Mark, reflects his sense of continuity, of Old Testament control, and a continuing concern for the Jewish people. The full eschatological event must happen there and the universal witness includes them. Here is his most distinctive mark. His resurrection narratives not only avoid appearances outside Jerusalem, they explicitly deny them, for such happenings would run counter to the theological assertions upon which his stories are based.

Chapter 17

LUKE—A REACTION TO MATTHEW

We are now in a position to draw together the conclusions of this section. Both the shape and the contents of Luke's Gospel are best explained on the supposition that Luke knew Matthew's Gospel as well as Mark's and that, while the latter was his primary source, he used Matthew as a second source with which to expand and update Mark. While this must of necessity remain at the level of hypothesis, Luke's Gospel can be explained without recourse to a hypothetical Q, and to do so does in fact give a more satisfactory account of the unity in outlook and belief that the third Gospel manifests so effectively.

Luke's primary source was Mark. I considered a number of arguments which have been adduced in support of the proto-Luke hypothesis with its supposition that some source other than Mark was primary for Luke. However, we found that Mark rather than anything else provided the structure on which Luke built his Gospel and that its influence was to be seen as determinative even when Luke was making use of other sources. The oft-repeated assertion that Luke used his sources in blocks rather than mingling them was seen to be only a half-truth and was in fact based on a pre-determined assumption of the limits of Lukan rewriting. The influence of Mark was all-embracing in Luke and determined the overall shape and outlook of the third Gospel.

This of course is not to deny the possibility of other sources which he might have used alongside Mark and which could have influenced his actual use of that Gospel. Lk. 22.24-27 for instance could be a rewriting and relocation of Mk 10.35-45, but it could equally well be the result of Luke's use of some other source, however much that was revised to serve the adequate expression of his own ideas. His Nazareth episode, though based on Mark to become an expansion of its scene and an explanation of its puzzle, may have been developed in the light of other sources whether originally associated with the rejection episode or not. Luke may have had other sources with which he filled out the Markan passion narrative. The possibility of such cannot be ruled out though there is little evidence to demand their existence. The unified viewpoint of the final work means that if they existed they are likely to have undergone a thorough revision. The point is, however, that such other material as Luke had remains secondary and supplementary to his Markan source.

Mark was Luke's primary and respected source. Nevertheless, what he undertook was nothing less than a thorough revision of the second Gospel, omitting a great deal, re-ordering many episodes, freely rewriting much, and reworking all to enable it to be pointed to the immediate needs of his readers which he believed were to be met only by his own particular presentation of the nature of Jesus and of God's work through him. Luke handled Mark freely, even drastically, to enable it to become the vehicle of his own proclamation. He engaged upon a thorough exercise in pastoral theology. Just how thorough an exercise it was is shown by the persistence of the proto-Luke hypothesis.

These results of a consideration of the relation of Luke to Mark have great implications for our approach to the Q hypothesis. Luke cannot be thought of as a conservative handler of the sources that came his way. If he handled his primary and determinative source, Mark, with such creative freedom, then any other sources he possessed are unlikely to have been used any less freely by him. Attempts to recreate Q become fraught with difficulties, for that bias towards the Lukan form which is usually found in attempted reconstructions of the original wording of Q is seen to rest on a very shaky basis. Our consideration of a number of such passages showed that the Lukan form of many of them could be explained on the basis of that evangelist's activity as easily as, and in some cases more easily than, the Matthaean form where such activity on the part of the first Evangelist is usually more readily admitted. Luke's form of a large number of passages is in fact explicable on the supposition of his creative handling of a Matthaean form, and in these many instances there is little or no need to postulate some third work to bridge the differences between the two.

That Luke was in fact using Matthew at these points is made more likely by the recurring need to explain the agreements between

Matthew and Luke against Mark. Though the so-called major agreements present a difficulty for any attempted solution of the Synoptic Problem which rests upon a supposed knowledge of at least one Gospel by the others, the difficulty is in fact less for that solution which believes that Luke had knowledge of both Mark and Matthew. At these points—for example, the narratives of the Baptist and of the temptations—Matthew added information to the Markan source which was of service to Luke in the unfolding of his understanding of God's action in Jesus. Luke could envisage Matthew's stories as improvements upon those of his Markan source. The messianic preaching of John which Matthew contained fitted his understanding of the Baptist's significance and could usefully supplement the Markan viewpoint, particularly as he moved the Matthaean material in a Markan direction. He handled other major agreements in the same way, using them as useful contributions to his portrait of Jesus but moving them nevertheless in the direction of his Markan primary source. The minor agreements again point to his knowledge of Matthew. As exampled in his version of the trial of Jesus before the Jews, they show Luke as using the first Gospel, not merely in the service of smoothing Markan rough edges but also to introduce significant points which served to make the Markan scenes more acceptable expressions of his own understanding. His rewriting of Mark may well have been influenced at various points by his knowledge of Matthew.

These considerations suggest that a large question has to be raised against the alleged existence of Q. Luke's creativity shows that it is less obvious than is often supposed and that in fact its introduction often does less than justice to Luke's method as that can be uncovered from his handling of Mark. Again, belief in Q fails to take seriously the ways in which Luke and Matthew agree so often against Mark. Together, these two factors virtually compel us to start from the assumption that Luke did in fact know Matthew and to face positively the difficulties that such an assumption raises.

The basic difficulty is that, if Luke knew both Matthew and Mark, he handled them in very different ways. Luke may have handled Mark freely—and we have seen that in actual fact he did so very freely—but, if he used Matthew, then he handled him with a freedom which was such as to be of a wholly different order from that with which he handled Mark. In part of course this can be explained from the supposition that Mark was his primary source to which everything else including Matthew was supplementary. Such priority given to Mark suggests that equally valued sources demanding equality of respect and usage were inherently unlikely.[1] But though this may account for a different handling of the two sources, it does not deal with the reality of the measure of the difference that is found in Luke's handling of Mark and Matthew. More than priority is involved: if Luke knew Matthew, he handled it with a freedom which shows that he gave to it a value which was wholly at variance with that which he gave to Mark. This comes out most clearly in the fact that Luke, with determined regularity, omits significant Matthaean additions to Markan scenes. Since we have established that many of Luke's episodes reflect the influence of both Mark and Matthew, the omission of these Matthaean additions takes on the nature of a deliberate rejection of what they contain to become a determined turning aside from the perspective which the Matthaean episodes reveal. Luke's handling of Matthew is seen to be one controlled by caution: it amounts to no more than a guarded use of the first Gospel's perspective and exhibits a critical attitude to much that it contains. Luke is in fact a critic of Matthew.

It is here that source criticism applied to Luke's Gospel has to take into account the conclusions of our first two sections. Luke, I showed, was a follower of Paul: he understood him and was influenced by him much more thoroughly than is often allowed. Though he interpreted the Pauline outlook to meet new circumstances, and in the light of his own understanding of the continuity expressed in the one developing saving action on the part of God, he assimilated and built upon Paul's insight that Law no longer had a part to play in defining either the boundaries of the people of God or the response that membership of that people both enabled and demanded. In this sense, the Law was at an end for Luke as much as it was for Paul even though he shied away from the complaints that the apostle made against it.

Our second section showed that Luke's perspective was therefore very different from that revealed in the first Gospel. Luke's Jesus has a much freer attitude to the Law than does Matthew's: if he is less

1. I would therefore dissent from Goulder's view that Luke was writing to reconcile the Gospels of Matthew and Mark. 'Luke is writing a reconciliation of Mark and Matthew to reassure Theophilus that the apparently dissonant Gospel tradition is trustworthy. It is just such a reconciliation which I have indicated above, and which is expounded in detail through the rest of this work' (*New Paradigm*, p. 200).

critical of it than Mark's presentation of him suggests, he nevertheless relates to it with a freedom born of a perspective which sees him as its eschatological fulfilment. Luke reduces the Law to a continuing mark of the Jewish people, good in itself when its true implications are seen but which becomes alien when its relation to its eschatological fulfilment is not acknowledged. There is in the third Gospel a lightness of touch which is wholly other than that attitude to it which is found in Matthew. Luke does not see it as a means of that higher righteousness which Matthew demands and which plays but little part in the third Gospel's presentation of the Christian response.

Again, Luke is consistently less hostile to the Jewish people than is Matthew. Harsh on their wilful rejection of Christ though he is, his God has nevertheless not turned his back on them to write them off in the way that Matthew suggests that he has. For Luke, they remain at least potentially the *laos* of God, and though they may be cut off from that people at the moment—to the extent that the rejecters among them forfeit all place in the covenantal community—nevertheless, God's continuing concern is with them and there is hope of a future eschatological incoming. Luke thinks in terms of a tragic situation: his community has not closed the doors against the Jewish people even though the realities of the actual situation make their coming in wholly unlikely for the present. Luke's community has nothing of that outlook of transfer, of its having done a takeover from the Jewish people, that is expressed so fiercely in Matthew.

And so Luke is somewhat less confident about the present than is Matthew. His kingdom, though actually already present in the heavens, remains hovering over, but not actually realized in the contemporary on earth. His church looks to the near parousia as a time of hope, as the time of revelation of that which at the moment though real is hidden by the realities of life as it is. He does not share in Mark's near despair for the present, but he is even further removed from Matthew's confidence which makes life in the church an anticipation of the kingdom even if the parousia is to effect a division of the sheep from the goats. Jesus is thought to be present in Matthew's understanding of the church in a way that he is not in Luke's.

Luke then has an understanding of the significance of Jesus' life which is very different from that found in Matthew. He recognizes the validity of that which Matthew set out to achieve, namely a reworking of Mark to enable his concept of a written Gospel to address and inform his own church faced with a new situation and in need of a different response. Both Mark and Matthew were essentially pastoral documents, designed to enable the message of the saving word to engage the churches of their times. Luke's church situation is other than that of Mark's though it is very close to that of Matthew's. Nevertheless, the answers he gives to the problems brought about by the passing of time are very different from those found in the first Gospel and amount to nothing less than a reaction against some of the basic stances of that Gospel. He sees Matthew's updating of Mark as right in conception but wrong in its overall execution and, at least at these fundamental points, he sets out to write a conscious response to it.

This explains Luke's omission of many of Matthew's additions to Mark and it also accounts for the breaking up of the Matthaean discourses. Their theological outlook is in fact inimical to Luke. It interferes with Luke's following of Mark's sense of movement and with that Gospel's concentration upon the future. Matthew's discourses arise out of his sense of the risen Lord's indwelling of his church which they enable him to address directly. Past and present cohere in an immediacy which is not taken over by Luke who retains a historical perspective to make an indirect address to the present by way of the past. Touches of this dimension are indeed found in Matthew, for instance, in the Lord's forbidding of the twelve to preach other than to 'the lost sheep of the house of Israel' (Mt. 10.5-6), but what appears in the first Gospel only cursorily is fundamental to Luke. The Matthaean discourses are therefore broken up and their material used selectively and for varied purposes. The sermon on the mount is reduced because neither its Matthaean status of a compendium of ethical requirements of the Christian disciple nor its dialogue with the Law is congenial to Luke's thought. The missionary discourse is used, at least in its more positive aspects, at the sending out of the seventy, but the distinctive parts of Matthew's parables chapter add nothing to Luke's understanding of the nature of the kingdom, while the direct ecclesiastical stance of Matthew 18 is alien to Luke's own perspective as this is unfolded in Acts where he pays but scant attention to the life of the established Christian communities other than that which he gives to the eschatological perspective of the life of the early Jerusalem church.

Luke expresses his own understanding of the eschatological dimension of Jesus' work largely by way of his presentation of Jesus' journey to Jerusalem. This played a fundamental part in his understanding of the nature of Jesus and of the community brought into being through him. Mosaic typology enabled the perspective of Deuteronomy to become the controlling factor in this section and allowed Luke to deal realistically with the tragedy of the Jewish rejection of Jesus without asserting that God's covenantal concern with the Jewish people was thereby brought to an end. By this means, Jesus of the past ministry is allowed to address, albeit indirectly, Luke's contemporary church from the perspective of one who is its living Lord.

We saw that Luke's use of Matthew as one of the sources of this section played a large part in determining the order of the first part of the journey narrative. The second part of the narrative made less use of Matthew which played almost no part in shaping its order which was determined rather by a logical development of those themes which the narrative as a whole expressed. Yet the rather rough edges at the joins of some of the narratives suggested that the Lukan special material was not wholly pliable to his purpose, and a number of the incidents (for instance, that of the healing of the man with dropsy) did not seem tailor made for the occasion. A number of passages that are paralleled in Matthew come from various parts of that Gospel and were not in any obvious order.[1] Luke's direct use of Matthew for this second half of the journey narrative was of the order of scavenging rather than of systematic gleaning and was quite unlike the use that he made of Matthew 10–17 in the first part of the central section.

We were therefore unable to follow Goulder's confidence that all of Luke's material parallel to Matthew in this section was necessarily derived from Matthew himself. Other floating traditions, either oral or written, cannot be ruled out. Nevertheless, on the other hand, we saw little need actually to accept Morgan's conclusions which allowed for some form of Q, a 'weak' Q, even a 'mini' Q. There are, it seems, very few cases where some source other than Matthew is required. Luke was scavenging at these points but his strong interest in Matthew and his determined reaction to it made such a method understandable. In the same way, Downing's disparaging of Luke's occasional production of his own version out of Mark and Matthew's is unnecessary.

1. See above, p. 340.

Luke's distinctive handling reflects his distinctive concerns and remains intelligible. Even his form of the Lord's Prayer, which could be the strongest candidate for being taken from what was to become the source of Matthew's version, does not run counter to the belief that Matthew was almost always Luke's source. Matthew's form may have been recently determined, the product of reflection by the group within his church whose outlook is reflected in his Gospel. Luke may be reacting against this newness. However, whether he brings its form back to something like its older version cannot be decided. All that can be said is that his form reflects his theology just as Matthew's reflects his.[1] Theology did not develop in a straight line. Great care must be taken in assessing what is more 'primitive'.

Finally, we considered Luke's infancy and resurrection narratives for these seem not merely to replace those of Matthew but to do so in such a way as to exclude the legitimacy of the Matthaean stories. It seems likely that Luke's position was such as to understand the significance of the Matthaean stories and consciously to reject it. Matthew's infancy stories reflect the first Gospel's hostility to the Jews and accept the inclusion of the Gentiles as taking their place. Such an outlook was alien to Luke's whole understanding of the work of God through Christ, and he therefore replaced them with a set of narratives which were parallel to Matthew's, which used his stories as a point of departure so as at times to build upon them—as in the narrative surrounding Mary and the birth of Jesus—and at others to react against them—as in his story of the coming of the shepherds. While the points which Matthew and Luke share may suggest a building upon a common tradition, such traditions play very little part in the rest of the New Testament. There is little in Luke to suggest that he was using sources of any kind other than Matthew for these first two chapters. It therefore seems more likely that he took over these ideas from Matthew and that he was dependent upon the first Gospel both for the

1. We may feel that at points Luke catches the outlook of Jesus more effectively than, say, does Matthew. This could be seen, for instance, in his suggestion (ch. 15) that Jesus made a habit of eating with tax collectors and sinners and that this reflected a characteristic activity on his part. Nevertheless, the fact that he uses the parable of the lost sheep in this context rather than in Matthew's church-discipline setting does not necessarily mean that he was earlier than Matthew (at least on this point). He may have been reversing Matthew in a way that reflected the tradition or it may just be a happy coincidence that his outlook, upon reflection, seems to be truer to that of Jesus on this point than is the Matthaean stance seen in Mt. 18.18.

general idea of infancy narratives and for the way in which he worked out his own particular approach based all the time, of course, upon his general understanding of the significance of Jesus and upon his own very particular appreciation of the Old Testament.

Luke would not have found Matthew's distinctive resurrection proclamation either congenial to his theology or a means of conveying his own understanding of the continuing work of Christ. Luke envisaged the ascension rather than the resurrection as the point of the glorification of Jesus. The period between the two events was for him one of explanation and commission as it was in Matthew, but these were worked out in his own distinctive, and we believe reactive, way. Jesus did not indwell his church but was exalted to the right hand of God. His ascension story therefore was, though a blessing, also a withdrawal. His continuing activity was mediated by way of the Spirit and by the Old Testament concept of 'the name'. Again, Luke did not find Christ in the observance of commandments but through the Scriptures and, above all, in the breaking of bread. His narratives therefore are very different. Once again, however, they parallel Matthew's and can be seen as having been built up in conscious response to those of the first Gospel. Jesus meets the doubters by giving demonstrable proofs of his resurrection to confound both them and those who would believe the Matthaean pointer to the Jewish false explanations. Luke shares Matthew's understanding of the risen Lord's commission but he does so in terms of a witness to the world which begins in Jerusalem rather than Galilee, does not break away from there but is consciously linked to its centre where the whole saving event had to happen in order that its full significance might be seen. The mission becomes a universal witness to Jesus rather than the establishment of a community in tension with the world. Luke looks to the return to establish God's promises to which the witness points and of which it is itself a guarantee.

Conclusion

Chapter 18

LUKE THE EVANGELIST

Luke was undoubtedly a Paulinist, an advocate of an interpreted Paulinism it is true, but a Paulinist nevertheless. Probably a God-fearer, one who came to Christianity out of a deep respect for Judaism and its institutions, having learned from Judaism yet forced to remain outside the covenantal people by reason of his uncircumcision, he accepted Christianity's promise of inclusion within the people of God without circumcision with wonder and joy. The whole outlook of Luke–Acts with its emphasis upon inclusion of outsiders seems most likely to have come out of his own experience; it became the bulwark of his own understanding of the significance of the work of Israel's God in Jesus of Nazareth. It was this which undoubtedly led him to become a disciple of Paul, for the very heart of the Pauline message would have struck deep chords in his own response to Christ. It was this fundamental conviction—that the Law was no longer that which marked out the boundaries of the people of God—that he had either learned from Paul or, perhaps more likely, that was shaped by Paul to become the very foundation of his outlook. Gentiles did not have to embrace the Law, for its significance as the badge of God's people had gone, and its moral seriousness was for him only an example and a making explicit of that moral outlook which he saw as part and parcel of the best of universal Gentile ethical concern. Luke as a God-fearer seemed to find the distinctiveness of the Jewish faith, not in an ethical stance, but in its covenantal understanding of making real and effective that unity with God which he saw as implicit in, but far from realized through, the universal Gentile religious quest.

So he embraced a Paulinism which inevitably differed from that which the apostle to the Gentiles actually expressed. Nevertheless, Luke's Paulinism was not so different as to deny either the basic tenets of Paul's beliefs or so to revise them as to evacuate his presentation of

Paul of the fundamental significance of those tenets. Time had moved on, and the fact that the earlier battles and conflicts had been fought and largely won meant that Luke could afford to mellow the polemic without belittling the fundamental insights.[1] Again, his experience of Judaism from without allowed him to be free of the pangs with which Paul expressed the change in outlook that the abandoning of the Law as a boundary marker required of him. National exclusiveness and pride was inevitable in the Jewish understanding of the Law even if individual legalism was not. Luke saw that brought to an end in Christ and he was free now to accept the Law as the identity marker of the Jewish people, as the means of acknowledging that which had enabled Christ and freed the universal Spirit which had now itself become the badge of the renewed and universalized people of God.

Luke could therefore reinterpret Paul to make him witness consistently to that priority of Israel which he acknowledged but which his own ministry was in danger of downplaying, to give him a determined ministry to the Jews which was in reality unlikely, to play down his sitting loose to the Law which his adversaries, not entirely justly but at the same time not without some justification, could accuse him of, and to give him an acceptance of the apostolic decree which his own dealings suggest was not real but which nevertheless, accepted as Luke understood it, was not out of character with Paul's own acknowledged concern with the weak. Luke revised Paul, but it was a revision which did not do despite to the apostle to the Gentiles and which is such as to mark Luke out as, though an interpreter of Paul, nevertheless not an illegitimate one.

It is as a Paulinist that Luke writes his two volumes. What caused him to do so? First, no doubt, his own nature—he himself. Recent study of him which has linked his art to that of Greek and Roman

1. It should not be suggested that a less confrontational theology is necessarily a less discerning one. The world did not come to an end and the original battles so fiercely entered into at the time of Paul did not have to be refought. His insights had necessarily to be adapted to meet both the continuing life of the church and the newer problems of a different situation. A change of Paul's outlook is not necessarily a disaster. It might in fact have been necessary in order to give value to God's actions in the world outside those found in Christ. The question must be whether re-interpretation does justice to the original insights to build legitimately upon them in a way which, while adapting, does not lose what is true in the original. I have argued that Luke is able to do justice to the original and that this interpretation is less bland than is often suggested.

literary movements—as well as the studied nature of his work which such a link underlines—shows him to be a man of letters, an artist with words, a man of imagination and insight, a person capable of the grand design. Whether he could have been a man of letters in the secular sense, capable of producing high-grade secular writings, we can only guess. Probably not, for it was his theme, his religious vision, which both gave the impetus for, and also provided the manner of his literary work. The impetus was his faith; that which encouraged him to write—apart from what in this area at least 'made him tick'—were his predecessors in the field, and that which gave him his programme and his means was the Old Testament which, as a man of letters and of faith, he had perused and pondered until it had really entered into his bones. A less all-embracing impetus, but one which was close to the surface most if not all of the time, was the fact that Paul was under attack, most probably not so much from Jewish outsiders (from whom we might suggest Luke would not have separated himself) but more seriously from within the church where he was being accused of abandoning the Law and so of denying both the old covenant and Christianity's embrace of it. Christianity's mission to the Jews, at least in the locality of Luke's community, had virtually come to an end. Paul was probably being blamed in part for this but, at the same time, in the light of its results, there was a growing bitter struggle between Christians and Jews as each side furthered their claims to be alone the covenantal people of God and to establish their inheritance as heirs of the Old Testament promises. Luke would find it hard in such a scenario not to take up his pen to unfold both his vision and his defence.

Mark seems to have been his primary source. He and his church had lived long with it and, congenial as it was by its Pauline stance, it had been a profound influence upon his thinking. He had embraced its thought though not without some criticism from the point of view of his own particular revision of Paulinism. Luke had entered into its eschatological stance and from it had deepened the Pauline expectation of an early parousia. But again, time had gone on and the church, though remaining an 'ecclesia pressa', was more established than Mark had allowed. So Luke saw the present as witnessing to the Lordship of Christ in a way which Mark's situation had made impossible. Nevertheless, the unfulfilment of Mark's confident expectation of an early parousia did cause problems, for it was no doubt shared by Luke himself as well as by large numbers of his readers. Luke could not rest in the security of the present for that security was fragile. Jewish perversity, Roman suspicion, much Gentile indifference and even hostility made the church of the present a very tender plant and the reality of its life hardly witnessed to the promises which propelled it. Luke's contemporaries suffered from a lack of confidence and it was in order to encourage them to meet this with legitimate vision, which avoided embracing false substitutes, that he wrote.

The immediate spur to writing was quite probably the discovery of Matthew's Gospel. Luke had lived long with Mark and, though the passing of time had made it inadequate for a church which had to come to terms with new situations and indeed with an ongoing history, its basic stance (revised as he revised Paul's) remained appropriate for his vision. With Matthew, however, it was otherwise. That Gospel reflected a stance which basically was inimical to his own. It ran counter to his attitude to the Law by advocating a mixed community living consciously in relation to it and responding to its terms. Its rigorism cut across the outreach which lay at the heart of his own understanding to encourage a closed community, living consciously in a stance of separation from those around them, self-consciously concerned with a standard which denied the legitimacy of those of a different persuasion, building up the status of the community as an anticipation of the kingdom of God, and deliberately denying the sphere of the kingdom to the people of Israel. Necessary though that stance may have been for the church at that time, and legitimate as it could be seen to be as an interpretation of Jesus and his resurrection, it represented neither Luke's stance nor his understanding of the significance of the gospel as Jesus himself was made to proclaim it in his Nazareth sermon.

Luke therefore wrote his two volumes as a witness to the gospel of God as he had come to understand it to a church which was perplexed by the hiddenness of Christ and by the failure of the response they could have expected, especially from the Jews, to the message of the freedom brought by God's outreach in Christ. He aimed to encourage the faint-hearted and to discourage them from taking refuge in what he would have regarded as inadequate substitute securities which would stop them from pushing forward to the prize which was within their grasp. His was fundamentally a message of hope based on the vision of God's wide embrace through Christ.

Luke and Matthew are to be brought into the closest possible relationship. Those who believe that Luke did not take all his material in the double tradition from Matthew itself but from sources which underlay the first Gospel would appear to suggest an even greater link, for their understanding would make it likely that Luke knew the traditions of at least a group within Matthew's church. Overall, we have seen little reason for the existence of such sources and have found it more likely that Luke worked from Matthew as it is. This would again suggest, however, a close, almost passionate, interest in that Gospel by Luke.

Such close links raise the possibility that Luke may have had direct contacts with Matthew's church and that, though he writes his Gospel as an individual's witness, he nevertheless writes it to a group who may have shared in something of his own concerns. Luke addresses his work to 'the most excellent Theophilus'. From the third century BC Theophilus was a name given to Jews of the diaspora. 'Most excellent' may be a courteous form of address of one who was esteemed, and the Gospel's dedication to him may suggest that he was intended to make it available for public consumption. As such, he was probably an influential member of a church and it may well be that he was regarded as the leader of the group which stood out as expressing an outlook which, though at one with that of Luke himself, may well have represented a minority viewpoint within his church as a whole.

We have seen that Luke and Matthew both reflect similar stages in the church's struggle for self-definition. Both represent a point at which the break with the Jews has taken on something of a finality in that there is little hope that the Jewish people will respond to the Christian proclamation. The church exists alongside, but apart from its Jewish neighbours. The future lies with the Gentile world where there remains hope of missionary success in spite of a certain ambivalence in attitude. Equally, we have seen that there was much the same situation in relation to the experienced delay of the parousia. Both Gospels, though they respond in different ways, are coming to terms with unfilled hopes of the return of Christ, and both can look back on the destruction of Jerusalem to see that it has not introduced the beginning of the end.

They reflect the same kind of situation to such an extent that it is no exaggerated flight of fancy to wonder perhaps whether they reflect the same actual situation so that both could have been occasioned by problems facing a single church. Are there in fact signs within the two Gospels of more immediate contact with each other? A number of points suggest at least the possibility of this.

One has to be careful however at this point, for substitutes in content or varied approaches to a particular theme may arise from a literary relationship rather than from a common link with a particular church. Though a sociological approach to the Gospels has encouraged us to relate their contents more directly to actual church situations, the relationship is not necessarily so exact as to enable a direct reading off of the one from the other. In the case of Luke this is made all the more difficult both by the historical method he has chosen to embrace and the very individual nature of the work which his preface suggests. The individual writer expresses his own message, his own response, and though this must inevitably make contact with the church to which it is addressed, it does mean that it is not necessarily to be taken as a point by point parallel to the situation. So, while common themes of attitudes to the Law, to Israel, to the parousia, to the kingdom, and even to riches may suggest a direct relationship between the actual Gospels, they do not necessarily mean a concern with a common situation. The general Christian tradition and the widespread Christian experience may well account for Luke's taking over Matthew's particular concerns.

Yet there are two factors in particular which would seem to suggest a much more direct overlap in the two Gospels' areas of concern. In the first place, both are interested in Peter, and the concern is of such a kind as to suggest that they are enshrining a picture of the apostle which is formed, not only in relation to each other, but which reflects a common background in a particular church. Peter is actually being claimed by both writings as an exponent of their own particular point of view; they are maintaining a tradition which is said to rest on him and which faithfully reflects his outlook.

To the Markan account of Peter's confession at Caesarea–Philippi, Matthew adds the Lord's promise to him and gives him the authority of binding and loosing, of that as standing as the true interpreter of the tradition and its stance. That is ratified in the final commission to the apostles as a group which is defined in its terms and of those of the sermon on the mount. These are linked together to authenticate the traditions that are maintained in Matthew's church and to give Dominical approval of that higher righteousness which is enshrined in Matthew's interpretation of the Law and which is seen to be endangered by those who would break free from that Law to place the emphasis upon a faith which Matthew at least sees as being dangerously free from works. Paul, or at least an interpretation of Paulinism, seems to have been regarded as a source of such beliefs. Peter is made to stand over and against an outlook which seems to do less than justice either to ethics or to the Law accepted, when properly interpreted, as still having a part to play in defining both the boundaries and the stance of the people of God.

Luke's portrait of Peter stands in conscious opposition to such an estimate of the apostle and seems in fact to rescue him from the clutches of Matthew's interpretation. He does not take over the Lord's praise of the apostle and his promise to him precisely because of the implications that Matthew draws from them. His Peter, however, is no less the source of authority as the determiner of the right relationship to the Law and its commands. We have seen the absolute centrality of the Cornelius episode for Luke and of the initiative of Peter in gaining the acceptance of its significance in terms which enshrine a Paulinism as Luke interprets it. The Law plays no part in defining the people of God and it is rendered superfluous as the definer of that people's stance. For both Luke and Matthew, table fellowship was no longer an issue as such because both seemed to accept a position regulated by the terms enshrined in the apostolic decree. What remained an issue, however, was the actual significance of the terms of the decree, of the meaning behind its regulations, of the interpretation of that meaning which the terms suggested. Matthew saw the Law as having some continuing significance in defining, not necessarily the area, but certainly the character of the holiness of the people of God: Luke, on the other hand, saw the Law as having come to an end on both issues. It had been caught up, not abrogated, into something greater to give it an irrelevance as far as the Christian community's inner being was concerned. Matthew made Peter an advocate of his interpretation; Luke denied that validity and claimed him for his own.

Mark had been completely unscrupulous in portraying Peter's weaknesses, and his Gospel had reflected the outlook of the Paul of Galatians. Both Matthew and Luke played them down, but the tradition was such that they could not ignore them. In Matthew, the rebuke of Peter is actually separated from his witness at Caesarea–Philippi and from the Lord's praise of him so that it becomes, not an expression of a fundamental weakness in the apostle's apprehension of messiahship, but a difficulty in accepting the manner in which that messiahship was to be enabled. The incident in Mark suggests continuing inability; in Matthew it reflects the beginning of a learning process. It is learned by the time of the final commission. Luke omits the rebuke altogether as he is also to omit Peter's attempt at walking on the water and as he is to play down the actual denial by him of Jesus at the time of the trial. The Lord's commissioning of Peter at the last supper maintains that Peter stumbled rather than falls and empowers him to move his brethren into a legitimate understanding of the significance of Jesus' establishing of the kingdom of God (Lk. 22.31). Matthew accepts Peter's weakness but attempts to see it as a temporary failure of perception; Luke plays down that weakness even more to make the denial a real learning situation which is completed by a personal resurrection appearance. He sees Peter thereafter as constant in his response to the full significance of the Cornelius event. His understanding is of such a kind as to leave no room for any real criticism of the apostle which would do justice to Paul's understanding of the significance of the Antioch incident. Luke most likely knows of the incident for in many ways it acts as a presupposition for a large part of his narrative.

Matthew on the other hand seems to be aware of the incident but wants to tell his story of Peter in such a way that it would make for conclusions which were other than those Luke was to draw. What does Matthew see as Peter's weakness? What was he criticising in Peter? In the light of the links between the Lord's acknowledgment, the later commissioning, and the sermon on the mount it could only have been Peter's temporary aberration from the stance of those three narratives. Peter's failure was seen by Matthew as a move in the direction of the later Pauline stance towards the Law. Luke recognizes that criticism and rebuts it by giving to Peter in the Cornelius incident a different significance which could not be denied.

One further point suggests the real possibility that both Luke and Matthew were associated with the same church. The apostolic decree refers both to food laws and to πορνεία. Matthew's Gospel revises Mark to move his outlook on both these issues in the direction of the stance taken in the decree. The Markan discussion on internal and external uncleanness (7.1-23) is rewritten to avoid its criticism of the actual food laws and to reduce it to an attack upon certain Pharisaic customs (15.1-20). Knowledge of the decree, though not explicitly revealed, for the contents of the Gospel could hardly allow its very specific regulations to be acknowledged, is nevertheless suggested, and it could be given, if not Dominical approval, then at least the status of being in accord with the Dominical stance. Luke omits this episode. It is unlikely that he could have included Matthew's version for he would not have wished Jesus to have appeared as a legalist however refined. Mark's version would not in itself have been inimical to him for it would have agreed with his Cornelius episode. Nevertheless, for Jesus himself to have advocated this stance during his ministry would have contradicted the Law in a way which Luke elsewhere avoids. His Jesus has a certain detachment from the Law but, as a Jew, he lived in relationship with it. There is nothing in the Cornelius episode to suggest that Luke himself was indifferent to Jewish food regulations. His Peter went beyond them as he ate with Cornelius, but he regularized the position by the acceptance of the apostolic decree.

Conflicting interpretations of the decree seem to lie behind Luke's and Matthew's divorce sayings. Matthew appears to have revised Mark with the introduction of the exception clause, not merely to make Jesus less hostile to the Law, but also to acknowledge the seriousness with which the decree understood πορνεία. In some way it threatened the purity of Judaism, and Gentiles therefore had to undertake to refrain from it. Where it occurred, divorce was actually demanded in a movement in the direction of the demands of the apostolic decree and in accordance with Matthew's own ethical stance. Paul himself had not acknowledged πορνειά as a grounds for divorce though he had acknowledged its gravity and given it his full condemnation (1 Cor. 6.16-17). Luke takes the Pauline stance on divorce (16.18) but, in having Jesus omit the exception clause, he denied Matthew's ethical rigorism without in any way undervaluing the high outlook on marriage which he affirms as the stance of Moses. We have seen the difficulties behind the interpretation of Lk. 16.16-18. Consistency is given to those verses when they are acknowledged as a response to Matthew's outlook. The actual form of the verses suggests something more than a response to Matthew's Gospel as such and seems rather to point to an actual church situation which was giving rise to the divergent approaches.

Kilpatrick[1] noted that Matthew's concern with Peter was perhaps the strongest reason for connecting that Gospel with the church at Antioch. Against such a connection was, however, in his view the lack of Paulinism in the first Gospel. Goulder, building on the work of C.H. Dodd, has attempted to find such an influence in it. He believes, for instance, that 'parallels between Romans 12–14 and the Sermon on the Mount are so frequent as to invite the hypothesis that the one has had a direct effect upon the other'. Parallels of material there may perhaps be, but the ideas expressed in such material are often very different indeed. The attitude to the Law, for instance, differs greatly in the two writers. Matthew's assertion that on the love of God and neighbour 'depend all the Law and the prophets' (Mt. 22.40), means that he sees the Law as that which enables love which itself allows the Law to be fulfilled. For Paul on the other hand, love takes the place of the Law which is no longer seen as enabling love but which rather makes the Law redundant. There is, as Benedict Green maintains,[2] between Matthew and Paul a fundamental divergence in their attitude to Law. What is distinctly Pauline is just not there in Matthew. But this does not necessarily mean that, as Kilpatrick suggests, there is therefore a problem with connecting Matthew with Antioch. Paul evidently lost out there as a result of the Antioch incident, and the position adopted by the church as a whole seems to have been that of the Petrine compromise in the light of the apostolic decree of which the gospel of Matthew is a very fair representation. Meier has recently made out a very strong case for taking the Antiochene connection of the first Gospel seriously. It must inevitably remain hypothetical but it is certainly one which can shed considerable light upon Matthew and at least one segment of early church history.

Tradition has, of course, also held that Luke was at one stage from Antioch. Though this may rest on little more than supposition drawn from the Acts of the Apostles, the tradition does at least point to the

1. G.D. Kilpatrick, *The Origin of the Gospel according to St Matthew* (Oxford: Clarendon Press, 1946), pp. 130-34.

2. *The Gospel according to Matthew*, pp. 34-37, 'For Paul (as for Jesus) God is gracious before he is demanding: for Matthew (as for the greatest of his Jewish opponents) God's graciousness is contained in his demand'. See also, O.L. Cope, 'To the Close of the Age', and R. Scroggs, 'Eschatological Existence in Matthew and Paul' in J. Marcus and M.L. Soards (eds.), *Apocalyptic and the New Testament* (JSNTSup, 24; Sheffield: JSOT Press, 1989).

strength of Acts as a basis for such a speculation. At least Acts may point to some Antioch traditions as underlying it. Fitzmyer[1] would limit such influence to the earlier stages of Antiochene Christianity but the links of Luke with Matthew and the likelihood that the Antioch incident and its repercussions forms at least one of the presuppositions of the work of the two evangelists suggests that Luke could well have been aware of later stages of that church's history. Luke–Acts could well reflect the situation of the church at Antioch and express an outlook of at least one of the streams of tradition which made up the complexity of the church's life there.

Luke–Acts reflects what could well have been the life of the Antioch church. There seems little reason to believe that it could not have arisen from within that church, and Esler has promised an article making just this claim. Yet we have seen that Luke–Acts retains very much the character of an individual's writing so that the actual situation of a church cannot easily be read-off directly from it. Its contents and an immediate church situation are not necessarily to be directly equated. Luke–Acts represents a church situation as it is seen through the eyes of an individual; there is about it something of an epistolatory character. Luke's work may therefore be the response to information rather than being the result of direct involvement in the church it addresses. Luke–Acts may have come from the area around the church out of which Matthew arose. Its idealization of the earlier history of the church, as this is seen for instance in the Acts picture of the solution of the Jewish–Gentile problems, may however suggest acquaintance with the situation, certainly of the past and most likely of the present also, only from a distance. It seems therefore more likely that Luke was written to Matthew's church from one who was outside, concerned but apart, theoretically rather than practically involved. Matthew's Gospel could have been derived from the Antiochene church; Luke–Acts could have been written to the Antiochene church. Its valuing of Mark's Gospel, its links with Paul's letter to the Romans (however re-interpreted), could suggest a Roman provenance, and its outlook concerning the Roman empire and its officials would not go against this. It is at least a fascinating possibility, no more than a hypothesis, but one at least which the contents of a fair part of the New Testament suggests is not entirely nothing more than armchair theorizing.

1. *Acts*, p. 46.

SELECT BIBLIOGRAPHY

Achtemeier, P.J., *The Quest for Unity in the New Testament Church* (Philadelphia: Fortress Press, 1987).

Alexander, L., 'Luke's Preface in the Context of Greek Preface-Writing', *NovT* 28 (1986), pp. 48-74.

Aune, D.E., *The New Testament in its Literary Environment* (Cambridge: James Clarke, 1987).

Bailey, K., *Poet and Peasant and through Peasant Eyes: A Literary-Cultural Approach to the Parables in Luke* (Grand Rapids: Eerdmans, 1983).

Banks, R., *Jesus and the Law in the Synoptic Tradition* (SNTSMS, 28; Cambridge: Cambridge University Press, 1975).

Barclay, J., *Obeying the Truth* (Edinburgh: T. & T. Clark, 1985).

Barrett, C.K., *A Commentary on the First Epistle to the Corinthians* (London: A. & C. Black, 1968).

—*A Commentary on the Second Epistle to the Corinthians* (London: A. & C. Black, 1973).

—'The Eschatology of the Epistle to the Hebrews', in D. Daube and W.D. Davies (eds.), *The Background of the New Testament and its Eschatology: Studies in Honour of C.H. Dodd* (Cambridge: Cambridge University Press, 1956), pp. 363-93.

—*Luke the Historian in Recent Study* (London: Epworth Press, 1961).

—'Stephen and the Son of Man', in *Apophoreta: Festschrift für Ernst Haenchen* (BZNW, 30; Berlin: Töpelmann, 1963), pp. 31-38.

—*New Testament Essays* (London: SPCK, 1972).

—'Pauline Controversies in a Post-Pauline Period', *NTS* 20 (1974), pp. 229-45.

—'Paul's Speech on the Areopagus', in M.K. Glasswell and E.W. Fasholé-Luke (eds.), *New Testament Christianity for Africa and the World* (London: SPCK, 1974), pp. 69-77.

—'Paul's Address to the Ephesian Elders', in J. Jervell and W. Meeks (eds.), *God's Christ and his People: Studies in Honour of Nils Alstrup Dahl* (Oslo: Universitetsforloget, 1977), pp. 107-121.

—'Theologia Crucis—in Acts?', in C. Anresen and G. Klein (eds.), *Theologia Crucis—Signum Crucis: Festschrift für Erich Dinkler* (Tübingen: Mohr [Paul Siebeck], 1979).

—*Essays on Paul* (London: SPCK, 1982).

—*Freedom and Obligation: A Study of the Epistle to the Galatians* (London: SPCK, 1985).

Barth, M., *The People of God* (JSNTSup, 5; Sheffield: JSOT Press, 1983).

Barton, J., *Reading the Old Testament: Method in Biblical Study* (London: Darton, Longman & Todd, 1984).

Beck, B.E., '*Imitatio Christi* and the Lucan Passion Narrative', in W. Horbury and B. McNeil (eds.), *Suffering and Martyrdom in the New Testament* (Cambridge: Cambridge University Press, 1981), pp. 28-47.

—*Christian Character in the Gospel of Luke* (London: Epworth Press, 1989).

Beker, J.C., *Paul the Apostle: The Triumph of God in Life and Thought* (Edinburgh: T. & T. Clark, 1980).

Black, C.C., *The Disciples according to Mark* (JSNTSup, 27; Sheffield: JSOT Press, 1989).

Blomberg, C., 'Midrash, Chiasmus, and the Outline of Luke's Central Section', in R.T. France and D. Wenham (eds.), *Gospel Perspectives,* III (Sheffield: JSOT Press, 1985), pp. 217-61.

Booth, R., *Jesus and the Laws of Purity* (JSNTSup, 13; Sheffield: JSOT Press, 1986).

Borg, M.J., *Conflict, Holiness and Politics in the Teaching of Jesus* (New York: Edwin Mellen, 1984).

—*Jesus: A New Vision* (San Francisco: Harper, 1987).

Borgen, P., 'From Paul to Luke: Observations towards Clarification of the Theology of Luke–Acts, *CBQ* 31 (1969), pp. 168-82.

—'Catalogues of Vices, the Apostolic Decree, and the Jerusalem Meeting' in *The Social World of Formative Christianity and Judaism* (ed. J. Neusner *et al.*; Philadelphia: Fortress Press, 1988), pp. 126-41.

Bornkamm, G., G. Barth and J.H. Held, *Tradition and Interpretation in Matthew* (trans. P. Scott; London: SCM Press, 1963).

Bovon, F., *Luc le théologian: Vingt-cinq ans de récherches (1950–75)* (Neuchâtel: Delachaux & Niestlé, 1978).

Bowker, J., *Jesus and the Pharisees* (Cambridge: Cambridge University Press, 1973).

Brawley, R.L., *Luke–Acts and the Jews: Conflict, Apology and Conciliation* (SBLMS, 33; Atlanta: Scholars Press, 1987).

Brown, R.E., *The Birth of the Messiah: A Commentary on the Infancy Narratives in Matthew and Luke* (London: Geoffrey Chapman, 1977).

—'Luke's Method in the Annunciation Narratives of Chapter One' in C.H. Talbert (ed.), *Perspectives on Luke–Acts* (Edinburgh: T. & T. Clark, 1978), pp. 126-38.

—'Gospel Infancy Narrative Research from 1976–1986, Part ii, Luke', *CBQ* 48 (1986), pp. 660-80.

Brown, R.E., and J.P. Meier, *Antioch and Rome: New Testament Cradles of Catholic Christianity* (London: Chapman, 1983).

Brown, S., *Apostasy and Perseverance in the Theology of Luke* (Rome: Analecta Biblica 36, 1989).

Bruce, F.F., *The Acts of the Apostles* (London: Tyndale Press, 1951).

—'Is the Paul of Acts the Real Paul?', *BJRL* 58 (1975–76), pp. 282-305.

—*Men and Movements in the Primitive Church: Studies in the Early Non-Pauline Christianity* (Exeter: Paternoster Press, 1979).

Bultmann, R., *The History of the Synoptic Tradition* (trans. J. Marsh; Oxford: Basil Blackwell, 1963).

Burchard, C., 'Paul in der Apostelgeschichte', *TLZ* 100 (1975), pp. 881-95.

Butler, B.C., *The Originality of St Matthew* (Cambridge: Cambridge University Press, 1951).

Cadbury, H.J., *The Making of Luke–Acts* (London: SPCK, 1958).
Caird, G.B., *Saint Luke* (Pelican Gospel Commentaries; Harmondsworth: Penguin Books, 1963).
—*The Language and Imagery of the Bible* (London: Duckworth, 1980).
Callan, T., 'The Preface of Luke–Acts and Historiography', *NTS* 31 (1985), pp. 576-81.
Carroll, J.T., 'Luke's Portrayal of the Pharisees', *CBQ* 50 (1988), pp. 604-621.
—*Response to the End of History: Eschatology and Situation in Luke–Acts* (SBLDS, 92; Atlanta, GA: Scholars Press, 1988).
Cassidy, R.J., *Society and Politics in the Acts of the Apostles* (Maryknoll, NY: Orbis Books, 1987).
Catchpole, D.R. *The Trial of Jesus* (Leiden: Brill, 1971).
—'Paul, Jesus and the Apostolic Decree', *NTS* 23 (1976–77), pp. 428-44.
—*The Quest for Q* (Edinburgh: T. & T. Clark, 1993).
Chadwick, H., 'All Things to All Men', *NGTS* 1 (1954–55), pp. 261-75.
Chance, J.B., *Jerusalem, the Temple and the New Age in Luke–Acts* (Macon, GA: Mercer University Press, 1988).
Chilton, B., 'Announcement in Nazara: An Analysis of Luke 4.16-30', in R.T. France and D. Wenham (eds.), *Gospel Perspectives*, II (Sheffield: JSOT Press, 1981), pp. 147-72.
Conzelmann, H., *The Theology of St Luke* (trans. G. Buswell; London: Faber and Faber, 1960).
—*An Outline of the Theology of the New Testament* (trans. J. Bowden; London: SCM Press, 1969).
—*Acts of the Apostles* (trans. J. Limberg, A. Thomas Kraable and D.H. Juel; Philadelphia: Fortress Press, 1987).
Creed, J.M., *The Gospel according to St Luke* (London: Macmillan, 1950).
Danker, F.W., *Jesus and the New Age* (Philadelphia: Fortress Press, 1988).
Davies, J.G., 'The Prefiguration of the Ascension in the Third Gospel', *JTS* NS 3 (1955), pp. 229-33.
Davies, J.H., 'The Purpose of the Central Section of St Luke's Gospel', *TU* 87 (1963), pp. 164-69.
Davies, W.D., *Paul and Rabbinic Judaism* (London: SPCK, 1948).
—'Paul and the People of Israel', *NTS* 24 (1977), pp. 4-39.
Davies, W.D., and D.C. Allison, *A Critical and Exegetical Commentary on the Gospel according to Saint Matthew* (Edinburgh: T. & T. Clark, 3 vols.; vol. 1 [1988], vol. 2 [1991].
Dawsey, J.M., *The Lukan Voice: Confusion and Irony in the Gospel of Luke* (Macon, GA: Mercer University Press, 1986).
Derrett, J.D.M., *Law in the New Testament* (London: Darton, Longman & Todd, 1970).
Dibelius, M., *From Tradition to Gospel* (trans. B. Lee Wolf; London: Nicholson & Watson, 1934).
—*Studies in the Acts of the Apostles* (ed. H. Greeven; London: SCM Press, 1956).
Dillon, R.J., 'Previewing Luke's Project from his Prologue', *CBQ* 43 (1981), pp. 205-27.
Dodd, C.H., *The Apostolic Preaching and its Development* (London: Hodder & Stoughton, 1936).

Donaldson, T.L., *Jesus on the Mountain: A Study in Matthaean Theology* (JSNTSup, 8; Sheffield: JSOT Press, 1985).
Donfried, P., *The Romans Debate* (Peabody, MA: Hendriksen, rev. edn, 1991).
Downing, F.G., 'Towards the Rehabilitation of Q', *NTS* 11 (1965), pp. 169-81.
—'Contemporary Analogies to the Gospels and Acts', in C.M. Tuckett (ed.), *Synoptic Studies: The Ampleforth Conferences of 1982 and 1983* (JSNTSup, 7; Sheffield: JSOT Press, 1984), pp. 51-66.
—'Compositional Conventions and the Synoptic Problem, *JBL* 107 (1988), pp. 69-85.
Drury, J., *Tradition and Design in Luke's Gospel* (London: Darton, Longman & Todd, 1976).
Dunn, J.D.G., *Unity and Diversity in the New Testament* (London: SCM Press, 1977).
—*Christology in the Making: An Inquiry into the Origins of the Doctrine of the Incarnation* (London: SCM Press, 1980).
—*Romans* (WBC; Dallas, TX: Word Books, 2 vols., 1988).
—*Jesus, Paul and the Law* (London: SPCK, 1990).
—*The Partings of the Ways* (London: SCM Press; Philadelphia: Trinity Press International, 1991).
Easton, B.S., *Early Christianity: The Purpose of Acts and Other Papers* (London: SPCK, 1954).
Egelkraut, H.E., *Jesus' Mission to Jerusalem: A Redaction-Critical Study of the Travel Narrative in the Gospel of Luke, Luke 9.51–19.48* (Europaische Hochschulschriften, Reike 23, Theologie 80; Bern: Herbert Lang, 1976).
Ellis, E.E., *Eschatology in Luke* (Philadelphia: Fortress Press, 1972).
—*The Gospel of Luke* (NCB London: Nelson, 1966).
Epp, E.J., *The Theological Tendency of Codex Bezae Cantabligiensis in Acts* (SNTSMS, 3; Cambridge: Cambridge University Press, 1966).
Esler, P.F., *Community and Gospel in Luke–Acts: The Social and Political Motivations of Lucan Theology* (SNTSMS, 57; Cambridge: Cambridge University Press, 1987).
Evans, C.A., 'Is Luke's View of the Jewish Rejection of Jesus Anti-Semitic?' in D.N. Sylva (ed.), *Reimaging the Death of the Lucan Jesus* (Frankfurt am Main: Anton Hain, 1990), pp. 29-56.
Evans, C.F., 'The Central Section of Saint Luke's Gospel', in D.E. Nineham (ed.), *Studies in the Gospels: Essays in Memory of R.H. Lightfoot* (Oxford: Basil Blackwell, 1965), pp. 37-53.
—*Saint Luke* (London: SCM Press, 1990).
Farrer, A.M., 'On *Dispensing with Q*', in D.E. Nineham (ed.), *Studies in the Gospels: Essays in Memory of R.H. Lightfoot* (Oxford: Basil Blackwell, 1957), pp. 55-88.
Farris, S., *The Hymns of Luke's Infancy Narratives: Their Origin, Meaning and Significance* (JSNTSup, 9; Sheffield: JSOT Press, 1985).
Fenton, J.C., *Saint Matthew* (Pelican Gospel Commentaries: Harmondsworth: Penguin Books, 1963).
Fitzmyer, J.A., *The Gospel according to Luke* (2 vols.; New York: Doubleday, 1981, 1985).
—*Luke the Theologian* (London: Geoffrey Chapman, 1989).
Foakes Jackson, F.J., and K. Lake, (eds.), *The Beginnings of Christianity*. I. *The Acts of the Apostles* (5 vols.; London: Macmillan, 1920–33).
France, R.T., *Matthew* (TNTC; Leicester: Inter-Varsity Press, 1985).

Franklin, E., 'The Ascension and the Eschatology of Luke–Acts', *SJT* 23 (1970), pp. 191-200.

—*Christ the Lord: A Study in the Purpose and Theology of Luke–Acts* (London: SPCK, 1975).

Freidricksen, T.A., 'The Matthew–Luke Agreements against Mark', in F. Neirynck (ed.), *L'evangile de Luc* (BETYL, 32; Leuven: Peeters, 1989), pp. 335-92.

Gasque, A.W. *A History of the Criticism of the Acts of the Apostles* (Grand Rapids: Eerdmans, 1975).

Gaston, L., *No Stone on Another: Studies in the Significance of the Fall of Jerusalem in the Synoptic Gospels* (NovTSup, 23; Leiden: Brill, 1970).

—'The Messiah of Israel as Teacher of the Gentiles', *Int* 29 (1978), pp. 25-40.

—'Anti-Judaism and the Passion Narrative in Luke–Acts', in P. Richardson with D. Granston (eds.), *Anti-Judaism in Early Christianity*. I. *Paul and the Gospels* (Waterloo: Wilfrid Laurier University Press, 1986), pp. 127-54.

Goppelt, L., *Apostolic and Post-Apostolic Times* (trans. R.A. Guelick; London: A. & C. Black, 1970).

Goulder, M.D., *Type and History in Acts* (London: SPCK, 1964).

—*Midrash and Lection in Matthew* (London: SPCK, 1974).

—*The Evangelists' Calendar* (London: SPCK, 1978).

—'The Order of a Crank' in C.M. Tuckett (ed.), *Synoptic Studies: The Ampleforth Conferences of 1982 and 1983* (JSNTSup, 7; Sheffield: JSOT Press, 1984), pp. 111-130.

—*Luke: A New Paradigm* (JSNTSup, 20; Sheffield: JSOT Press, 1989).

Green, H.B., *The Gospel according to Matthew* (New Clarendon Bible; Oxford: Oxford University Press, 1975).

—'The Credibility of Luke's Transformation of Matthew' in C.M. Tuckett (ed.), *Synoptic Studies: The Ampleforth Conferences of 1982 and 1983* (JSNTSup, 7; Sheffield: JSOT Press, 1984), pp. 131-56.

Grollenberg, L., *Unexpected Messiah* (London: SCM Press, 1987).

Guelich, R.A., *The Sermon on the Mount* (Waco, TX: Word Books, 1982).

Gundry, R.H., *The Use of the Old Testament in St Matthew's Gospel* (NovTSup, 18; Leiden: Brill, 1975).

—*Matthew: A Commentary on his Literary and Theological Art* (Grand Rapids: Eerdmans, 1982).

—'Matthaean Foreign Bodies in Agreements of Luke with Matthew against Mark: Evidence that Luke used Matthew', in F. van Segbroeck, *et al.* (eds.), *The Four Gospels* (BETL 100; Leuven: Peeters, 1992), 11, pp. 1467-95.

Haenchen, E., *The Acts of the Apostles* (trans. B. Noble, *et al.*; Oxford: Basil Blackwell, 1971).

—'The Book of Acts as Source Material for the History of Early Christianity' in L.E. Keck and J.L. Martyn (eds.), *Studies in Luke–Acts* (London: SPCK, 1966).

—'Judentum und Christentum in der Apostelgeschichte', *ZNTW* 44 (1963), pp. 155-87.

Hamerton-Kelly, R.G., *Pre-existence, Wisdom and the Son of Man* (SNTSMS, 21; Cambridge: Cambridge University Press, 1973).

Hann, M.D., 'The Freeing of the Bent Woman and the Restoration of Israel: Luke 13.10-17 as Narrative Theology', *JSNT* 31 (1987), pp. 23-44.

Hare, D.R.A., *The Theme of Jewish Persecution of Christianity in the Gospel according to St Matthew* (SNTSMS, 6; Cambridge; Cambridge University Press, 1967).
Harvey, A.E., *Strenuous Commands* (London: SCM Press, 1990).
Hemer, C.J., *The Book of Acts in the Setting of Hellenistic History* (WUNT, 49: Tübingen: Mohr [Paul Siebeck], 1989).
Hengel, M., *Acts and the History of Earliest Christianity* (trans. J. Bowden; London: SCM Press, 1979).
—*Between Jesus and Paul* (trans. J. Bowden; London: SCM Press, 1983).
Héring, J., *1 Corinthians* (trans. A.W. Heathcote and P.J. Allcock; London: Epworth Press, 1962).
Hiers, R.H., 'The Problem of the Delay of the Parousia in Luke–Acts', *NTS* 20 (1973), pp. 145-55.
Hill, D., *The Gospel of Matthew* (NCB; London: Marshall, Morgan & Scott, 1972).
Hooker, M., *Jesus and the Servant* (London: SPCK, 1959).
—*Continuity and Discontinuity: Early Christianity in its Jewish Setting* (London: Epworth Press, 1966).
—*The Son of Man in Mark* (London: SPCK, 1967).
—'In His Own Image?' in M. Hooker (ed.), *What About the New Testament? Essays in Honour of Christopher Evans* (London: SCM Press, 1975), pp. 28-44.
Houlden, J.L., 'The Purpose of Acts', *JSNT* 21 (1984), pp. 53-65.
Hurd, J.C., *The Origin of 1 Corinthians* (London: SPCK, 1965).
Jeremias, J., *The Parables of Jesus* (trans. S.H. Hooke; London; SCM Press, 1963).
—*The Eucharistic Words of Jesus* (trans. N. Perrin; London: SCM Press, 1966).
—*New Testament Theology: The Proclamation of Jesus* (trans. J. Bowden; London: SCM Press, 1971).
Jervell, J., *Luke and the People of God* (Minneapolis: Augsburg Publishing House, 1972).
—*The Unknown Paul: Essays on Luke–Acts and Early Christian History* (Minneapolis: Augsburg Publishing House, 1984).
Johnson, L.T., *The Literary Function of Possessions in Luke–Acts* (SBLDS, 39; Missoula, MT: Scholars Press, 1977).
—*Luke* (Sacra Pagina, 3; Collegeville, MN: Liturgical Press, 1991).
—*The Acts of the Apostles* (Sacra Pagina, 5; Collegeville, MN: Liturgical Press, 1992).
Johnson, M.D., *The Purpose of the Biblical Genealogies with Special Reference to the Genealogies of Jesus* (SNTSMS, 8; Cambridge: Cambridge University Press, 1969).
Jones, D.R., 'The Background and Character of the Lukan Psalms', *JTS* 19 (1968), pp. 19-50.
Juel, D., *Luke–Acts: The Promise of History* (Atlanta: John Knox, 1991).
Karris, R.J., 'Windows and Mirrors: Literary Criticism and Luke's Sitz im Leben', in P.J. Achtemeier (ed.), *SBL Seminar Paepers 1979* (Missoula, MT: Scholars Press, 1979).
—*Luke: Artist and Theologian* (New York: Paulist Press, 1985).
Käsemann, E., *Essays on New Testament Themes* (trans. W.J. Montague; London: SCM Press, 1964).
Keck, L.E., 'Will the Historical-Critical Method Survive?' in R.A. Spencer (ed.), *Orientation by Disorientation: Studies in Literary Criticism and Biblical Literary Criticism* (Pittsburgh: Pickwick Press, 1980), pp. 115-28.

Keck, L.E., and L.J. Martyn (eds.), *Studies in Luke–Acts* (London: SPCK, 1966).
Kee, H.C., *Christian Origins in Sociological Perspective* (London: SCM Press, 1980).
—*Good News to the Ends of the Earth: The Theology of Acts* (London: SCM Press, 1990).
Kilpatrick, G.D., *The Origin of the Gospel according to St Matthew* (Oxford: Clarendon Press, 1946).
Kim, S., *The Origin of Paul's Gospel* (WUNT, 24; Tübingen: Mohr [Siebeck], 1981).
Kingsbury, J.D., *The Parables of Jesus in Matthew 13* (London: SPCK, 1969).
—*Matthew: Structure, Christology, Kingdom* (London: SPCK, 1975).
—'The Developing Conflict between Jesus and the Jewish Leaders in Matthew's Gospel: A Literary Critical Study', *CBQ* 49 (1987), pp. 57-73.
Klein, G., 'Lukas 1–4 als theologisches Programmwerk' in E. Dinkler (ed.), *Zeit und Geschichte: für R. Bultmann* (Tübingen: Mohr [Siebeck], 1964).
Kloppenborg, J., *The Formation of Q: Trajectories in Ancient Wisdom Collections* (Philadelphia: Fortress Press, 1987).
Knox, J., *Chapters in a Life of Paul* (London: A. & C. Black, 1954).
Koester, H., 'GNOMAIDIAPHOROI' in H. Koester and J.M. Robinson (eds.), *Trajectories through Early Christianity* (Philadelphia: Fortress Press, 1971).
Kraabel, A.T., 'The Disappearance of the "God-fearers"', *Numen* 28 (1981), pp. 113-26.
—'Greeks, Jews and Lutherans in the Middle Half of Acts' in G.W.E. Nickelsburg and G.W. Macrae (eds.), *Christians among Jews and Gentiles* (Philadelphia: Fortress Press, 1986).
Kremer, J. (ed.), *Les Actes des Apôtres: Traditions, rédaction, théologie* (Bibliotheca Ephemeridum Theologicarum Louvaniensium 68; Gembloux: Leuven University Press, 1979).
Krodel, G., *Acts* (Proclamation Commentaries; Philadelphia: Fortress Press, 1981).
Kümmel, W.G., *Introduction to the New Testament* (trans. H.C. Kee; London: SCM Press, 1975).
Ladd, G.E., *A Theology of the New Testament* (London: Lutterworth Press, 1975).
Lambrecht, J., 'Paul's Farewell Address at Miletus (Acts 20.17-38)', in J. Kremer (ed.), Les Actes des Apôtres: Traditions, redaction, théologie (BETL, 48; Gembloux: Leuven University Press, 1979).
—*Once More Astonished* (New York: Crossroad, 1981).
Lampe, G.W.H., 'Acts', in M. Black and H.H. Rowley (eds.), *Peake's Commentary on the Bible* (London: Nelson, 1962).
—'Grievous Wolves', in B. Lindars and S.D. Smalley (eds.), *Christ and Spirit in the New Testament* (Cambridge: Cambridge University Press, 1973), pp. 253-68.
Larentin, R., *Structure et Théologie de Luc. 1–11* (Paris: Gabalda, 1957).
Leaney, A.R.C., *The Gospel according to St Luke* (London: A. & C. Black, 1958).
Linnemann, E., *Parables of Jesus* (London: SPCK, 1966).
Lüdemann, G., *Early Christianity according to the Traditions in Acts* (trans. J. Bowden; London: SCM Press, 1989).
Luz, U., *Matthew 1–7: A Commentary* (trans. W.C. Linss; Edinburgh: T. & T. Clark, 1989).
McNeile, A.H., *The Gospel according to Matthew* (London: Macmillan, 1915).
Maddox, R., *The Purpose of Luke–Acts* (Edinburgh: T. & T. Clark, 1982).
Marshall, I.H., *Luke: Historian and Theologian* (Exeter: Paternoster Press, 1970).

—*The Gospel of Luke* (Exeter: Paternoster Press, 1978).
—*Acts: An Introduction and Commentary* (Leicester: Inter-Varsity Press, 1980).
Matera, F.J., 'Responsibility for the Death of Jesus according to the Acts of the Apostles', JSNT 39 (1990), pp. 77-93.
Mattill, A.J., 'The Purpose of Acts; Schneckenburger Reconsidered', in W.W. Gasque and R.P. Martin (eds.), *Apostolic History in the Gospel* (Exeter: Paternoster Press, 1970).
—*Luke and the Last Things* (Dillsboro, NC: Western North Carolina Press, 1970).
Meeks, W.A., and R.L. Wilken, *Jews and Christians in Antioch in the First Four Centuries of the Common Era* (Missoula, MT: Scholars Press, 1978).
Meier, J.P., *Law and History in Matthew's Gospel* (Rome: Biblical Institute Press, 1976).
—*The Vision of Matthew: Christ, Church and Morality in the First Gospel* (New York: Paulist Press, 1979).
Minear, P.S., 'Luke's use of the Birth Stories', in K.E. Keck and J.L. Martyn (eds.), *Studies in Luke–Acts* (London: SPCK, 1966), pp. 111-30.
—'The Disciples and the Crowds in the Gospel of Matthew', *ATRSup*, 111 (1974), pp. 78-94.
Moessner, D.P., 'Luke 9.1-5: Luke's Preview of the Journey of the Prophet like Moses of Deuteronomy', *JBL* 102/4 (1983), pp. 575-605.
—'The Ironic Fulfilment of Israel's Glory', in J.B. Tyson (ed.), *Luke–Acts and the Jewish People* (Minneapolis: Augsburg, 1988), pp. 35-50.
—*Lord of the Banquet: The Literary and Theological Significance of the Lukan Travel Narrative* (Minneapolis: Fortress Press, 1989).
Mohrlang, R., *Matthew and Paul: A Comparison of Ethical Perspectives* (SNTSMS, 48; Cambridge: Cambridge University Press, 1984).
Moore, S.D., *Literary Criticism and the Gospels* (New Haven: Yale University Press, 1989).
Moule, C.F.D., 'The Christology of Acts', in L.E. Keck and J.L. Martyn (eds.), *Studies in Luke–Acts* (London: SPCK, 19665), pp. 159-85.
—*The Origin of Christology* (Cambridge: Cambridge University Press, 1977).
Munck, J., *Christ and Israel: An Interpretation of Romans 9–11* (Philadelphia: Fortress Press, 1967).
Neale, D.A., *None but the Sinners: Religious Categories in the Gospel of Luke* (JSNTSup, 58; Sheffield: JSOT Press, 1991).
Neirynck, F., *Evangelica: Gospel Studies: Collected Essays* (ed. F. van Segbroek: BETL, 60; Leuven: Leuven University Press, 1982).
Neirynck, F., (ed.), *The Gospel of Luke: Revised and Enlarged Edition of L'Evangile de Luc* (BETL, 32; Leuven: Leuven University Press, 1989).
Neusner, J., *The Beginning of Christianity* (London: SPCK, 1984).
Neusner, J., *et al.* (eds.), *The Social World of Formative Christianity and Judaism* (Philadelphia: Fortress Press, 1988).
Neyrey, J., 'Address to the Women of Jerusalem', *NTS* 29 (1981), pp. 74-86.
—*The Passion according to Luke: A Redaction Study of Luke's Soteriology* (New York: Paulist Press, 1985).
Nickle, K.F., *The Collection* (London: SCM Press, 1966).
Nineham, D., (ed.), *Studies in the Gospels: Essays in Memory of R.H. Lightfoot* (Oxford: Basil Blackwell, 1955).
Nolland, J., 'A Fresh Look at Acts 15.10', *NTS* 27 (1980), pp. 105-115.

—*Luke* (WBC, 35a, 35b; Dallas, TX: Word Books, 1989, 1993).

Ogg, G., 'The Central Section of the Gospel according to St Luke', *NTS* 18 (1971), pp. 39-53.

O'Neill, J.C., *The Theology of Acts in its Historical Setting* (London: SPCK, 1961).

Orchard, B., *A Synopsis of the Four Gospels in Greek* (Edinburgh: T. & T. Clark, 1983).

Orchard, B., and H. Riley, *The Order of the Synoptics: Why Three Gospels?* (Macon, GA: Mercer University Press, 1987).

O'Toole, R.F., 'Activity of the Risen Jesus in Luke–Acts', *Bib* (1981), pp. 471-98.

—*The Unity of Luke's Theology: An Analysis of Luke–Acts* (Wilmington, DE: Michael Glazier, 1984).

Parsons, M.C., *The Departure of Jesus in Luke–Acts* (JSNTSup, 21; Sheffield: JSOT Press, 1987).

Pervo, R.I., *Profit with Delight: The Literary Genre of the Acts of the Apostles* (Philadelphia: Fortress Press, 1987).

—'Must Luke and Acts belong to the Same Genre?', SBLSP, (1989), pp. 309-316.

Petrie, S., 'Q is only what You Make it', *NT* 13 (1959), pp. 215ff.

Pilgrim, W.E., *Good News to the Poor: Wealth and Poverty in Luke–Acts* (Minneapolis: Augsburg, 1981).

Porter, S.E., 'Thucydides 1.22.1 and Speeches in Acts: Is there a Thucydidean View?', *NovT* 32 (1990), pp. 121-42.

Przybylski, B., *Righteousness in Matthew and his World of Thought* (SNTSMS, 41; Cambridge: Cambridge University Press, 1980).

Radcliffe, T., 'The Emmaus Story: Necessity and Freedom', *New Blackfriars* 64 (1983), pp. 483-93.

Räisänen, H., *Paul and the Law* (Tübingen: Mohr [Paul Siebeck], 1983.

Reicke, B., 'Instruction and Discussion in the Travel Narrative', SE I/TU 73 (1959), pp. 206-216.

—*Gospel of Luke* (trans. R. Mackenzie; London: SPCK, 1965).

Rese, M., 'Die Funktion der altestamentlichen Zitate und Anspielungen in den Reden der Apostelgeschichte', in J. Kremer (ed.), *Les Actes des Apôtres: Traditions, rédaction, théologie* (Gembloux: Leuven University Press, 1979), pp. 61-79.

Richard, E., 'Luke—Writer, Theologian, Historian: Research and Orientation of the 1970s', *BTB* 13 (1983), pp. 3-15.

Richardson, P., *Israel in the Apostolic Church* (SNTSMS, 10; Cambridge: Cambridge University Press, 1969).

Ringgren, H., 'Luke's Use of the Old Testament', *HTR* 79 (1986), pp. 227-35.

Rist, J.M., *On the Independence of Matthew and Mark* (SNTSMS, 10; Cambridge: Cambridge University Press, 1978).

Robbins, V.K., 'Prefaces in Greco-Roman Biography and Luke–Acts', SBLSPS 14 (1978), pp. 193-207.

—'By Land and by Sea: The We-Passages and Ancient Sea Voyages', in C.H. Talbert (ed.), *Perspectives on Luke–Acts* (Edinburgh: T. & T. Clark, 1978), pp. 215-42.

Robinson, W.C., 'On Preaching the Word of God', in L.E. Keck and J.L. Martyn (eds.), *Studies in Luke–Acts* (London: SPCK, 1966), pp. 131-38.

Rowland, C., *The Open Heaven* (London: SPCK, 1985).

—*Christian Origins* (London: SPCK, 1985).

Sanders, E.P., *The Tendencies of the Synoptic Tradition* (SNTSMS, 9; Cambridge: Cambridge University Press, 1969).
—'The Argument from Order and the Relationship between Matthew and Luke', *NTS* 15 (1968–69), pp. 249-61.
—*Paul and Palestinian Judaism* (London: SCM Press, 1977).
—*Paul, the Law, and the Jewish People* (Philadelphia: Fortress Press, 1983).
—'Jesus and the Sinners', *JSNT* 19 (1983), pp. 5-36.
—*Jesus and Judaism* (London: SCM Press, 1987).
Sanders, E.P., and M. Davies, *Studying the Synoptic Gospels* (London: SCM Press; Philadelphia: Trinity Press International, 1989).
Sanders, J.A., 'From Isaiah 61 to Luke 4', in J. Neusner (ed.), *Christianity, Judaism and other Greco-Roman Cults* (Leiden: Brill, 1975), I.
Sanders, J.T., 'The Parable of the Pounds and Lukan Anti-Semitism', *TS* 42 (1981), pp. 660-68.
—*The Jews in Luke–Acts* (London: SCM Press, 1987).
—*Schismatics, Sectarians, Dissidents, Deviants* (London: SCM Press, 1993).
Schmithals, W., *Paul and James* (London: SCM Press, 1965).
Schneider, G., 'Zur Bedeutung von kayezêw im lukanischen Doppelwerk', *ZNW* 68 (1977), pp. 128-31.
—*Das Evangelium nach Lukas* (2 vols.; Gütersloh: Mohn, 1977).
—*Die Apostelgeschichte* (2 vols.; Freiburg: Herder, 1980–82).
Schramm, T., *Der Markus-Stoff bei Lukas* (SNTSMS, 14; Cambridge: Cambridge University Press, 1971).
Schubert, P., 'The Structure and Significance of Luke 24', in W. Eltester (ed.), *Neutestamentliche Studien für Rudolf Bultmann* (BZNW, 21; Berlin: Alfred Töpelmann, 1954), pp. 165-86.
Schürmann, H., *Das Lukasevangelium* (2 vols.; Freiburg: Herder, 1984).
Schweizer, E., 'Concerning the Speeches in Acts', in L.E. Keck and J.L. Martyn (eds.), *Studies in Luke–Acts* (London: SPCK, 1966), pp. 208-216.
—*The Good News according to Luke* (trans. D. Green; London: SPCK; Atlanta, GA: John Knox, 1984).
Scroggs, R., 'Eschatological Existence in Matthew and Paul'. in J. Marcus and M.L. Soards (eds.), *Apocalyptic and the New Testament* (JSNTSup, 24; Sheffield: JSOT Press, 1989).
Seifrid, M.A., 'Jesus and the Law in Acts', *JSNT* 30 (1987), pp. 39-57.
Senior, D., *The Passion of Jesus in Luke* (Wilmington, DE: Michael Glazier, 1988).
Sherwin-White, A.N., *Roman Society and Roman Law in the New Testament* (Oxford: Clarendon Press, 1963).
Simpson, R.T., 'The Major Agreements of Matthew and Luke against Mark', *NTS* 11 (1965), pp. 273-84.
Stanton, G.N., *Jesus of Nazareth in New Testament Preaching* (SNTSMS, 27; Cambridge: Cambridge University Press, 1974).
—*The Gospels and Jesus* (Oxford: Oxford University Press, 1989).
—*A Gospel for a New People* (Edinburgh: T. & T. Clark, 1992).
Stein, R.H., *The Synoptic Problem: An Introduction* (Leicester: Inter-Varsity Press, 1987).
Stempvoort, P.A. van, 'The Interpretation of the Ascension in Luke and Acts', *NTS* 5 (1959), pp. 30-42.

Stendahl, K., *The School of Matthew and its Use of the Old Testament* (Uppsala: Gleerup, 1954).
—'Quis at Unde? An Analysis of Matthew 1–2', in W. Eltester (ed.), *Judentum, Urchristentum, Kirche* (Berlin: Töpelmann, 1960), pp. 94-105.
—*Paul among Jews and Gentiles* (London: SCM Press, 1977).
Talbert, C.H., *Luke and the Gnostics* (Nashville: Abingdon Press, 1966).
—'The Redaction Critical Quest for Luke the Theologian', in D.G. Miller (ed.), *Jesus and Man's Hope* (Pittsburgh: Pittsburgh Theological Seminary, 1970), pp. 171-222.
—*Literary Patterns, Theological Themes, and the Genre of Luke–Acts* (SBLS, 20; Missoula, MT: Scholars Press, 1974).
—'Shifting Sands: The Recent Study of the Gospel of Luke', *Int* 30 (1976), pp. 381-95.
—*What is a Gospel?* (London: SPCK, 1977).
Talbert, C.H., (ed.), *Perspectives on Luke–Acts* (Edinburgh: T. & T. Clark, 1978).
—'Promise and Fulfilment in Lukan Theology', in C.H. Talbert (ed.), *Luke–Acts: New Perspectives from the Society of Biblical Literature* (New York: Crossroads, 1984), pp. 91-103.
—*Reading Luke: A Literary and Theological Commentary on the Third Gospel* (New York: Crossroad, 1984),
Tannehill, R.C., 'The Mission of Jesus according to Luke 4.16-30', in J. Eltester (ed.), *Jesus in Nazareth* (BZNTW, 40; Berlin: de Gruyter, 1972), pp. 51-75.
—'Israel in Luke–Acts; A Tragic Story', *JBL* 104 (1985), pp. 69-85.
—*The Narrative Unity of Luke–Acts* (Philadelphia: Fortress Press, vol. 1, 1986, vol. 2, 1990).
—'Rejection by Jews and Turning to Gentiles: The Pattern of Paul's Mission in Acts', in J.B. Tyson (ed.), *Luke–Acts and the Jewish People* (Minneapolis: Augsburg, 1988), pp. 83-101.
Taylor, N., *Paul, Antioch and Jerusalem* (JSNTSup, 66; Sheffield: JSOT Press, 1989).
Taylor, V., *The Gospels: A Short Introduction* (London: Epworth Press, 1960).
Theissen, G., *Psychological Aspects of Pauline Theology* (trans. J.P. Galvin; London: SCM Press, 1987).
Tiede, D.L., *Prophecy and History in Luke–Acts* (Philadelphia: Fortress Press, 1980).
—' "Glory to Thy People Israel": Luke–Acts and the Jews', in J.B. Tyson (ed.), *Luke–Acts and the Jewish People* (Minneapolis: Augsburg, 1988).
Trebilco, P.R., 'Paul and Silas—Servants of the Most High God (Acts 16.16-18)', *JSNT* 36 (1989), pp. 51-73.
Tuckett, C.M., *The Revival of the Griesbach Hypothesis* (SNTSMS, 44; Cambridge: Cambridge University Press, 1983).
Turner, M., 'Jesus and the Spirit in Lucan Perspective', *TB* 32 (1981), pp. 3-42.
—'The Significance of Receiving the Spirit in Luke–Acts: A Survey of Modern Scholarship', *TJ* 2 (1981), pp. 131-58.
—'The Spirit and the Power of Jesus' Miracles in the Lucan Conception', *NovT* 33 (1991), pp. 124-52.
Tyson, J.B., 'Conflict as a Literary Theme in the Gospel of Luke', in W.R. Farmer (ed.), *New Synoptic Studies* (Macon, BA: Mercer University Press, 1983).
—'The Jewish Public in Luke–Acts', *NTS* 30 (1984), pp. 574-83.

—*The Death of Jesus in Luke–Acts* (Columbia: University of South Carolina Press, 1986).

Tyson, J.B., (ed.), *Luke–Acts and the Jewish People: Eight Perspectives* (Minneapolis: Augsburg, 1988).

Vermes, G., *Jesus the Jew* (London: SCM Press, 1973).

Vielhauer, P., 'On the Paulinism of Acts', in L.E. Keck and J.L. Martyn (eds.), *Studies in Luke–Acts* (London: SPCK, 1966), pp. 35-50.

Walwasky, P.W., *'And So We Came to Rome': The Political Perspective of Acts* (SNTSMS, 49; Cambridge: Cambridge University Press, 1983).

Watson, F., *Paul, Judaism and the Gentiles* (SNTSMS, 56; Cambridge: Cambridge University Press, 1986).

Watson, N.M., 'Was Zacchaeus Really Reforming?', *ExpTim* 77 (1965–66), pp. 25-28.

Wedderburn, A.J.M., 'Paul and Jesus: The Problem of Continuity', *SJT* 38 (1985), pp. 189-203.

Weiser, A., 'Das Äpostelkonzel', *BZ* 28 (1981), pp. 145-67.

Wenham, D., 'The Paulinism of Acts Again', *Themelios* 13 (1988), pp. 53-55.

Wenham, J., 'Synoptic Independence and the Origin of Luke's Travel Narrative', *NTS* 27 (1987), pp. 507-515.

Westermann, C., *Isaiah 40–66* (trans. D. Stalker; London: SCM Press, 1969).

Wilckens, W., 'Interpreting Luke–Acts in a Period of Existentialist Theology', in L.E. Keck and J.L. Martyn (eds.), *Studies in Luke–Acts* (London: SPCK, 1966).

Wilcox, N., 'The God-fearers in Acts: A Reconsideration', *JSNT* 13 (1981), pp. 102-122.

Wilson, S.G., *The Gentiles and the Gentile Mission in Luke–Acts* (SNTSMS, 23; Cambridge: Cambridge University Press, 1973).

—*Luke and the Law* (SNTSMS, 50; Cambridge: Cambridge University Press, 1983).

Wilson, S.G., (ed.), *Anti-Judaism in Early Christianity: Separation and Polemic* (Waterloo, ON: Wilfrid Laurier University Press, 1986).

Winter, P., 'Some Observations on the Language in the Birth and Infancy Stories of the Third Gospel', *NTS* 1 (1954–55), pp. 111-21.

—'On Luke and Lukan Stories', *ZNW* 47 (1956), pp. 217-42.

Wolter, M., 'Apollos und die Ephesinischen Johannes jünger', *ZNTW* 78 (1987), pp. 49-73.

Wright, N.T., *The Climax of the Covenant* (Edinburgh: T. & T. Clark, 1991).

—*The New Testament and the People of God* (London: SPCK, 1992).

York, J.O., *The Last Shall Be First: The Rhetoric of Reversal in Luke* (JSNTSup, 46; Sheffield: JSOT Press, 1991).

Ziesler, J., 'Luke and the Pharisees', *NTS* 25 (1979), pp. 146-57.

—*Pauline Christianity* (Oxford: Oxford University Press, 1983).

INDEXES

INDEX OF REFERENCES

OLD TESTAMENT

NEW TESTAMENT

INDEX OF AUTHORS